AG 1 5 '14

SiTCOM

Wauconda Area Library
801 N. Main Street
Wauconda, IL 60084

Sitcom

★ ★ ★ ★ ★

A History in 24 Episodes
from *I Love Lucy* to *Community*

SAUL AUSTERLITZ

CHICAGO
REVIEW
PRESS

An A Cappella Book

Copyright © 2014 by Saul Austerlitz
All rights reserved
Published by Chicago Review Press Incorporated
814 North Franklin Street
Chicago, Illinois 60610
ISBN 978-1-61374-384-3

Portions of this book have previously been published in the *Boston Globe* and the *Atlantic Online*.

Library of Congress Cataloging-in-Publication Data
Austerlitz, Saul.
  Sitcom : a history in 24 episodes from I love Lucy to Community / Saul Austerlitz.
    pages cm
  Summary: "Obsessively watched and critically ignored, sitcoms were a distraction, a gentle lullaby of a kinder, gentler America—until suddenly the artificial boundary between the world and television entertainment collapsed. In this book we track the growth of the sitcom, following the path that leads from I LOVE LUCY to THE PHIL SILVERS SHOW; from THE DICK VAN DYKE SHOW to THE MARY TYLER MOORE SHOW; from M*A*S*H to TAXI; from CHEERS to ROSEANNE; from SEINFELD to CURB YOUR ENTHUSIASM; and from THE LARRY SANDERS SHOW to 30 ROCK. In twenty-four episodes, SITCOM surveys the history of the form, and functions as both a TV mix tape of fondly remembered shows that will guide us to notable series and larger trends, and a carefully curated guided tour through the history of one of our most treasured art forms"— Provided by publisher.
  Includes bibliographical references and index.
  ISBN 978-1-61374-384-3 (pbk.)
  1. Situation comedies (Television programs)—United States. I. Title.

PN1992.8.C66A97 2014
791.45'617—dc23

                    2013038098

Cover design: John Yates at Stealworks
Cover image: Warner Bros. Entertainment, via Photofest
Interior design: PerfecType, Nashville, TN
Interior images: pp. 7, 25, 39, 143, 159 © CBS Studios; p. 53 © NBC Universal; p. 67 © Calvada Productions; p. 79 © Turner Entertainment; pp. 95, 129, 207, 325 © 20th Century Fox; p. 113 © Tandem Licensing; pp. 175, 191 © Carsey-Werner Television; p. 225 © Castle Rock Entertainment; p. 243 © Partners with Boundaries Productions; p. 259 © Warner Bros. Entertainment; pp. 273, 309 © Home Box Office; p. 291 © DreamWorks; pp. 341, 355 © Universal Studios; p. 369 © Sony Pictures Television

Printed in the United States of America
5 4 3 2 1

To my parents, for everything

■ ■ ■

And in memory of Lisa Choueke Blank (1979–2012),
irreplaceable friend

Wauconda Area Library
801 N. Main Street
Wauconda, IL 60084

"One day the English language is going to perish. The easy spokenness of it will perish and go black and crumbly—maybe—and it will become a language like Latin that learned people learn. And scholars will write studies of *Larry Sanders* and *Friends* and *Will & Grace* and *Ellen* and *Designing Women* and *Mary Tyler Moore*, and everyone will see that the sitcom is the great American art form. American poetry will perish with the language; the sitcoms, on the other hand, are new to human evolution and therefore will be less perishable."

—NICHOLSON BAKER, *The Anthologist*

"More than jazz or musical theater or morbid obesity, television is the true American art form."

—KENNETH PARCELL (JACK MCBRAYER), *30 Rock*

"It's those TV networks, Marge. They won't let me. One quality show after another, each one fresher and more brilliant than the last. If they only stumbled once! Just give us thirty minutes to ourselves. But they won't! They won't let me live!"

—HOMER SIMPSON

Contents

Introduction

The form is so elemental, so basic, that we have difficulty imagining a time before it existed: a single set, fixed cameras, canned laughter, zany sidekicks, quirky family antics. Its very name is an imprecation, implying bloodless, prepackaged humor without subtlety or intelligence. And yet, having drawn our attention for more than half a century, the situation comedy is far more than its detractors would claim. Having first emerged in the youthful bloom of post–World War II American optimism and naïveté, the sitcom has grown in stature, developing from an afterthought into an art form.

And a peculiarly American art form it is. Thriving in the dim cathode-ray light of one hundred million living rooms, the situation comedy bloomed despite the benign neglect of a nation of captive viewers lulled into somnolence and the disinterest of high-mandarin cultural arbiters. Obsessively watched and critically ignored all at once, sitcoms were seemingly doomed to irrelevance by the creeping sense of being second-rate, a minor trifle. Sitcoms were a distraction, a gentle lullaby of a kinder, gentler America—until suddenly they weren't, not anymore, and the artificial boundary between the world and television entertainment collapsed. Archie Bunker and the Korean War replaced Lucy and Desi. The situation comedy grew naggingly familiar with its own inadequacies and absurdities, and found comedy in the knowledge of the form's delusions. The story of the sitcom is a capsule version of the twentieth-century arts—realism giving way to modernism, and then to postmodernism, all between the weeknight hours of 8:00 and 10:00 (7:00 and 9:00 central).

TV initially devoted itself to the charms and travails of the domestic, from Ralph Kramden to the Cleavers to the Ricardos. Sitcoms were a friendly neighbor, harmless and inoffensive and amusing. They were auxiliary members of the 1950s family, gently ribbing the postwar order without disrupting it. In its classical form, the sitcom revolved around the family: the solid, stolid father; the harried, loving mother; the kooky but well-meaning children. It rigorously adhered to a set pattern: thirty-minute length, a laugh track, a small recurring cast of characters, a domestic setting. And then there were the scrapes—an infinite series of easily resolved predicaments and indiscretions that plagued the sitcom families, demanding their immediate attention without ever lingering or affecting the unchanging dynamic of the families themselves.

Sitcoms exemplified the phenomenon of eternal return, promising endless variation without ever fundamentally altering the world that contained them. The words "forever" and "always" recur in this book in large part because the behavior of sitcom characters must be described as such; set along a single track, they continue to shuttle forward and scuttle backward, week after week, in an eternal recurrence of reassuring sameness.

And yet there was more to the sitcom than banal familiarity. There was, at times, the sense that within the comforting confines of its well-worn sets and well-worn punch lines, something surprising could happen. Sitcoms reflected America, but the mirrors they used could warp and bend reality into intriguing new patterns. Television could reflect not the America that was but the America that we wanted—one where Jewish families were as all-American as their Gentile neighbors; where women toiled at exciting, enlivening jobs in the big city; where African American families epitomized middle-class values. Sitcoms were also free to invent more individual fantasy worlds—where attractive Manhattan singles spent their abundant free time lazing around enormous apartments, where eight-year-old boys exhibited frightening intellectual precocity, where the pressures of show business created an ideal environment for emotionally blinkered narcissists to thrive.

The sitcom could also be politically subversive, introducing openly gay characters, like *Soap*, or parodying Nixon's Silent Majority, like *All in the Family*. But regardless of the laugh track, audiences would laugh when, and how, they chose. *All in the Family* became a hit not because people enjoyed ridiculing bigoted Archie Bunker but because they identified with him. TV, more than film, belongs to its audiences, and they determine the ultimate value—the ultimate meaning—of the shows they watch.

And then, over the past quarter century or so—dating approximately to the debut of *The Simpsons* in 1989, although already visible in such acclaimed series of the 1970s as *M*A*S*H* and *Taxi*—the sitcom burst its boundaries, finding humor in the disjunction between its family-values past and the dysfunctional present: Ward Cleaver, meet Homer Simpson. The sitcom expanded on the self-reflexivity of its earliest years, fully embracing the TV-centric self-mockery glimpsed on *I Love Lucy* and *The Dick Van Dyke Show*. Shows spoke to one another, commenting on past successes and failures, refracting familiar plotlines and story devices, aping the stylistic advances and compromises of their contemporaries and forebears. See how *Roseanne* offers itself as a Talmudic commentary to the holy sitcom text of *Leave It to Beaver*, or *Curb Your Enthusiasm* functions as an extended gloss on *Seinfeld*. In this alone, the sitcom is conscious of itself as a medium in its own right, with a tradition worthy of notice and a future worthy of recognition.

The sitcom became, more than ever, about itself—its past, its traditions, its unacknowledged conventions, its limitations. The genre became a series of questions in a never-ending interrogation: Just what is this thing we gather around our television sets to watch? Who is it intended for? How can it be reformed? The best series of the 1990s and 2000s, such as *Seinfeld*, *30 Rock*, and *Curb Your Enthusiasm*, are deeply self-reflexive, aware at all times of the peculiar nature of their chosen form.

Even the strict parameters of the form itself—the thirty-minute length, the laugh track, and so forth—proved surprisingly mutable. As with its older brother the American film, the seemingly impervious boundary between television comedy and drama is actually quite porous. As television matured, drama proved itself susceptible to the wooing of comedy, and comedy proved itself open to moments of uninflected drama. Series like *M*A*S*H*, *Moonlighting*, and *Freaks and Geeks* thrived in the slipstream between comedy and drama. Their example has proved enormously influential, and to ignore them in telling the story of the sitcom would be to render it a less capacious, less flexible genre.

But whether traditional or heterodox, a sitcom is defined by its episodes. Each episode is a self-enclosed world, a brief overturning of the established order of its universe before returning, unblemished, to the precise spot from which it began—or, as is increasingly the case in more modern sitcoms, some other place entirely. And great shows are often defined by their truly outstanding episodes—individual installments like *The Simpsons'* "22 Short Films About Springfield," *The Mary Tyler Moore Show's* "Chuckles Bites the Dust," *Seinfeld's* "The Pitch," or *Freaks and Geeks'* "Dead Dogs and Gym Teachers," in which Martin Starr's nerdy Bill takes comfort in—what else?—the pleasures of laughing at TV. We remember great television series in the context of their setups—the unchanging rules that govern their fictional worlds—but we cherish them most for the episodes that linger in our memories, their laughs growing sharper with the passage of time, rather than fading into the haze of the half-forgotten television past.

This book, too, is defined by episodes, each chapter springing from the consideration of a single representative entry. In twenty-four episodes, *Sitcom* will survey the history of the form, a TV mixtape of fondly remembered shows that will guide us to considerations of notable series (not just the ones reflected by the episodes) and of the larger trends in the history of the sitcom. Consider it a carefully curated guided tour from *I Love Lucy* to *Community*, pausing along the way to take in both the best of what the sitcom has accomplished and the most representative of its works.

In *Sitcom's* twenty-four chapters we watch the growth of the genre, following the path that leads from *I Love Lucy* to *The Phil Silvers Show*; from *The Dick Van Dyke Show* to *The Mary Tyler Moore Show*; from *M*A*S*H* to *Taxi*; from *Cheers* to *Roseanne*; from *Seinfeld* to *Curb Your Enthusiasm*; and from *The Larry Sanders Show* to *30 Rock*. The book's chapters are organized chronologically by the year of each show's premiere. For these purposes, shows are dated to when they began as stand-alone series, earlier appearances as sketch comedy notwithstanding—hence, *The Honeymooners* premiering in 1955, and *The Simpsons* in 1989.

Each chapter begins with a particular episode but ranges widely across television history, using memorable examples from other episodes and other series to illustrate the story of the sitcom's development. That said, this book is not, nor does it intend to be, entirely comprehensive. This is not an encyclopedia but a critical study of the history and growth of the sitcom. There are inevitably series—some more than worthy of closer study—that receive only a passing mention here, and others not even granted that privilege. And comedy series that do not adhere to the sitcom mode, like variety shows and sketch comedy series, are a story of their own, hence no *Your Show of Shows*, *Saturday Night Live*, or *Chappelle's Show*. Similarly, *The Tonight Show* and *The Daily Show* make for brilliant comedy but are not part of this book's purview. Like any mixtape worth its salt, there will be grounds for complaint over what is left off as much as what is included.

The passage of time, and the nearly universal acknowledgment of landmark shows like *Seinfeld*, *The Simpsons*, and *Arrested Development*, has rendered obsolete the ideological blinkers ("boob tube," "idiot box") that reflexively condemn television as inherently inferior or insipid. We can now value TV—and the sitcom in particular—as an underappreciated American art form. Being both the most popular and, for much of its history, the most critically ignored form of American culture, television falls into a peculiar netherworld of intimate familiarity without sustained consideration. Is it art if no one is paying attention? Is it art if *everyone* is paying attention? The arc of the sitcom follows the establishment of a carefully structured new mode of entertainment, ideally situated to reflect and cater to the postwar American middle-class consensus, and the eventual shattering of its conventions. Both halves of its story—the establishment of a tradition and its collapse— are necessary to comprehend the sitcom.

We will begin our tour like recurring guest stars, knocking at the door of each of these iconic TV shows, ushered in to reacquaint ourselves with the decor, the people, the overall ambience of these series, soaking in the applause. This book is about the artistry of the sitcom—its capabilities, and the ways in which the passage of time has seen it grow. It is a study of those who came into our homes and made us laugh.

1

I Love Lucy

"Lucy Does a TV Commercial"

May 5, 1952 ▪ CBS

L et us begin with a definition. The sitcom, in short, is about the preservation of equilibrium. Before we begin upsetting the sitcom's equilibrium ourselves, let us take a moment to settle it in its place. The sitcom is a jumble of mixed metaphors: the repetition compulsion of eternal sameness conjoined to a desire to overturn the established order; a profound aesthetic conservatism bundled with an ingrained desire to shock.

The sitcom, emerging at the tail end of the 1940s alongside the television itself, bore witness to the conformism borne of the horrors of the Second World War. A generation forged in the fire of the war sought placidity and sameness on the home front: stable nuclear families, a nation of identically constructed Levittowns. Television was a product of the same enforced consensus. It would mirror America, not necessarily as it was, but as it should be: peaceable, middle class, eternally unchanging.

The sitcom's arrival on television screens across America was a decade and a half in the making. Television, so profoundly intertwined with postwar American life, was actually a technological outgrowth of the 1930s. David Sarnoff of RCA, an early pioneer of television, pledged $1 million in 1935 for broadcasting experiments. Actors in Studio 3H at Radio City in New York's Rockefeller Center applied green makeup and purple lipstick for tests, the better to stand out on the tiny black-and-white screen. By 1939 RCA's NBC network was broadcasting an episode of *Amos 'n' Andy* from the grounds of the World's Fair in Queens. RCA was putting five-inch, nine-inch, and twelve-inch TVs on sale, with prices ranging from $200 to $600 ($3,300 to $10,000 in today's dollars).

The stage was set for television to succeed radio as Americans' principal source of home entertainment, but disputes over the new form's technical specifications, and the outbreak of World War II, pushed television's emergence back by almost a decade. During this "laboratory period," as Erik Barnouw describes the era in his book *Tube of Plenty*, a freeze on new stations meant that some cities, like New York and Los Angeles, had multiple television options, while others, like Little Rock and Austin, had no TV whatsoever.

But once television arrived in American cities after the war's end, its impact was immediate and incontrovertible. Movie theater receipts in cities with functioning TV stations decreased by 20 to 40 percent, while those cities without TV saw no drop-off at all. Television was usurping movies' central role in entertaining America, its immediacy and accessibility threatening to doom Hollywood to irrelevance. And no sitcom caught America's eye as immediately, or as thoroughly, as *I Love Lucy* (CBS, 1951–57).

I Love Lucy teetered on the balance between order and chaos, only reluctantly returning to the status quo. Lucy Ricardo (Lucille Ball), housewife and (eventually) mother, dreams of showbiz stardom, a beautiful bauble perpetually denied her by her husband, Ricky (Desi Arnaz), a nightclub performer. "You have no talent," Ricky bluntly tells Lucy, and he undoubtedly has a point. Lucy brays in an off-key, tuneless warble, unabashedly mugs for any audience she performs in front of, and lacks the suave polish of her showman husband. And yet, her copious deficiencies notwithstanding, Lucy hungers for fame, whatever the format or forum.

From the very outset, then, *I Love Lucy* winked at its audience, letting them in on the joke of the show's double identity. Lucille Ball embodied Lucy McGillicuddy Ricardo, frustrated housewife dreaming of showbiz triumph, even when viewers knew her as one of the most famous, instantly recognizable women in the world. This double sense—of a world within the television and another without—was compounded by *I Love Lucy*'s exploration of the fragile membrane dividing television from not-television. For someone desperate to appear on television, Lucy sure was on TV a lot.

The first-season episode "Lucy Does a TV Commercial," written by Jess Oppenheimer, Madelyn Pugh, and Bob Carroll Jr., is simultaneously one of Lucy Ricardo's many stabs at fame (in other episodes she replaces a baggy-pantsed comic in Ricky's act, auditions as a ballet dancer, works as a movie extra . . .) and a wink in the direction of the format itself. Lucy—the protagonist's name itself bearing witness to the overlap between art and life—bubbles with excitement on hearing that Ricky must hire an actress for a sponsor's commercial spot. She is, she asserts, an old hand in the ways of television programs: "Well, maybe not," she admits, "but I've watched them a lot."

In an effort to convince Ricky of her suitability, she enlists her neighbor, landlord, and occasional ally Fred Mertz (husband of Lucy's best friend, Ethel) to assist her with a proto-advertisement of her own. Cramming her head inside the empty frame of a television set, Lucy performs an impromptu cigarette commercial for her husband. "I can't get over how clear the picture is," Ricky, clearly amused, burbles. Lucy, as klutzy as ever, drops her pack of cigarettes through the screen and onto the floor. "Well, what do you know?" Ricky exclaims. "Third-dimensional television!" Lucy is both at home and on television, a star and a housewife all at once.

Lucy ultimately finagles her way into shooting the spot and is brought to the studio for a run-through of the ad before the broadcast. She is to tout the medicinal virtues of her product while also extolling its delightful taste. "Do you poop out at parties?" Lucy asks us, perfectly capturing the mock intimacy of a television huckster. The good news, she lets us know, is that Vitameatavegamin means "you can spoon your way to health!"

The director prompts Lucy to taste the product while delivering her pitch line—"It's so tasty, too!"—and Ball brilliantly telegraphs the shock of its unpleasant aftertaste, her face crumpling in a sour grimace as she swallows it down. Lucy is a two-year-old condemned to an eternally heaping plate of broccoli; on each encounter with the elixir, her lips curl into a frozen rictus, the skeleton of a smile without its flesh. Her eyes are two dead fish, her entire body tensing for the impact of another spoonful of Vitameatavegamin, communicating the broad sensations of discomfort and dissatisfaction. We are already in the realm of classic Ball physical comedy, but she then ratchets up the entire scene another notch. She reminds us that, as we have been told, Vitameatavegamin is 20 percent alcohol, and sets the bar for sitcom antics to come. Lucy does another run-through of the ad, brighter this time, ending with a surprise hiccup that rocks her body.

With each spoonful, Lucy gets a bit drunker, her smile more vacant, her eyes bulging slightly more, her words ever more slurred. Instead of cringing at the impact of each new dose, she eagerly anticipates it: "It's so tasty, too. Tastes like candy—honest!" The product's name undergoes a drunken reedit, now known as "Mitameatamigamin," which Lucy further informs us is chock-full of "megetables and vinerals." She spills much of the bottle on the floor and ends up swigging directly from the bottle and licking her fingers, and the spoon. She now offers a more heartfelt, if vaguer, encomium: "So everybody get a bottle of . . . this stuff!"

The episode is a classic example of Ball's enduring physical gifts. She is unafraid to make herself ridiculous in the pursuit of a laugh, and *Lucy* leans heavily on her perpetual fondness for costumes and imitations. In other episodes, Lucy disguises herself as a hobo musician to wheedle her way into Ricky's show, as a toothless hillbilly while posing as Ricky's date to a nightclub, and as an elderly biddy to ward off an older admirer. Lucy is fond of set-designing a fully rounded scene to win a point, be it the soiled version of her apartment, complete with rubber tires on the couch and lines of wash snaking across the living room—set up to fool a visiting photographer—or the steak she sets aflame to discourage her unwanted admirer, dousing it with a bottle of seltzer and then cutting it with a mallet and chisel.

The central set piece of "Lucy Does a TV Commercial," by imagining Lucy Ricardo / Lucille Ball as the impromptu star of a television commercial, was referencing an already familiar pattern of TV stars shilling for products on the air. Gertrude Berg, star of *The Goldbergs*, had plumped for Sanka as early as 1949, pledging that its decaf brand was safe any time of day, because "the sleep is left in." Television was in the business of entertainment, but that was paid for by the sponsorship of major corporations, meaning that television was ultimately in the business of providing eyeballs for commercials. The Depression and the war years had established a pattern of thrift and economizing that postwar advertisers needed to undo in order to sell their products. The first wave of TV commercials was dedicated to a kind of breathless hucksterism, boosting not only the product in question but the very notion of consumerism as the solution. It was, as Shellaby Jackson put it in a 1954 *New Republic* article, "a kind of frenzy. Sell, sell, sell—dozens of men with white teeth, pushing packages of cigarettes at you, dozens of well-groomed women batting their eyes and pushing packages of soap at you."

Between 1949 and 1953, television ad billings increased tenfold, from $68 million to $688 million. In that time, advertisers hired stars like Henry Fonda, Milton Berle, and Steve Allen as pitchmen. Ads were integrated into shows, with Alfred Hitchcock sardonically commenting on his commercial sponsors (with dialogue written by a copywriter) on *Alfred Hitchcock Presents*, and Jack Paar snapping photos of his guests with Polaroid Land Cameras. Berle and Dinah Shore would sing their sponsors' jingles on their shows. The early 1950s were a time of unconscious "advertainment" meant to escape the notice of viewers, when Jerry Lewis would shill for Colgate on the *Comedy Hour* sponsored by the brand, and Art Carney of *The Honeymooners* would pop in to *The Jackie Gleason Show* during an ad for Nescafé.

There was huge money to be made in television comedy, with CBS selling sponsorship of *The Jackie Gleason Show* at $90,000 a week in 1952. Phil Silvers smoked Camel cigarettes during episodes of *The Phil Silvers Show*, and the company was prominently featured in the show's opening credits. Even Ball made a habit of squeezing her sponsor into her shows, smoking Philip Morris cigarettes on *I Love Lucy* and doing ads in character as Lucy Ricardo; she would later do Westinghouse spots with Arnaz and pitchwoman extraordinaire Betty Furness on *The Lucille Ball–Desi Arnaz Show*.

As a new medium, television required adjustments to the very products being sold so that they could look as appealing as possible. Swiss cheese required the efforts of carpenters, who would make larger holes that would show up better on viewers' small television screens. Meat was always shown raw, and usually coated with petroleum jelly. The color white wreaked havoc on TV screens' contrast, leading to the strange spectacle of white cakes being dyed green in order to better show up as white.

But television ads, in this early era, were also generally presented live (although not on *Lucy*, which was shot on film, about which more momentarily), which led inevitably to mishaps and goofs. Live performers would shill for Lipton Tea while holding up a competitor's package, break into racking coughs after touting a cigarette's smoothness, get caught on camera dumping beer into a pail at their feet, or find themselves unable to turn off the electric shaver they were touting. They would open refrigerators and yank off the doors. They would, in short, act much like Lucy does in her Vitameatavegamin commercial. "Lucy Does a TV Commercial," then, perhaps is also a documentary of sorts, depicting the worst indignities of the early television advertisement.

Thus, the episode is a reminder that television was self-absorbed from practically the very beginning. "Television isn't going to last. It's just a fad," Lucy tells Ricky, but the joke was already self-evident, for TV was, by the early 1950s, an established fact of American life. In another notable episode of *Lucy*, Ricky is approached by a television executive, who solicits suggestions for a TV program with him as the star. "How about one of those husband-and-wife TV shows?" he offers. Which is precisely what we are already watching, of course. *I Love Lucy*, and the sitcom at large, demands that we simultaneously believe and not believe, trust in the efficacy of the fiction and also stand outside it, marveling at its verisimilitude. Celebrating its own domesticity, the sitcom was at home in our living rooms, making itself comfortable in a way the larger, more expensive, and more stolid movies never could. We did not have to go to television; television came to us.

And so while the sitcom, in its early years, sought shelter under the awning of domestic serenity and unchanging order, it also persistently drew attention to its newness, even as it pretended otherwise. Ricky successfully kept Lucy from stardom; and yet, in almost every episode, she sought escape from her comfortable domestic prison into the magical realm of celebrity. *I Love Lucy* pays obeisance to order while preferring the company of chaos. A pattern was established that would keep sitcoms busily active for the next half-century.

Lucy, though far and away the cleverest of its ilk, was not the first television series to exploit this sense of domesticity. Early TV was much more feminine than the macho bluster of the movies. The cinematic genre known as "the women's picture" had once catered to these audiences, with pictures starring Joan Crawford or Bette Davis, devoted to stories of downtrodden women emerging triumphant. By the early 1950s this brand of filmmaking was on its way to extinction, and television picked up the baton, turning over much of its early programming—especially its comic series—to women.

Many of these series leaned on a familiar brand of urban, ethnic humor, with raucous families anchored by a loving maternal figure. The antic Norwegians of *Mama* (CBS, 1949–57) and the eccentric Jews of *The Goldbergs* (CBS/NBC, 1949–56) were essentially the same family in different garb. Television took over where radio left off, with series like *The Goldbergs* and *The Life of Riley* making the transition from one form to the next, and others, like *I Love Lucy*, adapted from radio forebears.

The only real competition for Ball as a comic icon in this earliest era of TV was a pudgy Jewish matron with a similar itch to upend a stable but fragile domestic order. Echoing the journeys of so many other Jewish families in the aftermath of World War II, Molly Goldberg (series creator Gertrude Berg) and her family left the big city—in their case, East Tremont Avenue, the Bronx—and departed for the wide-open spaces of the suburbs, mingling with a Gentile world mostly unfamiliar to them. Having begun life as a highly popular radio serial, *The Goldbergs* made the transition to television in 1949, with the medium still in its infancy.

The Goldbergs is a remarkable document of early television, and a series that truthfully and humorously depicts the lives of American Jews. At a time when the (mostly Jewish) Hollywood moguls, deathly afraid of telling overtly Jewish stories, were taking their first tentative steps toward Jewish content with films like *Crossfire* (1947) and *Gentleman's Agreement* (1947), *The Goldbergs* was unashamedly Jewish. This is clearest in the immigrant malapropisms of Molly and her family, which often result in unintentional hilarity. "Should I boil you or fry you?" Uncle David (the brilliant Eli Mintz) asks at the breakfast table, and Molly tells her daughter "go and hang yourself in your closet" when she purchases a new dress.

Family happiness on *The Goldbergs* is threatened weekly by Molly's enthusiasms—for poetry, for psychoanalysis, for her daughter's singing career—but twenty-five minutes always bring about the resolution of all conflicts and the comforting ring of familial laughter. *The Goldbergs*, notably gentler than *Lucy*, was a progenitor of many of the family sitcoms that followed it, and the series remains remarkable for the loving attention it offers to the details of its Jewish family—the gefilte fish and the kugel, the squabbles over money and schoolwork, the tension between shtetl-bred parents and Americanized children. Like a classic sitcom that followed in its wake, *Seinfeld*, *The Goldbergs* makes Jews quintessentially American.

Television also became the province of has-beens and almost-familiar names, the place where movie stars went to be reborn. Many if not most of the popular sitcoms of the early and mid-1950s were star vehicles for movie character actors: Eve Arden in *Our Miss Brooks* (CBS, 1948–57), William

Bendix in *The Life of Riley* (NBC, 1949–58), Red Buttons in *The Red Buttons Show* (CBS/NBC, 1952–55), Ray Milland in *The Ray Milland Show* (CBS, 1953–55), Ann Sothern in *Private Secretary* (CBS, 1953–57), Spring Byington in *December Bride* (CBS, 1954–59), Walter Brennan in *The Real McCoys* (ABC/CBS, 1957–63), Charles Farrell in *My Little Margie* (CBS/NBC, 1952–55), Donna Reed in *The Donna Reed Show* (ABC, 1958–66). That many of these stars were women was no accident; as a domestic medium, the sitcom was the preferred home for a wave of female stars who found in its comforting familiarity the perfect habitat for their talents.

Sothern, who would later make a series of guest appearances with Ball on her *I Love Lucy* follow-up *The Lucy Show*, was a Lucy-like schemer on the modestly amusing *Private Secretary*, using her natural gifts for duplicity and double-talk to bend ostensible boss Don Porter to her desires. She smiles and snickers at Porter's fulminations on the telephone, one eyebrow perpetually raised in disbelief at the excesses of masculinity. "Still looking for the woman behind the man," her boss chides her. "Who's behind me—you?" She smirks.

Our Miss Brooks, like *Lucy*, gave a well-regarded Hollywood character actress with glints of comedic talent her own platform. Arden did her own version of Ball's scrunched eyebrows and bulging eyes, expressing perpetual surprise at the goings-on at the high school where she taught. But the show, compared with *Lucy*, is astoundingly slow. A single plot development—Miss Brooks being cajoled into jumping off the roof onto a waiting trampoline, or the school principal hiding meat in the school freezer—was stretched like stale taffy into a half-hour episode.

I Love Lucy was more successful at pairing order and subversion, at honoring normalcy while furtively undermining it. Lucy and Ricky are the television couple *par excellence*: cheerful, well scrubbed, and inoffensive. And yet traces of the exotic are present from the very outset. Ricky is Cuban, his occasional bursts of ill temper causing him to lash volleys of rapid-fire Spanish at his wife, and at the audience, neither of whom are expected to understand a word. Ricky is an alien presence in the guise of a familiar one, a deeply traditional 1950s husband and provider who is also a musician—and worse, a foreigner.

Husbands and wives speak different languages; *Lucy* only literalizes this familiar state of affairs. "Lucy, you got some 'splainin' to do," Ricky is forever demanding of his wife, his mangled English undermining his persistent urge for clarity in all his affairs. Ricky Ricardo is domineering and softhearted all at once, his traditional Cuban machismo (as the show sees it) partially offset by his tender acceptance of his wife's antics. Lucy is addle-headed and emotional, a creature of instinct incapable of reining in her unruly dream life. She can no more hide her emotions than a young child can; her two most prominent—petulance and sadness—arc over the full emotional palette of the toddler. She is an overgrown infant playing housewife, beating the bed with her fists and wailing like a police siren.

Ball and Arnaz were, of course, an offscreen couple as well as an onscreen one. Raised in Upstate New York, Ball got her start as a model, doing the occasional nude pictorial, before being recruited to Los Angeles for a supporting role in an Eddie Cantor picture. Within a decade, she was a well-regarded character actor in the movies, appearing alongside Katharine Hepburn and Ginger Rogers in the wisecracking backstage comedy *Stage Door* (1938), and in Dorothy Arzner's groundbreaking *Dance, Girl, Dance* (1941). Arnaz was a successful bandleader in his own right, with his biggest hit, "Babalu," destined to be resuscitated countless times on *I Love Lucy*.

Ball had pushed unsuccessfully to have Arnaz as her husband and costar on the CBS Radio program *My Favorite Husband* (1948–51), arguing that audiences would better believe a relationship with roots in real life. CBS cast Richard Denning instead, but changed the couple's name from the Cugats to the Coopers out of deference to Arnaz, whose Latin bandleader rival was named Xavier Cugat. The show was a notable hit, making Ball, in her late thirties, a household name for the first time.

When the show's sponsor wanted to adapt *My Favorite Husband* for television, Ball again pushed to work with her real husband on a similar show of their own. ("CBS said, 'We want you to go into television, but we think your husband, well, no one would believe *he* was your husband,' she later remembered. "And I said, 'Why not? We're married!'") She shot a pilot with the collaboration of Jess Oppenheimer, Madelyn Pugh, and Bob

Carroll Jr., who would serve as the brain trust for *I Love Lucy*. An executive at the advertising firm Young & Rubicam had suggested to Ball and Arnaz that they produce their own pilot, thereby retaining financial and creative control over their show—a decision that would reap untold rewards for them in the future.

With the casting of its central couple, *I Love Lucy* set itself partway along the path running to *The Adventures of Ozzie and Harriet*, in which Ozzie and Harriet Nelson and their real-life sons David and Ricky would accidentally create the world's first reality show by acting out pre-scripted adventures: a family playing at being a family. Although Ball and Arnaz did not play themselves, *I Love Lucy* thrived on reminding audiences of its stars' genuine romantic connection.

Lucy was the first sitcom to be shot on film before a studio audience, allowing Ball and Arnaz to re-create the sensation of performing for a crowd and feed off their energy, while avoiding the quality issues associated with live broadcasts. For the first few years of television, sitcoms were generally broadcast live on the East Coast, and the only way to record such a program was to film it off a monitor as it aired. This low-quality reproduction, called a kinescope, would then be used for the West Coast broadcast. Recording the performance itself on celluloid was far more expensive, but it allowed Ball and Arnaz to produce *I Love Lucy* from Los Angeles rather than moving out to New York, as CBS preferred. They could then edit the show together and provide high-quality copies for broadcast on both coasts.

Arnaz, credited as a producer alongside series creator Oppenheimer, had also founded the production company Desilu, its name formed out of the conjunction of Arnaz and Ball's first names. Desilu Productions was originally established for the purposes of producing a vaudeville show for Arnaz and Ball to star in, but the company would take off as a groundbreaking producer of scripted television series, beginning with *I Love Lucy* and continuing with classic sitcoms like *The Dick Van Dyke Show* and *The Andy Griffith Show*.

Arnaz also hired legendary cinematographer Karl Freund, who had photographed German Expressionist film classics like *The Last Laugh* (1924) and *Metropolis* (1927), to design a lighting system for the show. In order to capture different angles without fracturing the studio audience's experience by stopping to reset the camera, Arnaz wanted to shoot with three cameras simultaneously. Freund insisted that such a scenario was impossible; a different lighting setup would be required for each shot, depending on whether it was a wide, medium, or close-up shot. Shooting them all at once could never work. Arnaz, always a master manipulator, convinced Freund that the man who had invented the light meter should have no difficulty solving this problem, and the three-camera sitcom was born.

The even, flat lighting—allowing long shots and close-ups to be shot during the same take—is perhaps the single most immediately recognizable visual signature of the sitcom. The movies were dramatic, bold, eye-catching; television, a performer's medium, defined itself by its relative pictorial blandness. Whatever Freund's masterly work may have been intended to accomplish, this was ultimately part of the sitcom's appeal. It was intentionally dumpy, its ordinariness a silent passport for entry into homes across America.

Every sitcom possesses not just a routine that it perpetually seeks to overturn but also a particular style of fomenting that chaos. For *I Love Lucy*, it is the schemes playfully coordinated between an ever-rotating alliance of conspirators. Lucy and Ricky are matched, and balanced out, by Fred and Ethel Mertz, the older couple who are their landlords at 623 E. 68th Street in Manhattan. Ethel (Vivian Vance) is the quintessential busybody, walking into the Ricardos' apartment with a postcard for Lucy she has already seen fit to memorize. Fred (William Frawley), her husband, is devoted to his own creature comforts, treating Ethel like an old brown shoe he is too lazy to toss out. Fred is forever insulting his wife by overlooking all of her disguises; even clad in a men's suit, with a mustache penciled onto her upper lip, Fred walks right by her, having noticed nothing out of the ordinary about her getup. "How did you see through my disguise?" Ethel demands. "What disguise?" Fred innocently wonders.

Lucy is a four-handed vaudeville routine whose recurring theme is the prospect of revenge. In "Lucy Fakes Illness," Ricky catches on to one of

Lucy's schemes and hires an actor friend to turn the tables on her: "The show is called 'Getting Even with Lucy,'" he tells him. Someone is always getting even with someone else on *I Love Lucy*, and the institution of marriage itself is primarily a vehicle for petty gamesmanship and jockeying for position. The results are, occasionally, comically squalid—do Lucy and Ricky ever do anything *but* fight?—but also a television recreation of the adventures of Nick and Nora Charles in the *Thin Man* movies. Marriage was not necessarily a coffin built for two; it could be the license for unending, joyous competition.

In short order, *I Love Lucy* became the most popular show yet to appear on television, featured on more than ten million sets across the country every Monday at 9:00 PM eastern. When a campaign program for Democratic presidential nominee Adlai Stevenson preempted five minutes of *I Love Lucy*, it prompted thousands of outraged letters.

The program's success inspired the famously difficult cast to get along, or at least to keep their squabbling at a constant low simmer. Ball yanked off Vance's false eyelashes before one taping, telling her "nobody wears false eyelashes on this show but *me*." Vance, aware that *Lucy* was likely to be a hit, said of her costar and employer, "I'm gonna learn to love that bitch." The perpetually sozzled Frawley was also a nuisance, regularly calling Vance "bitch." She responded by referring to him as an "old coot." Vance would ultimately refuse what likely would have been a highly successful spinoff series after *I Love Lucy* called it quits because of her reluctance to go on working with Frawley.

The show was so popular that it eventually would expand the boundaries of what was allowed to appear on television. When Lucy becomes pregnant on the show, no one was allowed to describe her as such, only as "expecting" or "with child." "Pregnant" might have offended the delicate sensibilities of religiously inclined TV watchers, like the words "sex," "damn," and "hell," and even "for God's sake" and "darn." Nonetheless, by portraying a pregnant woman at all, *Lucy* expanded the spectrum of what made for acceptable family fare on television—a debate that would recur time and again in sitcom history.

Although television had emerged out of radio, it also owed a substantial debt to live theater, to which it bore a distinct resemblance. Why, after all, was there a live audience for the taping of a recorded television program? The audience lustily applauds Lucy and Ricky waking up in their separate beds, saluting them for appearing for our entertainment. With Arnaz an actual bandleader before being drafted to star in the show, and costar William Frawley a stage veteran, *I Love Lucy* carried distinct reminders of vaudeville. Practically every episode would pause for a musical number, be it Ricky onstage at the Club Tropicana, or former vaudevillians Fred and Ethel hoping to impress a new stranger—a television producer, a theater director—with some half-remembered bit of Ziegfeld Follies razzle-dazzle. It also owed a debt to the cinematic subgenre of the backstage musical, its musical interludes and comic numbers all justified by the show's plot. *I Love Lucy* was deliberately baggy, often extending its central comic bit to the expected half-hour running time with the addition of these interludes and asides. In so doing, *Lucy* would establish the sitcom style, dressed up with musical numbers and other asides, that would later serve the likes of *The Dick Van Dyke Show*, which likewise benefited from its show-business backdrop, and *The Cosby Show*, which imported performers like Stevie Wonder and Lena Horne.

But television was also something entirely new. It could be parodied or mocked, but its omnipresence could not be ignored. In one episode Lucy and Ricky get new neighbors, a husband-and-wife acting team with an upcoming TV gig; as they rehearse some dialogue, they note that it's pretty corny—even for television. In the episode "Lucy Gets Ricky on the Radio," Lucy proposes switching the television off for the evening and talking instead. To their chagrin, Lucy and Ricky, along with Ethel and Fred, find they have nothing to say to one another. Television filled in the dead air of American domesticity, and even its temporary absence reminded viewers—soon to be practically every American man, woman, and child—of its ubiquity.

The prospect of life without television was simply too painful to bear; when Fred, incensed by Ricky's flubbing the repair of the Mertzes' brand-new television, kicks a hole in the Ricardos' TV as payback, he is acting out

a primal scene of undiluted horror. Television was imagining its own evis-
ceration, encouraging viewers to cringe at the possibility of its disappearance. Later sitcoms like *The Cosby Show* and *Seinfeld* would self-consciously
avoid showing their characters' TV sets unless the story absolutely required
it, like superstitious medieval villagers afraid of drawing attention to what
they revered, and feared, most.

I Love Lucy was a touchstone of physical humor on television, with Ball
the inheritor of the gag-strewn comedy of the era of Charlie Chaplin and
Buster Keaton. In "Job Switching," one of the series' most beloved episodes,
Lucy and Ethel agree to switch responsibilities with their husbands to test
Ricky and Fred's assertion that housework is easier than earning a living.
The women are hired at a candy factory, where they struggle to keep up
with the chocolates skittering off the assembly line. Gamely attempting
to wrap each chocolate, Ethel eventually begins gobbling whole fistfuls to
keep up, while Lucy stuffs them down her shirt and into her hat. The entire
sequence is lifted wholesale from Chaplin's *Modern Times* (1936), and yet
Ball makes it her own, domesticating Chaplin's bittersweet grandeur for a
smaller format.

After running out of new permutations for its four leading characters,
I Love Lucy rejuvenated itself in its fourth season, in 1954–55, by moving
the Ricardos and the Mertzes to Hollywood. Following an epic cross-
country journey, Lucy is deposited in the white-hot core of American celebrity, breathlessly chasing after boldfaced names like a dog pursuing a table
scrap. She poses as a bellhop to sneak into Cornel Wilde's room, flinging his
newspaper in the bathtub when Wilde calls for it; she fakes a poolside chat
with Van Johnson to impress an out-of-town friend; and in "L.A., at Last,"
she hounds William Holden at the famed Brown Derby restaurant.

Sitting in an adjoining booth, Lucy spies Holden in her makeup mirror and is rattled when Holden stares back. She butters her hand instead of
a slice of bread, and gets tangled in a long strand of pasta she is unable to
unwind. (Ethel eventually snips it with a pair of scissors.) When Holden
comes up to their apartment to visit Ricky, Lucy hides behind a false nose
and glasses. Holden, lighting a cigarette, sets fire to Lucy's putty nose,

which she douses in a mug of coffee while still on her face (an inspired ad-lib on Ball's part). Lucy is a star impersonating a nobody, her relentless pursuit of Holden and the like a metaphorical stand-in for television's second-class status. Ball may have been somebody to us, but her medium was still a distinct afterthought in Hollywood.

Even more brilliant is Lucy's pas de deux with Harpo Marx, with whom she re-creates the legendary mirror scene from the Marx Brothers' film *Duck Soup* (1933). In the episode "Harpo Marx," Lucy poses as a series of Hollywood leading men to impress a visiting friend. After dressing as Gary Cooper and Clark Gable, she returns as Harpo—or so Ethel thinks. It is, of course, Harpo himself, handing Fred his leg to hold and playing "Take Me Out to the Ball Game" on the harp.

When Lucy shows up in her own Harpo costume, the real Harpo reaches for his chest, as if to assure himself of his own continued existence. Lucy steps into the Harpo role from *Duck Soup*, and Harpo assumes the Groucho role, trying to catch his imitator in a false step. After acting out a steadily escalating series of awkward gestures—a missed clap, a monkey face and belly scratch—Harpo and Lucy take off their hats to reveal identical mops of tight red curls. A baton is passed—from one red-haired clown to another, from one generation to the next, from the movies to television.

I Love Lucy lasted for six seasons and 180 episodes, ending as it had started: as the most popular show on television. *Lucy* transitioned into *The Lucille Ball–Desi Arnaz Show* in 1957, which offered the occasional new, hour-long Lucy adventure. Ball and Arnaz divorced in 1960, but Ball went on playing some form of Lucy for the rest of her television career, on *The Lucy Show* (CBS, 1962–68) and *Here's Lucy* (CBS, 1968–74). Ball's voice was smokier, more ragged, and less fluting than it once had been. Color, and the passage of time, were unforgiving. Where Ball had once been a beautiful woman masked as a clown, she had been transformed into a clown first and foremost, the blue eye shadow and carrot-orange hair an exaggeration of an exaggeration. On *The Lucy Show*, she was now Lucille Carmichael, dim-witted secretary, still embroiled in absurd hijinks: babysitting monkeys and filling in as a ventriloquist's dummy. The show reunited her with her *I Love Lucy* costar Vivian Vance, and its female-heavy cast gave rise to a nasty nickname: *The Dyke Sans Dick Show*.

Ball, while still enormously popular, was coasting on the fumes of Lucy Ricardo, her post-*Lucy* series intentionally blurring the lines between her most famous character and later incarnations. Ball had trouble moving on, but the sitcom itself did not. Fans preferred watching *I Love Lucy* reruns—a relatively new phenomenon beginning in the 1960s, when networks realized that old shows were a convenient schedule filler and a potential gold mine—to new episodes of *The Lucy Show*. "TV became a repository of popular culture," argues Stefan Kanfer, and "the storehouse of national memory." Television, only just emerging, already had a past worthy of note.

2

The Honeymooners

"Better Living Through TV"

November 12, 1955 ■ CBS

Awoman stands in her dilapidated kitchen in her threadbare apartment, plunging a clogged sink. Vigorously thrusting the plunger in and out until the foul bubbling subsides, she is a harried housewife at her occasionally rank daily work. It would be hard to imagine many of the other television programs of the 1950s featuring a clogged sink as prominently. *The Honeymooners* made it the very first scene of its first episode. The version of family life peddled by 1950s sitcoms like *Leave It to Beaver* was devoted to a prim aesthetic—separate beds, please!—and their scrapes magically remained antiseptic. But *The Honeymooners* was messy. Its pipes were regularly clogged, backed up by the brackish water of dissension and dissatisfaction and everyday human misery.

Jackie Gleason was perpetually frazzled bus driver Ralph Kramden, who never met an argument or a get-rich-quick scheme he didn't like. Ralph was the original television man-child, mothered by his ever-loving, ever-forgiving wife Alice (Audrey Meadows). He was also the living embodiment of the blue-collar sitcom—a thread that would be mostly abandoned after *The Honeymooners* and not picked up again for decades to come.

At the start of each episode, the audience would deafeningly applaud the entrance of Gleason and his costars, as if the curtain had been raised on the hit Broadway show of the season. *The Honeymooners* emerged from the variety show/vaudeville/radio nexus out of which the sitcom had been born. In its attitudes, the series reflected the same working-class, outer-borough milieu as Paddy Chayefsky's film *Marty* (1955).

The Honeymooners' constricted world was kitchen-sink drama (literally) with a laugh track, a pitiless exploration of man's inhumanity to man equipped with punch lines. "Never finished anything," Ralph says of himself in the episode "Young Man with a Horn," pacing around his wife while fingering the cornet his father had given him as a boy. "I could never hit the high note on anything I tried. . . . I mighta been the guy that built the Empire State Building if I'd stuck at that." The accidental lyricism melded indelibly with the Laurel & Hardy–esque hijinks of Ralph and his best friend, Ed Norton (Art Carney), the whole adding up to a sentimental sitcom take on *Waiting for Godot*. "I'm an important guy. I'm an important guy," Ralph repeats to himself like a mantra, before collapsing and admitting defeat: "I'm only important to me."

The show is a demonstration of the universality of misery, with Ralph a man dreaming of escape from sad-sack Brooklyn, and forever failing. The Kramdens live at 328 Chauncey Street—the address of Gleason's childhood home. *The Honeymooners* is attuned to the concerns, and speech patterns, of the Brooklyn of Gleason's youth. Ralph drives a bus, Ed works in the sewers, and everyone they encounter seems to have a similarly blue-collar job. When Ralph loses his job because of layoffs, he suggests to his wife that they "cut out this high living." Just what high living he might be referring to is a mystery to his wife, and the audience. Eschewing the traditional lifestyle sleight of hand of Hollywood, by which struggling artists reside in penthouse aeries and work is something that happens offscreen and out of sight, *The Honeymooners* was proudly grubby. Ed says "cherce," not "choice." Sitcoms such as *All in the Family* and *Roseanne*, preferring struggle to comfort, would follow in its defiantly working-class wake. (Amazingly, Gleason later turned down an opportunity to play another of the most legendary characters in television history, rejecting the role of Archie Bunker on *All in the Family* for being too vulgar.)

By "reflecting [Gleason's] humble origins," David Sterritt wrote, *The Honeymooners* "allow[ed] him to smack them away." The star's older brother had died when he was a boy, and his mother had tried to keep Jackie safe from harm by quarantining him at home. When Gleason was nine, his father disappeared, never to be heard from again, but not before first taking Jackie on a transformative trip to the theater. Jackie, soaking in the applause for a successful performer, had turned around to watch the audience clap and cheer, and had a revelation: "I want to be up there and look out at them applauding for me. That is what will feel the most natural."

Performance was a drug. "I got a laugh," Gleason later said of his early attempts at entertaining a crowd, "and it was like, I guess, ten spoonfuls of cocaine." But to return to those heights, he required chemical assistance of a more literal sort. Said Gleason about re-creating an early triumph, "I tried to remember what I had done and I knew the only way to remember was to go to the bar and have about fifteen drinks and it would come to me."

At first, Gleason was a popular, if uninspired, second-tier comic, swiping much of his material from Milton Berle and coasting on impressions of the likes of Peter Lorre. After creatively insulting Jack Warner at one gig, Gleason was signed as a contract player by Warner Bros., for whom he appeared in *All Through the Night* (1941) alongside Humphrey Bogart and

Phil Silvers. Theater was perhaps a better fit for Gleason, but he was often bored by the necessity of repeating the same material nightly. Wouldn't it be better if every performance could be a high-wire act, like those first alcohol-fueled triumphs?

Gleason made his earliest television appearance with a twenty-six-week run on the first TV version of *The Life of Riley* (NBC, 1949–58), his portrayal of blue-collar buffoon Chester Riley giving way to a more successful second incarnation of the show starring its original radio star, William Bendix. Bendix's Riley was a bug-eyed, hyperventilating shlemiel in the manner of Gleason, if without any of his charm or poignancy, turning his daughter's student-council election into a dirty-tricks campaign or convincing himself that his tonsillectomy was a life-threatening surgical procedure.

In 1950, Gleason moved on to a four-week contract as the fill-in host for the variety show *Cavalcade of Stars*, on the now-defunct DuMont Television Network. Pleased with his work, DuMont hired Gleason as the show's permanent host, giving him $50,000 a week with which to produce *Cavalcade*. The writers of the show's new iteration, looking to cut down on the monumental burden of crafting a completely original variety show each week, sought to create recurring characters for sketches. In the fall of 1951, they introduced a new one: dyspeptic bus driver Ralph Kramden. Ralph's perpetual squabbling with his wife was directly inspired by a popular radio program of the time, *The Bickersons*—perhaps too much so. When Gleason's booker/writer/assistant Joseph Cates asked if he wanted to license *The Bickersons* for his show, Gleason's answer had been delightfully blunt: "Fuck it, we'll make up our own."

Cavalcade brought in a cast of supporting performers soon to become household names in their own right. Art Carney was cast as Ed; Carney had been playing Newton the waiter on *The Morey Amsterdam Show* (CBS/DuMont, 1948–50), starring the future *Dick Van Dyke Show* mainstay. For Ed's wife, Trixie, Joyce Randolph was selected, because Cates had a crush on her roommate. (Elaine Stritch, later to hound Alec Baldwin's Jack Donaghy as his mother on *30 Rock*, also tried out for the Trixie Norton role.) Pert Kelton was cast as the original Alice, but was replaced by Audrey

Meadows in time for the show's most celebrated run. Gleason originally rejected Meadows as being too young and pretty for the role. She came back for a second audition dressed like Alice, without makeup, and fooled Gleason into thinking she was a different actress entirely.

"The Honeymooners" was one of the recurring elements of *Cavalcade of Stars*, and eventually became the linchpin of Gleason's own hour-long program, *The Jackie Gleason Show* (CBS, 1952–57; other, similar series featuring Gleason would stud the CBS schedule until 1970). By its third season, *The Jackie Gleason Show* was perched behind only *I Love Lucy* in the ratings.

The *Jackie Gleason* sketches parallel what would eventually be *The Honeymooners* in tone and format, although their running times vary wildly. Some installments are as long as a regular-length sitcom episode, while others are substantially shorter. But their concerns—Ralph's fluctuating weight, his squabbles with Ed and Alice, hated interruptions to his prized routine— are much the same as what would come. In "Ralph's Diet," a perpetually hungry Gleason goes berserk when a radio announcer suggests hitting the icebox for some "golden fried chicken." Ralph proceeds to smash his radio for its presumption to interfere with his weight-loss regimen. This is Ralph in a nutshell: slavishly devoted to a useless plan and punishing himself for his own failings.

Five seasons into his television career, Gleason was beginning to tire of the day-in, day-out grind of producing variety television, and he decided to switch to a sitcom format. It was not until 1955 that "The Honeymooners" was lifted from its live variety-show surroundings and turned into a filmed series in its own right for one lone season. The thirty-nine "classic" episodes of *The Honeymooners* form their own body of work, even as they are surrounded by other "Honeymooners" sketches and one-offs. Only in this context does the show truly function as a sitcom, much as *The Simpsons* only became a sitcom when it left the variety-show confines of *The Tracey Ullman Show*.

The Honeymooners is as much theater as television, the occasional flubbed lines of its performers, preserved for eternity, only adding to the sensation of the show as a stage, and not yet the window TV would become. (In a later episode, *The Honeymooners* would make the theatrical link literal, with

Gleason, Carney, and their castmates parting the curtains and stepping out to center stage to wish their audience—the people watching their performance, and by extension, those watching at home—a merry Christmas.) Gleason hated to rehearse, preferring the occasional mistakes that were testament to a fresh run through new material to the more polished patter of other shows. Everyone was to remain in character at all costs, even after an error or missed line. Eventually, the show's performers developed a secret language with which to communicate mid-show. If Meadows rubbed her stomach, that meant that Gleason should head for the refrigerator.

The medium itself was still young and unsure of both its capabilities and its responsibilities to realism. Ralph and Ed sneaking off for a fishing trip at 4 AM in "Something Fishy" are shot in the same broad, flat light as the rest of the series, with no hint of shadow or darkness visible. At other times, *The Honeymooners* was an accidental record of the production of a 1950s sitcom. When Ralph splashes paint all over his apartment in an effort to get out of his lease in the *Jackie Gleason Show* sketch "Moving Uptown," we can see the set's paper-thin walls shake on impact. The form of the sitcom had not solidified enough for it to know it was required to hide its imperfections from us.

But those imperfections are nothing compared to the imperfections of Ralph Kramden's life. Trapped in a nightmare of his own making, Ralph scrabbles desperately to get out, only to dig himself ever deeper in the quicksand of working-slob indignity. Meanwhile, the audience laughs heartily on the soundtrack. Were they sympathizing with the predicament of a place like Chauncey Street, or adding another subtle layer of mockery?

Ralph is forever solving his problems, seemingly erasing decades of hapless slobbery in a single stroke, only to fall victim to his own delusions of grandeur. We laugh at Ralph for his blindness, capable as he is of foreseeing everything except his own inevitable failures. In the episode "Ralph Kramden, Inc.," Ralph is notified he is being left a fortune by an elderly stranger, only to discover that Fortune is the name of her pet bird. In "The $99,000 Answer," he crams for a music-themed TV quiz show with Ed, who irritates him by regaling him with endless renditions of "Swanee River." On the show itself, Ralph is asked to identify that very song's composer, and finds, to his dismay, that he cannot ("Ed Norton?"). Ralph discovers a toothsome new dish of Alice's in "A Dog's Life," and immediately brings it to the attention of his bosses, dubbing it Kranmar's Delicious Mystery Appetizer. It is nothing other than dog food, and when he is alerted to his mistake, Ralph blanches, then collapses.

We come to know Ralph through his response to calamity—the beads of sweat on the forehead, the stammered rejoinders, the "humina-humina-humina." In "A Man's Pride," the last of the "classic" episodes, Ralph plays the swell with an old flame of Alice's and is stuck with the bill at a swanky restaurant. Summoning his courage, Ralph rolls his eyes heavenward, as if asking for deliverance from this trial, and tells his former rival, "I got a confession to make. My wife, Alice, has told me this once, she's told me a thousand times. That I shouldn't try to be somebody I'm not. I can't afford to pay this check." The episode ends in hilarity—his rival can't afford to pay, either—but the moment of swallowed pride lingers longer than the punch line.

Premiering at a time when many households were still yet to purchase their first set or were acclimating themselves to its arrival, *The Honeymooners* is explicitly about television's newfound centrality in American life. Its first episode, "TV or Not TV," was about a debate then taking place in millions of American homes: should the Kramdens buy a TV? Penny-pinching Ralph fights his wife every step of the way ("I'm waiting for 3-D television," he presciently tells his wife, fifty years ahead of his time), but when the television comes home, he is instantly transformed into a cathode-ray zombie.

Ralph squabbles with his neighbor Ed over what to watch—the kitschy *Captain Video* or a movie? Ed is already kitted out in his regulation Captain Video space helmet but is overruled by blustering Ralph, who threatens the space cadet's air supply if he disrupts the film again. Summoned to bed by his wife, bleary-eyed Ralph chooses the wrong door and stumbles down the front stairs. In a precedent that is rarely repeated, Ralph is given the honor of a partial triumph at the end of the episode. His wife acknowledges defeat: "Gotta admit it, Ralph, once in your life you were right. We never should have gotten a television set."

The Kramdens agreed, but America begged to differ. In 1946 there were a total of twenty thousand television sets in operation in the United States. Ten years later, there were forty million in circulation. Like the Kramdens, 85 percent of all American homes now owned a TV set. What had been a fringe interest of extreme early adopters, of technology buffs with enough expendable income to afford a $999 DuMont set, had become a mainstream leisure activity. The television set displaced the piano and the fireplace as the focal point and conversation piece of American living rooms. The average family was watching five hours a day of programming. TV had become America's hobby—and sitcoms were America's preferred entertainment. More people watched "Lucy Goes to the Hospital," to witness Ricky Ricardo Jr.'s arrival in the world, than tuned in to Dwight Eisenhower's inauguration as president the next day.

Television was here to stay, and by *The Honeymooners'* seventh episode, Ralph and Ed were dreaming not of watching TV but of starring on it. "Better Living Through TV," written by Marvin Marx and Walter Stone, is perhaps the most rip-roaring of *The Honeymooners'* thirty-nine episodes. It begins with yet another of Ralph's seemingly infinite array of schemes. This time, he and Ed plan to peddle an all-in-one kitchen gadget called the Handy Housewife Helper via live television infomercial, hoping to sell the product at a markup to the undiscriminating unwashed. Ralph and Ed practice their salesmanship until it becomes second nature. "Hello out there in television land!" Ed booms in his best announcer's voice. Ed is meant to be the stodgy chef of the past, revitalized and divested of his haul of useless implements, along with the purchase price of one dollar, by Ralph's wizardly chef of the future.

The medium, though, had ideas of its own, and the smoothly orchestrated, if stodgy, patter of their practice runs gives way to a disastrous live performance. Ralph freezes with stage fright, while Ed is hilariously unaffected by the presence of the cameras. Gleason looks queasy with panic, chewing his cud like a flatulent cow and fiddling hopelessly with his not-so-handy Housewife Helper. He eventually must be pushed into the spotlight like a reluctant toddler, eyes popping with fright, silently stammering as his gadget fatally guillotines an apple. Absolute television corrupts absolutely, even as its early practitioners sought to mold it in their own image.

Pop-eyed, nervous, skittish, Carney's Ed Norton is the ideal comic foil, the model sidekick to Gleason's perpetually agitated, overly well-fed, choleric Ralph. Carney is the Laurel to his Hardy, the beanpole to Gleason's tub of guts. ("The simp and the blimp," as Ralph's maid dubs the pair.) Ed is a crier like Laurel, forever sobbing when he gets himself into a pickle from which he cannot easily extricate himself. He reads Ralph's temperature by the glow of a cigarette lighter, and bawls when he sees Ralph has a fever of 111 degrees. Ralph's crime is the perpetual optimism of the easily duped. He and Ed are conjoined sitcom twins, doomed to terrorize each other without any hope of escaping the other's reach.

A few episodes into *The Honeymooners'* run, Carney started to get his own roar of applause with every entrance. The second banana had earned his own cheering section. Ed Norton paved the way for every notable television sidekick to come, including *Seinfeld*'s Kramer, who would eventually also stop the show each time he entered, receiving his due measure of acclaim. "I could do *The Honeymooners* with any Alice Kramden and any Trixie Norton that I picked up off the street," Gleason later said, in an unintentional swipe at Meadows and Randolph. "But I couldn't do it without Art Carney." Carney would go on to receive five Emmys for playing Ed Norton, while Gleason, to his chagrin, never won.

Much as it had been with Laurel & Hardy, *The Honeymooners* does not allow for the presence of any children, because Ralph and Ed are the designated infants here. (Little has changed in that regard; many of the Kramdens' squabbling sitcom descendants are childless as well.) Their wives are their full-time minders, doling out allowances and permission slips for their husbands' zanier exploits. And Ralph and Ed are perpetually bickering siblings, their harmonious play forever interrupted by explosions of peevishness and ill temper. "From here on in, *we* are deadly enemies," Ralph tells Ed in "The Man from Space," and some variant of the same recurs in nearly every episode. Ralph is prone to volcanic eruptions of anger, rising to his full height and pointing lazily at the front door: "Gee-et out!!" Offscreen,

Gleason and Carney were not quite deadly enemies, but contrary to the assertions of fan magazines and the actors themselves, neither were they best buddies. Years would often pass between conversations, and Gleason, mercurial and unpredictable at the best of times, retained all of his warmth for when the cameras were on.

Children would also have interfered with the tone of *The Honeymooners*. Kids require gentleness, instruction, forgiveness—all things the show scrupulously avoids. The emotional nub of *The Honeymooners* is perpetual dissatisfaction, be it Ralph's dissatisfaction with his lot in life, or Alice's with Ralph. Children would only dilute the primal intensity of its petulance. Ralph, in fact, seems only to know a small array of emotions: pride, juvenile pleasure, shame, and dyspepsia.

The series is pitched to the tune of the squabble. Everyone is bickering: Ralph and Alice, Ralph and Ed, Alice and Ed. In one episode, Ralph wagers that his mother-in-law will provoke a fight before three minutes have elapsed, and easily wins his bet. Ralph is forever threatening Alice with an array of baroque physical abuses, none of which ever come to fruition. "One of these days, one of these days, *pow!* Right in the kisser," Ralph snarls at Alice, his fist swiveling into an uppercut.

Ralph's most famous marital threat is one that gives the show's title an unexpected spin. It appears in a seemingly infinite series of varieties: "Do you want to go to the moon?" "The only place you're going is to the moon!" and so forth. (A nervous CBS executive once offered a creative note: "The moon is generally regarded as romantic. Could Ralph send her to Mars?") Ralph is constantly threatening his wife with violence, and yet the threats testify to his own beleaguerment rather than any real intent to harm. Many episodes end, too, on the same note of belated, weary acceptance, with Ralph reluctantly ceasing to grumble and making peace with Alice: "You know somethin', I did hit that high note once—the day I married you."

Gleason and Carney suck up much of the air on *The Honeymooners*, but the underrated Audrey Meadows's Alice has a wicked tongue of her own, with which she lashes Ralph mercilessly. In "Better Living Through TV,"

Ralph promises his wife that he is getting into the biggest thing he has ever gotten into. "The biggest thing you ever got into was your pants," Alice coolly responds. Meadows's dead-eyed gaze, trotted out only when she is truly furious with Ralph, is capable of turning her husband to ash with a single look. Alice jabs at Ralph's weight mercilessly, tormenting him even when ostensibly comforting him. "Nobody's gonna put you in a straitjacket," she consoles him in the *Jackie Gleason Show* sketch "The Little Man Who Wasn't There." "Where are they gonna find one big enough?" "You losing a pound," she tells him on another occasion, "is like Bayonne losing a mosquito." Alice has presumably learned from her own mother, who celebrated her union with Ralph by tartly observing, "I'm not losing a daughter, I'm gaining a ton."

Numerous episodes of *The Honeymooners* revolve around a role reversal in which male chauvinist Ralph must admit that his wife's work is even more soul-sucking than driving for the Gotham Bus Company. In "A Woman's Work Is Never Done," Ralph hires a maid (with what money?) to help out Alice after she complains of being overworked. "It may sound like work," Alice says of her "giddy" decision to spend her day washing the floor and windows, cleaning out the closet, shopping, and cooking a roast rather than ironing Ralph's shirt, "but it's fun!" The new maid is incorrigibly lazy (on hearing her employer's bell, she casually remarks, "If that's the Good Humor man, get me a popsicle"), and soon enough it is Ralph who must take over the housework.

In "Brother Ralph," Ralph is pressed into duty as a househusband when he is temporarily laid off and his wife must go to work. Almost instantly, husband and wife reverse roles: Alice comes home bone tired, demanding dinner and a back rub, and Ralph is in an apron, preparing dinner and complaining about lacking the money for steaks. *The Honeymooners*, at its core a product of the conformist 1950s, has a not-so-secret rebellious streak.

Ralph is, as he informs anyone who will listen, a king in his castle, master of his domain, but his insistence on reminding all and sundry of this fact reflects the uncertainty of his crown. He is, like *Father Knows Best*'s Jim Anderson, another paper tiger, ruling only with the consent of the governed.

As for Ed Norton, he tells a journalist that he is the unquestioned boss in his home but asks him not to print it: "If my wife reads that, she'll kill me." For all its macho chest-thumping, *The Honeymooners* acknowledges precisely who runs the Kramden and Norton households.

"Better Living Through TV" ends with Ralph near tears. Gleason's innate melancholy—the trampled dignity of the overweight, disheveled middle-aged man—supplies the surprising bittersweetness of this and so many other *Honeymooners* denouements, like a joke that catches in the throat, midway between a guffaw and a sob. Gleason handles another defeat elsewhere in the series by rubbing his nose with a meaty hand, mashing his face together wearily. Failure is an art form, a way of life.

As an actor, Gleason is endowed with a natural pathos that is second nature to him, and *The Honeymooners* is one of the landmarks in television history in large part because of his effortless summoning of the audience's sympathy. Before proceeding to commercial at the midshow mark in almost every episode, the camera pulls in for a close-up of Gleason's face, lost in thought as he ponders the enormity of the damage he has already caused himself, or swelling with pride at his heretofore hidden brilliance. *The Honeymooners* is a show about the same old shit, time and again, but unlike so many other sitcoms intent on repeating themselves, this one makes its characters at least partially aware of their own ruts. The show hits a metatextual peak with the 1956 *Jackie Gleason Show* sketch "Catch a Star," in which Ralph and Ed are rendered speechless by meeting those great stars of the small screen, Jackie Gleason and Art Carney. "Everybody's always talking about Jackie Gleason," Ed wickedly notes, "but if you ask me, that Art Carney's the whole show." This was self-referential television, four decades before *The Larry Sanders Show*.

Ratings actually dipped during *The Honeymooners'* single season, dropping Gleason all the way from second to twentieth in the Nielsen ratings for the year. Perry Como's variety show began to creep up in the ratings opposite *The Honeymooners*. After its relatively brief stand-alone sitcom run from 1955 to 1956, "The Honeymooners" would return as part of *The Jackie Gleason Show* for the 1956–57 season, and eventually make only irregular appearances. "I want to thank Perry Como for making me appear live again," Gleason said on announcing his return to the variety format. Gleason would stick with variety for the next decade through several different vehicles, only returning to regular "Honeymooners" sketches for the 1966–67 season. Ralph had been born out of Gleason's own childhood memories of deprivation and rage, but he, too, had been changed by success. Meadows was out now, replaced by a younger, prettier actress. In other words, Ralph had a new trophy wife, too.

In the mid-1950s, television was a phenomenon but not yet an institution. TV had arrived, but its place in the home—in American life—was still unsettled. *The Honeymooners* is explicit about the struggle over the integration of television—to TV or not to TV?—in a way that later shows, afraid of upsetting the unspoken, totemic form of the medium, notably avoid. TV would become the air we all breathed soon enough, but for this brief moment, its proper place in the larger culture still hung in the balance. *The Honeymooners* is a document of a medium still unsure of itself. Would any show following in its wake feel a similar need to proclaim its own existence, week after week, with an announcer calling out its stars' names, and the name of the program? (Perhaps only the 1970s sitcom *Soap*, which used announcer Rod Roddy in strictly tongue-in-cheek fashion to ape daytime soap operas and their overly florid narration.)

The next time you're in New York, take the subway—or better yet, the bus—to the corner of Eighth Avenue and Forty-Second Street. There, in front of the Port Authority Bus Terminal, stands sculptor Robert DuGrenier's ode to the most famous bus driver of all, Ralph Kramden. Ralph stands guard over the thousands of passengers streaming in and out of the world's most depressing bus station. Fact and fiction inextricably intertwine; what better place to pay tribute to America's most famous fictional bus driver than in front of its largest, only-too-real bus terminal? The statue was erected in 2000 by cable television channel TV Land, a nostalgia network devoted to old sitcoms like *The Honeymooners*. Like Falstaff, or James Bond, Ralph Kramden has become so familiar as to no longer be fictional. He has become, simply, part of the backdrop to the city.

Perhaps, then, we can imagine that on one of their excursions around midtown Manhattan, Joey Tribbiani or Miranda Hobbes or Tracy Jordan passed by Ralph as he watched traffic pass along Forty-Second Street. Scurrying on the way to their next wacky adventure, perhaps they briefly paused, nodding their heads in acknowledgment that without him, none of them would have existed. *To the moon, Alice . . .*

3

The Phil Silvers Show

"Doberman's Sister"

November 20, 1956 ▪ CBS

Sitcom heroes were crafty. For a form devoted to scheming of all kinds, this was practically a job requirement. Each new installment required a fresh plot, in both senses of the word. Lucy dreamed of show-business success; Ralph pictured that pot of gold at the end of the rainbow. Both were forever denied what they wanted most, because what would happen to us if they ever got it? The early sitcom, in its most essential incarnation, thrived on failure, and on the perpetual return to equilibrium. But what if chaos itself were a sitcom's default mode? And what if the scheming were less toothless and more disreputable? Could a sitcom be about an amoral con man and still be a sitcom?

These were the questions prompted by *The Phil Silvers Show* (also known as *Sgt. Bilko* and *You'll Never Get Rich*; like any good con man, the show traveled under a number of aliases), which ran on CBS from 1955 to 1959. *Phil Silvers* was never the ratings titan that *I Love Lucy* was, nor did it have the afterlife of *The Honeymooners*. So consider "Doberman's Sister," written by Nat Hiken, Leonard Stern, Tony Webster, and Billy Friedberg, as a route map to the sitcom road not taken, one laid out in detail and then mostly abandoned for close to four decades, until another set of clued-in, fearless Jewish comedians picked up where Bilko had left off.

Each episode of *The Phil Silvers Show*, created by former Milton Berle writer Nat Hiken (who had also written for a radio show called *The Magnificent Montague* that featured an up-and-coming performer named Art Carney) was a puzzle for us to unpack. How would Bilko (his very name hinting at what the good sergeant planned to do to each of his carefully cultivated pigeons) massage unyielding reality to bend to his desires? Who would give way before his assault of brown-nosing, misdirection, and shameless flattery? Occasionally—just to keep matters interesting—Bilko's schemes would fail. But the glory of Bilko was his ability to stay one step ahead of his humorless pursuers. For 1950s television, this was dazzlingly amoral territory to inhabit. "Nat's point of view pervaded on *Bilko*, which was very realistic and very satirical of human nature," *Phil Silvers* writer Coleman Jacoby observed of Hiken. "It was about a con man working his score. It was not a family show, like all those other shows at the time."

The series was designed as a star vehicle for Silvers, who as a child of the burlesque theater was a natural performer with a yen for the stage. "As a kid I just loved singing," Silvers writes in his autobiography. "If a five-year-old can have an orgasm—that's how I felt." Young Fischl Silver became known as "the reel-breaker-down singer," instant entertainment at the picture show when the movie inevitably broke down. At twelve, he was auditioning for theater owners in Brooklyn, his name massaged into the more felicitous Phil Silvers. He did a song-and-dance number with a little girl, and when they toppled over, Silvers looked out at the audience and said, "It's in the act." He got a huge laugh.

Later, when Silvers's voice began to change and his singing career came to an end, he became the child in the husband-and-wife vaudeville act of Flo & Joe. Silvers was a stage juvenile into his twenties, only graduating when MGM signed him as a contract player. He eventually spent nine years at 20th Century-Fox playing a string of roles he collectively characterized as "Blinky." He was, he later recalled, "the good-humored, bespectacled confidant of Betty Grable or John Payne." Silvers was always the sidekick and never the star; he never got the girl. That would soon change.

Flush off a Broadway success, Silvers was given a television show of his own, about a scheming sergeant in the US Army whose men also serve as the targets of his cons. Blinky was no longer. But CBS, unsure of the show, crammed the pilot into its vaults, unaired. In "a coup worthy of Bilko," a daring ad-agency representative rescued it from CBS's tomb and flew it out to North Carolina to show to executives at R. J. Reynolds, who loved Bilko and agreed to cosponsor the show. "The Camel people liked the way I smoked on the tube: I really bit into the cigarette," Silvers said. "I think they enjoyed that more than the show." *The Phil Silvers Show* was on the air, but its fate was still likely a dismal one. It had been scheduled opposite Milton Berle's *Texaco Star Theater*, long the most popular show on television. Ratings began dismally and then sank further, but by November 1955, *Phil Silvers* was gaining ground on Berle. By the next year, Berle was off the air and "Doberman's Sister," airing in November 1956, epitomized the inimitable Silvers magic.

In the episode, it is almost Family Day at Fort Baxter, located in the midwestern wilds of Kansas, and Sgt. Ernie Bilko (Phil Silvers) and his men are breathlessly preparing the base for the arrival of the men's mothers and fathers and, above all, for their sisters. "Start makin' trades!" Bilko orders, telling the soldiers to swap family obligations for dates to the base dance. The men immediately launch into a furious round of horse-trading, trotting out insider gossip and old recriminations. One soldier puffs out his cheeks to indicate that Gadowski's sister is too tubby for serious consideration. Another takes issue with his buddy having shown him a picture of Lena Horne the previous year and trying to pass it off as his sister.

As the negotiations rush toward their conclusion, one sizable speed bump emerges: what about the still-unseen sister of Private Duane Doberman (Maurice Gosfield)? Doberman is slovenly, portly, permanently unkempt, his chin dribbling into his neck like a melted puddle of ice cream. ("Doberman," Bilko calls out in another episode, snapping his fingers, "shower. That's an order!") His clothes hang limply off his shoulders, as if ashamed to reveal too much of their owner's dishevelment. Doberman has a small fringe of hair hanging lank over his forehead, a nose like a fishhook, and twinkling eyes that gaze up in dull wonder at Bilko each time he launches a new fishing expedition for his men's money. He is Bilko's designated whipping boy and mascot, the man he lectures about never being taken advantage of even as he has him scrambling to turn on faucets and fetch his shoes.

Doberman's popularity with audiences clearly rankled Silvers. "After a few weeks on our show he became a national celebrity," Silvers observes of Gosfield in his autobiography. "Off camera, Dobie thought of himself as Cary Grant playing a short, plump man." Gosfield's personal behavior found no more favor in Silvers's eyes: "Dobie never disappointed us in one of his talents: slobbery. His tie was always stained and his pants drooped. When he sat down to a meal he felt surrounded by enemies who would snatch his food if he didn't gobble it up first. He clutched his fork and knife as if they were weapons." (The book goes on for pages in this manner.) Clutching his own pen like a weapon, Silvers reserves the sharpest stiletto for last: "As the television shows and appearances rolled on over the years, Dobie began to have delusions. He believed he was a comedian." Coming from Silvers, no harsher indictment could be imagined.

Doberman's intellectual limitations are so severe as to make his physical limitations seem comparatively minor. So when Bilko raises the issue of Doberman's sister, and who might date her, his soldiers scatter to the four

winds. "Freeze!" Bilko orders, the natural mock affability of the grifter giving way to stern command when his men are hesitant to follow orders. Bilko
is bald and double-chinned, with a curved, beaky nose, but his perpetual
goofy grin is a hint of the whirring machinery inside.

Sensing a potential mutiny, Bilko sketches out a plan to turn Doberman's sister from a booby-trapped consolation prize into a highly sought-
after commodity. Bilko picks out one potential sap, Private Zimmerman
(Mickey Freeman), and offers him a side deal. If he'll agree to take Bilko's
steady girlfriend, Joan (Elisabeth Fraser), to the dance, Bilko will be freed
up to squire Doberman's sister. Zimmerman agrees, and Bilko breaks out
into ecstatic thanks, grabbing his underling's face in appreciation: "Bless
you! Yes!" Zimmerman leaves the barracks, and Bilko, his insight into
human weakness unparalleled, correctly predicts that he will be back in
under one minute, begging to be set up instead with Doberman's sister.

Bilko offers his men a scientific principle of attractiveness, gleaned from
years of intensive study of past Family Days: "The uglier the brother, the
more beautiful the sister." "If that's true," one member of his platoon quips,
"Doberman's sister is Miss Universe." That night, the men toss and turn in
their beds, each dreaming of the stunning, voluptuous Diane Doberman.
Bilko, master con artist, is so gifted that he even manages to convince himself. He tosses and turns in bed, dreaming of spotting the Marilyn Monroe–esque Diane at a movie premiere.

Bilko is rarely content to execute only one con when so many further
twists on the original scheme beckon. The next day, he crafts a fake tele-
gram about a sick ninety-six-year-old aunt to blow off Joan and have a shot
at squiring Doberman's sister. Then Diane arrives, and she is Doberman
in a blonde wig. No, literally: Gosfield gamely puts on drag for this shock-
cut visual punch line. Bilko's flowers immediately wilt, drooping down
the length of his arm. Having manipulated everyone around him so thoroughly, Bilko has mistakenly manipulated himself as well. But the final
joke redounds to his own benefit. Joan spots him with Doberman's sister
and realizes—well, "realizes," since Bilko himself is seemingly no longer in
on his own scheme—that all his contortions had been to protect a fragile

visitor from humiliation. Joan kisses him for his troubles, and Bilko smiles shamefacedly, a naughty boy rewarded for his flimflammery.

Bilko lives for competition—for a chance to show off his skill in the dark art of persuasion. Everything is an opportunity to get ahead. His soldiers are his designated ATM for an endless array of schemes: a football pool, a bed-making contest, a singing competition, uranium mining (seemingly a standard trope of 1950s sitcoms), a trip to Hollywood. The sweetest three words in the English language for Bilko are "money from home." Bilko can bilk his men with even the gentlest whiff of intrigue. He rents a store and has soldiers throwing money in his direction, certain he has a killer racket cooked up, even when he has absolutely nothing more than an empty storefront.

Even when Bilko's mostly hapless nemesis, Colonel Hall (Paul Ford), puts an end to his illegal gaming, Bilko and his men find a way. They turn a dry talk on Beethoven into an opportunity to place bets on the number of times a visiting lecturer twitches during her speech. The audience audibly counts along with each spasm, and when Mrs. Whitney hits twenty-five, the men cheer: "A new indoor record!" The arrival of a new soldier known as "the Stomach," who eats to excess when miserable, prompts Bilko to play an endless medley of sad wartime songs in the hopes of getting him psyched up for an eating contest. Weakness and disorder are Bilko's companions; without them, all his scheming is for naught. He hears that an army psychologist has cured the Stomach's ailment, and blurts out his true feelings before reining himself in: "That dirty . . . That's nice."

Flattery gets Bilko everywhere. He routinely engages in shameless puffery of his designated targets. He "confuses" a middle-aged nurse for Greta Garbo, and has her twittering and massaging his shoulders with alacrity, her native suspicion dissipated by his blitzkrieg of sweet talk. Colonel Hall's wife is mistaken for Betty Grable until Bilko corrects himself. "Imagine mistaking you for Betty Grable, Miss Monroe," he chuckles. An heir to a $200 million fortune comes to the base, and Bilko seeks out innovative ways of praising his new soldier. Coming to the motor pool where he works, he inspects a jeep carefully, pointing to one particular bolt with wonder.

"Who turned that screw?" Bilko exclaims, as if in the presence of a Vermeer of the Phillips head. "Is this a genius? Is this a genius?" he asks on another occasion. "They make a fuss about Edison!" Bilko's Yiddish inflections, his immigrant's line of patter, unexpectedly give way to a brilliant burlesque of the military bark when he is annoyed or harried. His voice deepens, his shoulders stiffen, and this icon of sloth is suddenly a ramrod-straight paragon of US Army discipline: "On-the-double-ee-ya-oh-up!"

Like any good huckster, Bilko is adept at the long con, at setting a scene for his rubes. A politician visits the base, and Bilko paints a compelling portrait of deprivation in the hopes of winning increased government funding for Fort Baxter. At lunch, Bilko generously offers to carve the meat, slicing a single hot dog and serving it to his guests. They are also welcome to take as many beans as they like—three *or* four, he does not mind.

Occasionally—*very* occasionally—Bilko is foiled. His plot to field a tone-deaf crew for an a cappella singing contest, and make a killing by betting against his men, is stymied when a new recruit unexpectedly has a golden voice. "You got a radio on?" Bilko innocently wonders when he first hears him singing, only belatedly realizing the collapse of his intrigues. An attempt to wrangle a seat at a legendary navy craps game results in Bilko and his cronies only narrowly avoiding the brig—and penury. These reversals keep things interesting enough, although *The Phil Silvers Show* is generally more concerned with how Bilko proceeds than whether he succeeds. Beware of Pickpockets, reads the prominently placed sign in Bilko's office, but the warning is ironic, the shark warning the minnow of the dangerous characters swimming around the neighborhood.

Bilko is eternal. He is the emblem of American skullduggery and amorality and calculation, its homegrown antidote to patriotic treacle. He puts on a pageant for the one hundredth anniversary of Fort Baxter in "The Centennial," offering a rapid-fire revue of American history in his own image. There Bilko is, selling whiskey to Native Americans, sentencing a Civil War soldier to death in order to romance his wife, and turning over military secrets to a sultry spy during the Spanish-American War. In another memorable episode, "The Revolutionary War," Bilko stumbles across an ancestor's military medal and wonders about past Bilkos' acts of bravery. "There was a Bilko in the Revolutionary War?" Colonel Hall exclaims. "And we won?" Silvers takes the stage as his 1776 incarnation, selling boat tickets for the crossing of the Delaware ("Wine, women, Hessian girls") until there are no seats left. "General, I'm afraid you're going to just have to stand," he tells George Washington as the boat sets out. Upon closer investigation, the war hero's medal is indeed genuine, but it was awarded by King George III.

Phil Silvers exists on the borderline between the first and second waves of television—the urban first adopters, living along the Eastern Seaboard, who made stars of the sophisticated likes of Milton Berle and Sid Caesar, and the rural audiences who came to television later, and brought with them a taste for less challenging fare like *The Beverly Hillbillies* and *Green Acres*. Embodying the clash to come between television past and television future, Bilko is the savvy Jewish schemer outclassing the fatally slow hicks of the army.

The show was produced early enough in the history of television that Silvers's flubbed lines were not edited out of the final shows, preserved for eternity as an accidental measure of sitcom realism. *The Phil Silvers Show* is otherwise little interested in realism. Its version of the US Army is a stumblebum hodgepodge of malcontents, buffoons, and mediocrities. Fort Baxter, ostensibly located in the Midwest, appears to be peopled entirely by soldiers from Brooklyn, Queens, and New Jersey. *Phil Silvers* is a New York show artificially relocated to a Kansas that seemed to exist, as in the famous Saul Steinberg *New Yorker* cover, just over the river from Ninth Avenue.

Bilko is forever stumbling across unacknowledged phenoms—boxers who can soak up punishment like champs, competitive eaters with wooden legs for the storage of hamburgers. These individuals are not only Bilko's targets but also occasionally future sitcom stars themselves. The show emulates its star, seeking out unappreciated talent, laying the groundwork for future long cons. Channeling future flashback episodes of *The Dick Van Dyke Show*—or perhaps laying the groundwork for that series' recurrent interest in military life—Dick Van Dyke guest-stars as a green recruit in the episode "Hillbilly Whiz." Here, Van Dyke is Private Lumpkin, a country bumpkin whose Doberman-like mental deficiencies are more than made up for by his ability to nail an infinitesimally small target with a stone from 150 feet away. Doberman, as is his wont, immediately crushes Lumpkin's hand in the door of a jeep. Lumpkin, entirely unconcerned, tells Sgt. Bilko not to worry—he can pitch with the other hand just as well. Bilko immediately breaks into sobs of gratitude and relief.

Bilko sees an opportunity to penetrate the inner sphere of some *real* charlatans and hustlers: the owners and players of Major League Baseball. He wants to sell Lumpkin to the New York Yankees, but the pitcher protests. As a good Tennessee boy, he could *never* play with any Yankees. Not to worry, Bilko insists; the Yankees—ranging from Mickey "Moonshine" Mantle to Colonel Casey Stengel—are all country boys, too. The perennial con man arranges for some of the Yankees to visit the base and prove their down-home decency. Someone mentions that Yogi Berra, that famed purveyor of accidental wit, reminds them of Doberman, and Berra is curious to catch a glimpse of his malaprop-spouting television doppelganger. Bilko enters a room with famously tightfisted Yankees boss Dan Topping, and as they emerge, Topping is apologizing to *him* for not being able to offer his client more money.

Van Dyke is the eternal naïf, a goof to be molded to Bilko's specifications. There is little sign here, as of yet, of the wit or intelligence of his Rob Petrie from *The Dick Van Dyke Show*. This is Bilko's show, and there is no room on *The Phil Silvers Show* for any competitors. But Silvers's inborn ability to talk his way out of any sticky situation is the eventual inspiration for Rob's gift of comic gab. In another time and another place, Bilko would have made a great comedy writer.

Still bearing traces of puppy fat on his cheeks, that other future icon of sitcom decency stops in to tempt Bilko in the episode "Bilko the Art Lover." Years before achieving television immortality as *M*A*S*H*'s Hawkeye Pierce, Alan Alda is almost unrecognizable here, too conventionally polished to bear much resemblance to the bathrobe-wearing, perpetually disheveled Hawkeye. But a line can be drawn from the garrulous, silver-tongued Bilko to his student and fellow military iconoclast. Both Bilko and

Hawkeye never met a rule they didn't assume applied only to others. Both find a way to turn army discipline into an optional endeavor. And both lend the fatally polite sitcom a touch of genuine anarchic vigor.

There is also a line to be drawn between *The Phil Silvers Show* and *M*A*S*H*, the last and most successful of the military sitcoms. But *M*A*S*H* took its setting far more seriously than its predecessor, for which it was merely a convenient foil. The latter perspective may seem odd to contemporary viewers, for whom military service is both somewhat exotic and not at all comic. In television's early years, however, lighthearted military sitcoms were a regular presence. Following *Phil Silvers* were the likes of *McHale's Navy* (ABC, 1962–66), starring Ernest Borgnine as a World War II PT boat captain; *F Troop* (ABC, 1965–67); the POW camp comedy *Hogan's Heroes* (CBS, 1965–71); and the *Andy Griffith Show* spinoff *Gomer Pyle, U.S.M.C.* (CBS, 1964–69). The idea behind all of them was, as critic John Leonard put it, "that you could enlist or be drafted into a family." Barracks were alternate-world living rooms, and platoons were haphazard families for a form looking to re-create the familiar sitcom blend of intimacy and conflict in new surroundings.

In another important respect, though, *Phil Silvers* and its successors parted company, thanks to a dramatic shift in television audiences. We think of TV as coming into existence all at once in the late 1940s, but in truth, TV was rolled out in the United States in limited release. Having begun in cities like New York and Los Angeles, television only slowly made its way into the interior of the country. Rural areas were especially tardy in receiving access to TV signals. As television penetrated deeper into the less populated pockets of the country, the nature of viewership changed. Series such as *The Phil Silvers Show* were unlikely to appeal to this new, less sophisticated brand of television watchers. Thus, in the late 1950s and early 1960s, the sharp-edged urbanity of the early sitcoms, most of which seemed to be set in Brooklyn or Manhattan or peopled by natives of the five boroughs, was replaced by a distinctly middle-American mind-set. Creatively, the sitcom took a decided step backward, in large part because its new audience demanded a different kind of programming less given to artistic daring.

The idea of a laugh track in a Nazi POW camp seems, to contemporary ears, like a bad joke—no, the very definition of a bad joke. And yet, *Hogan's Heroes* was a sizable television success just half a decade after Adolf Eichmann went on trial in Israel for the mass murder of the Jews of Europe. This was the revised version of World War II, in which the wised-up Americans ran circles around their fatally gullible German overlords. It was Bilko at war, with the Germans the stand-ins for Bilko's regular flock of pigeons. If they were so smart, why hadn't the Americans, led by the calculating Colonel Hogan (Bob Crane), escaped from the clutches of monocled, hare-brained Colonel Klink (Werner Klemperer) and his jolly, roly-poly associate Schultz (John Banner)?

Gomer Pyle is *Bilko* in reverse, with Gomer (Jim Nabors) a Doberman figure getting his slow-witted revenge on the scheming Sgt. Carter (Frank Sutton). Mayberry's dimmest bulb is sent to infiltrate the US Marine Corps and kill it with kindness. Carter is a failed Bilko, outgunned by a yokel, his crew cut a landing strip for his endless worries, his mouth twisted into a permanent curl from the agony of handling Pyle. The marines are a sort of permanent summer camp here, a place to leisurely shoot the breeze, or as Gomer might say, "the bray-az." Gomer is a Forrest Gump type, bearing a distinct physical resemblance to a future sitcom military recruit: *Arrested Development*'s Buster Bluth.

Bilko and Gomer and the POWs of *Hogan's Heroes* were each, in their own distinctive way, representative of the sitcom's new preferred mode: the fish-out-of-water story. A new array of backdrops heretofore unfamiliar to television were summoned in order to maximally juxtapose an array of freaks and oddballs. *The Phil Silvers Show* took place in a Kansas that was really Brooklyn; a number of these new shows, even when they were set in Beverly Hills, occupied an Appalachia of the mind.

The Beverly Hillbillies (CBS, 1962–71) was devoted to the quasi-surreal juxtaposition of the luxurious and the penurious: a misfiring Model T cruising down Rodeo Drive, a moonshine still built next to the backyard pool, a down-home wingding in a gleaming modern living room, complete with squealing pig in the kitchen. Its yokels-in-California aesthetic was lifted from *The Real McCoys* (ABC/CBS, 1957–63), the first rural sitcom to find an audience, starring legendary character actor Walter Brennan as a font of ignorant down-home wisdom.

Hillbillies is nearly unwatchable now, a hodgepodge of faux down-home humor, squabbling womenfolk, and painful Southern California jokes. Jed (Buddy Ebsen), busted for a minor indiscretion, is told, "You do make more racket than a jackass in a tin barn," and the same verdict could stand for the series as a whole. Yet *The Beverly Hillbillies*, all its surface flaws notwithstanding, was the top-rated show in the United States for the 1962–63 and 1963–64 seasons, and it hovered around the top ten for the bulk of its ten-season run.

The same absurdist Ruraltania was the setting of *Petticoat Junction* (CBS, 1963–70) and *Green Acres* (CBS, 1965–71), which both bear the imprint of *Hillbillies* producer Paul Henning. In *Petticoat Junction*, Bea Benaderet, *The Beverly Hillbillies'* Cousin Pearl, was cast as a hotelier with three nubile daughters to protect from the depredations of the masculine world, enlisting her own wiles, her shotgun, and her irascible uncle Joe (Edgar Buchanan) as a last line of defense. *Petticoat Junction* is studied cornpone with a slightly absurdist tilt, courtesy of the W. C. Fields–like Buchanan and the series' taste for musical numbers and crossover episodes with its sibling *Green Acres*.

Green Acres makes the geographic displacement of the 1960s sitcom literal, yanking European cosmopolitan Eva Gabor and her husband Eddie Albert out of New York City and moving them to the country. *Green Acres* is a rural comedy with some of the zany spirit of its contemporary *Get Smart*, channeled primarily through the figure of Arnold Ziffel—a television-loving pig who is doted on by his human "parents" and treated like a child by all the local townsfolk. Arnold communicates his grocery list to the local shopkeeper in grunts and squeals, and is warned on his way out not to play baseball with the other kids on his way home. (Arnold is close television kin to the talking horse of *Mister Ed* [syndicated/CBS, 1961–66], another exemplar of 1960s sitcoms' interest in the humdrum surreal perhaps exemplified by those twin freakshow families, *The Munsters* [CBS, 1964–66] and *The Addams Family* [ABC, 1964–66].) Television shows grew aware of each other's presence in the firmament. *Green Acres* characters watch *The Beverly Hillbillies* on their TV sets, even putting on a theatrical adaptation of the show at their local playhouse.

By this point, *The Phil Silvers Show* had long since reached its terminus. The series ended in 1959 after four seasons and 143 episodes, with "The Weekend Colonel." Colonel Hall has finally crafted a foolproof system for stopping his nemesis, and it involves the use of a technology we have all grown familiar with: television. Training his cameras on Bilko, the colonel catches him in all manner of indiscretions, tracking down his top-secret illicit craps game via internal security system. (Hadn't audiences been conducting the same surveillance of Bilko all along?) The colonel, it turns out, is not quite as amused by watching Bilko on television as audiences were. And Bilko's tall tales no longer hold water in this era of mass-media sophistication: "That story might have held up twenty years ago," the colonel lectures him, "because we didn't have television then." Silvers smiles foolishly at the camera when the colonel points it out, only too aware of its power to educate and mislead.

In the series' final scene, Colonel Hall sits in front of a television, enjoying the spectacle of Bilko filling his screen. He is amused less by the man than by the setting: a jail cell, where Bilko and his associates now languish. The colonel, for once, gets the last word about this TV show: "And the best part is that as long as I'm the sponsor, it'll never be canceled." Well, *almost* the last word. Before we go, we see Bilko once more, channeling Porky Pig in fond farewell to his audience: "Th-that's all, folks!"

Bilko is, at long last, being punished for his crimes against humanity, but he has learned no lessons and accepts no blame. His fate anticipates that of another troupe of amoral schemers who would close out their legendary sitcom serving their own stint in prison. Between the end of Bilko and the emergence of *Seinfeld* some three decades later, this would be the road not taken for the sitcom—a model that eschewed warmth and sentiment in favor of the cold appeal of the hustle. The sitcom would have to belatedly learn once again the lesson originally taught by Bilko: how not to be polite.

4

Leave It to Beaver

"Beaver Gets 'Spelled"

October 4, 1957 ▪ CBS

The 1950s sitcom is the source of much deeply flawed wisdom. It will come as a shock to contemporary viewers to hear a television character announce, in all seriousness, that "women are much too interested in themselves to worry about anyone else." *Father Knows Best*, *Leave It to Beaver* (CBS/ABC, 1957–63), and the other family sitcoms of the era present a carefully pruned version of American life—white, suburban, middle class, patriarchal, vaguely Protestant—as universal. *Father* was even set in that most blandly American of places: Springfield. (Eventually, another landmark sitcom would borrow the same location, simultaneously everywhere and nowhere, for its own series.) They were field guides to the new postwar consensus, an effort to simultaneously reflect the lives of their audiences and subtly steer their behavior.

These series were testaments to the authority and infallibility of parents—particularly fathers—in the guise of gentle parodies. Kings had once employed jesters, whose mockery of royalty allowed the monarchs to demonstrate their genial tolerance. Similarly, shows like *Father Knows Best*, constructed as a burlesque of all-knowing fatherhood, only burnished the credentials of the patriarchy they reflected. Not only were fathers in charge, they were even capable of laughing at their own foibles. *Leave It to Beaver* and *Father Knows Best* have become less notable television series than symbolic stand-ins of an era, perfect representatives of a bygone time, for better and for worse.

It would be worthwhile to acknowledge, some six decades later, just how repetitive these shows could be. Charming, occasionally; funny, *very* occasionally. But to see one episode of *Leave It to Beaver* is functionally to see them all. Like a Mad Lib, an episode of *Leave It to Beaver* follows a pre-printed template that only requires the insertion of nouns and verbs. Beaver (Jerry Mathers) gets himself into hot water by [fill in the blank]; big brother Wally (Tony Dow) and best friend Eddie Haskell (Ken Osmond) gamely assist by [fill in the blank]; dad Ward (Hugh Beaumont) fulminates; mom June (Barbara Billingsley) coos encouragingly; and the misunderstanding is settled by [fill in the blank]. Each episode is crisp, uncomplicated by side plots or unresolved emotions. The show is a well-oiled machine: fill it with the tiniest drop of narrative—Beaver gets a pet alligator! Wally purchases an old clunker!—and the jalopy sputters to life, cruising efficiently through three acts in twenty-five minutes.

Consider one representative episode, written by the show's creators, Joe Connelly and Bob Mosher, the first episode after an abortive pilot with different actors in the roles of Ward and Wally. In "Beaver Gets 'Spelled" (i.e., "Expelled"), Beaver (asked if that is his given name, he responds, "Yes, ma'am—my brother given it to me") is perturbed when his teacher gives him a letter to take home to his parents. He is convinced that the letter spells his academic doom, and nothing his brother tells him dispels that impression. "You'll be the first kid to ever be thrown out of the second grade in the history of the school," blurts Wally.

Beaver and Wally are not bad kids, exactly. Instead, they are endlessly, innocently mischievous, and it is this mischief that sets the show in motion. Possessed of their own idiosyncratic morality, they have an ingrained notion of what they can and cannot do. Wally refuses to open the letter from Beaver's teacher, insisting that it would be dishonest. That he says so while emptying the dirt from Beaver's pet turtle's enclosure into the bath, in order to fool his mother with a plausible-looking ring around the tub, only says that he is possessed of a flexible sense of what dishonesty might consist of.

In order to escape from his imagined purgatory, Beaver tells his teacher that his father is in the hospital after a fire. June is, needless to say, a bit suspicious when her husband receives flowers from a mysterious woman, and he is no better equipped to explain than she is. (Eventually, one suspects the Cleavers are willfully dumb to not immediately suspect Beaver as the source of all their kerfuffles, but since this is only the first episode, they are still deserving of a pass.) Beaver plays hooky from school in the hope of avoiding the problem, gazing into the window of a travel agency at an advertisement for flights to Chicago and Miami. When a trip on the Orient Express falls through, Beaver resorts to hiding in a tree, from which he is eventually coaxed down by his parents. The letter does not announce Beaver's expulsion, but merely requests his participation in the school play. Order is restored, and the parents chuckle over their son's scheming as June washes the dishes and Ward dries.

Leave It to Beaver premiered in 1957–58, the first season after the end of *I Love Lucy*'s triumphant six-year run. It had begun as a pilot called *It's a Small World*, featuring Mathers and Billingsley alongside Casey Adams as Ward and Paul Sullivan as Wally. Most tantalizing of all, a young Harry Shearer—the future voice of *The Simpsons*' Mr. Burns, Principal Skinner, and many others—was the Eddie Haskell equivalent, brown-noser Frankie Bennett. Mathers was cast as Beaver after wearing a Cub Scout uniform to his audition and scheming to skip out early from his tryout so as not to miss his weekly meeting. Beaver was based on show cocreator Joe Connelly's son Ricky, but some of Mathers himself seeped into the character as well.

Every episode of *Leave It to Beaver* revolves around a similarly miniscule crisis. Beaver loses his money on the way to the barber shop and has Wally give him what turns out to be a proto–Travis Bickle Mohawk; he leaves a pop-up snake in his teacher's desk as a prank; he is mistaken for a genius when another boy in his class swaps test papers with him.

Often, it is Ward who overreacts to his boys' small scrapes. He is convinced that Beaver smuggling a Chihuahua to school inside his jacket, or spending his money on a new baseball glove, is an impending sign of the apocalypse. Ward is forever lecturing his sons on responsibility, concerned their latest run-in is symbolic of aimless youth gone astray. Actor and role became intertwined; Beaumont drafted an open letter to viewers that could have been mistaken for another of Ward's pep talks. Beaumont was proud that *Beaver* taught young viewers the value of gestures like pulling out a chair for your mother: "To us, things like helping mother with the dishes, wearing a jacket or tie on a date . . . are more than just surface attributes—we think of them as symbols of respect."

Ward is meant to be fallible, engaging in mistaken shenanigans of his own, like taking over his sons' paper route and delivering the wrong day's papers. June is the softer presence, keeping not only her sons but also her husband in check, saving him from his occasional outbursts. In its collisions between parental clout and youthful exuberance, *Leave It to Beaver* is a demonstration of the benignity of authority. Ward and June are often mistaken, and occasionally flawed, but they are never malign. Theirs is a genial sort of dictatorship.

But perhaps the point of the show is to be found in just how little happened on it. The sitcom was meant to soothe, not ruffle, and only a decade or so after a war that had shipped millions of American men across the ocean to fight, and killed more than four hundred thousand of them, perhaps it was a comfort to hear—or even better, to see—that the war was over and life comfortably resumed.

There were no real problems to be found in *Beaver*'s Mayfield, just like in *Father Knows Best*'s Springfield: no mention of *Brown v. Board of Education* or Sputnik or Little Rock (Although in "Beaver and Chuey," Beaver befriends and accidentally insults a new friend coded as Mexican but identified as Spanish). "It's always spring or fall," Mathers says of Mayfield in his memoir *And Jerry Mathers as "the Beaver,"* "and it never snows. It's usually sunny, unless the plot calls for rain." Mom always wears pearls, never a housecoat, and Dad keeps his tie on at the dinner table. This is the boredom of peace. Even the working world is too burdensome, too likely to interfere with the calm of domesticity; we never do learn what Ward Cleaver does for a living.

The real lives of *Beaver*'s cast and crew had a nuance, and a dramatic heft, deliberately lacking from the show itself. Beaumont's mother was killed and his wife and son injured in a car accident shortly before he joined the show, leaving him often short-tempered with the show's cast and crew. Mathers was dyslexic and required his mother's assistance with scripts in order to memorize his lines. During the Bel Air fires in the early 1960s, Joe Connelly, according to Mathers's memoir, "broke through the police barricades, climbed to the top of his roof with fire hose in hand, and watered down his house and grounds. Then he fended off the evacuation teams with a .45 from his extensive gun collection. The result was that his was one of the few houses to survive the fire." Not quite the polite behavior one might expect from the cocreator of *Leave It to Beaver*. After the show's termination, Ken Osmond served as an officer in the Los Angeles Police Department for seventeen years. Untold numbers of car thieves and crooks were unknowingly apprehended by none other than Eddie Haskell.

Television had displaced older hobbies as the prime leisure pursuit of American families, so it was no surprise that television programming sought to reflect both family life and the newfound habit of watching TV. It had first carried over familiar radio characters like *The Goldbergs*' Molly Goldberg and Mama from *Mama*. These were genial white-ethnic maternal figures, and their shows' warmth and familial cohesion were echoes of an earlier era, a comforting tale of the old neighborhood as the middle-class family packed up and headed for the suburbs. Soon enough, though, the shows changed, themselves moving from the inner city to suburbia. And if TV, in its early years, was a kind of illustrated guide to the mores of postwar American middle-class life, then how could it not also be, at times, about television itself?

The Anderson family of *Father Knows Best* (CBS, 1954–60) gathers around their television in the episode "Father Is a Dope" in order to watch *their* favorite sitcom, *Father Does It Again*. In it, Jackie Gleason–inspired numbskull George cajoles his wife to allow him to participate in a surefire uranium deal with his neighbor. (Ralph had been reminded by his wife, in *The Honeymooners*' "Better Living Through TV," of a failed uranium field proposition in Asbury Park.) Meanwhile, his son shows up wearing a hard hat in the kitchen, in search of a road-gang job to support the family when his father's latest harebrained scheme falls through. If you were to ask frustrated family patriarch Jim Anderson (Robert Young), the show should be called *Father Is a Dope*: "Oh, these ridiculous TV family situation shows," he clucks regretfully, shaking his head. Dopey George finally melts on seeing his daughter wanting to sell her clothes to save the family, holding his wife's shoulders and uttering what we can immediately tell is his trademark expression: "Doll baby, you're the most of the mostest."

Father Does It Again, with its squabbling couple, its moneymaking schemes, and its closing clinch between husband and wife, is clearly intended as a takeoff on *The Honeymooners*. And yet *Father Knows Best* is less interested in parodying television for its own sake—this is not *Saturday Night Live*, or even *Your Show of Shows*—than in wielding it as another weapon in the further education of clumsy father Jim Anderson. Annoyed by *Father Does It Again*, Jim becomes convinced that family life is a conspiracy to rob fathers of their innate dignity. "Hey, how come mothers are so much smarter than fathers?" his son Bud asks him. Jim bristles, muttering, "Only on television."

As "Father Is a Dope" continues, Jim is beset by the demands of his three children—a ride to a birthday party, assistance with an important meeting, ministering to an illness—and he comes to believe that all these problems are imaginary, meant to keep him from a planned duck-hunting expedition with a neighbor. Family life, it seems, is a collaborative fiction intended to keep men from their rightful leisure. Jim is convinced he is on a mediocre television show of his own, cast against his will as the idiot father by his wife and children. The family's whining, he tells his neighbor, "sounded like a rehearsal to that television show *Father Does It Again*." Asked by his children what kind of father he is to leave them behind in their hour of need, he responds, "Oh, just a regulation simple-minded stumble-bum father you see on your TV set."

Eventually, of course, Jim realizes what the show has long since telegraphed to its audience. Bud (Billy Gray) really is sick, teenage daughter Betty (Elinor Donahue) really is nervous about her job interview, and little Kathy (Lauren Chapin) really doesn't have a ride to her party. Jim's wife, Margaret (Jane Wyatt), really does want him to go on his hunting trip. Jim apologizes to his wife, who feigns ignorance about his perceived misdeeds. Betty asks her mother if she really doesn't know why her father apologized, and Margaret explains: "Of course not. It's amazing the ideas some men pick up watching that TV box." Wyatt playfully looks at the camera out of the corner of her eye—the only character on the show regularly accorded the privilege of winking at the audience—a reminder that, its title to the contrary, the show's family is a closet matriarchy.

The Anderson household settles in to watch their favorite show once more, and this time Jim enjoys himself too, chuckling good-naturedly at his sitcom stand-in's foolishness. Jim has once again learned a valuable lesson while attempting to teach his children, this time about his own limitations. "They made George entirely too smart," he observes of *Father Does It Again*, smiling in recognition of his own well-demonstrated foolishness. "We fathers don't have half that many brains."

Father Knows Best began life as a radio serial with the more ambiguous title *Father Knows Best?* Kent cigarettes, the show's commercial sponsor, demanded the removal of the question mark, but it hung in the air, ghost punctuation to this sitcom about a father who managed to be simultaneously bungling and omnipotent. It was a show whose protagonist could credibly tell his children, without setting off an avalanche of canned yuks from the laugh track, that "you're just going to have to learn that I'm an ordinary human being, with a reasonable amount of intelligence. . . . Just because I'm your father doesn't mean that I'm infallible."

At the same time, Young, one of the first movie stars to make the transition to television, is clearly designated as the puppet leader of the Andersons, good-naturedly manipulated by his family. In "New Girl at School," Jim is pleased by how tough-minded Bud has become about his new crush, April, relieved to see him behaving like a true Anderson man. No sooner have the words left his mouth than Margaret asks him to bring her a cold drink and a properly fluffed pillow to prop her up. As he rushes to assist her, she saucily raises an eyebrow at the camera, letting us in on the joke of her husband's paper crown.

Father Knows Best, like its compatriots, offered the weekly inculcation of moral lessons—loyalty, honesty, decency to strangers, trust in one's family members to do the right thing. The show ritually presented the weekly crisis—Kathy breaks a window with an errant baseball; Bud may elope with his girlfriend—while never leaving in any genuine doubt the ultimate stability of the family unit. Even what seems like a fairly serious cause for concern, in the episode "Betty Earns a Formal," is handled without any genuine panic. Jim and Margaret seem relatively untroubled by the thought that Betty might be moonlighting as a burlesque dancer in order to earn the $89 she needs in order to purchase a formal gown. One suspects that the parents on *The Cosby Show*, for example, would have rained fire and brimstone if their daughter Denise had been suspected of a similar offense. The face these earlier family shows turned toward the world was one of unceasing optimism and positivity. Problems are raised only to be resolved. Life carries on as it always has and as it always will. The uniformity of these family sitcoms transforms them into a collective chorus, drowning out dissenting voices.

Advice was the currency of these shows, passed out by sitcom parents like so many crumpled dollar bills. Donna and Jeff Stone (Donna Reed and Paul Petersen) of *The Donna Reed Show* (ABC, 1958–66) are pillars of the community, a pediatrician and his loving wife, offering guidance to their children and his patients in roughly equal doses. There is a sense of quasi-sexual competition among the mothers to impress Dr. Stone in an early episode, hoping to win favor for their offspring in a cutest baby contest, but the show mostly skims over such complicated, impolite emotions.

In the episode "A Very Merry Christmas," a remarkable guest appearance by silent film legend Buster Keaton gestures at the complexities this show, and those like it, normally eschewed. As a hospital janitor pressed by Donna into service as Santa Claus, Keaton stumbles into the hospital wing and shakes the sick boys' hands with comic solemnity, his eyes heavy-lidded and rimmed with sadness. Even in his diminished state, some three decades after *The General* (1926), Keaton is representative of all the things the sitcom could not—would not—do.

These family shows, essentially fantasies about an orderly America that did not quite exist, were devoted to their own homely brand of realism. *Father Knows Best* was shot on sets with four walls, rather than the usual three, as if to subtly encourage viewers in the belief that the Andersons' was a real suburban house. On *The Adventures of Ozzie and Harriet* (ABC, 1952–66), the opening credits made a big fuss about pointing out that stars Ozzie and Harriet Nelson and their sons were a real family, and the show was even filmed in an exact replica of the Nelson home. *Ozzie and Harriet* was so devoted to maintaining its freakish sitcom simulacrum of realism that eventually the real-life wives of sons David and Ricky were added to the cast.

Ozzie Nelson was another bumbling, well-meaning sitcom father in the vein of Jim Anderson, always wringing his hands over his boys' nonexistent problems. Ozzie is even more mild-mannered than his sitcom-father compatriots, more of an older brother to his sons. Much of the show, in its earliest incarnation, is about dating and girls, with Ozzie and Harriet's guidance intended, we are meant to understand, to assist their sons in forming stable, satisfying partnerships like their own. (An added irony given that, according to David Halberstam, Ozzie "had in effect stolen the childhood of both of his sons and used it for commercial purposes; he had taken what was most private and made it terribly public.")

In one episode, Ozzie, prompted by his wife, begins keeping a list of quirky or humorous events from his day to share with Harriet—itself a kind of symbolic stand-in for the work of this sitcom, and those like it, which sought to report back to American families a heightened, modestly more amusing version of the workaday world. And these shows' imaginations could, not surprisingly, have an impact on the world they sought to depict. After an *Ozzie and Harriet* episode of December 1957, in which Ozzie, following a craving, goes off in search of his favorite dessert, there was a national run on tutti-frutti ice cream.

Other sitcom fathers interlaced their saccharine good cheer with the slightest hints of vinegar. Danny Thomas of *Make Room for Daddy* (ABC/CBS, 1953–64) is another itinerant performer in the style of Ricky Ricardo (with whom he shares a stage, and an antipathy to free-spending wives, in a crossover episode with *The Lucille Ball–Desi Arnaz Show*), an all-American father with a retinue of fractious Lebanese relatives and an inextinguishable array of hangers-on in need of guidance. (A young, button-nosed actress named Mary Tyler Moore auditioned for a role on the show as Thomas's daughter and was rejected: "Nobody would believe that was my daughter with *that* nose!")

Fred MacMurray of *My Three Sons* (ABC, 1960–72), a veteran of Billy Wilder's *The Apartment* and *Double Indemnity*, is a far more substantial presence than Ward Cleaver or the other sitcom fathers, even as his show is every bit as weightless and indistinct: widower father raises his children with the assistance of his gruff father-in-law (*I Love Lucy* vet William Frawley, irascible as ever), and later, a gruff uncle. MacMurray's perpetually raised eyebrow is both a commentary on his sons' endless minor scrapes and, presumably, on the material itself, in need of a knowing wink it sorely lacks.

If *Leave It to Beaver* and its colleagues seem too impossibly repetitive for contemporary viewers, it is worth remembering in this era of Netflix Instant that we no longer watch these shows in the manner in which they were created. When *Leave It to Beaver* premiered in 1957, there were no DVD boxed sets, no VCRs, no DVRs. Shows were on once a week, in a particular time slot. Between airings, the show disappeared into the ether and old episodes could not be revisited—at least until its syndicated premiere, when past installations were haphazardly reintroduced. *Leave It to Beaver*, like every other sitcom of its time, existed in a perpetual present, its past sluiced away at the end of each half hour, unlikely to soon return.

This meant that television series could get away with endlessly repeating themselves; barring the occasional Thanksgiving or New Year's marathon, there would be no opportunities to see more than one episode at a time. The mind-boggling degree of sameness endemic to *Leave It to Beaver* could go relatively unnoticed. *Beaver* was like a trusted after-school snack, dependably filling an empty stomach. It was never intended to be studied or even revisited. Each episode strives toward a platonic ideal of Beaverness, of that perfect blend of familial harmony rattled and restabilized. To say that it is repetitive is only to restate the obvious; like so many other family series of its time, it was *meant* to be repetitive—comfortingly so.

This is the foundation upon which the sitcom built itself. Having received its initial push, and its first wave of stars from radio and film, the family sitcom was the first throbbing of an organic television form. Hardly anyone would claim that *Leave It to Beaver* is in the same class as *I Love Lucy* or *The Honeymooners* or even *The Andy Griffith Show*. But it establishes a baseline from which we can profitably measure the sitcom's growth.

In "Beaver's Short Pants," from *Leave It to Beaver*'s first season, Beaver is flummoxed when visiting babysitter Aunt Martha insists on his wearing shorts to school. The plotline, complete with Beaver generously wearing the ludicrous outfit in order to bid his aunt farewell, so as not to hurt her feelings, could have been transplanted wholesale to *The Andy Griffith Show* (CBS, 1960–68). *Andy Griffith* was created by former *Phil Silvers* writer Aaron Ruben as a *Make Room for Daddy* spinoff, and Aunt Martha can be seen as a precursor to that show's Aunt Bee (Frances Bavier).

If *Leave It to Beaver* is set in some magical, opalescent Midwest, *Andy Griffith* takes place in an idealized South of the mind called Mayberry. Accents are molasses-thick, work is casual, and supper is always about to be placed on the table. In "The Guitar Player," an itinerant musician is arrested for disturbing the peace, but is in luck—Aunt Bee is making chicken and dumplings for dinner. Andy Griffith's Sheriff Andy Taylor is a sly fox, using good humor and untutored reverse psychology to convince others to do his bidding. Encountering a pair of feuding families in "A Feud Is a Feud," Andy orchestrates a duel between the rival patriarchs, convinces them both that the other is out for blood, then sends them scurrying for home by firing a single shot in the air.

A family show with copious interludes for Sheriff Andy to encounter townsfolk and wandering strangers, and for his deputy Barney (Don Knotts) and his outraged harrumphing, *Andy Griffith* is less burdened than *Beaver* by the need to be ideally representative of America. (The link with *Father Knows Best* is stronger; Elinor Donahue, that show's Betty, is Andy's girlfriend Ellie here.) Its Mayberry is the kind of place where boys with cowboy hats and toy pistols fire at the sheriff on the street ("I'll die a little later on if I get the chance," Andy graciously offers) and women carrying parasols might be drafted as impromptu batters for a pitching exhibition. It was deceptively genial, and smarter than it initially looked.

Everything was filtered through Griffith's jovial, homespun wisdom. Teaching his son Opie (Ron Howard) about *Romeo and Juliet* to prep the audience for the star-crossed lovers of "A Feud Is a Feud," Andy offers some guidance: "They said 'hark' a whole lot back then." Opie is unfazed by his first taste of the classics: "Boy, that *Romeo and Juliet* would sure make a good TV show."

Like *Beaver*, there is often a moral lesson directly imparted at the end of each episode of *The Andy Griffith Show*, but its characters are more likely to surprise us with their stubbornness, irascibility, and wit. Even its designated Beaver figure, Opie, has more spark than the other irrepressible young boys common to the sitcoms of the era. (And we would be hearing from Ron Howard again. In a way, the history of the sitcom is the story of Howard's ascendancy from freckle-faced little boy to respected veteran. Without him, the sitcom would look—and sound—quite different.)

Unlike the variety show, or the western, the family comedy was an early television genre that stuck around. The *Beaver / Father Knows Best* strain never disappeared from television; it was only subsumed by bigger, shinier new inventions. Each generation of children had their own *Beaver*: the fantasia of remarriage in *The Brady Bunch* for the 1970s; topical, melodramatic series like *Growing Pains* and *Family Ties* for the 1980s; blue-collar, yuk-intensive *Home Improvement* for the 1990s. Some even had the Beav himself: *The New Leave It to Beaver*, running on a variety of channels from 1983 to 1989, brought back Mathers and Dow as fathers with children of their own, and Billingsley as the maternal eminence grise.

Perhaps the most influential successor to *Beaver* was *The Cosby Show*, which updated its predecessor's sunny tone and good cheer for another time and a distinctly different kind of family. Eventually, entire cable networks—Nickelodeon, the Disney Channel, ABC Family—were devoted to offering the kind of wholesome family entertainment *Beaver* had once symbolized.

Father Knows Best and *Leave It to Beaver* became more than old television shows, fondly remembered; they became code for, depending on who you asked, an earlier, better time, tragically trampled underfoot, or a benighted era whose glib platitudes had ignored messy American reality. It would be most accurate, perhaps, to say that these family series reflected American life as it wanted to be, not necessarily as it was. Either way, television was now, in some fashion, our collective memory. Had that happened to us or to our friends on-screen? It was a distinction without a difference. The 1950s were Beaver's time.

5

The Dick Van Dyke Show

"Forty-Four Tickets"

December 5, 1961 ▪ CBS

From the outset, television had been aware of itself, like an infant regarding its reflection in a mirror, or some great beast of yore making out its image in the ripples of a clear lake. Ralph and Ed had appeared on television to hawk their flawed Handy Housewife Helper, Jim Anderson had confronted the scourge of dim-witted sitcom fathers, and Lucy had had her run-ins with the recorded image, most memorably her failed, alcohol-aided commercial for Vitameatavegamin. TV had known that in some ways, its preferred subject was television itself, whether it was the box sitting in living rooms across America or the picture-perfect families that gathered around the box to be amused and distracted.

The fundamental advance of *The Dick Van Dyke Show* (CBS, 1961–66) over shows like *Leave It to Beaver* and *Father Knows Best*, then, was twofold. First, it elevated the sitcom's interest in television to an explicit, persistent concern, and second, it melded this self-referential focus with an interest in the suburban hijinks of the ideal white American middle-class family. With one foot in the old and one in the new, *The Dick Van Dyke Show* burst onto the scene in 1961, a highly traditional, family-oriented television show that was also about the making of a television show.

The TV show about TV was born, unsurprisingly, on the set of a TV show. Carl Reiner was a writer on the groundbreaking comedy variety series *Your Show of Shows* (NBC, 1950–54), writing for star Sid Caesar alongside future comedic luminaries Woody Allen, Neil Simon, and Mel Brooks. Commuting home every night to his young family in Westchester County (including his son Rob, who would eventually play his own crucial role in the story of the sitcom), Reiner had an idea: wouldn't it be original to create a series set in the writers' room of a television comedy series, with the harried head writer heading home in the evenings to his suburban castle? The idea was for Reiner to write himself and his experience as a television comedy writer into his own version of *Leave It to Beaver*. Reiner wrote a sheaf of scripts for the show, which he called *Head of the Family*, during his family's summer vacation on Fire Island and planned to cast himself in the lead role. One can only imagine the disaster that would have ensued had he succeeded.

Actually, one need not imagine; the pilot episode still exists, and it makes for an ideal controlled experiment in the mysteries of comedy. To be sure, Reiner's show is far wittier than *Father Knows Best*, its explicit influence, ever was. Everything is in place—the careful balance of work and family life, the wisecracking paterfamilias, the interest in mundane happenings as a wellspring of comic invention—and yet the show itself is a complete flop. The characters all have the same names, but there is none of the magic of *The Dick Van Dyke Show* yet. Such are the perverse demands of the medium that Carl Reiner was unable to play a character fundamentally based on himself. Executive producer Sheldon Leonard told Reiner to recast the show. Luckily, Reiner was willing to consider a replacement lead, Leonard caught a performance of *Bye Bye Birdie* on Broadway with an appealing young star, and *The Dick Van Dyke Show* was born.

Watching the new Rob and Laura Petrie—Van Dyke (Reiner had also considered a young television personality named Johnny Carson for the role) and a little-known twenty-four-year-old actress named Mary Tyler Moore, discovered at an audition—put through the same paces makes clear all the reasons why *Head of the Family* didn't work and *The Dick Van Dyke Show* did. The endearing charm of *The Dick Van Dyke Show* is found in three things, of which Reiner's pilot possesses only one. The self-referential "What about this joke?" aesthetic of the fictional *Alan Brady Show*'s writers' room is present in spades. Without Van Dyke's balletic physicality and the easy charm of Rob and Laura's marriage, though, *Head of the Family* lies flat on the screen. In the retooled version, Reiner smartly relegates himself to the role of Alan Brady, at first only a disembodied, dyspeptic voice before appearing in a number of episodes late in the show's run.

Van Dyke was the animating spirit of the show, his loose-limbed gawkiness suggesting some jury-rigged combination of Fred Astaire and Stan Laurel. Where Reiner seemed like he was holding an inexplicable grudge against his family and colleagues on *Head of the Family*, Van Dyke's lightfooted grace kept the show nimble. Van Dyke was an expert musician, and his instrument was his body; for all the show's many charms, *The Dick Van Dyke Show* was at its best when Rob was left to his own devices. Seeing Rob wheeling an enormous German shepherd into his bedroom in a baby crib, and singing it a lullaby, in "The Unwelcome Houseguest" is to be in the presence of a comic master.

One need only watch the extended interlude in the first-season flashback episode "Where Did I Come From?" to see Van Dyke's remarkable comedic powers expressed in physical movement. Laura is pregnant with their son Ritchie, and Rob is increasingly panicked by every sigh escaping his wife's lips, sure she is about to give birth. The ringing of the alarm clock unleashes a frenzy of discombobulated suitcase-grabbing and pajama-shedding. When Rob is cajoled back into his bed (1961 was still the era of separate beds on television, even for married couples), he furtively pulls the phone under the covers, his finger resting on the dial. Rob even practices rapidly putting on his hat, flipping it off the ledge and onto his head. The next morning, hearing the phone ring, he and Laura both pick up simultaneously, and Rob becomes convinced that Laura has taken herself to the hospital without him. Hearing her protest that all she is doing is boiling water, Rob is transported into further heights of delusional amazement: "What a woman!"

Previous sitcom heroes—Ralph Kramden and Lucy Ricardo and the like—had been bumblers, well-intentioned buffoons with a propensity for getting into trouble. Rob Petrie, by comparison, is more like a less conniving Bilko, endlessly charming and witty, the best of company. The fact that he, too, has a propensity for getting into trouble is part of the show's appeal. It is also a reminder that *The Dick Van Dyke Show* straddles both worlds, with Rob both an intellectual (or the TV version thereof) and a regular-Joe suburban father. But *The Dick Van Dyke Show* did not immediately connect with audiences. CBS actually canceled the series after its first season, relenting only when Sheldon Leonard flew to Cincinnati to beg Procter & Gamble to sponsor the show and when summer reruns proved surprisingly popular.

In "Forty-Four Tickets," written by Carl Reiner, from the show's first season, *The Dick Van Dyke Show* nails the perfect sweet spot of balancing comedy-room geekery and miniature suburban dilemma. Rob has forgotten that he promised forty-four tickets to his show to the local PTA, and he scrambles to gather them before imperious PTA honcho Mrs. Billings (Eleanor Audley) shows up at the theater with her party. The episode is essentially a drawn-out version of the famous opening sequence of subsequent seasons in which Van Dyke trips over the living-room ottoman, taking an acrobat's flip onto the carpet. Here, Rob plummets in slow motion over the hurtling abyss of coming up ticketless before forty-four demanding New Rochelle women.

Rob's conscience weighs him down, so that even a friendly game of bridge is infected by his crime: "Four no tickets. Did I say that? I mean forty-four no trump." Resolving the confusion, if only for himself, Rob turns back to the game: "Well, let's play tickets." Laura worries about what might happen if Rob fails to come up with forty-four show tickets, but her husband is nonchalant as only a television writer could be: "Oh, no problem. We'll change our names, and sell the house, and move to a new neighborhood."

Rob recruits his fellow writers, the sardonic Buddy (Morey Amsterdam) and witty single girl Sally (Rose Marie) to help him out of his jam— roles they are regularly recruited to play, being found in Rob's living room as often as in their office. "I got an idea!" Buddy exclaims, as Rob clutches his forehead in frustration. "Beginners' luck," Sally mutters to herself. (The advantage of setting your comedy series in a comedy writers' room is that you have a readymade explanation for why all the characters are trying to be funny all the time. Even better, you have a reason why they succeed.) "Easy," Buddy goes on. "You get a drunken bus driver, and he crashes into a lamppost." Choosing not to dispose of the PTA in such callous fashion, Rob and his fellow writers proceed to steal a fistful of tickets from the show's producer and designated whipping boy, bald-pated Mel Cooley (Richard Deacon, who also played Ward Cleaver's business rival on *Leave It to Beaver*), but honest Boy Scout Rob cannot bear the guilt and admits to the ploy.

The night of the show, Rob and Laura search for scalpers outside the theater, to little avail (though they do obtain one ticket from an elderly lady, who tells them she makes sure to get passes to all her favorite shows, having no television set at home). "Now I know how Custer felt," Rob cheerily observes before his guests arrive. He settles on the truth as his only out: "But I'm going to do it so charmingly that there's a very good chance they won't kill me." At the very last minute, as he stands on a bench, set to break the bad news to his guests, he has a brainstorm: why not cast his forty-four albatrosses as extras in the night's finale? Suitably pleased, the New Rochelle PTA is marched off, and Rob slumps in relief. Rob and Laura return home, where he has a request for his wife: "Honey, will you remind me never to forget anything again?" Rob proceeds to forget himself once more, tripping this time over his briefcase and catapulting to the floor in resounding fashion.

Reiner was on to something when he decided to emphasize the commingled boredom and hilarity of the writers' room. It gave the show a certain savvy that its contemporaries lacked. This was a show whose characters actually laughed at each other's jokes, who were witty and urbane and deliberately charming. Rob's comrades Sally and Buddy—one endlessly looking for a mate, the other endlessly looking to ditch his, Pickles—are the show's free-floating gag lines, present mostly to punch up otherwise hopelessly drab plotlines with a touch of writers' room sophistication. The office establishes its own routine. Rob does push-ups to stay limber, Buddy sleeps on the couch, and Sally obsesses over her latest beau or lack thereof. The writers' room is a boys' club, with Sally, intriguingly, accepted as one of the boys. When Rob is prompted by Laura to treat Sally more like a lady by complimenting her outfit, she responds like a true comedy writer: "You like it? It's yours!"

Buddy saves his best wisecracks for the show's producer, Mel, who gets jabbed with an endless array of jibes about his baldness, his stupidity, and his earning the job by nepotism. Buddy and Mel's ceaseless animosity is the clear inspiration for the more memorable antagonism between another writer and his stuffed-shirt foil: Murray and Ted on *The Mary Tyler Moore Show*.

A television show so emphatically about television also meant commentary on TV's unspoken rules and taboos, still a relatively new endeavor in the early 1960s. "What's the one thing that's never been done on television?" Rob asks Buddy in "The Return of Edwin Carp." "You can't do that on television," Buddy instantly retorts, implying all the risqué matters that television so adroitly sidestepped in its artistic infancy. Even Rob and Laura's son Ritchie (Larry Mathews) takes on a TV-centric view of the world. He tells his parents he is happy to have been born, because otherwise "I wouldn't be here, and I'd miss all my best television programs."

One suspects that Ritchie would have enjoyed the zany sitcom created by Reiner's onetime comedy partner Mel Brooks, *Get Smart* (NBC/CBS, 1965–70). Rob likely would have chuckled at it, too—occasionally. Like *The Dick Van Dyke Show*, *Get Smart* was television that poked at the invisible boundaries of the form. This sarcastic spy series was lightning-quick, studded with visual gags and throwaway quips.

Get Smart occupies a funhouse-mirror universe in which all manner of bizarre and outlandish developments are calmly accepted. Television's naive commitment to realism was wearing away under the assault of the new. (NBC's *I Spy*, starring Bill Cosby, also premiered on NBC in 1965; it was like *Get Smart* without the avalanche of puns, and with more realistic backdrops to its action. *The Man from U.N.C.L.E.* [NBC, 1964–68] found a similar sweet spot at the intersection of comedy and spy games.) Shot almost entirely in close-up and medium shot—perhaps a reflection of the show's chintzy aesthetic—*Get Smart* has a shallow feel endemic to 1960s television. The wide shot was too realistic; its revelations might crack the fragile membrane of the sitcom.

Maxwell Smart (Don Adams) combats a feisty ship's captain in the episode "Ship of Spies," untroubled by his unexpected maneuver: "The old gun-in-the-pegleg trick. It's the second time I've fallen for it this year." Maxwell is the secret agent as used car salesman, always selling down after his first, boldest lie fails the smell test. Caught on his knees with his tie caught in a rival agent's briefcase, he gives it his best shot: "Would you believe a Jolson medley?" He promises the US 7th Fleet is steaming to a rescue, and if not them, "how about a school of angry flounder?" Brooks's fondness for shallow puns is everywhere. On spotting Captain Grauman's "Oriental servant," Maxwell cracks, "So that's Grauman's Chinese."

Like Adams's secret agent, the three comedy-writer characters on *The Dick Van Dyke Show* hurl one-liners like stilettos, looking for the comic upthrust that will simultaneously impress their fellow writers and allow them to finish their script and head home. "Good night, folks," Buddy offers as a potential show closer one evening, "and remember: a friend in need is a pest." Sally accepts the plaudits for a good joke with another one: "Please don't applaud, just send phone numbers of single men." To be a writer in the world of *The Dick Van Dyke Show* is to be a natural performer. The fact that Buddy and Sally seem like far more gifted comedians than the ostensible star of the show they write for is a mystery that is never entirely addressed or settled.

Rob gets into the act, too, winning over his new colleagues (as we see in the flashback episode "I Was a Teenage Head Writer") with a dazzlingly inventive routine in which he singlehandedly impersonates a car—polishing his grill, having his tires kicked, getting stolen by a gunman. Van Dyke does a superb Stan Laurel imitation (Laurel's gormless clumsiness being the clear inspiration for Van Dyke's own brand of pratfalls) and a more than passable turn as *The Honeymooners*' elbow-flapping Ed Norton. On more than one occasion, Rob saves the show from sure disaster by seemingly improvising brilliant routines from scratch. In "The Sam Pomerantz Scandals," a former mentor of Rob's wants to bring back supposedly lowbrow slapstick humor, and Van Dyke turns the routine into an impromptu lecture on sophisticated contemporary audiences rejecting such uncultured approaches, all the while slamming his fingers in drawers, clobbering his chin on the desk, and getting his foot stuck in the garbage can.

The entirety of *The Dick Van Dyke Show* has a variety-show feel, a loose allegiance to advancing the plot that leaves room for all manner of performances: novelty numbers like the catchy hit song "Bupkis" in the episode of the same name, Buddy and Sally's musical act at a local roadhouse in "The Secret Life of Buddy and Sally," and Rob's expert array of impersonations. The show trusts its star to entertain its audience, granting entire episodes to Van Dyke trapped in an elevator, hanging upside down from the ceiling as he attempts to crawl out, or living out his John Wayne gunslinger fantasies at a remote cabin. Emerging a brief dozen years after the first sitcoms appeared on TV, *The Dick Van Dyke Show* is still loose enough to be composed of essentially anything within its star's wheelhouse: musical numbers, Laurel & Hardy tributes, dance shuffles with Moore, rapid-fire verbal warfare with his fellow writers.

The episode "Never Bathe on Saturday" is a highlight of the series' fourth season and perhaps the most pleasurable episode in the show's run. During a weekend getaway with his wife, Van Dyke is first given permission to run through his lover-man persona ("Give me a kiss, baby!" "Darling, what about the bellboy?" "You first") and ascot-wearing David Niven impression ("Don't toy with me, you saucy wench!"). Then Laura gets her toe stuck in the faucet of the hotel bathtub, and Rob must swing into action to rescue her. He feels the locked bathroom door, assessing its pressure points like a kung fu black belt poised to strike. Eventually, he commandeers the house detective's revolver to blow the lock off the door. "You guys want to see something ridiculous?" he chuckles, before realizing his wife's delicate position and raising the gun threateningly at any strange men who might want to enter. Oh, and in playing Niven, Rob draws a mustache on himself with Laura's eyebrow pencil, and cannot scrub it off. Just another weekend in the life of the Petries.

Part dancer, part vaudevillian, part silent comedian, part model husband and father, Van Dyke was the ideal representative of the Kennedy era, which valued the casual grace he effortlessly embodied. (The show's pilot, in a symbolic convergence too delicious not to mention, was filmed on the day of John F. Kennedy's inauguration as president.) Television, in its youth, required the talents of a single performer charming enough to be invited back into viewers' homes, week after week.

But *The Dick Van Dyke Show*'s enduring appeal owes an enormous debt to the actress recruited to play Van Dyke's wife. Mary Tyler Moore embodies the cheerful, well-scrubbed, progressive suburban wholesomeness of *The Dick Van Dyke Show*. Moore's Laura Petrie is the model happy postwar homemaker and mother, even as the show occasionally hints at her half-buried desire to return to the stage. Rob is threatened when Laura enjoys her brief interlude as an *Alan Brady Show* hoofer in the episode "To Tell or Not to Tell," and the buried link between *The Dick Van Dyke Show* and the governing dynamic of *I Love Lucy*—showman husband, frustrated ex-showgirl wife—is briefly exposed. (Lucy and Laura even both commit themselves to one hundred strokes of the hairbrush before bed, good girls to the last.) Ball once visited the set of *The Dick Van Dyke Show*, walked past Moore, then turned, looked her in the eye, and told her, "You're very good." Moore never forgot it.

The fundamental tension of the show, one it found so rich in possibility that it returns to it regularly, is the danger of outside agitators threatening the Petries' domestic harmony. Their marriage is persistently tested by all manner of rivals and doppelgangers. Dishy actresses, schoolgirls with puppy-love crushes, voluptuous blondes on trial for murder (Rob leaps out of the jury box to retrieve her dropped tissue in "One Angry Man")—the show introduces no end of potential rivals to Laura, threatening to overturn the happy placidity of the Petries' home. And for someone who married her husband at the tender age of seventeen, Laura appears to have no shortage of handsome ex-boyfriends who pop in to ruffle Rob's feathers. *The Dick Van Dyke Show* simultaneously promises an unthreatening marital bliss straight out of *Leave It to Beaver* and, in its own naive way, raises the possibility of all that satisfaction disappearing like hissing air from a leaky balloon. It also places itself above the domestic run-of-the-mill by virtue of its self-awareness. "You sound exactly like one of those wives in a situation comedy," Rob chides Laura when she complains about a comely friend of her husband's visiting the house.

Rob's daydreams notwithstanding, the series was constructed on the bedrock of Rob and Laura's relationship, one of the most charming ever depicted on television. Rob and Laura Petrie were such paragons of attractive American domesticity that they were employed to advertise household products like Cheer detergent, Joy dishwashing soap, and Kent cigarettes, in character, after their programs. They were the anti–Lucy and Ricky, their easygoing vitality a stark contrast to the early sitcoms' preference for relentless marital squabbling.

The series as a whole exudes a vague liberal uplift, with the Petries representing a wholesome politics of inclusion extending beyond their well-heeled suburban enclave. In the flashback episode "That's My Boy??" a petrified Rob is convinced that the hospital has given him the wrong baby. He calls the other new parents from the hospital, convinced the Peters family has his son and the Petries theirs. When they come to the house, all such concerns are wiped away with perhaps the biggest single laugh of the entire series: the Peterses are African American. In a later episode, "Show of

Hands," Laura and Rob both accidentally dye their hands black before Rob is to receive an award from a civil rights organization. Rob seeks to cover up the damage with gloves but eventually removes them to prove a point: "I can't wait till the day when understanding between everybody is such a commonplace thing that they don't have to hand out awards for it."

The Dick Van Dyke Show furthers the sitcom's self-contemplation, being not just about television but about a comedy writer who—like Reiner himself—draws on his own home life for inspiration. In "Ray Murdock's X-Ray," Rob tells a persistent television interviewer (TV again!) that all the jokes he writes for *The Alan Brady Show* are autobiographical, offering copious documentation of Laura's having inspired the array of nutty housewives on the show. (Reiner always said that most of the show's domestic plotlines were inspired by his home life with his wife, Estelle.) Rob, knowing he has badly flubbed it, comes home hell-bent on distracting Laura from watching the show, adjusting the television reception, moving the furniture, even dancing to keep her from the TV set.

The show would return to this self-reflexive material time and again. Rob catches Laura going through his mail in "The Curious Thing About Women" ("I feel silly I wasted all those years learning how to read!" he exclaims) and transforms it into a sketch about a nosy young wife named Laura who opens a tantalizing package addressed to her husband, which turns out to be a self-inflating raft. Laura takes offense at the way her friends assume the sketch is about her, but when a tantalizing package arrives at the Petrie home addressed to her husband, she cannot help herself. It is—guess what?—a self-inflating raft. Life imitates art imitating life. (Thirty years later a similar premise, a stand-up comedian collecting material from the odd and funny happenings of his day, would provide the initial inspiration for Larry David and Jerry Seinfeld's "show about nothing.")

In *The Dick Van Dyke Show*'s final episode, Rob finally finishes the memoir he has been working on, only to find book publishers entirely uninterested in a story of suburban domestic hijinks. There is, however, a ray of light: Alan Brady is interested in optioning the book for his next television series. Rob is to serve as head writer on a show inspired by his own life—a show, presumably, not unlike *The Dick Van Dyke Show*. Carl Reiner has written a show in which a character based on himself pens a book on his own life, which looks and sounds a lot like Reiner's, and sells it to a character played by himself. With that one flourish, Reiner completes the self-referential loop of *The Dick Van Dyke Show*, making TV about TV about TV, and inscribing his own show into the imaginary world he has created.

6

Gilligan's Island

"St. Gilligan and the Dragon"

February 13, 1965 ▪ CBS

A number of years have passed, and the sitcom has subtly shifted ground. We are no longer in a suburban living room or a cramped office but amidst the overgrown shrubbery and tangled vines of a Pacific island. A handful of huts and shacks dot an otherwise untouched landscape abutting a hidden cove. Beyond, the endless ocean beckons and divides, keeping a colorful crew of castaways—rich man, movie star, ship's captain, farm girl—from civilization. But hark! The faint strains of a melody appear over the horizon, and the sound of a folk choir. Perhaps *they* can fill us in on what we've missed . . .

"Just sit right back and you'll hear a tale / A tale of a fateful trip / That started from this tropic port / Aboard this tiny ship." *Gilligan's Island*, premiering on CBS in the fall of 1964, took a short trip with a long afterlife, but its journey perfectly represents television during its awkward adolescence, caught between its adorable early years and a more sophisticated adulthood. It is, by nearly all measures, mediocre television, but it also embodies the sitcom in transition.

To begin with, we are now watching television in color; the deserted island's plant life, seen in black and white during the show's first season, was just not as impressive in shades of grey. The characters are also color coded for our benefit: the doltish assistant in the red pullover, the lumpish boss in his royal-blue polo shirt. Everything has been carefully coordinated for maximum comprehension with minimal effort—just like that expository earworm of a theme song.

(Why is it, anyway, that television shows have theme songs? Why must they announce themselves so formally? In part, it is due to the precedent established by television's older siblings, radio and the movies. But it also owes something to television series' overwhelming urge to make themselves instantly recognizable. We hear the melody—*Gilligan's* sailors' ditty, the carefully picked acoustic guitar of *M*A*S*H*'s "Suicide Is Painless," the bouncy melody of *The Mary Tyler Moore Show*'s "Love Is All Around"—and know we are in safe hands. The song is the promise of the familiar.)

The theme song was key to the creation of *Gilligan's Island* (CBS, 1964–67). Creator Sherwood Schwartz had been looking for a setup that would allow him to force disparate characters together without the ability to leave. "All my shows, actually, are how do people learn to get along with each other?" Schwartz would later note. He pitched a show to his longtime agent about seven desert-island castaways trapped together and got an unexpectedly virulent answer: "Sherwood, you're out of your fucking mind. Who the hell is going to watch the same goddamn seven people on the same goddamn island every week?" He changed agents.

Schwartz wrote out thirty-one two-to-three-sentence story ideas on a long roll of butcher paper he tacked up in his office, then rolled it up and brought it to his next meeting. CBS bought the show almost immediately, but network president Jim Aubrey was insistent that it required far too much explanation of its guiding premise each week to be viable. Schwartz believed otherwise, arguing that an introductory theme song would solve all such problems. Schwartz originally had a Harry Belafonte–inspired calypso rhythm in mind but was ultimately convinced to abandon it in favor of the sea chantey style of the final version, introducing the five passengers, the three-hour tour, and the tiny ship getting tossed.

Originally, show creator Sherwood Schwartz envisioned none other than Jerry Van Dyke in the role of Gilligan. Dick Van Dyke's brother, who had played a recurring role as Rob Petrie's sleepwalking sibling on *The Dick Van Dyke Show*, turned it down in favor of James L. Brooks and Allan Burns's legendary mediocrity *My Mother the Car* (NBC, 1965–66). In his stead, Schwartz drafted former English teacher Bob Denver, already familiar to audiences as goateed beatnik Maynard G. Krebs on *The Many Loves of Dobie Gillis* (CBS, 1959–63). Hard as it may be to imagine, Denver's simpleminded first mate could have been paired up with a Skipper played by Archie Bunker. "I needed someone who was going to be physically bigger than poor little Bob Denver's Gilligan, and who would berate him and bawl him out for this and that, and just be annoyed with him all the time," said Schwartz. "I really needed a sort of Hardy who would suffer the tortures Laurel put him through. . . . We tested everyone here in town whom we could think of, and when they didn't work out, CBS sent for four or five actors from New York who were primarily stage actors at that point. Carroll O'Connor was among them. Obviously it has nothing to do with talent that he didn't fit the part. . . . It's the luckiest thing that could happen to Carroll O'Connor when he didn't get the part. If he'd become identified with the Skipper, no way would he have been chosen for Archie Bunker."

After running through his options, Schwartz spotted Alan Hale Jr. across a crowded restaurant and insisted to his wife that he had found his Skipper. Schwartz ended up having to chase him down on the set of a western in a remote Utah canyon, but Hale agreed to take the role.

In "St. Gilligan and the Dragon," written by Arnold and Lois Peyser, Gilligan, the Skipper, and the other male castaways—intellectual jack-of-all-trades the Professor (Russell Johnson), and blue-blooded millionaire Thurston Howell III (Jim Backus)—have frustrated their female companions by making only meager efforts to address the island's lack of privacy. The ladies—sultry actress Ginger Grant (Tina Louise), well-scrubbed country girl Mary Ann (Dawn Wells), and hoity-toity society belle "Lovey" Howell (Natalie Schafer)—decide to stage a full-on male vs. female confrontation. There will be no more cooking and no more washing until the men break down and give the women space of their own.

Thurston immediately cracks up at the notion of women sharing equal rights with men. Soon enough, though, the men are left to their own devices in the kitchen and the open-air laundry, scrubbing clothes and slicing coconuts. Thurston, clad in a chef's hat and apron, is disappointed by his fireside failures: "I am a good cook when I have a chef working for me!" The men seek their own form of revenge for this tame TV version of Aristophanes's *Lysistrata*, constructing an elaborate Trojan horse beast in order to scare the ladies into submission. They are instantly caught in the act, and Gilligan falls back on a typically hapless excuse: "We were on our way to a masquerade party . . ."

Gilligan is ultimately a show about dressing up and playing make-believe. In "St. Gilligan and the Dragon," it falls to the men to imagine a world more to their liking, with women less inclined to complain about their lot. Each gets a lavishly art-directed fantasy of their own. The Skipper, lamenting the women's failure to "just act the way we wanted 'em to," pictures himself as an Oriental maharajah, bedecked in silks and surrounded by submissive houris of all shapes and sizes. Mr. Howell, he of the permanently clenched jaw and tendency to weep over the vagaries of his blue-chip stocks, imagines the women as worker bees, dutifully, lovingly treating him to a manicure and pedicure. His wife, no stranger to servicing his whims, is poised by his feet, offering to do "anything to make you happy."

The Professor, his exotic fantasies more deeply buried under a facade of scientific dispassion, transforms himself into a teen idol in the mold of Frank Sinatra, under assault from a small army of shrieking bobby-soxers. They shred his clothes and claw at his chest as he does Tony Curtis doing Cary Grant. In perhaps the most unlikely transformation, Gilligan becomes a thin-mustachioed Spanish bullfighter, surrounded by a squadron of dark-haired, pale-skinned Goya beauties.

Many of *Gilligan*'s episodes, like "St. Gilligan and the Dragon," revolve around fantasy adventures far from the island. Gilligan becomes a Napoleonic potentate in a tricornered hat or Secret Agent Gilligan, clad in a tuxedo and trench coat. Mary Ann apes *Pygmalion* as an Eliza Doolittle type, while the Professor is imagined as a caveman scientist inventing the wheel. Lovey is transformed into both Mary Poppins and Cinderella. Even when taking place within the confines of the island, episodes often concern matters elsewhere. One might think, given the brute economic realities of life on an uninhabited island removed from civilization, that its residents might be a trifle less concerned than they are with the windfalls to be gained from the discovery of gold on the island, or the deed to an oil well Mr. Howell sells to Gilligan.

Gilligan's Island is a series trapped in its own concept. Where does a show with seven characters and a single small island go to roam? The show never grows tired of introducing new, temporary castaways: drifting surfers, hapless socialites, Russian cosmonauts. It also luxuriates in mock-tribal hoo-ha and high-colonialist nonsense about terrifying natives and drum-beating savages, with the bucktoothed, malaprop-spouting Japanese soldier introduced in "So Sorry, My Island Now" as perhaps the worst offender of a sorry lot. (Sophisticated fare this was not.)

The castaways' famous radio, never running down its batteries, always broadcasting news of immediate import to their lives, is representative of the show's casual surrealism: spells to levitate tables, pigeons on treadmills, gorillas named Gladys, magical bottles offering three wishes (hints of *I Dream of Jeannie*, about which more momentarily). In perhaps the most inspired of its surrealist touches, Gilligan is transformed by a smack in the jaw into a radio in "Hi-Fi Gilligan," with the other castaways demanding he entertain them with the programming of their choosing.

In "St. Gilligan," the fantasies of female subjugation run their course, and we return to the island—albeit with a sinking feeling of familiarity—and to the sight of another masterfully crafted Trojan horse, this time in the shape of an enormous ladybug. The women are unimpressed, calling on the men to step out of their contraption, only to panic when they see their ostensible rivals also gawking at the oversized critter. The natural order of *Gilligan's Island* is mercifully restored, with the women running gladly into the paternal embrace of the men, in search of protection and comfort. The buffoon once more restores equilibrium through calamity; with stories of dragons implanted in his head, Gilligan convinces himself that he must slaughter the beast to protect his friends. As the Skipper and the Professor mutually realize that the oversized ladybug is actually a weather balloon, their potential salvation, Gilligan rushes forward, lance in hand. Taking the balloon's hot air for the fiery breath of a dragon, Gilligan stabs it, instantly piercing the inflated hopes of his compatriots once more.

This is a series about paranoia, with Gilligan as the designated punching bag. The Platonic ideal of a *Gilligan's Island* episode exiles Gilligan from the rest of the gang due to some misunderstanding whereby he comes to believe he is a vampire or a Kupakai headhunter, or hideously deformed by baldness or a busted nose. Eventually, Gilligan is reunited with his friends, but not before temporarily coming to believe that he no longer belongs in their company.

Gilligan's klutziness is the show's eternal bad-luck charm; he is forever spoiling the others' best-laid plans for rescue by the sheer excess of his enthusiasm, to the frustration of the island's natural leaders, the Skipper and the Professor. Gilligan is the fuckup son to the Skipper's angry father, and his cry of distress—"Skipper!"—sounds like a nervous toddler desperately in search of his mother. The Skipper's "little buddy" is part son, part brother, part pet, and all indentured servant.

The show delegates different brands of humor to each of its characters, the most consistently amusing being Ginger's array of raised eyebrows and libidinous whispers, and Thurston Howell's clenched-jawed WASP detachment. Tina Louise is a self-aware vamp, trotting out her entire bag of seductive tricks for our amusement. Jim Backus's Thurston Howell is the oligarch as helpless babe, with only his money to protect him from his own inadequacy. "Good heavens, Lovey, how do you work one of these?" he wonders when pressed into manual labor, wielding a shovel from the wrong end. Luckily for him, he is often able to lull others into doing his work with promises of bottomless wealth. He and his wife are convinced that social status will protect them when nothing else will. "A shark bite a Howell?" he roars. "He wouldn't dare!"

Gilligan and the Skipper are granted the show's permit for physical comedy, always clanging into each other to a soundtrack of big-top circus music. Their routines are drawn directly from vaudeville and the silent film, the pratfalls like rusty third-hand Buster Keaton, and the verbal tomfoolery of Laurel & Hardy minus the warmth or the inventiveness. Gilligan torments the Skipper with his lack of agility, regularly butting heads with him, dumping pots of glue on his head, or clocking him with ladders. Gilligan takes his fair share of licks, too; the Skipper is often close to crushing his little buddy with his excess bulk, his hammock perched dangerously close to Gilligan's own.

Gilligan's Island owes its most direct debt to *Robinson Crusoe*, its characters carefully recreating American life out of tree bark and coconuts. Part and parcel of the recreation, of course, is the careful slotting of each person into their appropriate place. Mr. Howell assumes a position of authority over the others merely by virtue of his now-meaningless wealth, and the men take unquestioned charge of the decision-making process. It is only in "St. Gilligan and the Dragon" that the women demand what is rightfully theirs, momentarily exposing the sexist underpinning of these gentle fantasies.

In this, *Gilligan's Island* marched in lockstep with the other fantasy-oriented shows of the era. Most clung to notions of women as mystically oriented helpmeets that would, in short order, come to appear hopelessly naive. Suburban hausfraus were now possessed of magical, mysterious powers: Samantha (Elizabeth Montgomery) of *Bewitched* (ABC, 1964–72) is a witch, descended from a long line of witches, who attempts to transform herself, out of love for her husband Darrin (Dick York, and later Dick Sargent), into a plain-vanilla suburban housewife. Jeannie (Barbara Eden), of *I Dream of Jeannie* (NBC, 1965–70), is a bare-midriffed, plunging-necklined blonde imprisoned in a bottle by a lovelorn Arabian djinn some two thousand years prior, and set free in prim, respectable 1960s America. (Sally Field, as the title character in *The Flying Nun* [ABC, 1967–70], is a variation on this same essential theme.) In both cases, the women, imbued with remarkable capabilities, accept a life of dull conformity as the price of their happiness. The shows are similarly rigid, firing an endless array of potential calamities at their protagonists while always returning to exactly where they had begun at the top of the half-hour.

The pleasures of both *I Dream of Jeannie* and *Bewitched* come from watching their protagonists bend the seemingly unyielding rules in their favor. Try as they might, neither can help herself from disrupting the established order. Jeannie crosses her arms, blinks her eyes, nods her head, and disappears in a puff of lavender smoke, the sound of a boinging spring the aural corollary to her magic. Samantha wrinkles her nose to work her witchcraft, scored to a soundtrack of twinkling magic wands. (*Gilligan's Island*, too, offers its own moth-eaten magic, its sped-up footage of Gilligan escaping his tormentors a sitcom version of the old silent-film chase sequences.) Samantha, who professes devotion to the suburban ideal of being a wife and mother, is cajoled and taunted by her carefree fellow witch and mother, Endora (played by that veteran of Orson Welles's theatrical company, joyously slumming it on television, Agnes Moorehead). *Bewitched* is constructed as a series of threats—younger women preying on Darrin, Endora's enticements to witchery, various supernaturally inclined relatives—to the smoothly oiled machine of suburban contentment.

Jeannie, meanwhile, is Ginger Grant minus the star's sense of entitlement. The 1960s shirtsleeved idealism of Larry Hagman's Tony Nelson—he is literally an astronaut—is undercut by the whiff of the Arabian Nights imported in Jeannie's bottle. His brawny, well-meaning American masculinity is sabotaged by scheming womanhood. Jeannie simultaneously exacerbates and solves all of her new master's problems, all at once. And that title—"master"! Could *I Dream of Jeannie* have been any more blatant about its masculine wish fulfillment? And yet, if the setup of *Jeannie* was blatant pandering to some of the more regressive fantasies of men, the show was devoted to Jeannie's occasional rebellions. The battle of the sexes is the subject here as much as it had been on *The Honeymooners*, if with more levity and less raw heat.

Both *Jeannie* and *Bewitched* tiptoe around their primary attraction, which is, of course, sex. Darrin the talented adman (Don Draper before his time) and Major Nelson the astronaut are twin ideals of masculine verve—selling America to itself, exploring the universe—and yet their home life is ever so slightly off. Jeannie is a certain kind of bachelor's dream girl, submissive and subservient, if also clingy and unpredictable. And Samantha, well scrubbed and polite, finds secret reserves of stubborn individuality, hinting at just why her husband prefers her to their suburban neighborhood's Stepford wives.

Jeannie pushes back against her master's expectations that she naturally assume the duties of homemaker, while also hiding in her genie's bottle whenever the doorbell rings. The show offers up a series of rivals to their unacknowledged domestic bliss: smoldering secretaries and lascivious movie stars for him, an array of Tony's colleagues and friends for her. *Jeannie* goes to some trouble to introduce the word "platonic"—a word Jeannie does not entirely comprehend—into its working vocabulary, but whatever its initial insistence to the contrary, the show promises the pleasures of the harem cloaked in a NASA jumpsuit. "We don't do this in Cocoa Beach," Tony tells Jeannie in the show's first episode, having discovered her wriggling out of the bottle that imprisoned her, but she never quite unlearns her natural carnality. Eventually, toward the end of the series' run, Jeannie and Tony marry, as if to fulfill their destiny, but *I Dream of Jeannie* clearly prefers the ambiguity.

Gilligan's Island, meanwhile, like its hero, is mostly asexual. Five healthy, unattached young men and women (and the married Howells) are marooned alone on an island, and no one pairs off, no one sneaks off for a quickie in the bushes, and no one lusts after one of his or her companions. The series does raise the possibility of sexual intrigue as motivation; slinky Ginger, who testifies repeatedly to her erotic manipulation of Hollywood's powers that be, regularly attempts to win over one of the recalcitrant men— usually Gilligan—with the implicit promise of blissful movie-star sex. And yet no one exchanges so much as a kiss, as if the island were a cloister and its inhabitants a septet of nuns. Poet Philip Larkin's farcical belief that "Sexual intercourse began / In nineteen sixty-three . . . / Between the end of the 'Chatterley' ban / And the Beatles' first LP" notwithstanding, American television in 1964 was still an erotically sparse landscape. The sitcoms of the mid-1960s persistently gestured at sexual freedom without ever being able to offer more than a glimpse of it.

The special effects on *Gilligan's Island*, *Bewitched*, and *I Dream of Jeannie* are the television equivalent of those found in 1950s monster movies. Noses magically grow to enormous size, envelopes slip themselves under doors and into mailboxes, and canteens tighten their lids as if by sorcery. The black wires are not quite visible, but they feel as if they might just be. On the DVD reissues of *My Favorite Martian* (CBS, 1963–66), the wires lifting off the spaceship of visiting alien Martin (Ray Walston) from the fairgrounds *are* highly conspicuous. Martin passes himself off as an earthling under the protection of his supposed nephew, intrepid reporter Tim O'Hara (Bill Bixby), but is perpetually tempted, like Jeannie and Samantha, to expose his Martian abilities in order to bend the arc of the mundane world in his favor. Forever on the brink of fixing his rocket ship and returning to Mars, Martin is repeatedly undone by the unexpected bursts of fancy of an otherwise hopelessly square America. In "Rocket to Mars," his spaceship is co-opted for a kiddie ride at the local fair, leaving Martin steaming: "I just set myself back a thousand years." The point is less to wow us—these series are hardly the stuff of James Cameron—than to amuse us, to demonstrate television's capacity for upholding and subverting domestic bliss all at once.

And speaking of casual surrealism, what could be more effortlessly surreal than *Bewitched* replacing one Darrin, the stolid Dick York, with another, the irascible Dick Sargent, in 1969 without ever acknowledging the substitution? (When *Roseanne* substituted Sarah Chalke for Lecy Goranson as Becky Conner, the show felt compelled to crack some nervous jokes about Becky suddenly looking different.) The sitcom's bland facade—wholesome entertainment for a nation of families gathered around television sets in suburban living rooms—could mask a surprising strangeness.

Sitcoms had begun to understand that the normal was an illusion, and they were intent on passing off the deliriously strange as a simulacrum of normalcy. Another gang of mismatched types marooned together, another painfully explanatory theme song: *Gilligan* creator Sherwood Schwartz would regroup after the cancellation of the show with *The Brady Bunch* (ABC, 1969–74). *The Brady Bunch* is, like its predecessor, a fantasy offering an effortless ideal of social harmony between strangers. Widower Mike Brady (Ralph Reed) and his three sons join with Carol (Florence Henderson) and her three daughters and form a new, intertwined family. *The Brady Bunch* gestures at the post–*Leave It to Beaver* complexities of American domestic life, but its plot hook notwithstanding, the series prefers to re-create the cozy, unthreatening atmosphere of the 1950s sitcom, newly outfitted with shag carpeting and sideburns. If *The Brady Bunch* has a single recurring visual image, it is the children's open-mouthed sighs of gratitude when one of their niggling problems has been solved, as if to say, "Gee whiz, aren't parents swell?" Greg Brady (Barry Williams) in particular is a Mary Ann dreaming of becoming a Ginger, latching on to half-baked ambitions of taking the mound for the Dodgers or rocking out as teenybopper star Johnny Bravo. In keeping with *Brady*'s sustained interest in uplifting pablum, those dreams of stardom are always jettisoned. Who needs success when you already have family?

Gilligan's Island also dreams of Hollywood success, seeing being marooned on a desert island as no impediment to making it big. After all, what else is there to dream of? In the episode "The Producer"—perhaps the only one of the nearly one hundred installments of the show that is actually laugh-out-loud funny—the brilliant Phil Silvers shows up as Hollywood mogul Harold H. Hecuba, a fedora on his head, a cravat wrapped around his neck, a cigar stub jammed wetly into the corner of his mouth. "I don't put in with negative thinking," he tells the castaways. "Do you wanna know why? Because it's negative!" In true Bilko fashion, Hecuba has them doing his bidding in no time, carrying his bags, giving up their lodgings, and putting on a show for his entertainment.

Ginger tries and fails to impress him with her range as an actress by passing herself off as an earthy Italian peasant à la Anna Magnani. ("Brea-ad! You want-a bread!") Instead, the gang puts on a musical version of *Hamlet*, with Gilligan (who else?) as the Danish prince, Ginger as Ophelia, and the Howells as Gertrude and Claudius. The know-it-all producer immediately takes command of the show, casting himself in every role, lumbering off the stage for another quick-fire costume change. He runs through the show in double time before steaming back to civilization with his latest, pilfered, production in hand. Silvers's Harold Hecuba is every bit the gadfly and charlatan his Sgt. Bilko had been, running circles around the dim-witted castaways with murderous aplomb. One wonders why *Gilligan's Island* so rarely had guest stars of Silvers's ilk on the show—then one remembers how poorly the other cast members come off in comparison and marvels that he ever made it on.

Watch enough television, and sitcoms begin to talk to one another. Gilligan is meant to be a charmed buffoon in the vein of some of his sitcom predecessors, forever stumbling into chaos and scrabbling his way out. Like Lucy Ricardo, he is a one-man whirlwind, reaping disorder in his wake and blind to the consequences of his doltishness. As if to highlight his own antecedents, the episode "Gilligan vs. Gilligan" re-creates the famous mirror scene from the Marx Brothers' *Duck Soup*, with Gilligan pitted against his scheming Soviet doppelganger. One suspects, though, that the true inspiration was less Groucho and Chico than Harpo Marx's guest appearance on *I Love Lucy*, matching wits with Lucy Ricardo. Gilligan eventually catches out his Communist double by feigning a sneeze, finger poised precariously under his nose. Bob Denver was no Harpo Marx—or Lucille Ball, for that matter—but the sitcom continued to pay homage to its predecessors with self-referential glee.

Two raft-in-a-package episodes: A box purporting to contain a raft washes ashore in the episode "It's Magic," and as the castaways struggle to open it, one is instantly reminded of *The Dick Van Dyke Show*'s "The Curious Thing About Women," in which Laura Petrie, tormented by curiosity, opens a package addressed to her husband and watches to her chagrin as a massive life raft automatically inflates in her living room. The *Gilligan* package proves to be a box of tricks belonging to a magician named the Great Raftini, not a raft, but the impression lingers that these series were in communication, exchanging whispers, symbols, plot points, and helpful hints. Cynics might argue that they were drawing on the limited pool of amusing sitcom tropes, repeatedly echoing each other consciously or otherwise. But dedicated watchers could sense that something was afoot—that the closed universes created by each sitcom were in silent, worshipful communion.

And the strange spell cast by *Gilligan's Island* lingered for decades. In "Sherwood Schwartz: A Loving Tribute," a *Roseanne* episode from 1995, the Conner family indulges in an impromptu fantasy revival of the show, with Laurie Metcalf's Jackie Harris as Gilligan, John Goodman's Dan Conner as the Skipper, and Roseanne as Ginger. Sara Gilbert's Darlene Conner is Mary Ann, a self-described "dumb girl from the country with an amazing rack." Johnny Galecki's David Healy remains himself, trudging angrily through the sand and muttering to himself, "I don't even like this show. I wanted to be on *Friends*."

Goodman, game as ever, does a spot-on imitation of the Skipper's bluster, and Roseanne, embodying Ginger only insomuch as she, too, dons a spangly evening gown for no particular reason, is kidnapped by those always-pesky cannibals. She curses them one last time before disappearing into their human-size stockpot: "I hope I give your whole village the trots!" *Roseanne* strands itself on the familiar island, and then adds to the sense of mystical communication between the closed universes of the sitcom by depositing none other than Gilligan, Ginger, and the Professor in Lanford, Illinois, in the Conners' house, playing the Conners—Denver as Jackie,

Louise as Roseanne, and Johnson as Mark. The audience roars in recognition, perhaps less because the stars of *Gilligan's Island* are still recognizable thirty years later (they mostly aren't) but in tribute to the eternal nature of the sitcom.

Gilligan's Island only lasted three seasons before being unceremoniously canceled by CBS in 1967. The network had moved it around on the schedule numerous times, and according to Schwartz, even its modest success was not enough to overcome the disapproval of network chairman William Paley. Reappearing in syndication, the show found an unexpectedly vast new audience, appealing particularly to children. As one wag notes in a documentary on the show's enduring appeal, "Everyone hated it except the audience." The renewed interest in the castaways was potent enough to stimulate three follow-up movies: *Rescue from Gilligan's Island* (1978), *The Castaways on Gilligan's Island* (1979), and most hilariously of all, *The Harlem Globetrotters on Gilligan's Island* (1981). (What marketing meeting from hell spawned this odd amalgam of faux ensembles with next to nothing in common?)

The sitcom had divested itself of its workaday trappings, preferring the fantastical (talking pigs, like *Green Acres'* Arnold) and the supernatural (all those witches and genies and Martians) to the humdrum domestic world of *The Honeymooners* and *The Dick Van Dyke Show*. In the midst of a growth spurt, the sitcom was ready to burst its boundaries, spilling into genres and styles wholly distinct from what it had initially been. For now, sitcoms were each marooned on their own desert islands, adrift from the world they could only partially, faultily re-create.

The sitcom's evolution closely tracked that of the society that gave birth to it, if belatedly, with staggered enthusiasm, and at a distance. The 1950s sitcom had been determinedly domestic, interested in relations between the sexes, the raising of children, and family harmony. The television was both screen and mirror; entertaining America, it also reflected back what America—or the part of America considered to be worth acknowledging—saw itself to be. It was a nation of fathers and mothers, parents and children, husbands and wives, and if chaos dominated, it never reigned. Their setups were disarmingly simple, capable of being summed up in a sentence—if an entire sentence was even necessary. "Happy families are all alike," wrote Leo Tolstoy, and little the author of *Anna Karenina* might have seen on 1950s television, other than *The Honeymooners*, would have been likely to disabuse him of the notion or force him to consider the adjoining notion of the unhappy family. Eventually, *All in the Family* would inaugurate a wave of sitcoms about dysfunctional families that would prove as amusing as their more contented counterparts and break the sitcom out of its self-imposed straitjacket of satisfaction.

Prior to that, the mid-1960s saw the sitcom in transition. No longer content with the familiar, it yearned to expand its horizons, to reach beyond the familiar domestic realm. But the form did not yet know how to become what it wanted to be—something better-rounded, and more diverse, than it already was, mature enough to embrace sophistication and self-referentiality as a rhetorical device. In 1964, the year *Gilligan's Island* premiered, the Beatles made their American debut on *The Ed Sullivan Show*, soon to remake pop music in their half-mocking, half-cerebral image; and Stanley Kubrick turned nuclear holocaust into *Dr. Strangelove*, the darkest black comedy ever made. (Gilligan, in the episode "X Marks the Spot," rides a runaway rocket in a manner immediately reminiscent of Slim Pickens's Major "King" Kong in that film.)

In comparison, television was a backwater, a haven for the hackneyed and shopworn, its audience preferring to be lulled into submission rather than shocked with unforeseen pleasures. As history unfolded in the streets—riots, assassinations, protests, a society in the throes of wrenching change—television reflected nothing and understood nothing. The new wave spilling onto the airwaves and soon to take over the movies would eventually come to television as well. The sitcom would drift back ever closer to the mainland, shepherding itself into a stronger communion with the world it still mostly eschewed. Within a decade, *The Mary Tyler Moore Show* and *M*A*S*H* would remake the sitcom as something knottier, more personal, and more politically charged than it had ever been before. The era of Gilligan would seem a distant memory, even further off than more naive forebears like *I Love Lucy*.

In the meantime, though, the sitcom had to crawl through this fantastical "vast wasteland." (The man who coined that term, FCC chairman Newton Minow, was the namesake for *Gilligan's Island*'s ship, the S.S. *Minnow*.) Consider *Gilligan* and its kind, then, a necessary but awkward phase in the growth of the sitcom—an attempt at doing something more than it had been capable of in the past, but without any sense of what that might entail.

7

The Mary Tyler Moore Show

"Chuckles Bites the Dust"

October 25, 1975 ▪ CBS

I t all started at a five-thousand-watt radio station in Fresno, California . . . Well, before we let Ted Baxter have his say, let's begin instead with Mary Richards. Or perhaps we should call her Laura Petrie? A number of years after *The Dick Van Dyke Show* went off the air in 1965, writers James L. Brooks and Allan Burns were recruited by producer Grant Tinker to develop a concept for a new sitcom for Mary Tyler Moore. Moore had just

starred with her old costar in a special called *Dick Van Dyke and the Other
Woman*, where they dueted on the number "Life Is Like a Sitcom," and she
now felt ready for a return to television.

They had the idea of bringing Moore back as a character not unlike
Laura, if more world-weary: a divorced woman moving alone to a new city,
with a new job as a stringer for a gossip column, and new friends. After
all, given the remarkable chemistry between Moore and her costar on *The
Dick Van Dyke Show*, observed Burns, "Where was that magic likely to happen again as between the two of them?" CBS, which had aired *The Dick
Van Dyke Show*, loved the idea of a new vehicle for Mary Tyler Moore but
had a few problems with the scheme. "There are four things Americans
won't stand for," a CBS executive named Mark Golden told them. "Jews,
men with moustaches, New Yorkers, and divorced women." And besides,
wondered another CBS executive, "Wouldn't people think she had divorced
Dick Van Dyke?"

Those bits of wisdom in hand, Brooks and Burns reconsidered, and
made Mary Richards a single woman newly arrived in Minneapolis after a
breakup, working as a TV news producer at a third-rate station. They rapidly put together a ten- or twelve-page treatment for the show that included
what ended up as much of the pilot's dialogue.

In testing, the show's pilot was wildly unpopular. Audiences did not
like any of the lead performers, and mutterings about replacing some of the
actors were heard. Tinker called Brooks and Burns with a simple directive:
"Fix it." They chose not to panic and just made some minor adjustments to
the script. The show went on to win four Emmys its first season, and to an
eventual perch in the top ten.

The urban setting was deliberate counterprogramming to CBS's wildly
popular lineup of family-friendly cornpone shows like *The Beverly Hillbillies*
and *Green Acres*. The enormous success of *The Mary Tyler Moore Show* (CBS,
1970–77) would ultimately lead, instead, to the wholesale purge of those
still-popular series from the CBS schedule, to be replaced by a new slate of
sophisticated urban programming. Jim Aubrey, once the president of CBS,
had noted that "we program for the people we fly over," but *The Mary Tyler

Moore Show was intended for a younger, hipper audience than the bulk of CBS's more staid programming, reflecting changing American mores—or at least the shifting desires of advertisers.

Fred Silverman, head of programming at CBS, argued that older, rural audiences "really weren't sellable and we were a national advertising medium." Originally, *The Mary Tyler Moore Show* was put on preceding *Hee-Haw*—precisely the wrong audience for the former show. "We have a bunch of junk on Saturday night. We ought to move one of those hillbilly shows and put this there," Silverman told CBS president Bob Wood. Once it was switched to Saturday nights, where it initially aired after *The New Dick Van Dyke Show*, *MTM* would become a harbinger of the new sitcom of the 1970s, leading the way for more sophisticated series like its eventual Saturday-night compatriots *All in the Family*, *M*A*S*H*, and *Taxi*. James L. Brooks would go on to become an icon of the American sitcom, and other key *Mary Tyler Moore* staff, like director Jay Sandrich, would have a hand in landmark series to come.

For 168 episodes, Mary was introduced to the tune of Sonny Curtis's "Love Is All Around," flinging her hat into the air with gleeful abandon. The freeze frame at the end of the credits left viewers with the same snapshot of delirious freedom, week after week, that lingering moment of ecstasy serving as the defining image of *The Mary Tyler Moore Show*'s delight in shattering the sitcom's cozy domestic platitudes.

The ecstasy was not confined to Mary and her choice of headgear but instead dependent on the steady accretion of one well-honed line of dialogue after another. The sophistication was less in the subject matter—although *The Mary Tyler Moore Show* boldly ventured, on occasion, where its predecessors might have feared to—than in its craft. The sitcom was no longer content merely to entertain. It wanted to succeed within the structure it had built and the rules it had written for itself.

This is nowhere more evident than in the most famous of *The Mary Tyler Moore Show*'s episodes, and one of the most beloved individual episodes of any sitcom in the history of television. "Chuckles Bites the Dust," from the show's sixth season, is a one-joke masterpiece, a rolling snowball of inappropriate humor. The show boldly tackles taboo by laughing at that most inappropriate of subjects: death. More than a cavalcade of bad taste, "Chuckles Bites the Dust," written by David Lloyd, is also an impassioned defense of laughter as the best—the only—medicine for sorrow, and of the sitcom as an instrument flexible enough for all human emotions, not just the bluntest form of seltzer-down-your-pants comedy. Mourning Chuckles, *Mary Tyler Moore* also displaces him.

In "Chuckles Bites the Dust," newscaster Ted Baxter (Ted Knight), always childishly enthusiastic over recognition of any kind, is delighted to hear he has been summoned by the circus to serve as the grand marshal of their annual parade. News director Lou Grant (Ed Asner), protective of the station's dignity, refuses to let him go, and Chuckles the Clown, kiddie-show host, is sent in his stead. Mary defends Lou, telling Ted that he has always been treated like a responsible adult. "Then why won't he let me go to the circus?" Ted pouts, breaking down in childlike sobs. In the next scene, Lou stumbles into the newsroom, breathing heavily. "Something terrible has happened," he announces. "Someone we all know is dead."

After refusing numerous entreaties to tell them the identity of the deceased, Lou finally spits it out, and the hilarity begins: "Chuckles the Clown is dead. It was a freak accident. He went to the parade dressed as Peter Peanut, and a rogue elephant tried to shell him." Lou dashes off to tell Ted but stops first to share a seemingly irrelevant detail with writer Murray Slaughter (Gavin MacLeod): "The elephant's name is Jocko." Ted, still sulk-ing over his abandoned circus appearance, hardly takes in the news: "Stop trying to cheer me up, Lou."

The news team gathers, and everyone trades memories of Chuckles, opening the floodgates to the inevitable mockery. Ted recites Chuckles' famous motto ("A little song, a little dance, a little seltzer down your pants") on the air, and offers a tribute to his art: "I like to think that somewhere up there tonight, in his honor, a choir of angels is sitting on whoopee cushions." Murray, his reserves of tact weakened by Chuckles' indisputably comic exit, lets loose a stream of zingers. He suggests the Chuckles tribute show be titled "Requiem for a Peanut" and expresses relief that no one else had been hurt: "After all, you know how hard it is to stop after just one peanut." Lou clucks at Murray's insensitivity but then bursts into laughter himself. The characters are wrestling with the same impulses as the show itself. How far can you go in search of a laugh? At what point does the cool relief of humor become the hot silence of the tasteless?

Prim Mary is repulsed by everyone's laughter and attempts to guilt everyone into silence before they head to Chuckles' memorial service. (Mary asks Ted for a ride to the service, and he responds, tactfully as ever, "The more the merrier.") Inevitably, Mary weakens under the onslaught of rich comic material fondly remembered at the service. The list of Chuckles' characters—Mr. Fee Fi Fo, Billy Banana, Aunt Yoohoo—is the first chink in her armor, and when the minister refers to the "deeper meaning" of the clown's work, she weakly passes off her first snickers as coughs.

Gripping her mouth in a tight rictus of barely contained hilarity, Mary throws her head back in seeming pain, swallowing heavily. The minister speaks about how Mr. Fee Fi Fo would "pick himself up, dust himself off, and say 'I hurt my foo-foo,'" but Mary—teary-eyed, shoulders silently heaving—only bursts into shrieks of laughter when he, too, solemnly quotes Chuckles' fondness for seltzer in his pants. The minister has the shamed Mary stand, asking her to laugh for Chuckles, as that was what he lived for. Mary immediately bursts into tears.

The lesson of the episode is encapsulated in Lou's earlier pronouncement on the medicinal value of laughter. "It's a relief," he says. "It's like whistling in a graveyard. Ya laugh at something that scares ya. We laugh at death because we know that death will have the last laugh on us." Murray echoes Lou, if in slightly less philosophical terms: "Somewhere out there, there's an elephant with your name on it."

There was also an elephant lurking in the room for *The Mary Tyler Moore Show* as a whole, and its name was marriage. What was wrong with Mary Richards, viewers unconsciously wanted to know, that no man had yet snapped her up? As if to get it out of the way as soon as possible, the very first episode of *The Mary Tyler Moore Show* sees Mary dismissing her long-time boyfriend after he stumbles over the words "I love you." "Take care of yourself," he tells her as he is escorted out the door, and Mary briskly kisses him off: "I think I just did." Mary is not grumbling about her missing ring. She wants marriage, but only on her terms. *MTM* ends with its single career girl, astonishingly, still single.

In this, it was riffing off another series with *Dick Van Dyke Show* roots and proto-feminist ambitions: *That Girl* (ABC, 1966–71). Created by *Dick Van Dyke Show* writers Bill Persky and Sam Denoff and starring Marlo Thomas as another ingénue in search of her big-city break, *That Girl* similarly insulates its protagonist from marriage. *That Girl* is a 1960s mod show in stuffy 1960s TV style, which means no sex, no drugs, and no rock 'n' roll. Even without those stimulants, Thomas is impossibly perky, excitable, and rambunctious, her eyes perpetually widening in unadorned pleasure, often at the romantic doings of her boyfriend Don (Ted Bessell). Her Ann is the force behind this appealing series, plucked out from the masses of indistinguishable young women, week after week, and selected as "that girl." "I wanted to play the person that had the problem, not the person who assisted the person with the problem," said Thomas of *That Girl*. "Girl" she is; her disapproving father still stops by regularly with the laundry, inevitably catching Ann in a seemingly compromising moment. By comparison, Mary Richards is a paragon of enlightened maturity.

The inherent complexity of navigating career and personal life—one that has not gotten demonstrably easier in the ensuing forty years—is the driving force of *The Mary Tyler Moore Show* at its outset. In nearly every episode in *MTM*'s first two seasons, Mary meets an intriguing—or baffling, or nauseating—new man, and Moore's parry and thrust with another eligible bachelor is one of the show's recurring comic pleasures. Mary is audited by an IRS man, who tells her that "I've enjoyed doing you more than anybody I've done before"; she is courted by a short man who has her practicing her Groucho Marx stoop-walk in order not to tower over him; she meets a series of middle-aged grotesques at a divorcées' club offering discounted European trips.

Mary is the graceful, polite, stubbornly single small-town girl—the golden girl whose biggest disappointment in life is that she won election as student class president by a comparatively small margin. Moore, a gifted physical comedian, supplied her with a palette of physical gestures that would become second nature to viewers: the quick swipe across the body with one hand to wave away unpleasant thoughts, the bobbling head when engrossed in an internal debate, the agitated sputtering that the show's writers referred to as "fumphering," the guffaw that erupts from nowhere, surprising Mary as much as anyone else.

She remains firmly grounded, however, a realistic heroine offset by two exuberant caricatures. There is self-satisfied married woman Phyllis (Cloris Leachman), the classic underminer; and Rhoda (Valerie Harper), a loud-mouthed Jewish New York transplant swaddled in fortune-teller scarves. Rhoda is willing to say anything, or be anyone, in order to snag a man. Their friendship is the classic marriage of opposites, on-screen and off. Harper was a Democrat, a feminist, and a fan of Betty Friedan's *The Feminine Mystique*; Moore was a Republican, a Catholic, and a traditionalist. The sitcom's timidity partially undercuts the comparison; Rhoda, intended to be dumpy and shrill in comparison with Mary, is played by the lissome Harper. When Rhoda loses twenty pounds and wins a beauty contest in "Rhoda the Beautiful," viewers might be confused: was Rhoda supposed to have been overweight?

Mary exists simultaneously in two realms: the personal and female, and the professional and male. More than just a relationship sitcom, *MTM* is also a workplace show in the model of *The Dick Van Dyke Show*, with Mary the lone straight woman to a series of male comic foils. If Mary is a revived, revamped Laura Petrie, Murray is a shrunken Rob Petrie, still quick with a wisecrack, if shorter, balder, and dumpier than his predecessor. Network observations about the presence of Jews in sitcoms to the contrary, MacLeod delivers his lines like a Catskills tummler, hitting his consonants explosively, every punch line a shiv in the guts.

The show's creators had initially intended Murray to serve as Mary's workplace nemesis, and Ted as her love interest. But after considering MacLeod for the role of Lou, they ended up casting him as Murray, a character based on a gay colleague of Brooks's from his days working as a copywriter at CBS News, who used to keep skates in his desk and spend his lunch hour at the Rockefeller Center ice rink. MacLeod's innate gentleness made him an unlikely antagonist.

And who could picture the ideal young woman falling for the likes of Ted Baxter? Ted is a classic—at times, *too* classic—dummkopf, his narcissism and dim-wittedness making him the ideal target for Murray's zingers. Ted is the overgrown infant being collectively raised by the newsroom staff, his puppy-dog desire to please matched by an equally strong petulant streak. Murray hears a news report about a man's award-winning 115-pound turnip and retorts, "What's so amazing about that? We have a 165-pound vegetable doing the news every evening!"

The role of boss Lou Grant ultimately went to Ed Asner, after he blew his first audition. After thinking over his mistakes, Asner marched immediately back into the audition room and castigated the show's staff: "You just sat there on your asses and let me bomb like that? I was terrible. And you know it was terrible and you were too polite to tell me. Don't be so fucking polite. Tell me what you want in this character."

Much of *The Mary Tyler Moore Show* revolved around the small indignities of work. Many of these were feminist in iteration: why was it that only Mary could be trusted to make coffee for her male coworkers? But the show itself is a paean to a bygone time, one that, in this era of high unemployment and job insecurity, must be translated for contemporary audiences like cuneiform tablets. *Mary Tyler Moore* is about people devoted to their workplace and their coworkers, and the strange affection that crops up between people who spend all their days together in a common pursuit of excellence—or, knowing Ted Baxter, a minimum of embarrassment.

MTM was an aspirational series for a new generation of women. Mary is idealistic and a bit naive, but pressure reveals the innate toughness underneath. (This is to be contrasted with Rhoda, whose Bronx-tough facade covers up the unprotected flesh below.) The show was a reflection of millions of young American women who, like Mary, were belatedly, tremblingly asserting their authority, in the workplace and in their private lives. Every time Mary stood up to her boss, or successfully navigated a treacherous assignment, she was a stand-in for all her offscreen counterparts. Part of the inspirational quality of *MTM* was Moore's beauty and her seemingly unflappable poise; only on television could a woman be awakened from a deep sleep at 2 AM by her best friend and her date and emerge with her hair and makeup in perfect condition. This is the sort of show on which it might take years to fully resolve the burning issue of where Mary's bathroom might be located.

The show is a lot like its protagonist: politely rebellious. *The Mary Tyler Moore Show* does little its 1960s predecessors wouldn't have in terms of form, but its content pushes the envelope of propriety for the prudish networks. Mary's mother, visiting her apartment, says, "Don't forget to take your pill," and both Mary and her father respond, "I won't." Mary's father looks askance at her, but a point has been scored in favor of honesty on television. Laura Petrie would never have been able to do it.

The Mary Tyler Moore Show also expanded the sitcom's horizons by allowing its stories to spill across multiple episodes—sometimes entire seasons. Lou's divorce and his ex-wife's remarriage, Ted's romance with Georgette (Georgia Engel)—*MTM* trusts enough in its audience's loyalty to let its characters grow with the passage of time. Syndicated reruns required series whose episodes could be reencountered haphazardly, out of broadcast order, but *The Mary Tyler Moore Show* demanded a slightly deeper absorption in its plot development. Everything did not necessarily return to normal at the end of thirty minutes.

Mary is rarely troubled by such developments or by the everyday slings and arrows of an unequal workplace, cheerily making the best of matters. She is an eternal optimist only lightly dinged by the show's parade of small humiliations. And yet Mary is at her best—and her funniest—when she finally ceases being polite. Mary, so preternaturally assured, almost inevitably cracks under stress, and this is where the comedy of *The Mary Tyler Moore Show* truly begins. On a disastrous election night broadcast in season one's "The Snow Must Go On," she threatens to fire Ted if he declares a winner before the station receives its own results. She succeeds in making him toe the line but still sulks afterward like a child deprived of a favorite toy: "But I'm supposed to be *in charge*." When Lou questions what he sees as her careerism, she lashes back with a satirical outburst: "You guessed it, Mr. Grant. I want to go out there and scratch and claw for power. I'll stop at nothing in my ruthless fight for the top."

In these early seasons, Asner's Lou Grant is conflicted about whether he is a male chauvinist pig or a gentleman, Archie Bunker or Heathcliff Huxtable. Lou is belligerent, old-fashioned, an unrepentant hard drinker, and a shouter. "Somebody put wastepaper in my wastepaper basket!" he exclaims to nobody in particular, searching for his liquor bottle in its usual hiding place. Lou is mostly a kindly father figure to Mary, but flashes of a generation gap emerge unexpectedly. Unlike her coworkers, Mary can never bring herself to call him by his first name, only Mr. Grant. Lou defends paying Mary less than her male predecessor because "he had a family to support. You don't. Why don't you come back when you have an answer to that?" She eventually does, countering that financial need should play no role in the amount that workers are paid. There are times where *MTM* feels like a construction kit for the making of young feminists, parceling out arguments and attitudes like Gloria Steinem with a laugh track appended. Lou is a straw man against whom feminist points can easily be scored: "Mary, don't wear pants to the office anymore," he announces during one episode, apropos of nothing.

It is not until the show's third season that it jettisons some of the meta-new-guy filler and replaces it with a more acid depiction of 1970s womanhood. "Now I feel like I represent women everywhere," Mary observes in the first episode of the season, and the show grows to take on that very burden. Female writers like Treva Silverman expanded the show's focus, gleaning comedy from places male writers would not have known to go. For Silverman, what made *Mary Tyler Moore* special was that it was a show about the quirks of human behavior, not just a compendium of punch lines.

As Brooks noted, there was a world of comedy inside his wife's purse, but he did not know quite how to reach it. In direct contrast with their forebears, Brooks and Burns were open to hiring inexperienced female writers as long as they grasped the kinds of stories the show was looking to tell. New writers took their own experiences and granted them to Mary and

Rhoda. Sybil Adelman gave Rhoda a joke about her imagined wedding announcement, with her parents "relieved to announce" her engagement. Karyl Geld quoted from a letter written by her mother, composed in the hospital after giving birth to her.

Silverman was a one-woman reeducation program for boorish sitcom writers. On hearing that the staff had Mary in a scene, watching Ted flipping through his little black book, with women sorted by their hair color, she dissented: "You know, you can't have Mary standing there. Get her out of the scene—or she's gotta have a rejoinder. She can't stand there and let that pig remark go." Sitcoms were now not only about women but also, sometimes, by women.

Mary turns down a suitor's marriage proposal, surprising herself with the realization that she does not *need* to get married in order to be satisfied. Her parents move to Minneapolis, and she and her father, who love each other but have little to say to each other, have a heart-to-heart. "Mary, are you ever lonely?" he wonders. Mary, quietly touched, responds, "No, not too often, Daddy. I have a good life."

Lou is now more solidly cast as Mary's protector, marching into the ladies' room to comfort her when her comedian boyfriend's performance goes disastrously wrong in "But Seriously, Folks." He yanks the towel out of its bathroom dispenser, dragging the entire roll in her direction so that she can blow her nose. And Mary is now the worrying daughter to an occasionally pig-headed father, always protecting Lou from his own tendencies toward mawkishness and drunken hostility.

In the show's fourth season, Rhoda is packed off to her own series. (Phyllis unceremoniously disappears as well; she would eventually turn up on a spinoff of her own.) *Rhoda* (CBS, 1974–78) reunites many familiar faces from *Mary Tyler Moore*: Harper as Rhoda, and Nancy Walker and Harold Gould as her parents, adding Julie Kavner (later the voice of Marge Simpson) as Rhoda's sister Brenda and David Groh as her husband, Joe. (The producers had initially wanted to cast future *Taxi* star Judd Hirsch as Joe, but dueling commitments forced him to back out.) Rhoda, now returned to her hometown ("New York, this is your last chance!" she playfully threatens in the show's opening credits) is now the glamorous one, with Brenda taking over the role of occasionally jealous sidekick.

The aura of cautious feminism, carried over from *MTM*, is still beset on all sides by ignorance and incomprehension. Rhoda's mother's first lines on the show are classics, and perfectly indicative of the series as a whole: "So, how come you're not wearing a bra?" Rhoda and Mary are blood sisters, their frames of reference practically identical. "Oh, I thank you, *Ms.* magazine," Rhoda exclaims after summoning the nerve to ask a man out on a date. "I never could have done it without you!"

The Mary Tyler Moore Show became so influential that its imprint could be felt on shows that otherwise hardly resembled it at all, such as *Alice* (CBS, 1976–85), which offered the spectacle of a mostly female workplace sitcom staffed by kooks and weirdos. *Maude* (CBS, 1972–78) emerged from the stable of producer extraordinaire Norman Lear as a spinoff of the wildly successful *All in the Family*. Maude Findlay (Bea Arthur) is a left-wing, feminist inverse of her cousin by marriage Archie Bunker, wildly spewing invective at a variety of juicy targets like the Vietnam War, boorish men, and Richard Nixon. *Maude*'s setup is a carbon copy of *All in the Family*: loudmouth protagonist, long-suffering spouse, adult child. *Maude* pokes fun at *The Mary Tyler Moore Show*'s gentle tweaking of the country's moral code. "She went out on a date and she stayed out all night," Maude's conservative neighbor tut-tuts about a mildly racy *MTM* episode. "You can sneer all you want, Maude, but as Mary Tyler Moore goes, so goes America."

"Life is trial and error," observes Maude, a liberal Jewish firebrand awkwardly disguised for television audiences in Gentile garb. She is speaking of her new husband, her fourth, but she might as well be referring to her penchant for following an argument through to the bitter end, no matter the consequences or the facts. Maude is always in a low boil about something, and the Findlay household is another quarrel-happy home, the Bunkers in slightly posher digs. She is a passionate liberal, regularly undermined by the ferocity of her ardor. *Maude* finds its humor in the scrapes its heroine gets into in the name of proving a point: looking to buy marijuana to get herself arrested, or pushing her husband to divest from an investment in a slum property. Maude is both more and less enlightened than Mary Richards; for an impassioned feminist, Maude is extremely punctual about putting dinner on the table for her husband every night.

But the show's sensitively handled exploration of abortion, in the episode "Maude's Dilemma" (written by future *Soap* and *Golden Girls* creator Susan Harris), could not have been possible without the feminist idealism of *The Mary Tyler Moore Show* to guide the way. Of course, *All in the Family*'s fearlessness about the minefield of current events was an inspiration, too. Like *All in the Family*, *Maude* is at its best when jabbing its meaty finger at the hotbutton issues of the day—never more so than with the two-part "Maude's Dilemma," first broadcast in November 1972. Maude, forty-seven years old and already a grandmother, discovers she is pregnant, and wrestles with the idea of having an abortion. Maude, as the show clearly indicates, is not looking forward to being a mother again, nor is she adequately prepared for the task. Her neighbor asks her if she is nursing, and the heavy-drinking Maude responds, "No, I was just having coffee." The 1970s' new-age motherhood sets Maude off on another impassioned rant: breastfeeding is now "an art, like French cooking." Humorously, more of "Maude's Dilemma" is devoted to the question of whether or not Walter will get a vasectomy—a clear case of barring the barn door after the cow has escaped. Ultimately, Maude and Walter decide not to have another child: "For you, Maude, for me," Walter argues, "in the privacy of our own lives, you're doing the right thing."

Another sitcom's protagonist may have been a mousy middle-aged man with thinning hair and a receding personality, but on close examination, much about *The Bob Newhart Show* (CBS, 1972–78) is modeled on *The Mary Tyler Moore Show*. The balance of work and home life, the upwardly mobile midwestern milieu—psychologist Bob Hartley (Bob Newhart) and his wife, Emily (Suzanne Pleshette), even live in an apartment that looks like an exact duplicate of Mary's later, ritzier digs. The show is revolutionary, too, in its own quiet way; while rarely drawing attention to it, much of the action finds Bob and Emily in the bed they share together. Rob and Laura Petrie and their matching twin beds had been left far behind.

Created by *MTM* and *Rhoda* producer David Davis, along with Lorenzo Music (who worked with him on *Rhoda*), and directed by *MTM* veteran Jay Sandrich, *The Bob Newhart Show* expertly re-creates the straight-man-and-oddballs aura of *The Mary Tyler Moore Show*. Davis and Music both felt that Newhart "listened funny," and made him a psychologist to capitalize on their star's gifts. Bob plays armchair therapist to his wife and friends, while also fighting gamely to mask his own low-grade neuroses. The action, such as it is, generally revolves around the minor psychological hang-ups of Bob, his friends and family, and his patients. Newhart, a stand-up comedian with a string of successful comedy albums to his name, is indeed a master spectator, and his series—the first of two hit shows to bear his name, followed by *Newhart* (CBS, 1982–90)—allows him to quietly observe, and occasionally intercede, in the low-temperature kerfuffles of others. There are no "very special episodes" of *The Bob Newhart Show*.

In "Goodnight, Nancy," a standout episode from the show's first season, friends and colleagues are convinced Bob is cheating on his wife when he reencounters an old girlfriend. Bob hastily attempts to dampen the fire of Emily's burgeoning jealousy but finds himself accidentally fanning the flames in bumbling Mary Richards fashion. He insists Emily not purchase a new dress for their dinner with his ex-girlfriend Nancy and her husband, then is caught wearing new loafers. "Well, I had to—to go with my new suit," he explains sheepishly, gesturing awkwardly with the back of his hand at his new ensemble. The camera freezes on Bob's mock-placid expression of horror at hearing Nancy tell him she and her husband are thinking of splitting up, cutting to commercial at the peak moment of Bob's awkwardness.

It only gets worse from there, with Nancy insisting on reaching across the table and feeding Bob a bite of her salad, cooing at him while sensuously sliding the fork out from his mouth. Bob, sure she is interested in rekindling their romance, plans to let her down easy at lunch the next day. As it turns out, Nancy is not interested in Bob at all, and it is Bob who is crushed. The nuanced psychological insight of *The Bob Newhart Show* and *The Mary*

Tyler Moore Show was a departure from the raucous but often single-note character studies of 1950s and 1960s sitcoms. Characters were allowed to contradict themselves, to develop beyond their initial outlines.

After the departure of Rhoda and Phyllis from *The Mary Tyler Moore Show*, Mary is now thrown in all the more closely with her work gang, and Ted evolves, ever so slightly, from being a caricature to being a caricature with a personal life. Two memorable new characters are introduced: Ted's equally dim-witted but well-meaning girlfriend (and later wife) Georgette, and Sue Ann Nivens (Betty White), "the Happy Homemaker," whose cooking show is also filmed at the station. Sue Ann is another in the series' array of comic grotesques, a sex-starved virago with an eye for disheveled Lou. Lou calls out to her, "Sue Ann, can you do me a favor?" White smiles, her bubbly enthusiasm for any and all men never diminished by perpetual rejection, and drawls, "Well, maybe on my lunch hour."

Sue Ann is primarily present as an irrepressibly raunchy foil to Mary, her Martha Stewart household-cleaning tips somehow never standing in the way of her dirty mind. Introduced in *MTM*, White would become a television fixture dreaming of bygone days in St. Olaf on the 1980s NBC hit *The Golden Girls*. Georgette, meanwhile, is Ted's selfless helpmate, her blank-faced patter providing an accidental critique of her husband's skinflint ways: "Ted and I are going to the movies this afternoon," she tells Mary as she makes her way out the door, "and I have to go home and make the popcorn."

With "Chuckles Bites the Dust," the new, Rhoda- and Phyllis-less *MTM* reaches the pinnacle of the series' ambitions, as well as the first signs of its imminent demise. There was an elephant with *The Mary Tyler Moore Show*'s name on it, although the show soldiered on through seven seasons. There was no visible diminution in the show's writing or acting, but the plotlines had worn a bit thin, with numerous episodes revolving around characters almost quitting or being fired and such not-quite-hot-button topics as Mary's dependency on sleeping pills. *MTM* was no longer a cost-benefit analysis of the single life but a touching, occasionally sentimental portrait of work as family.

After seven seasons of furtive discussion of firing the incompetent Ted, the station comes under new management in "The Last Show," the series' final episode, and everyone is fired—except for Ted. Mary, Lou, Murray, and Ted gather one last time in the newsroom. Lou, his voice shaking with emotion, tells his staff, "I treasure you people."

Mary gets the opportunity to deliver her own farewell speech—one replete with meaning for the many millions of American women for whom she was a symbol, stand-in, and role model. "Sometimes I get concerned about being a career woman. I get to thinking my job is too important to me, and I tell myself that the people I work with are just the people I work with, and not my family. Last night, I thought, what is a family, anyway? They're just people who make you feel less alone, and really loved, and that's what you've done for me. Thank you for being my family."

Never one to end on an exclusively somber note, the show has its entire ensemble gather for a teary group hug, collectively shuffling over to Mary's desk to pick up tissues like a multiheaded, bleary-eyed octopus. The moment was born out of an improvisation during rehearsal, and adopted, over Burns's opposition, for the show itself. "Now for the hard part," Murray wonders. "How do we leave this room?" Mary famously takes one last look before turning the lights out permanently on the WJM newsroom. The shot had to be taken twice, because the crew member in charge of dimming the lights, engrossed in the moment, flubbed his cue.

Lou would move on to *Lou Grant* (CBS, 1977–82), a newspaper show set in Los Angeles. As if to emphasize the peculiar amalgam of comedy and sentiment that *The Mary Tyler Moore Show* embodies, *Lou Grant* is, of all things, an hour-long drama. Lou is still Lou—shambling, gruff, hard-nosed, unsentimental in a misty-eyed way—but the laugh track has dissipated, and the last-place television station has been replaced with a crack team of ace investigative journalists. That no one burst out laughing at the concept was proof of his character's solidity; no one was constructing a drama around Thurston Howell III. *M*A*S*H* would also inspire the drama *Trapper John, M.D.* (CBS, 1979–86), and a decade later the acclaimed drama *Hill Street*

Blues would attempt to reverse the feat, spinning off Dennis Franz into the mostly comic *Beverly Hills Buntz* (NBC, 1987–88).

What 1970s shows like *The Mary Tyler Moore Show* and, soon, *M*A*S*H* were introducing to television would become the default mode of the sitcom. The sitcom family of *The Adventures of Ozzie and Harriet* and *Leave It to Beaver* had frayed, and in its place new families—jury-rigged, misshapen, self-selected—would emerge.

8

All in the Family

"The First and Last Supper"

April 6, 1971 ▪ CBS

It remains one of the great ironies of television history that the inventor of the sitcom's most beloved racist hatemonger was a card-carrying liberal humanist. Norman Lear, creator of *All in the Family* (CBS, 1971–79), had intended for Archie Bunker, played by Carroll O'Connor, to parody the Silent Majority: the beleaguered white-ethnic Americans who had supposedly been President Richard Nixon's strongest supporters. But a funny thing happened on the way to television immortality: audiences *liked* Archie. Not in an ironic way, not in a so-racist-he's-funny way; Archie was TV royalty because fans saw him as one of their own. *All in the Family* was not parodying the Silent Majority; the show embodied it. And the weekly squabbles between Archie; his wife, Edith (Jean Stapleton); his daughter, Gloria (Sally Struthers); and his son-in-law, Michael "Meathead" Stivic (Rob Reiner, whose father, Carl, had created *The Dick Van Dyke Show*) were a version of America in microcosm—a national debate confined to a single Queens living room and boiled down to thirty minutes of comically aggrieved low-level warfare. It was not the response Lear expected, but it was the one *All in the Family* deserved.

Like its predecessor *The Honeymooners*, *All in the Family* is a thirty-minute prison sentence in the constricted confines of a working-class living room dominated by a single, overwhelming masculine presence. Archie is composed of two parts rage to one part ineffectual action. Like another sitcom landmark, *I Love Lucy*, it is a four-handed act, with two wildly disparate couples, their alliances perpetually shifting, engaged in perpetual combat. And yet, for all its links with the sitcom past, Archie Bunker's first steps onto the screen are revolutionary. Archie demolishes most of the rules of television propriety that had existed before his arrival. He is crass where his predecessors had been mostly polite, outspoken where they had been reticent, flatulent where they had been bodiless—a willful demolition expert of the unspoken liberal order of the sitcom.

Lear had gotten his own start, after failed endeavors as a hot-plate manufacturer and baby-photo entrepreneur, as a writer for Danny Thomas, and then for Dean Martin and Jerry Lewis. He met Bud Yorkin on Martin and Lewis's staff, and branched out into feature films, writing *Come Blow Your Horn* (1963) for Frank Sinatra and *Divorce American Style* (1967) before returning to television as a showrunner. *All in the Family* arrived at the end of a long wave of meek family programming. "We followed a whole bunch of shows like *Father Knows Best*, *Leave It to Beaver*, *Green Acres*, and other shows of the '60s," said Lear. "They were all fine shows, but you would think by watching them that America had no blacks, no racial tension, that there was no Vietnam."

Perched on his worn, tan-colored armchair like a decidedly minor deity, Archie is the tin-pot tyrant of the Bunker household, ruling by dint of what he sees as his natural masculine authority. O'Connor's bulldog jowls and perpetually hooded eyes are physical manifestations of the contempt and suspicion with which Archie views the world beyond his purview. He is the strident, furious voice of white working-class rage, with his feckless college student son-in-law in particular the representative of all that is new and noxious in the world at large. "Archie, oppressed, oppresses," observes Donna McCrohan in her book *Archie & Edith, Mike & Gloria*, in as precise a summary of the show as anyone has yet offered.

Archie's attacks spray his targets with endless fusillades of verbal fire: Jews, Puerto Ricans, feminists, McGovern supporters, hippies, students, Catholics. Archie sees himself as the last defender of old-fashioned decency, an average American man defending his natural prerogatives from being claimed by the undeserving hordes. He is, even to those around him, a relic. In "Archie and the Editorial," from the show's third season, Archie goes to visit a local television station to complain about an anti–gun rights editorial, and the station manager, breathless with excitement, asks to have a colleague sent in: "There's something I want him to see before it's extinct." In an expression of the sitcom's eternal forgetfulness, Archie is forever learning his lesson about the costs of intolerance, only to begin each new episode with his reservoir of hatred brimming over afresh.

If Archie can be said to have a bête noire, so to speak (if you'll pardon the accidental pun, worthy of Archie himself), it is unquestionably African Americans. *All in the Family* premiered at a time when it was still permissible—even funny, given the right situation—for someone like Archie Bunker to say "coon" on television. He mostly avoids the even harsher "nigger," but it is a word that is clearly much on his mind. Lionel Jefferson, son of the Bunkers' African American neighbors, subtly ridicules Archie by honoring his intolerance. Whenever he mentions his career plans, Lionel deliberately lapses into mock dialect, making sure to tell Archie he hopes one day to become a "'lectrical engineer." Archie is crafty enough, though, to occasionally turn the tables on his antagonists. When Meathead uses the word "snigger," Archie politely corrects him, wittily observing "Don't you know that the delicate word for that is 'snegro'?"

Fans made ARCHIE BUNKER FOR PRESIDENT T-shirts and buttons in 1972, and once more in 1976. But not everyone enjoyed or approved of Archie. "Why review a wretched program?" John Leonard wondered after *All in the Family*'s premiere. "Some watch the show and love Archie because they think he's right," said sitcom icon Bill Cosby. "Names have a tendency to stay. Names like kike, nigger, and the rest of them never seem to die. Archie says them in his home where in his mind it's safe. I guess what I dislike most about him is he never says what he does is wrong."

Archie is offset, and to a degree undermined, by his wife, Edith. She passively takes Archie's abuse ("Edith, will you stifle?"), her stupidity a kind of subversion, her naive compassion partially counteracting his blunt prejudice. Like her husband, Edith is a social commentator, albeit of an unknowing sort. Her uninformed view of African American life is an implicit critique of the brand of entertainment-as-uplift that Lear's shows sought to undermine: "Two years ago, they was nothing but servants and janitors. Now they're teachers and doctors and lawyers. They've come a long way on TV." It was also reflective of the tortured depiction of African Americans in the sitcom, which had begun late and petered off relatively early, about which more momentarily.

In "The First and Last Supper," written by Jerry Mayer, from *All in the Family*'s first season, Archie is alarmed to learn that an African American family, the Jeffersons, are moving into their white, working-class Queens neighborhood. Even worse, Edith has accepted an invitation to their home for dinner. "There's one thing Archie Bunker ain't never gonna do," mutters Archie, in self-referential mode, "and that's break bread with no jungle bunnies." After making this pronouncement, Archie must contend with

Meathead, who takes issue with his outspoken racism. "What has any of this got to do with hate, you dumb Polack?" Archie wonders.

Archie cancels dinner but is outmaneuvered into hosting the Jeffersons at his house. Edith sets the table with candles, and Archie complains that given the low light, he won't be able to make out their guests at all unless they smile. The stakes are raised even higher when a neighbor comes around with a petition to keep the Jeffersons, and any other black families, out of their community. As Archie takes out his pen to sign it, the Jeffersons ring the doorbell ("Them colored people love to play with bells," Archie mutters). Archie hustles his white-supremacist compatriot out the back door as his new African American neighbors come through the front door.

In one fleeting image, *All in the Family* epitomizes all of Archie's worst fears. Stepping back into the living room, he finds Edith inviting Henry Jefferson (Mel Stewart, holding down the fort until Sherman Hemsley's George Jefferson arrives on the scene a few seasons later) to sit in his favorite armchair. Archie does his trademark slow burn, silently seething as his unwanted neighbor literally takes his spot in the world. The white man has been supplanted by the black man, and no one but Archie Bunker cares enough to intervene.

All in the Family is not content to leave it at that, by any means, and Archie and Henry tussle for a few more rounds. Henry delivers a mocking toast before dinner, offering tribute "to good neighbors—they come in all colors. White, off-white, lily-white . . ." Soon enough, Archie and Henry take their argument to its illogical extreme, and debate God's racial makeup. Archie asks, in all ignorant innocence, "God is white, ain't he?" He finally settles on another, more pointed argument: "I was made in God's image, and you'll note that I ain't black." Henry wants none of his racial superiority complex: "Well, don't complain to me about it."

Archie sees himself as the protector of the old verities—home, family, neighborhood—against the onslaught of the newer and lesser. He defends the eternal truths of white Anglo-Saxon Protestantism, even as he perpetually fails to remember his own minister's name. He wields the Bible more as sword than shield. He hears the doorbell ring on a Sunday and plaintively moans, "Don't people stay home and read their Bibles no more? What happened to Christianity, anyhow? Whoever that is, tell them to get the hell out of here."

Archie offers an endless array of unpleasantly frank observations, not all of them politically charged. Archie comes home complaining of a subway trip interrupted by a jumper on the tracks: "He couldn't do it in the middle of the day? He's got to hold up the rush hour!" He is a serial malaprop artist, present for us to chuckle at his dim-witted insensitivity. He refers to a Jackson Pollock show as a "Polack art exhibit," and when he is corrected, notes, "Well, he sure paints Polish." He pictures Mass as "some Catholic priest sprinkling incest over everybody."

Norman Lear had lifted the Bunkers from a British television series he had heard described but had never seen called *Till Death Us Do Part*. Mark Golden (the same CBS executive who told James L. Brooks and Allan Burns that Jews and mustaches were verboten from TV) had caught the show on a business trip to London, and came back singing its praises. Lear, struck by the idea, could not believe he had not come up with it first: "How did I never think of this?! That's my *father*." Lear turned *Till Death*'s Alf Garnett into Archie, adapting the series for a US audience and a moment— the early 1970s—still sorting through the frenzy of American political and social upheaval.

ABC, not CBS, ended up purchasing the rights from Lear and shot two pilots for the show, in 1968 and 1969. At first called *Justice for All* and then *Those Were the Days*, neither pilot satisfied the network enough to make it to air. After one abortive pilot screening, ABC president Tom Moore told head of programming Leonard Goldberg, "We in senior management are going to pretend this pilot never happened. And for your own future, I would suggest you do the same." In 1971 Lear's series was back at CBS, which hoped the show would help improve its abysmal ratings among younger viewers. CBS initially booked a thirteen-episode commitment, with an option to bail after three.

Lear had originally wanted Mickey Rooney for *Justice for All* before settling on O'Connor. Rooney rejected the show's premise and suggested an alternate one: "Listen to this: Vietnam vet. Short. Blind. Private eye. Large dog!" Lear had also cast Candice Azzara and Chip Oliver as Archie's original daughter and son-in-law, more boy- and girl-next-door types than their eventual replacements Reiner and Struthers. Struthers in particular had gotten the role of Gloria by auditioning with laryngitis and winning over the show's producers with her increasingly hoarse attempts to fight back.

Lear wanted to cram as much shock value as possible into the premiere episode. "I felt we had to get the network wet completely," remembered Lear. "Once you're completely wet you can't get wetter. I wanted the audience to hear all of Archie's epithets, to see his sexual hang-ups, to meet the whole family." CBS steeled itself for furious protests, running the episode with a disclaimer meekly pleading that the show cast "a humorous spotlight on our frailties, prejudices, and concerns," but received only one thousand phone calls after *All in the Family*'s premiere, far less than expected, and with 60 percent of the callers expressing favorable views. CBS president Bob Wood compared *All in the Family* to "breaking peanut brittle with a ballpeen hammer," but were audiences laughing at Archie or with him? Chuckling condescendingly or guffawing approvingly? *All in the Family*, learning quickly from its unexpectedly intense popularity, skirted the distinction between approval and condemnation of its prime instigator.

All in the Family is deliberately ugly, not only in Archie's benighted opinion-mongering but also in the symphony of noxious browns and yellows of its living-room set. Lear had originally considered shooting *All in the Family* in black-and-white, and the drab colors served as a substitute palette. It is the precise inverse of predecessors like *The Dick Van Dyke Show* and *Leave It to Beaver*, which depicted domestic life as a comfortable, warm respite from the outside world. The Bunker living room is a cage where the beasts pace restlessly, in search of any stimulation or distraction—even, or especially, a fight. Archie is primarily pitted against Meathead and Gloria, representatives of the new order—for them, tolerance and sexual freedom;

for him, immorality and chaos. But even the new order is occasionally fractured. For Michael, in the episode "Gloria Discovers Women's Lib," liberalism stops at the foot of his bedroom door. His version of total equality of the sexes depends on women admitting their total inferiority—grounds, no one would be surprised, for a knock-down, drag-out fight between husband and wife. Soon enough, *All in the Family* embraces its flintiness as a comic trope, consistently delivering the familiar clashes between left and right, old and young.

There would be fights between Lear and the network as well—over a storyline about Mike's temporary impotence, or the use of the word "Mafia." There would even be a battle over showing Mike and Gloria's baby being diapered, with CBS fearful of audience response to momentary full-frontal nudity even when the nudity in question was that of an infant.

All in the Family has the dubious honor of having introduced bathroom humor to American television, its flushing toilet an all-purpose punch line for this and all future Lear shows. "Edith, let me tell you something about beer," Archie tells his wife as he comes out of the bathroom (not actually seen on the show, only heard). "You can never buy beer, you can only rent it." "With that first flush, you know," observed *M*A*S*H* creator Larry Gelbart, "all of television's inhibitions and ridiculous rules went down the drain, literally." The working-class humor of Lear's series would go on to directly influence later blue-collar sitcoms like *Married . . . with Children* and *Roseanne*, whose crassness was like a perpetually flushing toilet.

All in the Family would also come to serve as the template for a new wave of sassing, impolite comedies about African American life. By including the Jeffersons within his circle of contempt, Archie would, perversely, open the door to families like theirs becoming regular presences on television, prime-time neighbors to the Bunkers.

In earlier decades, the television landscape had been for black performers a vast wasteland of demeaning roles, many imported from already popular radio programs. African Americans were servants, like Eddie "Rochester" Anderson on *Jack Benny*, or buffoons, like the protagonists of *Amos 'n' Andy* (CBS, 1951–53). *Amos* had been a wildly popular radio series for almost thirty years, created by two white men, Freeman Gosden and Charles Correll, who also provided the voices for their African American characters. In adapting *Amos 'n' Andy* for television, Gosden and Correll were forced to cast African American performers Alvin Childress and Spencer Williams in the roles they themselves had once played. *Amos 'n' Andy* ran on television for three seasons until a protest campaign orchestrated by the NAACP drove the show off the air.

The show is undoubtedly offensive, an unending parade of tired stereotypes, but judged on the admittedly meager merits of the early sitcom, *Amos 'n' Andy*, at least in its television incarnation, does not entirely bear the burden of its ultraracist reputation. The bulk of *Amos 'n' Andy*, its name to the contrary, is about Kingfish (Tim Moore), a schemer much like Ralph Kramden, plagued by persistent bad luck. Even Kingfish's unexpected good fortune—having a $3,000 ring fall into his box of Cracker Jack at a Yankees game, or wheedling $500 from his Uncle Clarence for his imaginary new baby—inevitably ends in chaos and continued penury. "Whether the characterizations presented a more objectionable stereotype than those of *Sanford and Son* is for the sociologists to debate," argues Alex McNeil in *Total Television*. Kingfish is a dim-witted buffoon with an unerring penchant for getting himself in trouble. But was this really so different from the likes of *The Honeymooners*?

More recently, Bill Cosby had won three straight Emmys as secret agent Alexander Scott on the wildly popular *I Spy*. And *Julia* (NBC, 1968–71), starring Diahann Carroll, had been among the first to feature an African American woman in a leading role. (The latter series is name-checked by Edith Bunker.) But it was *All in the Family* that, by opening the sitcom to discussing matters of race, touched off a wave of African American and minority-themed programming. In its wake would follow an array of series on African American life—*The Jeffersons*, *Sanford and Son*, *Good Times*, *What's Happening!!*—many of them produced by Norman Lear. They were mostly mediocre, but the very fact of their existence was a sign of progress Archie himself would have hated.

The Jeffersons (CBS, 1975–85) was a most logical spinoff of *All in the Family*, taking the African American family next door to the Bunkers and giving them a series of their own. Henry was long gone and Lionel was mostly an afterthought, making way for nouveau-riche couple George and Louise "Weezie" Jefferson (Sherman Hemsley and Isabel Sanford). In each week's credits, the Jeffersons relive the quintessential journey of their lives, from working-class Queens to the entitled Upper East Side. George, now the owner of a flourishing chain of dry cleaning establishments, high-steps into his new, cushy life, the two halves of his body dancing to different rhythms like two spinning tops stacked end to end.

George is so pleased to have arrived on the East Side, in fact, that he is forever seeing pending developments—Lionel's palling around with a millionaire's son, or erroneously believing that he is descended from African royalty—as further proof of the rightness of his success. George's up-from-bootstraps spiel is so familiar to his wife that she is able to move her lips along with her husband each time he trots it out. He is intent on living up to his new lifestyle, insistent on the necessity of a grand piano so luxurious it crowds out the rest of their living-room furniture. Records, he contends, don't go with his new tuxedo.

The Jeffersons are constantly at each other's throats, their dialogue drizzled with elaborately choreographed disses. The show is a loose array of setups constructed around a skeleton of insults and barbed asides, punctuated by the "oohs!" and "all rights!" of the energized studio audience. The sensation is of an endless game of the dozens, its sameness tempered only by George's occasional bursts of pathos at the prospect of being stripped of his hard-won success. "I don't want to go back to the ghetto," he moans to Weezie after telling her his nightmare about being trapped on an A train full of zebras and cockroaches. We come to understand that this is George's primal motivation, and the source of his insecurity.

George would undoubtedly agree with Archie that "white should only dance with white." He is eternally aware of the need to preserve his dignity in the face of white assaults on his manhood. George brings home a watermelon from the store in a bowling bag "'cause I don't want whitey to see it." George is intended as an affirmative-action Archie—another in Lear's series of two-bit dictators endlessly tussling with their wives and children, resentful of those unlike them. Like Archie, George is unabashedly racist, observing with dismay the mixed marriage of his upstairs neighbors (and future daughter-in-law's parents) Helen and Tom Willis (Roxie Roker and Franklin Cover). Helen and Tom are his punching bags, sparring partners, and all-around fill-ins for Meathead and Gloria.

The parallels between Archie and George are indicative of Lear's 1970s-progressive strain of liberalism, which stubbornly insists, against all evidence to the contrary, that black and white racists, and racism, are precisely identical. Archie finds harmony with Henry Jefferson on *All in the Family* only in collaborating to keep a Puerto Rican family out of the neighborhood, joining forces in mutual hatred. If only George Jefferson could learn to be as accepting as Meathead Stivic or his own son Lionel, the show's unstated logic insists, all of America's homegrown race problems would be overcome. In Lear's world, there appear to be just as many Georges as Archies, with equally pernicious results stemming from their bigotry. This nonsensical false equality was perhaps the only way that Lear could create characters as outspokenly politically incorrect as he did, but gives both *All in the Family* and *The Jeffersons* a strange never-never land quality.

Executive produced by Lear and Bud Yorkin, *Sanford and Son* (NBC, 1972–77) contemplates the prospect of an African American Archie minus the conservative outrage. *Sanford* is another working-class show, without the work; we rarely see the Sanfords at their business, although junk-dealing did help account for the slapdash quality of their home's decor. Redd Foxx's Fred Sanford is a font of countrified wisdom, eternally lamenting the foolishness of his beleaguered son Lamont (Demond Wilson) with his plaintive cry, "Ya big dummy!" *Sanford and Son* is another show about familial strife, sanded down to a single recurring squabble between father and son, unsophisticated experience doing battle with youthful vigor.

Fred offers the doctor treating his heart ailment a swig from his bottle of Ripple and treats every minor setback as an invitation to eternity. "You hear that, Elizabeth?" he asks his late wife, looking up to the heavens and clutching his chest. "I'm coming to join ya, honey!" And there is the occasional pinch of political humor, although Fred Sanford seemed an even less likely source than Archie had: "This bed is so full of bugs, I feel like I'm sleeping at the Watergate!" The non-Lear sitcom *Chico and the Man* (NBC, 1974–78) is practically the same show, complete with the scruffy blue-collar setting (here an auto mechanic's garage) and a hard-drinking protagonist with a penchant for talking to his dead wife. Only here, Ed Brown (Jack Albertson) is "the Man," the white garage owner who reluctantly employs Chico (Freddie Prinze), a singing, dancing, Hispanic force of nature. Ed gets off zingers like "In those days, Mexicans knew their place: Mexico!" but the show belongs to the charming, irrepressible Chico.

All in the Family was so immensely popular that its spinoffs begat spinoffs of their own. In *Good Times* (CBS, 1974–79), housekeeper Florida Evans (Esther Rolle) from the *All in the Family* spinoff *Maude* is transplanted from Westchester County to a Chicago housing project, along with her hardworking husband, James (John Amos, in a notable departure from his role as Gordy the weatherman on *The Mary Tyler Moore Show*). The show is ostensibly a comedy about hardscrabble working-class African American life, punctuated by financial crises and homespun wisdom about scraping by in America. "Let's face it, James," Florida tells her husband, "this family ain't Ozzie and Harriet."

There are moments when it lives up to its own self-inscribed promise, but the bulk of *Good Times* is sideswiped by eldest son J.J. (Jimmie Walker), *Amos 'n' Andy*'s Kingfish returned, a shucking, jiving stereotype outfitted in an array of ridiculous headgear and a trademark catchphrase: "Dy-no-*mite!*" "He can't read or write. He doesn't think. The show didn't start out to be that," Esther Rolle complained about the character. "They have made J.J. more stupid and enlarged the role." J.J. mugs for the camera incessantly, and his antics rapidly become the focus of *Good Times*, pushing his parents and their quasi-realistic concerns to the margins.

What's Happening!! (ABC, 1976–79) was an even more degraded copy of the Norman Lear formula (without Norman Lear), the kind of sitcom that would have no qualms about devoting a two-part special episode to the evils of bootlegging rock concerts. ("Doobie or Not Doobie," from the show's second season. And yes, of course, the episode stars the Doobie Brothers as the rock stars in question.) The theoretical uplift was consistently trumped by the ratings lift granted to stupidity, with Fred Berry's hapless Rerun—an intimate friend of J.J.'s, no doubt—noisily swiping the show from his more polished friends. Raj (Ernest Thomas) the outlaw journalist and star student was all well and good, but audiences clamored for the boy in the red beret, maroon vest, and rainbow-colored suspenders. "Hey-hey-hey!" Rerun, Raj, and Dwayne chimed in echoing unison when any pretty girl passed their way, like a chorus of randy mockingbirds.

Still to come would be an array of strangely similar shows about adorable black children and their nurturing white surrogate families, like *Diff'rent Strokes* (NBC/ABC, 1978–86) and *Webster* (ABC, 1983–87). Though the black sitcom trend spawned by *All in the Family* had succumbed to severely diminishing returns, eventually it would lead to the greatest of African American sitcom families, and a peak of the art form: *The Cosby Show*'s Huxtables.

Racial issues aside, *All in the Family* also introduced a cornucopia of hot-button topics previously verboten on television: gender politics, Watergate, unions, rape, the sex life of the married couple. Michael and Gloria sneak off for a quickie when Archie and Edith are at church in the *All in the Family* pilot, and the show remains equally fearless (for its time, at least) in its cracking open the closed doors of the sitcom. Lear's writers, aware of their place in the hierarchy of television programming, cast a cynical glance at their fluffier rival. "*The Mary Tyler Moore Show* got wind of the fact that we're doing a two-parter on abortion," said one wag who wrote for both *All in the Family* and *Maude*. "They're retaliating; they're doing a *three*-parter on mayonnaise." Consider *All in the Family*, then, the television equivalent of *Bonnie and Clyde* and *The Graduate*—a deliberately pointed expression of the new youth culture, intended to slay elderly dragons of propriety and order. The only difference was that *All in the Family*'s protagonist was a *conservative* flamethrower, and many of the pieties he was undermining were liberal ones.

Archie is, in *All in the Family*'s estimation, the ideal representative of, and stand-in for, the presidential administration of Richard M. Nixon and its ambivalent relationship with morality and decency. Archie is forever turning to President Nixon to provide justification for his own hardline stances. "Well, I happen to agree with my government," Archie argues to his son-in-law about his own snooping. "If you ain't got nothing to be ashamed of, you don't need no privacy." He daydreams of being honored on television after penning a letter in "Writing the President," picturing Nixon paying tribute to him: "In your president's opinion, Archie Bunker is one great American." That this was, for Lear, an ambiguous honor at best, was part of the complex political canvas of *All in the Family.*

The 1970s sitcom still existed in a gray zone between the overt theatricality of 1950s shows like *The Honeymooners* and the more aggressively realistic, character-growth-intensive sitcoms of the 1990s and after. *All in the Family*'s laugh track is itself a symbol of the show's hothouse growth, booming and echoing as if emerging from a vacuum-sealed chamber of mirth-enhanced robots. Each episode is self-contained and transitions are nonexistent, in a fashion jarring to those raised on the serial likes of *Friends* or *The Office.* In "Edith's Christmas Story," from the show's fourth season, Edith is rattled when she discovers a lump on her breast. By the start of the next episode, Archie is suggesting she shake her head so the plumber can hear the water on her brain, and nothing about her health scare is ever mentioned again.

Gloria complains, in a later episode, that she has grown bored of the house remaining eternally unchanged, and the same could be said for *All in the Family* as a series. It was a victim of its own success, outliving its initial burst of inspiration and eventually reduced to supping on the remnants of its comic feast. Like *M*A*S*H*, *All in the Family* perpetually introduces new characters in an attempt to keep the show fresh, like wacky neighbors Frank and Irene (Vincent Gardenia and Betty Garrett), Hispanic boarder Teresa (Liz Torres), and spunky nine-year-old Stephanie (Danielle Brisebois). Adjustments are made to the status quo—Michael and Gloria have a baby, Archie opens his own bar—but the results are more of a diversion from the show's central dynamic than an expansion. The same could be said, though, of nearly any comedy series—few shows' later seasons are as consistent as its earlier ones.

As the show progresses, however, Archie does undergo a subtle transformation—from a grotesque of the American id to a figure of pathos, left behind by progress. In "Gloria Has a Belly Full," Archie is overjoyed to learn that he is to be a grandfather. Coming home from work with an oversized teddy bear in his arms, he is the last to learn that Gloria has suffered a miscarriage. The camera claws closer to Archie's face as he takes it in, setting the bear gently down: "She lost the baby?"

Archie is still unkind, inappropriate, and intemperate, but he is also prone to occasional fits of melancholy. Turning fifty in "Archie Feels Left Out" is a bittersweet reminder of the pleasures he never had: "I never rode a horse," he mournfully notes, "and I never had oysters Rockefeller." (In Archie's inimitable Queens brogue, "oysters" become "ersters," "oil" is "erl," and "toilet" is "terlet.") In "Archie and the Bowling Team," he is left off a competitive bowling team in favor of an African American. "You can't fight it—the world's changing," his friend tells him, and Archie offers an all-purpose rejoinder: "And every time it changes, it gives me another kick in the butt."

All in the Family is so much a product of its time that it is hard to watch today. It is like a time capsule stuffed with the gewgaws and trinkets of the precise day it was packed for posterity. Lacking the emotional and political context for its air of perpetual combat, the show often feels like being trapped in a too-small living room with a foursome of argumentative loudmouths who derive a perverse pleasure from endless warfare. (The belligerent Bundys of *Married . . . with Children* could never have existed without the Bunkers to show them the way.) Archie in particular is a challenge for contemporary viewers, for whom he will likely have crossed over from provocative to unacceptable. As any student of Hollywood knows, racial humor is the most sensitive of all brands of comedy, and the least likely to age gently. In 1971 Archie hugged the boundary of what was shocking; more than forty years later, much of the humor of *All in the Family* has curdled.

9

M*A*S*H

"Yankee Doodle Doctor"

October 22, 1972 ▪ CBS

Television comedy series had generally followed a number of unstated rules. They had, for the most part, taken place in the present (the past was, by its very nature, inherently less funny). They had stuck to a single tone of voice: funny episodes were funny, the very occasional serious episode was serious. Confusion of tone was a sin no sitcom was foolish enough to commit. And they were shot on familiar sets, with fixed cameras—usually three. Otherwise, how would anyone know it was a sitcom?

Suddenly, in the pilot episode of *M*A*S*H* (CBS, 1972–83), a hand places a golf ball on a tee, and the established rules of the sitcom are unceremoniously dismissed. To begin with, there is the title on the screen, declaring our having entered another time, another place: KOREA, 1950—A HUNDRED YEARS AGO.

As a series of zooms and telephoto-lens shots—visual language borrowed directly from the show's source material, Robert Altman's 1970 film *MASH*—silently introduces each of the show's main characters, the camera catches its crew of army surgeons and nurses at play: tossing a football around, hitting golf balls (one explodes a land mine in the distance), playing footsie under the mess-hall table. The mood is light, joshing, a college campus with khaki uniforms. Then the whir of helicopters, faint at first, roars across the soundtrack, and the playful interlude comes to a halt. The medical staff rushes in the direction of the helicopters, where wounded soldiers are being unloaded for emergency medical treatment, and the series' haunting theme song—Johnny Mandel's "Suicide Is Painless," lifted from the Altman film—kicks in.

M*A*S*H bears the imprimatur of a greater commitment to realism than its sitcom predecessors. Where earlier sitcoms had paid homage to the realistic by limiting themselves to a small set of familiar locations—living room, bedroom, kitchen—*M*A*S*H* zoomed out, beyond home, beyond the borders of the United States, to a conflict taking place overseas, and to a group of Americans very far from home and from all they knew. We were, as the sign on the camp's main road reminded us, 5,610 miles from Burbank, and by extension, far from the concerns of other series native to television's hometown.

Set in Korea, *M*A*S*H* was a show whose roots were elsewhere. As viewers had already grasped from Altman's film, an enormous critical and commercial success upon its release two years prior, Korea was merely a stand-in for Vietnam, an inharmonious stalemate filling in for a pointless quagmire. A nation of television watchers had grown accustomed to seeing graphic footage of the war on the network news each night; now, Vietnam was a sitcom.

The TV adaptation of the Altman film was the inspiration of 20th Century-Fox president William Self. With the original sets from the film still in hand, Self envisioned a cheaply produced sitcom with the lavish look of a feature film. CBS agreed to shoot a pilot for the series without seeing a script—a rarity in the television business at the time. The network brought in Larry Gelbart as showrunner. Gelbart had been a gag writer for Danny Thomas while still in high school, had traveled to Korea with Bob Hope in 1951, and had been part of the legendary writing staff of *Caesar's Hour* (NBC, 1954–57) alongside Mel Brooks, Carl Reiner, and Neil Simon. Gelbart had also written the play *Sly Fox*, which on its abortive national tour starred none other than Jackie Gleason.

At the outset of the series, Gelbart kept a map of Korea, a US Army handbook, and a list of Korean men's names on his desk for guidance. The first season of *M*A*S*H* was a matter of trial and error, subtracting unnecessary characters (farewell, Spearchucker) and clarifying the show's style. "We didn't realize we could go straight with the material—we thought the audience wanted high jinks and hilarity, which were also in the film," said Gelbart. There were also fights with network censors over the use of words like "breasts" and "virgin." (Gelbart lost the latter battle, then had his revenge by having a soldier in a later episode be from the Virgin Islands.) *All in the Family* was a touchstone for Gelbart, as well as a cudgel with which to beat the CBS censors: "Norman Lear was busting barriers every week! So we could always say, 'How come they can do *that*, and we can't do *this*?'" Then *M*A*S*H* was moved into the prime slot after *All in the Family* on Saturday nights, and its ratings skyrocketed. "We could have repaired flat tires in that time slot and gotten a good rating," said Gelbart.

Even more importantly, Gelbart and future executive producer Gene Reynolds visited Korea after the second season, returning with twenty-two hours of taped conversations with doctors, nurses, helicopter pilots, and orderlies to rummage through for plots. "We cherished those notes," Gelbart said, and they often served as the raw material of the show, inspiring future episodes. *M*A*S*H*'s language is drawn from the store of experiences native to Korea. When Hawkeye (Alan Alda, who had made his TV debut on another military series, *The Phil Silvers Show*) compliments a comely nurse as "the best thing to hit this place since dry socks," the show's writers have captured something precise about the mind-set of its characters.

The show's realism stemmed, in large part, from the steady reminders of its characters' secret hurts, and of the war taking place just beyond the borders of the screen. (It did not come, needless to say, from its laugh track, perhaps the least justifiable in sitcom history. Where, exactly, was the audience supposed to be sitting?) The mess-hall food is terrible, the cold blistering and the heat maddening, surgical conditions less than optimal, and bickering a constant companion. After a long session in the operating room, B.J. (Mike Farrell) is inconsolable at the thought that with each day that passes in Korea, his daughter remembers him ever so slightly less.

*M*A*S*H*'s realism is to be found in its focused commitment to the lives of doctors and nurses forged in the crucible of war, regardless of what oddball hijinks they might get up to in any particular week. But in the midst of those hijinks, Hawkeye might bring his surgical instruments into the mess hall to eat lunch or gambol naked around the camp. In part, this is further evidence of the insanity of war, but it is also indicative of a show whose commitment to realism is intense but intermittent.

*M*A*S*H*, in its earliest phase, coasts in the slipstream separating work and play, drama and comedy, sex and death. Its protagonists Benjamin Franklin "Hawkeye" Pierce, Captain John "Trapper" McIntyre (Wayne Rogers), and Colonel Henry Blake (McLean Stevenson) are surgeons in a mobile surgical hospital, their sexual libertinism—another day, another nurse—the only respite from their living nightmare of eternally recurring gore and pain. Their operating rooms were self-replenishing: one soldier, his first chin hairs just sprouted, would be lifted from the surgeon's table, only to be replaced, almost instantaneously, by another.

The surgeons are the guardians and maintenance men of an endless, pointless war—pardon me, police action. They face the brutality and inhumanity of war with a good cheer born of terrible darkness and a desire to pierce the delusions of "the good war." "Korea's pretty much the same story," Hawkeye writes home in a letter to his father. "The fighting goes on—the hatred, the violence, the senseless brutality, men behaving like animals. Then, of course, there's the war." The tug-of-war between professionalism and fatigue, caring for wounded men while hating the war that delivered them, is the fulcrum on which *M*A*S*H* rests.

There had been other shows set in the past whose run overlapped with *M*A*S*H*'s, such as *Happy Days*. There had been other shows about the military, like *The Phil Silvers Show*. And there had been other sitcoms that took place in wartime, like *McHale's Navy* and the POW-camp comedy *Hogan's Heroes*. But *M*A*S*H* was the first sitcom to be inspired by the American New Wave of filmmakers like Altman and Coppola and Scorsese, transforming its grab bag of emotions and styles, and its abiding cynicism, into a functionally new television format.

Decades before *The Office*, *M*A*S*H* leaned on the conventions of the documentary to place its fictional characters in a suitably realistic context. Sitcoms had been a window, offering an unobstructed view on the goings-on within; this was, self-consciously, a canvas, providing ample evidence of its own construction. *M*A*S*H* emphasized its clash of visual formats, playing off the friction of newsreels and home movies and old films. In doing so, it also exploded the conventions of the war film, upending the tidy conclusions of John Wayne pictures by transforming the Korean War into the subject of an eleven-year sitcom run. In other words, the war lasted approximately three and a half times as long on television as it had in real life.

The series is also about undercutting the smug mush of which so many other military-themed films, novels, and television series consisted. *M*A*S*H* is devoted to building up patriotic straw men, time and again, in order to cut them down anew. The majesty of war is propped up, at least in the psyches of some of its more delusional warriors, so that it can be torn down all the more authoritatively. "Those two," nurse Margaret "Hot Lips" Houlihan (Loretta Swit) complains about Hawkeye and Trapper, "they're ruining this war for all of us!" Hawkeye and his wingman—Trapper, and later B.J.—combat the low-grade fascists of the US Army with good humor and panache and a still full of gin. The bathrobe-clad Hawkeye exercises his bile on the show's parade of prigs and warmongers and standers on ceremony, wielding his well-documented and much-needed surgical skill as a weapon to ward off the designated representatives of a morally hollow order.

"Yankee Doodle Doctor," written by Laurence Marks, from the show's first season, is perhaps the most striking expression of the series' synthesis of stylistic and moral choices. A documentary film crew comes to the 4077th and attempts to corral messy, disordered reality into a preconceived framework of "saints in surgical garb." The disjunction between its shrink-wrapped patriotic bromides and the reality of war is emphasized in the subtle contrasts of its editing. As the MASH doctors are called "real soldiers" on the voiceover, we watch Hawkeye and Trapper drunkenly dancing and swilling martinis out of their homemade still. "Any of you done any acting?" the director wonders. Hawkeye immediately launches into his best snarling James Cagney impression: "You dirty rat . . ." The director asks a patient, being ministered to by Hawkeye, if he would mind smiling for the cameras. The camera interferes with the doctors' work, coming between surgeons and patients in the operating room.

Hawkeye and Trapper are insulted by the final film, which they consider a tissue of lies and misdirection—an amalgam of all the milquetoast war movies and TV shows that *M*A*S*H* seeks to undermine. No stranger to cruel pranks, they expose all the director's film, damaging the footage beyond repair. In its stead, they make their own version of the movie—a stand-in for the work of the show itself, drawing mustaches and rabbit ears on others' empty platitudes. The first version's jingoistic voiceover has been laid atop silly footage of their own devising. A farcical patriotic drama has become an all-out farce, with Hawkeye casting himself as a stoop-walking, saw-wielding Groucho Marx type and Trapper as the horn-honking Harpo, pulling surgical equipment out of his oversized trench coat. "Wait a minute, have you got a reservation?" Hawkeye-Groucho asks Radar (Gary Burghoff), playing a patient. "You shoulda booked ahead. Come to think of it, you should've booked the rest of the body, as well." Playacting is more than a game; it is a means of staying alive, of preserving one's spirit against the depredations of war. Korea was less *Sands of Iwo Jima* than *Duck Soup*.

At their film's conclusion, Hawkeye abruptly drops the Marx Brothers shtick and gets momentarily serious while sitting at a patient's bedside: "We win some, we lose some . . . no promises, no guaranteed survival. No 'saints in surgical garb.' . . . Not a very happy ending for a movie, but then no war is a movie." Hawkeye walks out of camera range, and the film sputters to a stop, ambushed by a barrage of honesty. Hawkeye and Trapper are stand-ins for the show itself. This was no John Wayne picture. The cavalry was not riding to the rescue.

The remarkable episode "The Interview," from the show's fifth season, is a successor to "Yankee Doodle Doctor." Shot in black-and-white, "The Interview" is a mock-documentary of its protagonists, with another camera crew tramping through the MASH unit. The long takes of personal testimony are photographed in an unusual-for-sitcoms array of close-ups and jagged traveling shots. And the interviewees are caught in revealing moments. B.J. offers a defense of what might seem like excessive drinking among the doctors and nurses: "We do considerable drinking as opposed to sitting at home. We do not enough drinking as opposed to being here."

Father Mulcahy (William Christopher) testifies to being moved by watching the surgeons warming their hands on a brutally cold day over the steam expelled by the wounded bodies on the operating table (itself a story inspired by the collected testimony of the Korea-vet surgeons). "The people at this MASH," the voiceover concludes, "are doing the work that they do best, but that they would rather not be doing at all, in a place they'd rather not be."

Earlier sitcoms had mostly established a pattern and slavishly kept to it. Lucy made a game lunge at fame before creating a mess and cleaning it up at the last possible second. Archie Bunker attacked then retreated, his zealotry temporarily muted after the roar of pitched combat. *M*A*S*H* is not entirely different. Its characters booze and woo and operate and banter. But *M*A*S*H* is, in this regard, more than a sitcom. It is a show whose laugh track cuts in and out, its irrepressible banter covering a perpetually bleeding heart. It is also a series intent on growing over time. "We very much wanted our characters to progress," said Reynolds. Margaret's marriage and divorce and Hawkeye's personality changes epitomize *M*A*S*H*'s refusal to stagnate.

Hawkeye is the chief prankster, angry young man, and moral conscience of the show. As a nurse accurately pegs him, "Anger turned inward is depression. Anger turned sideways is Hawkeye." Simultaneously impish and socially conscious, Hawkeye is the spirit of the show personified, its paragon of waggish, humane cynicism. He is the military hero with no interest whatsoever in military formality. Hawkeye often appears either in scrubs or his bathrobe, mocking the pressed and starched military brass with his rumpled demeanor. (You can count the number of times Alda appears in full dress uniform on two hands, and each time it serves a particular narrative purpose.)

He is, at the outset, *M*A*S*H*'s official lothario. The sultry young things in the show's first seasons parading in and out of his bed read today, contrary to its intentions, as a grotesque parody of masculine bluster. In later seasons, as *M*A*S*H* settles in for a long stay in Korea, the nurses introduced for one-off roles get notably less beautiful, and Hawkeye keeps his hands more to himself. The show's primary focus moves away from erotic frolicking and toward its trademark blend of anger and bittersweetness. Sex is no longer the matter at hand.

The series' putative hero is, in the words of a frustrated nurse, an utter bastard: "You're cynical and you're selfish, and when you're not in the operating room, all you ever think about is your pleasure." *M*A*S*H* mourns a moral clarity it could no longer locate. When its characters watch John Ford's classic 1946 film *My Darling Clementine* and sing its title song in the operating room, its chorus becomes a dirge for an innocence trampled into the blood and viscera of the MASH operating room.

M*A*S*H is bittersweet in a manner no preceding sitcom had managed to pull off—or really even try. Sitcoms had had the occasional tender moment before—think of *The Honeymooners'* exhausted declarations of love or *The Mary Tyler Moore Show*'s paeans to friendship—but they were more the outgrowth of their natural emotional effervescence, an overspilling of comic energy into sentiment. *M*A*S*H*'s heart-tugging moments lean on the element of surprise, of exposing a hidden reality trapped beneath the placid sitcom surface. Houlihan, an unflagging martinet to her subordinates in "The Nurses," is wounded by others' coldness: "Can you imagine what it feels like to walk by this tent and hear you laughing, and know you're not welcome?" Father Mulcahy, in "Blood Brothers," rages against Hawkeye's indifference to his concerns about a visiting cardinal's arrival, until he learns that Pierce has just had to inform a soldier he has incurable leukemia. Mulcahy's shoulders slump, his eyes bulge, and his mouth goes slack with shame at his self-absorption. Radar's farewell party in the show's eighth season is interrupted by the arrival of fresh wounded, leaving the beloved company clerk standing alone. After scraping a finger fondly through his good-bye cake, he presses his face against the window of the OR, where Hawkeye, in mid-operation, notices his presence. He sighs, then salutes, raising a stiff, bloody hand to his forehead.

Even its most exaggerated caricatures, like the khaki-clad buffoon Frank Burns (Larry Linville), are allowed occasional moments of tenderness. When Houlihan flies off after her whirlwind wedding to join her officer beau, Frank watches wistfully as the helicopter ascends, offering, sotto voce, his final farewell to his former lover and comrade. *M*A*S*H* has it both ways, undercutting the rigid formality of military life, draped in a metaphoric bathrobe of hilarity while drawing on the bank of emotions associated with war to heighten the emotional resonance of the series' occasional dramatic endeavors. In so doing, *M*A*S*H* is the first sitcom to successfully merge drama and comedy, its Santa Clauses, as in the episode "Dear Dad," all flying off to the front to minister to the wounded.

In addition, numerous episodes of *M*A*S*H* challenge conventional dogma about what a comedy series could (and could not) do on television by devoting themselves, like in "Yankee Doodle Doctor," to experiments in sitcom narrative. "Point of View" dedicates an entire episode to the perspective of a wounded soldier, with surgeons and nurses crowded around the injured man, directly addressing the camera. The utterly remarkable "Life

Time" superimposes a clock at the bottom right of the screen, precious seconds ticking by as doctors scramble to treat a soldier requiring an emergency graft to his damaged aorta.

The lighter-hearted "The Long-John Flap" follows the tormented journey of a single pair of double-knit long johns. Hawkeye receives them in the mail from his father and gives them to sickly Trapper, who loses them to Radar in a card game, who plans to offer them to a luscious nurse as a romantic enticement but instead trades them to the mess-hall cook for a leg of lamb with a side of mint jelly. The cook gives them to Major Frank Burns when threatened with demotion. Frank gives them to his girlfriend, Margaret, when she demands proof of his ardor. Cross-dressing Corporal Klinger (Jamie Farr) swipes them from Houlihan and gives them to the priest as absolution for his sins. Father Mulcahy offers them to Colonel Blake to give to the neediest soul, where Hawkeye comes across them once more.

Blake, meanwhile, needs an emergency appendectomy, and Hawkeye tells Radar to get ready: "Go get Nurse Beddoes—we're cutting him open." Radar is astonished by Hawkeye's seeming thirst for revenge: "Just because he stole your underwear?" An entire world of intimate, occasionally claustrophobic relationships is summoned, and summarized, by the travels of a much-needed pair of long johns. And *M*A*S*H* has once more encoded its realism into the comic fabric of its stories; why is there so much pent-up desire for long underwear, if not to combat the hellish cold of a Korean winter?

Even within otherwise unremarkable episodes, there are moments of terrifying, nerve-jangling intensity. "Mulcahy's War" has the unit's mild-mannered chaplain shamed into seeking a taste of the front after a patient chides him for his empty spiritual blandishments. Having snuck aboard a jeep headed to rescue a soldier, Father Mulcahy notices the wounded man struggling for breath. He is forced to perform an emergency tracheotomy using a penknife and the plastic tubing from his eyedrops, with Hawkeye and the other doctors talking him through the procedure via radio. *M*A*S*H* had never shied from depicting the graphic side of combat and surgery, but this is something else entirely. There is no comforting sheen of expertise, no semblance of order. Bombs explode from every direction, and a man with no more medical expertise than the viewers at home is slicing a hole in a man's neck, his fingers trembling from the horrific effort of cutting away human flesh.

M*A*S*H's decade-long run was in large part accidental—it is doubtful that CBS or creator Larry Gelbart could have known at the show's inception that it would be as popular as it was—but it is also emblematic of its central point. War is not just a matter of discrete moments of pain, or sacrifice; it is a matter of duration, of sitting on a cot in a tent in a foreign country as one's children grow older and less likely to remember your face. As the series matured, much of the booze-fueled good times fell away. Perhaps influenced by Alda's burgeoning feminism, *M*A*S*H* revealed a broad sentimental streak that cut against the laughs. (The laugh track also grew more intermittent, in keeping with Gelbart and Reynolds's dissatisfaction with its presence and discomfort with its implementation.)

For a show that lasted eleven seasons, constant change was necessary to keep things fresh. Gelbart left after the fourth season, and Reynolds after the fifth. Alda would go on to write and direct a substantial percentage of *M*A*S*H*'s episodes after Gelbart's departure. "One of the reasons Larry Gelbart claims he left the show," argued *M*A*S*H* writers Thad Mumford and Dan Wilcox, "was because he felt he couldn't say 'war is hell' any more in a fresh way." By the second half of its run, *M*A*S*H*'s writers had shifted from developing plots out of their sources' stories to thinking of new ways to bring, say, Charles and Margaret together for a fresh adventure.

Trapper is subbed out after the show's third year (Wayne Rogers quit the series), and his shoes are filled by Mike Farrell's B. J. Hunnicutt, who is essentially the same character minus the Southern accent and plus a wife and daughter. Most shockingly, at the conclusion of the same season, McLean Stevenson's Lt. Colonel Henry Blake, laid-back commander and older-brother type, prone to boozing and whoring alongside his surgeons, is unceremoniously killed off. Violating all the standard television rules about the protection of its favored characters, Blake is shot down (offscreen) over the Sea of Japan on his way home, after a long, boozy, sentimental farewell.

M*A*S*H had reneged on its promise of safe, antiseptic hijinks. We could no longer be confident in the sitcom as a cocoon from the world's ills.

Blake is replaced by Col. Sherman Potter (Henry Morgan), no-nonsense grandpa with an endless array of quirky backwoods expressions ("Mule muffins!") imported from his native Missouri. Radar departs, and the cross-dressing Klinger, desperate to escape the army for the homely comforts of his native Toledo, is promoted from a supporting eccentric occasionally decorating the edges of the screen to Potter's foil and assistant. And Frank—conservative, sex-obsessed, judgmental, a mediocre surgeon—is replaced by the patrician Charles Emerson Winchester (David Ogden Stiers) in the show's sixth season; he serves as Hawkeye and B.J.'s foil without always being their enemy. New executive producer Burt Metcalfe, who had been looking for a William F. Buckley type for the show to replace Larry Linville, spotted Stiers as the station manager on *The Mary Tyler Moore Show* and knew he had found his new star.

M*A*S*H's final episode, the two-and-a-half-hour "Goodbye, Farewell and Amen," broadcast on February 28, 1983, was for twenty-seven years the most-watched program in the history of American television (it was eventually surpassed by Super Bowl XLIV, between the New Orleans Saints and the Indianapolis Colts). Fifty million households tuned in to watch Hawkeye, Hot Lips, B.J., and the rest of the 4077th bid adieu to Korea. Of the television sets in the United States that were turned on at the time, 77 percent were tuned to the *M*A*S*H* finale. It was, and remains, a model of the satisfying series finale. (If only *Seinfeld* had studied it more carefully.)

The Korean War ends, and yet the war never truly comes to a conclusion. On the day of the planned ceasefire, a radio broadcast announces the arithmetic of the damage: four hundred thousand Korean civilians dead, two million total killed and wounded, one hundred thousand orphans with no parents to return home to. The surgeons and the nurses look up, disoriented by the sudden silence of the guns, only to immediately resume the drone and bustle of surgery. The camera retreats to a distance, with a table of surgical equipment in the foreground and the operating tables in the distance. We have begun our own retreat from Korea, but for the men and women of the 4077th, the ceasefire is only a brief respite.

Like a Shakespearean comedy, this one ends with a wedding. Klinger, the character most anxious to flee Korea, is the one who ends up staying behind, marrying a Korean woman and pledging to assist her in tracking down her family. The 4077th's signs—BURBANK 5610 MILES—are taken down and hauled off, each to return to the veterans' hometowns.

True to its mission to provide comfort and affliction in roughly equal doses, not everyone leaves happily. Father Mulcahy's hearing is badly damaged in an explosion. Hawkeye is psychologically scarred by seeing a Korean woman smother her own child during a bombing raid. These familiar faces, present in our homes for more than a decade, tenderly take their leave from one another. Charles unexpectedly gives Margaret his cherished copy of Elizabeth Barrett Browning's *Sonnets from the Portuguese*. Hawkeye grabs Hot Lips and kisses her as Potter, B.J., and Charles awkwardly pace nearby. Potter rides off on his horse. "Well, boys," Potter tells B.J. and Hawkeye in summation, "it would be hard to call what we've been through fun, but I'm sure glad we went through it together." Hawkeye, unable to make out B.J.'s final words over the sound of the helicopter bearing him away, spots his best friend's note, laid out with stones on the scarred landscape they are at last leaving behind: GOODBYE.

The farewell is directed at us at much as Hawkeye, a last glimpse of the familiar turf of one of the most popular and beloved sitcoms of all time. The last moments echo the show's very first, in reverse; a helicopter was now taking off, not landing, and instead of patients arriving for treatment, the doctors were departing, planning to begin their own healing. The experience of war had come to an end, and the 4077th's time in purgatory was no longer.

10

Taxi

"Latka the Playboy"

May 21, 1981　■　ABC

The sitcom depended on its sidekicks. Stars had always required a doltish counterbalance. The idea was to emphasize the stars' more appealing qualities—their attractiveness, their intelligence, their perspicacity—by the relative absence of those qualities in their second bananas. But what would happen when the sitcom no longer revolved around stars? Where would the television comedy series go when sidekicks ruled?

Ed. Weinberger, James L. Brooks, and Stan Daniels had made their names on *The Mary Tyler Moore Show*, crafting a seemingly endless array of variations on a single theme: the zany, eccentric workplace. The threesome eventually left MTM Productions, run by Moore and her husband, Grant Tinker, and were attracted to a new property: a *New York* magazine article by Mark Jacobson on the drivers of the Dover Cab Company in Manhattan's Greenwich Village. The motley array of nighttime drivers, Jacobson found, included "a college professor, a couple of Ph.D. candidates, a former priest, a calligrapher, a guy who drives to pay his family's land taxes in Vermont, a Rumanian discotheque D.J., plenty of M.A.'s, a slew of social workers, trombone players, a guy who makes 300-pound sculptures out of solid rock, the inventor of the electric harp, professional photographers, and the usual gang of starving artists, actors, and writers." Brooks and Co. saw the glimmers of a television show much like *Mary Tyler Moore*, with cabbies on "shape-up"—awaiting the cab tradeoff between daytime and nighttime drivers—swapping banter and hanging out.

Taxi (ABC/NBC, 1978–83) is a New York sitcom for the financially strapped, crime-ridden era of FORD TO CITY: DROP DEAD. Its characters include muggers and burnouts and runaways, and even its tourists have a wish list of sights particular to that dystopian time and place: "garbage strike, blackout, urban blight." In *Taxi*'s opening sequence, a lone cab sets out, week after week, over the Fifty-Ninth Street Bridge, to the tune of Bob James's insidiously funky theme song, out to face the wild world of the New York streets.

The show never found the audience it deserved. Sputtering through four seasons on ABC beginning in 1978–79, and one final season on NBC after ABC dropped it, *Taxi* is the middle link between *The Mary Tyler Moore Show* and *Cheers*, though it never reached the cultural ubiquity of either of those shows. It is a high-classical sitcom with slight tweaks, like the filming setup designed by director James Burrows (soon to play an outsized role in the creation of future sitcom landmarks like *Cheers* and *Friends*), which added a fourth camera to the sitcom's traditional three to accommodate the show's larger-than-customary sets.

Taxi was founded on the bedrock principles of the workplace comedy established by *MTM*, but the balance of power had subtly, and then increasingly not so subtly, shifted. The series was initially constructed around Alex Reiger (Judd Hirsch), mouthpiece, mascot, and guru to a crew of slashes: cabbie-slash-boxer, cabbie-slash-actor, cabbie-slash-art-dealer, and the like. Alex is the kindly Jewish uncle to the "only in New York" assembly of types, close kin to other sensitive leading men of 1970s sitcoms, like *M*A*S*H*'s Hawkeye Pierce. If Alex is the father figure, Elaine Nardo (Marilu Henner) is the den mother, offering encouragement and discipline in roughly equal doses to her troop of wayward sons. And yet, for all the emphasis on the rough-hewn good sense of Alex and Elaine, and the tamped-down attraction between the never-quite-couple, the show's center of gravity begins shifting almost as soon as it is established. They are not, nor will they ever be, Sam and Diane from *Cheers*, or *Friends'* Ross and Rachel.

The dependable Alex and Elaine, along with the less compelling figures of Bobby Wheeler (Jeff Conaway) and Tony Banta (Tony Danza), are counterbalanced by two, and eventually three, unhinged sidekicks: immigrant mechanic Latka Gravas (Andy Kaufman), dyspeptic garage dispatcher Louie De Palma (Danny DeVito), and, joining the cast in the series' second season, the Reverend Jim Ignatowski (Christopher Lloyd). The sidekicks overwhelmed the heroes, and *Taxi* would eventually dedicate itself to their propagation.

If the show's producers had stuck with their first choice for the lead role of Alex, it's hard to imagine him giving up quite so much of the show's spotlight. Originally, producers had considered Tony Curtis, of *Some Like It Hot* fame. After abandoning the idea, Brooks, Weinberger, and Daniels turned to Judd Hirsch, who initially turned them down but then reconsidered. The casting process also saw other changes to the planned makeup of the show. Tony Banta, the dim ex-boxer eventually played by Tony Danza, was originally Phil Ryan, an older, more punch-drunk former pugilist. Danza had in fact been a boxer before turning to acting, with a lifetime record of 4-3, and gave Tony Banta some of his own boxing stories. (Banta and

Henner's character, Nardo, were named after *Mary Tyler Moore Show* writers Gloria Banta and Pat Nardo.) The role of Bobby was initially intended for an African American performer, with Cleavon Little of *Blazing Saddles* among the actors called in to audition for the part before Jeff Conaway was cast. And after a trip to the Comedy Store in Los Angeles, where they saw him perform his Foreign Man character, the producers cast Andy Kaufman as Latka.

If sidekicks can be understood as loud, colorful personalities sideswiping otherwise sedate series, then "Latka the Playboy," a standout episode from *Taxi*'s third season, offers the unusual sight of a sidekick swiping the limelight from a sidekick. That both characters were scrabbling for power inside the body of Andy Kaufman only added to the sensation of an all-out, no-holds-barred battle for sitcom domination.

Over the course of three seasons, Kaufman's Latka, an immigrant from some unnamed, highly peculiar Ruritanian state, had been granted an assortment of colorful mannerisms, including a tendency toward overexplanation and a steady stream of malapropisms. Latka's slightly off-kilter relationship with American ways and his doggedly literal frame of reference are the source of some of *Taxi*'s best lines, as when he tells his hosts at a dinner party, "I am so hungry I could eat a dog," or expresses puzzlement about American sports: "This team called the Redskins, but they are almost all black." With his boyish manner and high-pitched voice, Latka is *Taxi*'s good-natured mascot, his impish spirit of fun part and parcel of the show's easygoing charm. When Louie demands that Latka empty his pockets, he reveals an array of effects worthy of Harpo Marx: a paintbrush, a telephone receiver, a sandwich, windshield wipers, cat cookies, and then the cat, too.

Latka's highly casual relationship with the English language was complemented by a fictional native tongue whose most recognizable words include the all-purpose noun "yakabei," and the you-can't-do-that-on-television pastime "nik-nik." (Latka's favorite television shows? "*The Honeymooners* and *I Nik-Nik Lucy*.") To teach Latka's language to Carol Kane, who played his girlfriend (and later wife) Simka on the show, Andy Kaufman took the actress out to dinner and refused to speak to her in English.

Kaufman was less an actor than an instigator, famous as a stand-up comedian for such inspired gambits as boring an audience stiff with a reading from *The Great Gatsby*. When the audience grew restless, Kaufman would ask them if they would prefer to listen to a record instead. Kaufman would drop the needle—onto a record of him reading *Gatsby*. On the set of *Taxi*, Kaufman introduced his combative alter ego Tony Clifton, who was played sometimes by Kaufman himself and sometimes by an accomplice. "Clifton" verbally abused cast members and cavorted with prostitutes until the show's producers had no choice but to dismiss him. Kaufman insisted that Clifton be fired in public on set.

"Latka the Playboy," written by future *Cheers* creators Glen and Les Charles (and also featuring future *Cheers* sidekick George Wendt as a gruff exterminator), would introduce a new, Cliftonesque dynamic to *Taxi*, and the show would never be quite the same again. Tired of being perpetually ignored by women, Latka devotes his vacation to studying back issues of *Playboy* magazine and cassettes of FM radio DJs' patter. He comes back as alter ego Vic Ferrari, whose passions include "Italian cars, Technics stereos, Australian films, and beautiful ladies." Where Latka stumbles over basic English phrases, searching his ever-present phrase book for guidance, Vic—a loose approximation of Buddy Love from Jerry Lewis's *The Nutty Professor*—keeps up a steady stream of hipster mumbo-jumbo. "I don't like this authority trip that you're always laying on me, man," Vic tells Louie. Latka's friends plead for his return, but to no avail. Vic is Latka's revenge on his puppy-dog reputation. He makes idiotic faces and mocks Louie's gruff shape-up-or-ship-out talk, far more tickled by his own antics than anyone else. Vic is not funny, precisely; instead, he is humorous for his blissful obliviousness, tuned to his own private channel of amusement.

Latka's friends eventually glimpse him trapped inside Vic, pleading to be released. "I cry at night," he tells them. "I'm stuck inside of here. I don't like this guy. I don't remember how I got in. I don't like the fast lane." Vic/Latka parts his lips, seeking to release Latka's distinctive, vaguely European (Yugoslavian? Romanian?) accent from beneath Vic's affectless patter. Kaufman grits his teeth and flares his nostrils, squinting from the pressure of his effort, before leaning back, his eyes familiarly bulging, a vacant smirk playing across his lips. Latka is back, and *Taxi* is relieved of the pressure of Vic's queasy self-satisfaction. Or is it? The episode ends with a freeze-frame on Latka's shifting eyes, darting nervously to and fro, hinting that creepy Vic still resides somewhere behind Latka's mock-placid mug.

In a deliberate echo of Kaufman's own manipulation of his Tony Clifton character, Vic would become Latka's nemesis in subsequent episodes, stealing his girl and tormenting him with proof of his superiority. The standoff between Latka and Vic is *Taxi*'s daffiest moment of frenzied weirdness, even if it is not precisely its funniest. "You made love with another man right under my nose," the furious Latka accuses Simka. Latka plots his revenge on the villainous Vic, observing that "I would hate to be in his shoes." He is, of course.

Latka is hardly *Taxi*'s only resident eccentric. Danny DeVito's Louie is the embodiment of a New Yorker outsiders enjoy disparaging and locals secretly celebrate: the hard-as-nails bastard, only looking out for number one. Locked in his dispatcher's cage primarily to keep the drivers from getting their hands on him, Louie is a malevolent elf with a barbed tongue and an appetite for humiliating his adversaries—who consist, at one time or another, of every other employee of the cab company. He is, when he wants to be, surprisingly sprightly, leaping out of his cage and sliding across the hood of a cab to swipe a blank check from Jim's estranged father, or shoving an old lady down the stairs out of spite.

Louie is afraid of human frailty—primarily his own—and as a result, he is forever being belatedly schooled in the ways of his fellow humans, and forever backsliding. Try as he might, Louie cannot quite muster any lingering sense of compassion for his fellow man. They are the "losers," as he ceaselessly reminds them, and he is their superior. Even Louie's abortive romance with the forgiving Zena (Rhea Perlman) does not find him in a particularly romantic mood: "I like your goodies," he tells her by way of wooing her. He cannot say Zena's name without emitting his trademark evil chuckle, each "heh-heh" a staccato burst of creepy malevolence.

Louie regularly calls out for "Nardo," his taunting laced with traces of guilt and stymied desire. Louie is present to jeer at the series' other regulars, his essential callowness and selfishness a counterpart to their white-bread decency. (Speaking of white bread, for a show about 1970s New York City taxi drivers, how come *Taxi*'s cast is made up entirely of white men, with one white woman for color?) Louie is the untrammeled id run amok, funny precisely for his inability to summon *any* grace, or compassion, or decency.

Christopher Lloyd's Reverend Jim Ignatowski is introduced as a regular in the show's second season, effectively replacing Randall Carver's bland newbie driver John Burns. "I am the living embodiment of the '60s," Jim announces by way of introduction, and what that proves to mean is less a devotion to political activism than a fondness for recreational drugs and a loose relationship with what we informally refer to as reality. Jim always sounds as if he is simultaneously reaching the peak of an impromptu sermon and the summit of a drug-fueled frenzy. Jim had once been, as we learn in a flashback episode, a straitlaced Harvard student, remonstrating with his girlfriend for having nagged him into having premarital sex. But one bite of a pot brownie sets Jim into permanent orbit. Jim tells his new friends about the time he was arrested in the 1960s. "Did they get you on drugs?" he is asked. "No," he responds, "I was already on drugs."

In a clever two-part episode from *Taxi*'s third season, "On the Job," the drivers are all temporarily laid off and must find other employment. Jim sets out as a door-to-door salesman, offering a practiced spiel about the magical cleaning powers of his vacuum cleaner to a skeptical housewife. (Lucy had engaged in a similar, equally hopeless scheme on *I Love Lucy*.) He carefully scatters cigarette ashes, dirt, and milk on the carpet, then reaches into his bag to pull out—a set of encyclopedias.

Jim is a man of many enthusiasms and hidden abilities. In "Jim Joins the Network," he is recruited by a television executive to assist with putting together a prime-time schedule after he has revealed a hidden knack for programming. "Louie, I need the rest of the afternoon off," he tells De Palma as he leaves the garage. "I'm going to save television!"

The late 1970s may have been the era when the second banana took over TV, but sidekicks had been a sitcom staple since the days of Ed Norton and Fred and Ethel Mertz. Crashing through closed apartment doors, running their clammy hands all over the carefully guarded treasures of others, interfering, gumming up the works, sidekicks were the collective deus ex machina of the sitcom, setting into action the inevitable oil slick of chaos, and the hasty cleanup crews scrubbing the floors and wiping down the counters before the onset of the next disaster. The sitcom was devoted to a certain kind of star—one whose familiarity and affability encouraged viewers to return, week after week, for our scheduled time with them. But even the most appealing sitcom stars—Lucille Ball, say, or Dick Van Dyke—required someone off whom they could bounce some of their comic ideas, someone to ease some of the terrible burden that came with thirty minutes a week of empty air to fill. They were the inheritors of a tradition already crafted by the movies, where Peter Lorre dogged Humphrey Bogart's footsteps and Edward Everett Horton always tangled in Fred and Ginger's affairs.

And so for every Ball there was Vivian Vance and William Frawley, and for every Van Dyke there was Morey Amsterdam and Rose Marie. They were the unrewarded grunts of the sitcom, the middle management, the back office. They received neither the profits nor the adulation. Without them, though, the laughter dried up. Rob Petrie is more appealing by virtue of being set against the crabby antics of Buddy Sorrell, and Ralph Kramden appears a veritable prince of intellect when placed next to Ed Norton. Jittery Barney Fife throws the aw-shucks everyday decency of Sheriff Andy Taylor on *The Andy Griffith Show* into yet starker relief. Good egg Danny Williams (Danny Thomas) of *Make Room for Daddy* (ABC/CBS, 1953–64) is sharpened by the hectoring presence of his old-country Uncle Tonoose (Hans Conried). Even the occasional antics of Wally and the Beav are set into contrast by the presence of brown-nosing, vainglorious Eddie Haskell. Try as they might, the Cleaver boys can never be as mercenary, vain, or callous as Eddie—and that is why he is there. Sidekicks were like insurance policies taken out against any possible claims of weakness, vanity, or lack of dignity. By hauling away all those negative traits and dumping them atop these paragons of the second-rate, the glow of stardom was preserved for another day, another episode.

By the 1970s, however, the sitcom was tugging at its leash, demanding more freedom, seeking liberation from the 1950s strictures it was still saddled with. The sitcom had begun as family entertainment, meant to placidly occupy the entire family gathered in the living room for an evening's gentle fun. Now, series began to subvert their own carefully laid routines by elevating sidekicks to heroes, demoting the well-meaning but fatally bland family to secondary status. Sidekicks were now the stars.

In some cases, this was quite literal. Henry Winkler's Fonz burrowed into the center of *Happy Days* (ABC, 1974–84) after beginning as an afterthought, slowly taking over the show from Ron Howard's Richie Cunningham and the white-bread Cunningham family. Snapping his fingers and banging demonstratively on the jukebox ("Ayyyy!"), holding out his leather-jacketed arms to keep from losing his cool, fresh from a date with the Aloha Pussycats, Fonzie is the untrammeled id of this otherwise deliberately square ode to 1950s nostalgia. Most of *Happy Days* is meant to be just like *Father Knows Best* or *Leave It to Beaver*—or close enough to the warm, fuzzy innocence of those 1950s sitcoms to split the difference. "The kids on *Father Knows Best* never walk out on Robert Young!" Mr. Cunningham (Tom Bosley) complains to his children.

It is only Fonzie who breaks out of that dead end, granting *Happy Days* a touch of much-needed outlaw panache. He struts down the aisle to belatedly receive his high school diploma in "Graduation," thwarting the efforts of a school administrator to keep him from participating by having his diploma delivered by postman. Called in for a pre-draft exam in "The Physical," Fonz informs the drill sergeant that he must leave by noon for his date with the Hooper triplets. And Fonzie, to his eternal credit and shame, is the sitcom character who—quite literally—jumps the shark, water-skiing over a tiger shark in the episode "Hollywood: Part 3." (Cue *Community*'s Troy Barnes: "Oh, and for the record, there was an episode of *Happy Days* where a guy *literally* jumped over a shark. And it was the best one.")

Fonzie's unparalleled success prompted *Happy Days* to introduce an array of other colorful supporting characters, eventually to be spun off to successful series of their own. Fonzie's outrageous, intellectually impoverished pals Laverne and Shirley (Penny Marshall and Cindy Williams) are the kind of women who, given chewing gum to make it through a rough flight, stick it in their ears. *Laverne and Shirley* (ABC, 1976–83) is a show composed of nursery rhymes ("Schlemiel! Schlimazel! Hasenpfeffer Incorporated!") and the women who sang them. They are good-natured buffoons, sidekicks who come packaged with sidekicks of their own: Lenny and Squiggy (Michael McKean and David L. Lander). The two scuzzy greasers, Fonzies without the charm, are regularly summoned by the force of Laverne and Shirley's disdain. "What sort of cheap, pathetic freeloader," Laverne wonders as they prepare themselves for the departure of their much-anticipated Great Lakes cruise, "would stow away aboard a ship?" Cue Lenny and Squiggy, bursting breathlessly into their stateroom.

Robin Williams's Mork, the "shazbat"-spewing alien from Ork, had also been introduced on *Happy Days* as yet another quirky sideshow act before being spun off into his own successful series, *Mork & Mindy* (ABC, 1978–82). Mork is simply a funnel to channel Williams's frantic stand-up routines, his extraterrestrial unfamiliarity with the details of life in 1970s Colorado allowing him to creatively misunderstand America. Mindy (Pam Dawber) tells him that having a baby is less of a solo endeavor and more a union, and Mork nods knowingly. "Oh sure, I hear about 'women in labor' all the time."

Ensemble series such as *Welcome Back, Kotter* (ABC, 1975–79), *Barney Miller* (ABC, 1975–82), *Soap* (ABC, 1977–81), and *WKRP in Cincinnati* (CBS, 1978–82) either placed their eccentrics front and center as the show's stars or adopted a madhouse format in which all characters were equally unhinged. *WKRP* is a head-on collision of stark opposites: Howard Hesseman's weary, ironic DJ Johnny Fever; Tim Reid's strutting, pimp-suited Venus Flytrap; Loni Anderson's station receptionist Jennifer Marlowe, all wood and silicone. *Kotter* allows the lunatics to take over the asylum, granting the wildly exaggerated Sweathogs—especially John Travolta's lunkhead

Vinnie Barbarino and Ron Palillo's walking stereotype Arnold Horshack—time that might otherwise have gone to ostensible star Gabe Kaplan.

Soap, which ran for four increasingly hallucinatory seasons on ABC, is a soap opera parody defined by the absence among all the members of its two intermingled families, the Tates and the Campbells, of anyone who might be confused for a straight man. In Susan Harris's critically admired sitcom, there is no Alex for its array of Latkas and Reverend Jims. Harris adopted the show's open-ended, permanently unresolved narrative ("These questions, and many others, will be answered on the next episode of *Soap*") because of her difficulty with crafting traditional sitcom endings for each installment. A brief précis of the show's narrative arc would include defrocked priests, alien probes, sex changes, demonically possessed infants, religious cults, teacher/student relationships, secret doubles, Mafia killings, interracial romances, psychotic exes, Marxist rebels, and evil karate masters.

Barney Miller is emblematic of the new hybrid series, a sitcom taking place on the set of a drama. It is a cop show in the vein of *Dragnet* and *Hawaii Five-0*, but *Barney Miller* is less interested in the action of police work—chasing perps or cracking cases—than in the everyday boredom of hanging out at the precinct. The series empties out the drama from perhaps the most wearily familiar of dramatic-series locales, leaving only the faintly absurd aftertaste. Theatrical and occasionally bittersweet, *Barney Miller* is a series of unusual encounters with New York's oddest. Many of them, as it turned out, are uniformed members of the NYPD, including Abe Vigoda's cranky, wizened Fish. His jutting jaw his most prominent feature, his skin stretched tight over his hairless skull, Vigoda is the elderly mascot for this shambling band of brothers. "What can I do in 3-B?" Fish asks when checked out by the comely blonde next door on a stakeout. "I can't even eat fried foods!"

Barney (Hal Linden) is the moral enforcer for this colorful, multiracial band of cops. The show is the middle term in the set bookended by *The Goldbergs* and *Seinfeld* titled "Funny Jews on TV." Everyone, including the Japanese cop and the guy at the deli, seems to have gotten their training in the Catskills. Foreground and background had switched, or merged; these shows, devoted as they were to their parade of freaks, denied the primacy of leading men and women, preferring the warmth of the collective.

Eventually, network dramas would take up where shows like *Barney Miller* had left off. *Barney Miller* is a comedy in the guise of a drama; acclaimed dramas of the 1980s like *Hill Street Blues* and *St. Elsewhere* would import a touch of *Barney Miller*'s wacky-workplace cynicism, stocking their subplots and supporting characters with cranks who would have fit in right alongside Fish. The moat ringing the drama was partially drained, and shows of all kinds were now granted permission to make us laugh.

After *Taxi* and the left-field success of Latka and Reverend Jim, an entire wave of daffy sidekicks, many of them explicitly modeled on *Taxi*'s supporting cast, crashed on the beach of the sitcom. Instead of Latka, there is *Perfect Strangers*' Balki (Bronson Pinchot); instead of Reverend Jim, there is *Newhart*'s George Utley (Tom Poston). But the conservatism of the 1980s and early 1990s meant that many sitcoms once again relegated these quirky second bananas to supporting roles, afraid of giving their weirdos too much leeway. There were drips like *Family Ties*' Skippy (Marc Price), *Full House*'s Kimmy (Andrea Barber), and *The Fresh Prince of Bel-Air*'s Carlton (Alfonso Ribeiro); geeks like *The Wonder Years*' Paul (Josh Saviano) and *Saved by the Bell*'s Screech (Dustin Diamond); wild children like *Blossom*'s Six (Jenna von Oÿ) and *Growing Pains*' Boner (Andrew Koenig); loyal followers like Vinnie (Max Casella) of *Doogie Howser, M.D.*; and wrenches in the works like *Charles in Charge*'s Buddy Lembeck (Willie Aames). The new generation of sitcoms sought to balance comfort and peculiarity, often offloading their desire to amuse on this array of interchangeable eccentrics who rock the boat of sitcom familial order without ever capsizing it.

Post-*Seinfeld*, ensemble shows again began to muddy the easy distinction between leading and supporting roles. Dwight Schrute is a traditional sidekick, following his boss and mentor Michael Scott around *The Office* like a wounded puppy hungry for affection, but then so is Michael himself, his dim-wittedness, penchant for ill-timed motivational schemes, and lovelorn cluelessness revealing him as the direct descendant of both Ralph Kramden and Ed Norton. Who is star and who is sidekick on *30 Rock*? Even

Community, which features a supremely traditional leading man in Joel McHale's Jeff Winger, mocks its own proclivities by perpetually parodying his magical white-man ability to band together his team of community college rivals with a slick speech. The leading-man role had become a hollow shell, a mask covering an abyss. The sidekicks had taken over.

As for the series that pioneered the sitcom's devotion to its house eccentrics, *Taxi* was in most other ways a show devoted to preserving, not overthrowing, the existing order of television. Punch lines are telegraphed minutes in advance, the familiar ritual—luckless cabbies shooting the breeze—is forever restored at the close of each half-hour, and the comedy is liberally larded with heart-tugging moments of pathos. Indeed, the series evinces a wide sentimental streak it has no interest in repressing. Watching *Taxi* from a post-*Seinfeld*, post-*30 Rock* perspective, it is hard to fathom the show's devotion to plotlines like Alex's encounters with his ex-wife, or Tony's return to the boxing ring to honor the wish of a boy in a wheelchair. (That episode alone deserves a special place in the sitcom cliché hall of fame.) Even Louie is regularly summoned, late in the show's run, to supply some emotional heft, falling in love with a blind woman (with DeVito taking the Chaplin role from *City Lights*) or movingly describing his experiences shopping in the boys' husky department at a clothing store. The tender moments rarely fit comfortably with the cabbie hijinks of the rest of the series.

Conventional as it may be, *Taxi* is aware, as many of its predecessors were not, of its place in the world of television sitcoms. A film producer played by Martin Mull, soon to be a fixture on *Roseanne* as the title character's buttoned-up gay boss, visits the garage in "Hollywood Calling," and Alex regales him with cabbie stories. Mull lets him down gently, sharing his opinion that Alex's small-bore stories aren't entirely appropriate for the big screen: "He said they were more like television," says Alex. Television was marking its own territory, distinct from film and operating in a discrete emotional and comedic register all its own.

Mull is not the series' only reminder of the strange lives of character actors, passing through one sitcom on the way to the next, inhabiting one brief, memorable life before being shunted off to another. Jeffrey Tambor makes a brief appearance as a lovelorn politician in "Elaine and the Lame Duck," years before *The Larry Sanders Show*'s Hank Kingsley or *Arrested Development*'s George Bluth were more than a speck in their creators' eyes. And Wallace Shawn romances Elaine on the way to hanging out with the Huxtables as their nerdy, sexually repressed neighbor Jeffrey. Sitcoms— particularly long-in-the-tooth series that had already exhausted practically every permutation involving its main characters—depended on these guest performers for a shot of adrenaline, a temporary sidekick to the sidekicks. They also created an uncanny sense of drift between wildly disparate shows, as if the distance between a New York cab company and the set of a late-night talk show in Los Angeles were only a matter of steps.

Taxi itself reaches across the gap between sitcom universes to poke fun at some of its rivals. The sound of a flushing toilet reminds one of the cabbies—and not just us viewers at home—of Archie Bunker: "They're watching a rerun of *All in the Family* here." In "Alex's Old Buddy," from the series' final season, Jim is frustrated when his spec script for *M*A*S*H*, with emergency surgery on Colonel Potter interrupted by an alien invasion and the queen of the Zaxelonians falling in love with Klinger (the closest thing to a Reverend Jim on *M*A*S*H*), is rejected by the show. Jim's pithy description of his script sounds suspiciously like a subtle poke at the occasionally pompous modus operandi of that far more popular series: "Comedy, tragedy, and a statement against war. And a pie fight."

Never a ratings stalwart, *Taxi* coasted for its few seasons in the drift of the inexplicably popular *Three's Company*, which it followed on Tuesdays. After the show's third season, *Taxi* was moved to Wednesday nights, where it languished in fifty-third place. ABC summarily canceled the series, only to be taken aback when Hirsch, Lloyd, and Kane all won acting awards at that year's Emmys. NBC picked up the series, where it lasted for one more season before being permanently taken off the air.

Around that same time, as young comics named Jerry Seinfeld, Larry David, and Garry Shandling were gathering material in comedy clubs and doing *Tonight Show* appearances for what would become epoch-shattering additions to the sitcom form, the last and perhaps most successful of the classical workplace sitcoms would appear. A bar, like a police precinct or a taxi garage, was a gathering place for solitary souls of all sorts, and another station of sitcom purgatory. *Taxi* had begun the process by turning over the keys to Latka and Jim and Louie. It would take another decade for *Seinfeld* to cement the change, but in the meantime, *Cheers* would carry the torch for the sidekick as sitcom hero.

11

Cheers

"Strange Bedfellows, Pt. 2"

May 8, 1986 ▪ NBC

W ould they, or wouldn't they?" had never been a question the sitcom
had much concerned itself with. To begin with, the query assumed
an instability foreign to the unchanging order of the sitcom. If everything
always reverted to a comforting order at the end of thirty minutes, how could
any nagging questions linger from one episode to the next? More than that,
there was a matter of technical housekeeping preventing television from

such concerns. Each episode was a self-enclosed world, meant to require nothing from viewers beyond the faintest passing notion of the show's characters. "Would they, or wouldn't they?" required a familiarity with past developments that might pose a barrier to entry for casual fans of a series not fanatically committed to following each and every plot twist.

As its title might indicate, the *Cheers* (NBC, 1982–93) episode "Strange Bedfellows, Pt. 2," written by future *Frasier* cocreator David Angell, was neither the start nor the conclusion of the saga of its star-crossed lovers, Sam Malone (Ted Danson) and Diane Chambers (Shelley Long). There had been previous installments of their story, and there would be more to come—even a "Strange Bedfellows, Pt. 3" the next week. We catch Sam and Diane as they were meant to be, in medias res, torn between love and hate, eternal commitment and eternal enmity. As we enter, their relationship has undoubtedly hit a low. Sam is dating an elegant local politician named Janet Eldridge (Kate Mulgrew), hobnobbing with celebrities and basking in the reflected glow of fame. Diane is lonely and frustrated.

The episode begins, just like almost every other episode of *Cheers*, at the bar, surrounded by Red Sox memorabilia and a wooden Indian and fish mounted on the wall, the gang discussing their evening plans. Diane stews as Sam struts around the bar in his tuxedo, crowing about growing accustomed to his "monkey suit." "You know," she replies, a smile breaking across her heretofore somber visage, "I never realized until now just how appropriate that nickname is." Sam grumbles, and Diane gently prods him further: "My, aren't we a grumpy primate."

Diane uses humor and sarcasm as emotional repellent, keeping herself protected from her lingering feelings for Sam by the sting of her own wit, but "Strange Bedfellows" is intent on her humiliation. When former presidential candidate Gary Hart walks into the bar to return Sam's coat and compliment his Trivial Pursuit skills, Diane devolves into a shrieking, babbling twelve-year-old in the presence of her teenybopper idol. Always intent on preserving her own inflated sense of dignity, Diane eventually catches herself, and awkwardly covers her tracks: "I was just showing you how silly it looks. . . . Please, don't do it again."

As Sam plans for his evening with Janet at the mayor's house, Diane crows about the evening she and her beau of the moment have planned: theater, dinner, and dancing. "Boy, does that bring back memories," Woody coos from behind the bar. Diane, touched, asks if he remembers similar dates of his own. Woody, distractedly adjusting Sam's bowtie, offers an example of the misdirection that is *Cheers'* métier: "No, I just remembered your date called and canceled." Diane gulps and replies that it wasn't like she had just spent $312 on a new dress. Woody is relieved to hear it: "Then you'd really feel dumb!" *Cheers* thrives on these deliberate misunderstandings—on one character taking another's innocuous cue and running with it at top speed in the wrong direction.

Broad comedy, on *Cheers*, is always balanced by an innate tenderness. And the tenderness is always undone by the humor, in an eternally oscillating pendulum of the naughty and the nice. As Diane is fending off Sam's irrepressible good cheer, she is also gently scolding her other ex-flame, Frasier Crane (Kelsey Grammer). Frasier, considered by the show's cocreator Les Charles as an unthreatening Ralph Bellamy type treading on Sam's Cary Grant territory, is having a beer with Jim (Max Wright, soon to serve as the long-suffering Willie on *ALF*), who has just endured a "shellacking" in the election that returned Janet to office. Jim is now interested in pursuing campaign volunteer Diane, and Frasier kills him with misguided kindness. "Well, I think that's wonderfully open-minded of you," he coos, "considering her operation." Jim stammers and stutters, shuffling rapidly out of the bar when Diane arrives. "Frasier, have you been telling people that I had a sex-change operation again?" Diane asks. "No," Frasier insists, "he guessed."

That evening, Diane gets trapped in the bar, lurking by the bathrooms as Sam and Janet return from their night out. She hides, panicked, underneath the bar as Janet quizzes Sam about his romantic past. What was the longest relationship he'd ever been part of? Sam stutters and stumbles before admitting that it was with Diane, though whether out of embarrassment or lingering tenderness remains uncertain. Janet wonders, feigning casual interest, why Diane stays on at the bar. Would Sam lose business if she were to leave? "Matter of fact," he acknowledges, "I'd probably get a few back if I did let her go." Diane looks miffed as she perches under the bar, and near tears as Janet skillfully guides Sam to deciding to fire Diane, supposedly for the good of Diane's career. As the episode goes to its commercial break, Sam shuts off the bar's lights, and the camera tilts downward to take in Diane, crying on the floor.

When we return, Sam quizzes grouchy barmaid Carla (Rhea Perlman) about whether she thinks Diane belongs there. "You mean this bar, or this planet?" she replies. Either way, Carla offers, she agrees that she does not. Carla is the eternal cynic regarding Diane, and any purported changes to Sam under Diane's tutelage. Diane takes Sam to an art gallery, in the episode "Affairs of the Heart," and when Sam is faintly enthusiastic about the day's activity, Carla challenges him directly: "Name any piece of art in the world." Later, after Sam and Diane have broken up for the first time, Carla hears talk of Diane and pleads for an update: "Did she die? Is she dying? Is she suffering in any way? Throw me a bone here." With her gruff intonation and evil snicker, Carla is a less flamboyant—but equally misanthropic—version of *Taxi*'s Louie De Palma (played, perhaps not coincidentally, by Perlman's husband, Danny DeVito).

Carla's disapproval of Diane is so fierce that its predictability, too, becomes a joke. "Let me see if I'm following this," barfly Norm (George Wendt) observes from his bar stool, wielding a pretzel in his hand like a laser pointer. "Now Carla, you think Diane is bad for Sam . . ." Carla goes on to tell Sam that he is not, nor has he ever been, a "one-woman guy." This fling with Janet is merely that, reminiscent of what she calls the "great sickness." It takes Sam a moment to realize that Carla is referring to his relationship with Diane.

Sam nervously awaits Diane's arrival, but when she shows up at the bar, she preempts him, interrupting his speech to hand him an envelope. Sam opens it cautiously, flipping through its pages—its many, many pages. (Diane is never one to use one word where twenty multisyllabic ones will do.) "Does this mean you're quitting?" he asks. "Isn't that what it clearly states on page five?" she barks. Sam and Diane trade the baton, one stewing, the other crowing. First Diane is in control, proud of asserting her own dignity. Then it is Sam, asserting his own when she retracts her letter of resignation, refusing to make this final parting easy on him. Diane dares him to fire her, and Sam leans in close for the final kill: "You're fired." "Too late," Diane crisply responds. "I resign."

Sam and Diane, as mismatched as ever, go on to squabble over whether she has resigned or been fired. Eventually, they agree to disagree, their emotional dispute translated into a linguistic scuffle. "See you in the funny papers," Sam offers as a final kiss-off, and Diane takes umbrage not so much with its content as its form. Tottering toward the door in her black heels, she snipes at Sam once more: "Oh, that's perfect. The funny papers. Don't say another word. Let that be the last utterance I remember. And now I'm off to begin a new life. I shall forget you in a trice." At that last word, Sam is off like a cannon, rendered as insensible by her pretentious mannerisms ("in a trice"!) as she is by his boorishness. Diane storms out as Sam crumples her letter, returning for one more last word: "You troglodyte!" Make that one in a series of last words; Diane goes on to deliver an impromptu final address to the bar's patrons, ending with a spirited promise: "But there's one thing I know: you will never ever see me again." She storms out but realizes she has forgotten her coat. Diane snakes her arm back through the door, but Carla spots her and slowly, steadily tilts the coat rack away from her until Diane tumbles back inside. "Hey, look everyone!" Carla cackles. "It's Diane!"

There would be no end—at least, not this season, nor the one to follow—to the saga of Sam and Diane. Diane would get trapped again, this time under Sam's desk, while he and Janet talk marriage. "You have to make some choices," Janet later tells him forcefully, "some commitments. It's called growing up." The season finale ends with Sam picking up the phone in the darkened bar and proposing marriage—to whom, we do not know.

When the fifth season picks up, we discover that Diane was the recipient of the proposal. Almost as soon as the glorious news emerges, the pinnacle to which all of *Cheers* had been building to, it begins to fizzle, undone by Diane's pretentiousness and Sam's lunkheadedness. The game of love is back on, but Diane has been rendered no less annoying by romance. "*Bonsoir, mon coeur,*" she coos into the phone, and Sam mutters confusedly, "Right, right."

Sam formally proposes in person in "The Proposal," this time on a boat. When Diane turns him down flat, Sam forces her to leap into the water as punishment for once again foiling his romantic plans. Diane, choosing to view Sam's proposal of marriage as open-ended, later marches into the bar and positively shouts, "Yes!" Once Sam sorts out what she is affirming, he demurs: "The statute of limitations on that proposal ran out the second your feet hit the water."

Cheers is, in the form of the ballad of Sam and Diane, the longest exploration yet by a sitcom of romantic uncertainty as the emotional through-line for an otherwise lighthearted series. (Rachel and Ross, picking up where *Cheers* left off, would keep the same dance going for ten full seasons on *Friends*, doubling up on Sam and Diane's record.) The prime mover for the show's first five seasons is the tempestuous relationship between the lothario and the overeducated barmaid. "We wanted to create a show around a Katharine Hepburn-Spencer Tracy relationship," said James Burrows, the show's regular director and cocreator. Like with Hepburn and Tracy, the squabbling was more fun than the making up. "*Moonlighting* had the same problem: Everyone wants the two characters to be together, but then once they are, it's not that much fun," said writer Heide Perlman (younger sister to Carla herself, Rhea Perlman).

Upon closer look, of course, they are badly matched. Diane is a grind and a pedant, insistent on lugging a troupe of beer-swigging lugs to the opera for an evening so tedious that even she falls asleep. When she drafts another letter of resignation from the bar on an earlier occasion, she composes it partially in French. Sam is a recovering drunk with a persistent addiction to sleeping around. He admits to having had four hundred lovers when first taking up with Diane, before realizing the error of his ways and attempting to massage his answer into "four honeys." Sam's unconscious male swagger takes physical form in his loose-limbed walk, rolling forward on the balls of his feet, always en route to the next assignation.

Like *The Cosby Show*, with which it ran neck and neck in the Nielsen ratings for much of the 1980s, *Cheers* was part of the retrenchment that marked the television series of the era, retreating from the more political or experimental series of the 1970s into a comfortable, audience-pleasing routine. It was a show with an impressive sitcom lineage, created by *Taxi* writers Glen and Les Charles and director James Burrows, who had worked not only on *Taxi* but also on *The Mary Tyler Moore Show*, *Rhoda*, and *The Bob Newhart Show* (and would go on to direct episodes of *Friends*, *Will & Grace*, and *Frasier*). Like *Seinfeld*, *Cheers* was a product of NBC's patience. Nearly canceled after a single low-rated season, *Cheers* would bloom into a top-ten staple for almost a decade. There would be other classicist sitcoms after *Cheers*; one of its characters, Frasier Crane, would star in perhaps the best example of the form. But after *Cheers*, the style became defensive, an expression of aesthetic conservatism rather than a default point of view.

Either way, such series were consciously choosing to opt out of the sitcom's aesthetic reinvention, preferring the old, solid ways to the danger and promise of the new. None of this was, in any way, *Cheers'* fault. But falling where it did on the grid of the sitcom's history, it was inevitable that *Cheers* would have to bear the mantle of sitcom formalism soon to be upended by its successors.

A few weeks into the production of the series, Burrows realized that the relationship between Sam and Diane was the show's heart. "Sam and Diane is our money," he told a staff writer. "We have to go back to them, regardless of what the story is, [every] episode." Even knowing all the flaws of their alliance, we still root for them to end up together; like Diane, we are sure that fate will insist on the happy union of the prude and the ladykiller. This is what television does to us; it makes us crave the happy endings we know are bad for us.

The structure of episodes from the high-Diane era of *Cheers* generally follows the outline of "Strange Bedfellows Pt. 2." Each new installation ends with a tense, anguished standoff between Sam and Diane, usually in the bar's back office, or another round of sexually charged squabbling. The encounters, always promising a resolution to their tangled alliance, inevitably, slowly fizzle out. Prudish Diane is turned off by Sam's swashbuckling style, and Sam is bored by Diane's pseudointellectual trappings. The two still find themselves drawn together, almost against their wills, by the force of their physical attraction. Sex is the gravitational pull that keeps their mis-aligned bodies from spinning apart. A solemn pledge by them to go without sex for a month, in the episode "Personal Business," gets steadily whittled down until all that is left is fifteen minutes—enough time for the two of them to safely get back to Diane's apartment.

Sam and Diane's relationship is constructed out of the competitive streaks of two mismatched lovers, each grappling for superior position. Diane discovering Sam's hidden stash of her letters, lovingly tied up with a bow, is less a cause for a change of heart than an opportunity to crow at the revelation of Sam's gooey romantic streak. The mixture of sentiment and banter was one that would profitably serve another contemporary show devoted to the same questions of perpetually thwarted romance: *Moonlighting* (about which more in chapter 19).

Sam and Diane's fortunes wax and wane, the ebbing and flowing of their affections the metronome underscoring the show's melody. Diane leaves Sam for her therapist, Frasier, then leaves Frasier at the altar at the end of the third season to go back to Sam. Following the boat proposal, Diane eventually has Sam arrested for assault. Sam proposes marriage once more, this time to avoid a jail term. "It's the classic American love story," Sam avers sarcastically—proposal, denial, proposal, denial, court case. This time, the engagement sticks for a while, only to come unstuck once more. Sam feels emasculated by Diane's incessant chatter about fingertip towels and china patterns, and mutters to himself, "We better get married quick or I'm gonna kill her."

Their wedding—taking place, of course, at the bar—is undone by Diane's signing a book contract to write a novel and, stepping briefly out of the diegetic realm, Shelley Long's leaving *Cheers* for the temporarily brighter pastures of film. All of which ensures that Sam and Diane make it to the altar without actually marrying. "Do you agree that we shouldn't get married?" Sam asks. "I do," Diane reluctantly responds. Carla shrieks, and money changes hands furiously between all the Cheers regulars, their betting over Sam and Diane's abortive nuptials finally resolved. Weddings exist on *Cheers* primarily in order to be interrupted.

In its early days, *Cheers* was notably reluctant to depart from its three-room setup: bar, poolroom, back office. The show did its utmost to set even the most unlikely scenes—weddings, television broadcasts, costume parties—within its confines, and so viewers became used to seeing all manner of life inside the bar. Like the Huxtables' living room, the *Cheers* bar also became the repository for stories dragged in from the great outdoors. Bars are natural homes for raconteurs, and *Cheers*, like *The Cosby Show*, is a show about coming back home—or in this case, to the bar—with a story to tell. Someone (Sam, Frasier, Carla . . .) walks into Cheers with news from the outside world, and the interconnected wheels of *Cheers'* internal clock spring into action. There is no shortage to *Cheers'* array of one-liners (271 episodes worth!), but they are grounded in a strong sense of place and close observation of character.

Each character is an archetype, a familiar figure rounded by the seemingly infinite variations provided by the show. They are as dependable as a mug of cold beer on a hot day. *Cheers* characters are instantly identifiable—by their turns of speech, their routines, even their gait. Norm is a man whose fondest ambition, realized twice over the course of the series, is to be locked in the bar alone; Cliff (John Ratzenberger) is loveless, lives with his mother, and is passionately devoted to the US Postal Service; Coach (Nicholas Colasanto) is a take on Yogi Berra, so slow he never realizes how far he's fallen behind; Woody (Woody Harrelson) is Coach 2.0, a hick who is polite even when he is trying his utmost to be rude; Frasier is an over-educated boob who overcomes his infatuation with Diane to end up under the thumb of his eventual wife, the icy, brisk Lilith (Bebe Neuwirth).

Viewers had grown so accustomed to their faces gathered around the great wooden slab of a bar—Sam, Diane, Carla, and Woody or Coach doling out drinks, and Norm and Cliff and Frasier sucking them down—that the notion of the gang gathering anywhere other than Cheers seemed a mistake, a sort of cosmic error in which refugees are removed from their homes and relocated somewhere entirely foreign to their way of life. The Cheers gang—*outside* the bar?

Cheers is, like its predecessor *The Mary Tyler Moore Show* and its successor *Friends*, a fantasia about people who spend all of their time together, and the ways in which close friends can become something more. The Charles brothers and Burrows had initially planned to call their production company A Jew and Two Mormons, and one mismatched family gave birth to another. As the Charles brothers told an NBC executive when pitching *Cheers*, "This is about a family; it just happens not to be a group of brothers and sisters."

And we are, by extension, part of the gang, another onlooker at a nearby table, a positioning subtly underscored by the show's visual language. In one of *Cheers'* most basic shots, anonymous bar patrons pass by in the foreground as two characters talk in the middle distance. The intention is not so much to keep us at a distance from *Cheers'* characters as to realistically embed them within the sphere of the bar. With its array of two- and three-shots spelled by the occasional zoom into a close-up, and a limber camera given to tracking shots across the length of the bar, *Cheers* is intent on framing its characters within the context of their environment.

In one of *Cheers'* favorite set pieces, barfly extraordinaire Norm enters the bar, to the unfeigned pleasure of fellow drinkers ("Norm!") and an inevitable question from the bartender—first Coach, and then after Colasanto's death following the show's third season, Woody. (Norm's trademark was actually borrowed from Colasanto, who in his drinking days used to frequent a bar where regulars were greeted by name.) "What's going down, Mr. Peterson?" Woody wonders in "Strange Bedfellows." "My cheeks, on this bar stool," he replies. Norm is eternally quickstepping toward the bar stool permanently imprinted with his behind. "What do you say to a nice beer, Normie?" he is asked in another episode. "Going down?" he quizzically replies. "How does a beer sound, Norm?" Coach asks him as he walks in on another occasion. "I don't know, Coach. I usually finish them before they get a word in."

Sam and Diane are offset, in a way, by the similarly symbiotic and dysfunctional relationship of master barflies Cliff and Norm. They call each other, adorably enough, Cliffie and Normie (or, in a more precise phonetic rendering of Cliff's inimitably delicious Massachusetts brogue, "Nahmie"), and spend all their leisure time on side-by-side bar stools at Cheers. Norm, intent on preserving his superiority to Cliff the screwball know-it-all, deals out a steady stream of wisecracks intended to put his drinking buddy down. And Cliff is, truth be told, a handful; he spends an entire season of the show enthusing about the magical properties of vacationing in Florida and another lovingly fondling his crop of homegrown vegetables. Interrupting his own soliloquy about giving his veggies a shampoo, Cliff wonders about himself: "Is it me, or is this getting a little weird?"

Norm, too, has his rituals, all of which, apparently, revolve around the consumption of beer. He stops in solo at the bar during a date (while briefly separated from his eternally offscreen wife, Vera), having skipped out on *Gandhi* to quickly slake his thirst before returning to Richard Attenborough's Academy Award–winning slog. On another occasion, when Cliff asks Norm what time it is, Norm asks him how many beers he has drunk that evening. When told that he is up to his eleventh, Norm tells Cliff it is 8:05.

When the show returned for its sixth season in 1987–88, Diane had left Sam for good. Shelley Long, who had antagonized her fellow castmates with what they felt was preferential treatment and a Diane-like tendency to excessively question the nuances of her role, had taken off for a movie career that never quite blossomed. (According to assistant director Thomas Lofaro, Long believed herself to be "the new Lucille Ball"; appropriately enough, the show had engaged in negotiations with the real Lucille Ball to play Diane's mother, but she eventually demurred.) Diane is gladly forgotten. "I'm never going to take a woman away from you," Sam promises Frasier, leery of a repeat of earlier misadventures. "What about Diane?" Frasier wonders. "And didn't God punish me with a vengeance?" Sam argues.

With Diane out of the picture, the emotionally charged drama of the series mostly dissipates. Long is replaced by Kirstie Alley's Rebecca Howe (after a number of other candidates, including future *Sex and the City* star Kim Cattrall, were considered) and Sam, horndog extraordinaire, chases her as well: "She's almost as great-looking as I am," he moans, distinctly impressed. Their cat-and-mouse game, though, is keyed to a lower, earthier register. Sam is after Rebecca's body and nothing more (with a brief, mistaken detour, in the show's tenth season, toward them having a baby together). Rebecca, virtuous yuppie, is entranced by a series of wealthy cads and (mostly) turned off by Sam's muscular sexuality. Sam gamely continues to make his pitch—by one count, on 4,659 separate occasions: "Have sex with me twenty-five times, and if at the end of the night, you're still not sure . . ."

Rebecca, having learned a few lessons along the way from the corporate wizards she lives to brown-nose, is forever promising herself to Sam in exchange for some favor—locating her lost earrings, recovering a company executive's runaway dog—and then reneging, to his dismay. Sam is like a dog in search of a flavorful bone, always slobbering at the opportunity even if he knows, deep down, he will go home unsated once again. "I want to get my hands on Rebecca's jewels," he pants, hot on the trail of one of her wild geese, "but first I've got to find her earrings."

Cheers had been built around Sam and Diane's flickering romance, but in its absence, the show keeps on chugging, without any of the emotional heft it had once borne—but also without a hitch. When Rebecca finally accedes to Sam's charms, there are no emotional fireworks, but there *is* Woody's jumbo-sized betting chart, pulled out from underneath the bar. Who had this month? Who had "very good" for a verdict on Sam's performance?

After eleven seasons, the show packs it in with the three-part "One for the Road." It is a summation, a farewell, and a retroactive justification of *Cheers*' stylistic choices. "I like things you can count on," Woody observes, frustrated at the feeling of waking up each morning only to discover that something else has changed for the worse. *Cheers* was television you could count on. It would not quite be the last of its kind, but there was something of the antediluvian clinging to *Cheers* that rendered it simultaneously uncool and timeless. The show had done precisely what it intended to do, offering audiences more than a decade of evenings hanging out aimlessly at the bar.

Norm comes in one last time, preaching the gospel of a man's love for his neighborhood local to Sam. "You want to know what I love?" he asks. Sam nods at him from behind the bar, a beatific smile on his face: "Beer, Norm?" Norm treats Sam's response as an offer, glances at his watch as if to assess the time, and grunts, "Yeah." We have been set up, against our will, for one last walking-Norm joke, one last misunderstanding. Norm hobbles back to his stool for one last last one for the road. As if aware that a tender moment has been undercut—albeit for a superlative joke—he offers one of the more touching encomiums in the history of the sitcom, and undoubtedly the best ever granted by a man to his seat: "I love that stool! If there's a heaven, I don't want to go there unless my stool is waiting for me."

But first *Cheers* brings back Diane for one last fling with Sam. Diane is now a successful screenwriter, and when Carla spots her on television, she is sure she is having "one of my spells." And when Diane returns to the bar, Carla yelps, bowls of pretzels flying in every direction, shrieking anew each time she takes her in. Sam, freshly besotted, plans to leave for California with her. Will they, in the end?

Cheers was that rare show with an afterlife. Most hit series departed from the small screen never to be heard from again except in the eternal afterlife of reruns. Some shows attempted to spin off popular characters for new series of their own, either before or after the parent show gave up the ghost, but most ended up in the junkyard of well-intentioned flops: *Three's Company* (ABC, 1977–84) begat *The Ropers* (1979–80), *Barney Miller* begat *Fish* (ABC, 1977–78), *M*A*S*H* begat *AfterMASH* (CBS, 1983–84), *The Golden Girls* begat *The Golden Palace* (CBS, 1992–93), *Friends* begat *Joey* (NBC, 2004–06). Even *Cheers* had *The Tortellis* (NBC, 1987), which moved Carla's sleazy ex-husband (Dan Hedaya) and his showgirl wife to Las Vegas and did no better. But with its later, much better-known spinoff, *Cheers* actually managed to propel its success into a successor show with a decade-long run of its own.

In one of the vanishingly few successful acts of sitcom cross-pollination, Frasier Crane was bodily ejected from his seat at Cheers and deposited, unharmed, in a radio station some three thousand miles away, in Seattle. Frasier had been the odd man out at Cheers, the bourgeois intellectual surrounded by working slobs. The interest in the classical form of the sitcom familiar from *Cheers*—setup and punch line, variations on a familiar theme—abides, but *Frasier* (NBC, 1993–2004) inverts the equation. It provides new shadings and nuances to a character already familiar from a decade on television by replanting him in an unabashedly brainy milieu.

Frasier is still a psychiatrist, although now he works as the host of a popular therapeutic radio program, doling out psychological nostrums to an audience of the lonely and confused. A barfly no longer, Frasier has become a latte-sipping patron of Cafe Nervosa, surrounded by an array of doubles and foils. There is his equally pretentious, even more neurotic fellow-psychiatrist brother Niles (David Hyde Pierce); his cantankerous ex-cop father (John Mahoney), who moves in, depositing his puke-green armchair in the exact center of Frasier's high-modernist living room; his down-to-earth producer, Roz (Peri Gilpin); and Daphne (Jane Leeves, the virgin temptress of *Seinfeld*'s "The Contest"), the quirky, occasionally psychic caretaker for Frasier's father and the object of Niles's obsessive fixation.

Like its predecessor, *Frasier* is devoted to the pleasures of small talk. Frasier is no longer the yuppie twit he was on *Cheers*, there to provide a counterpoint to the workaday schlubs who populate the bar. One of the pleasing variations *Frasier* provides on its much-lauded predecessor is its devotion to the quiet exercise of wit. In fact, one of the most sheerly enjoyable episodes of the series, "My Coffee with Niles," consists almost entirely of the two brothers at a café table, talking. Niles wants to know one thing: after a year in Seattle, is Frasier happy?

The episode consists entirely of the interruptions between question and answer: Frasier's demanding coffee order, their father's anger when his sons forget his birthday, the hunt for a café table that will provide shelter from a traditional Seattle downpour, Frasier turning the tables and asking whether Niles is in love with Daphne. "Couldn't you find some beefy Eastern European scrubwoman who reeked of ammonia?" Niles pleads about their father's caretaker. "Well, I asked, but it was an Olympic year," Frasier responds. "The agency was fresh out."

The difference between *Frasier* and *Cheers* is the difference between a bar and a coffee shop. The raucous bonhomie of the former has given way to the free-flowing, if occasionally strained, conversation of the latter. Still, both are tributes to the richest node of the classical sitcom: its endless reservoirs of chatter.

"I am not your mother!" Sam shrieks at his regulars in *Cheers'* series finale, when they nag him about getting back together with Diane. "This is not your home!" Sam is right to stand his ground, but he is also entirely mistaken. Not only is it their home, it is also ours.

Sam eventually leaves Diane again, their brief dalliance a reminder of why, for all their magic, the form's most famous not-quite-couple never did belong together. Instead, Sam returns to Cheers, where Norm offers a benediction intended for us as much as for his longtime friend: "You can never be unfaithful to your one true love. You always come back to her." When asked who that might be, Norm turns back on his way out the door: "Think about it, Sam."

After a moment, Sam smiles to himself, standing behind the bar and muttering to himself: "I'm the luckiest son of a bitch on Earth." He straightens a picture on the wall (a photo of Geronimo that had belonged to Colasanto, a fitting, muted tribute to his departed colleague), then walks back toward the poolroom, and into the darkness. The shadows of leaves tremble against the exterior of the bar, and the credits roll one last time. We would never see Cheers again.

12

The Cosby Show

"Pilot"

September 20, 1984　▪　NBC

"Hard to get good help, isn't it?" Heathcliff Huxtable (Bill Cosby) gently picks his way through the minefield of detritus that is his teenage son's bedroom floor, displacing a small mountain of dirty clothing to create a tiny perch for himself on the bed. Theo (Malcolm-Jamal Warner) has come home with a report card of Cs and Ds, and his father has been dispatched upstairs to explain the future consequences of poor grades.

Theo insists that unlike his father the doctor and his mother the lawyer, he only wants to be a regular person, with a regular job. Cliff pulls out a packet of Monopoly money, prompted to teach his son an impromptu lesson in economics. Doling out $1,200 in monthly pay to Theo, Cliff begins taking it back: $350 in taxes (because "the government comes for the regular people first"), $400 for a Manhattan apartment (Theo, taking back $200: "I'll live in New Jersey!"), $300 for a car (Theo takes back $100, claiming he'll ride a motorbike instead; Cliff reclaims $50 for the helmet), $200 for clothes and shoes (at Theo's insistence: "I want to look good"). "What does that leave you with?" "Two hundred dollars," crows Theo, beaming at having avoided his father's rhetorical flourish, "so no problem!" "There is a problem," Cliff observes through gritted teeth. "You haven't eaten yet." Theo announces he is capable of getting by on baloney and cereal, and Cliff unsheathes his final saber: "You plan to have a girlfriend?" He takes the rest of his Monopoly money.

Theo, still unsettled on the subject, asks his father later in the episode to accept him as he is, flaws and all. "Maybe I was born to be a regular person, and live a regular life. . . . If you weren't a doctor, I wouldn't love you less, because you're my dad. Maybe you can just accept who I am and love me anyway, because I'm your son." The studio audience warmly applauds his sentiment. Another hoary sitcom trope has been trotted out, and Bill Cosby, old pro of television cliché, waits for the clapping to die down before rising out of his seat. "Theo," he calls out, "that's the dumbest thing I ever heard in my life!" Not content to leave it there, Cliff shifts into an even higher gear of rhetorical ire: "I am your father. I brought you in this world, and I'll take you out." Papa don't take no mess; *The Cosby Show* (NBC, 1984–92), as its title unabashedly indicates, was all about Cliff. Bill Cosby became television's most famous father by undercutting all the lazy politesse of the sitcom, and he begins right here, in the very first episode.

Cosby, a stand-up comic and a TV star for two decades, was weary of television's stale clichés. "I don't want to see one more car moving sideways down the street for two blocks—passing a (white) hooker talking to a black pimp—before crashing into a building in front of a man who drops to his knees with a .357 magnum. End of story," he said. Instead, he proposed a detective series about an investigator who never pulled his gun while solving cases. The networks passed, and Cosby returned with a new series idea based on the domestic observation of his stand-up work. "There's a war going on here between parents and children," he told NBC executives, according to then–network VP Warren Littlefield, "and we parents have no intention of losing." The show was originally to be called *The New, Improved Bill Cosby Show*, and marketed like a soda or a deodorant.

After a lengthy detour away from family life, toward workplaces, passels of friends, and childless couples, the sitcom had returned home, aping the format and reassuring feel of the classic 1950s series while updating their content for the go-go 1980s. Nuclear families—amiable father, no-nonsense mother, lovably perky children—were back in vogue, products, in one fashion or another, of Ronald Reagan's conservative resurgence. Instead of having their milk money swiped by bullies, these kids were having sex and getting arrested, but Dad (and Mom too, if in slightly blurrier focus) was still bailing them out of trouble. The guardianship of children was now a full-time occupation; sitcom parents' primary purpose was to inculcate positive values and steer their kids away from ever-present danger.

The 1980s were the era of fatherhood resurgent. Father knew best once more, reigning from living-room thrones, wielding kitchen-table scepters. (Weren't all of these fathers, in one way or another, reflections of that ultimate father as protector, the Gipper himself?) These fathers were kinder, softer presences than their predecessors, signaled by their Mr. Rogers–esque sartorial and grooming choices. Cliff had his garish sweaters, *Family Ties'* Steven Keaton (Michael Gross) his salt-and-pepper beard, and Dr. Jason Seaver (Alan Thicke) of *Growing Pains* had his array of sensitive-man cardigans and turtlenecks. Parents and children were allies and rivals all at once.

The soft-pedaled conflict of these new family sitcoms was between the old generation and the new. *Family Ties* pitted former hippie parents against children wholly uninterested in changing the world for the better. In the show's first episode, the Keatons revel in a slideshow of their 1960s activist days while their children are horrified by their gauche outfits and political causes. "The '60s are over, Dad," their son Alex, played with tweed-jacket-and-tie panache by Michael J. Fox, bluntly informs his father, and the sense of gently clashing sensibilities informs the show. The parents meant well, espousing all the liberal platitudes television preferred to peddle, but Young Republican Alex (one of whose girlfriends would be played by future *Friends* star Courteney Cox) was entirely preferable as comic company.

Although Alex Keaton would likely have found a cold shoulder in the Huxtable home, on first view there is little that might distinguish *The Cosby Show* from contemporaries such as *Family Ties* and *Growing Pains*. The setup of the show's pilot—aimless son runs headfirst into the hard-fought wisdom of worldly father—could have been imported from any other sitcom not only of its time but of the time of *Father Knows Best* and *Leave It to Beaver*. Future episodes would be devoted to the similarly gentle scrapes of not only Theo but also his older sisters Sondra (Sabrina Le Beauf) and Denise (Lisa Bonet) and younger sisters Vanessa (Tempestt Bledsoe) and Rudy (Keshia Knight Pulliam). The innovation of *The Cosby Show* was, paradoxically, to be found in how utterly ordinary its plotlines were: dead goldfish and adolescent dustups and meandering life lessons from Dad.

It is Cosby, and to a slightly lesser extent, Phylicia Rashad's Claire Huxtable, who anchor the show, with a no-nonsense attitude to child-rearing and, by extension, sitcom-building. Cliff and Claire are more irascible than their sitcom forebears, more willing to turn their rapier wit on their children. Cliff Huxtable is sweet and sharp and exasperating in equal measure—so effortlessly brilliant that it is only too easy to lose sight of how consistently good Rashad is as well. Their middle-class ordinariness endeared the series to average Americans who might otherwise have been uncomfortable with the series' unique twist: this sitcom family was African American. Little took place on *The Cosby Show* that had not happened on dozens of other shows countless times before, but the sheer fact of the Huxtables being who they were made it notable and worthy.

By the time of *The Cosby Show*'s premiere in 1984, Bill Cosby was already a legendary figure in television history. He had been the first African American star of a prime-time drama series with the gently charming spy show *I Spy* (NBC, 1965–68). Cosby was the comic foil for partner Robert Culp, but *I Spy* was notable for its distinctly unpatronizing tone toward Cosby. Cosby was a master of heavy-lidded comic understatement, coiled violence and coiled humor in the same tightly wound package. (Cosby won three Emmys for best actor in a drama series for *I Spy*, rendering it all the more astonishing that not only did he never win an Emmy for playing Cliff Huxtable, he was never even nominated.) Even in the mid-1960s, Cosby's story was intertwining with that of the sitcom; in the episode "It's All Done with Mirrors," he tangles with a scenery-chewing *Manchurian Candidate*-style brainwashing expert, played with gleeful affect by that fellow future sitcom icon, Carroll O'Connor. One would not have expected Cliff Huxtable and Archie Bunker to meet under such circumstances.

Cosby went on to headline the first sitcom named after an African American performer, *The Bill Cosby Show* (NBC, 1969–71), also becoming the first African American man to star in a sitcom since *Amos 'n' Andy*'s Tim Moore. *Bill Cosby* was demonstrably more multicultural and diverse than the shows that had preceded it on television, with Cosby playing dashiki-clad Chet Kincaid, a physical education teacher at a Los Angeles high school who persistently finds himself embroiled in others' imbroglios.

In the show's first episode, a small gem of the kind of shaggy dog storytelling that would become a Cliff Huxtable staple, Chet sets out for a jog, answers a ringing pay phone, and finds himself in pursuit of a man named Calvin. Chet is simultaneously being hunted by the police, who suspect him in a string of robberies. In another episode, Chet is in search of a new valve needle to blow up his saggy basketballs and must negotiate the thicket of educational bureaucracy in order to acquire one. He eventually commandeers the school's janitor to move a file cabinet in order to procure the necessary requisition form before learning that furniture moving, too, requires a special form.

Bill Cosby's star is its beleaguered voice of reason, his innate decency shining through even when blustering through an algebra class as a substitute, or when bachelor Chet must face a sex education class of inquisitive girls, telling them that he only believes in taking the pill when he has a headache (Mary Richards would likely have offered different advice). Like its far more famous successor, *The Bill Cosby Show* is anecdotal, low-key, and inclined toward the mundane. Cosby, at his best when interacting with children, is cast as a teacher so that he can offer wickedly realistic counsel to an array of troubled adolescents.

For *The Cosby Show*, the star collaborated with Ed. Weinberger, who had cocreated *Taxi* (and before that, *The Bill Cosby Show*) and written for *The Mary Tyler Moore Show*. The *Cosby Show* team also included Jay Sandrich, who had directed the bulk of the episodes of both *MTM* and *Soap*. Weinberger and Sandrich's presence alongside Cosby ensured that *The Cosby Show* was a veteran enterprise from the outset. It also meant that something of *Mary Tyler Moore*'s character setup, an ensemble piece revolving around a single unchanging protagonist, was imported to *The Cosby Show*. Mary Richards, meet Cliff Huxtable.

Originally, the Huxtables were to be a working-class family, with Cliff a driver and Claire a plumber. With no pilot or script to show, Cosby's representatives shopped the series to ABC. The network rejected it, and NBC swooped in to pick up the Cosby vehicle. In the process, Cliff and Claire became white-collar professionals—Cliff an obstetrician, Claire an attorney—with Cosby seeking the advice of the OB/GYN who delivered his five children for crafting the character of Dr. Huxtable. The new show was to be filmed in New York, near Cosby's home, and not in Los Angeles, where most sitcoms were made. "I'd like to be canceled a little closer to my home this time," said Cosby.

Like almost every other sitcom of its era, *The Cosby Show* was drastically limited in its physical scope: the living room and kitchen, with occasional detours to the bedrooms upstairs. A traditional multicamera sitcom, *The Cosby Show*'s setup required flat, even lighting. Eschewing so much of the film director's traditional palette, sitcoms are a writer's and performer's medium, requiring acting and dialogue to do the work that lighting and camera movement cannot. But Cosby's penchant for physical comedy and his storyteller's flair are built into the foundation of the series.

Cliff is forever recounting and recreating his adventures outside the house: begging to make a purchase at the electronics store after his wife forbids the proprietors from selling to him, or taking Theo to an army recruiting office as punishment after an out-of-control party at their house, encountering other parents with ropes around their children's necks or guns cocked in their pockets. The show leaves ample room for Cosby to show off his physical gifts, whether he is sneezing directly into a box of tissues or slowly, carefully lowering himself onto a couch as a pregnant man in the fantasy episode "The Day the Spores Landed." (He eventually gives birth to a ten-foot hoagie, followed in short order by a bottle of soda.)

Cliff and Claire are near-ideal parents, but much of *The Cosby Show* is devoted to the sheer maddening frustration of parenthood. In the very first episode of the series, Claire confronts her husband at the front door as soon as he comes home: "Cliff, why do we have four children?" (She hasn't lost track of the number; in the pilot, Sondra had yet to be added to the cast.) When Theo wonders how to be alone, his father offers a simple formula: "Get a job, get a house, get married, and have no children." When Denise, unsure about attending college, pontificates at length about learning from the university of life, Cliff sagely observes, "I understand that some of its graduates go on to move back with their parents."

In an episode from the first season, Cliff jokes that his name should officially be changed to "Dad-Can-I," in order to simplify matters for his children and their incessant demands. "The United States of America is a wonderful place," Cliff complains, "but they don't have anything where you can get rid of your kid." In the episode "The Shirt Story," Theo enthuses about the quality materials and design of a dress shirt he covets, and Cliff wearily asks, interrupting his son's consumerist aria, "How much?"

Cosby is regularly paired with the gifted Malcolm-Jamal Warner as his foil. In the episode "Independence Day," Theo gets an earring, and as Cliff maneuvers to catch a glimpse of the illicit jewelry, father and son lean back in tandem until they are practically supine. Cliff and Theo have a similar hide-and-seek dynamic in an episode early in the series' second season, when Cliff drapes himself over Theo's shoulder, curious about what is captivating his son's attention inside the refrigerator.

Cosby and Warner have superb chemistry and execute a seemingly infinite series of variations on the theme of disappointed father and disappointing son. When Sondra announces she has decided against law school, the high-school-aged Theo is inspired to give up on his own higher education, seeking to claim his college tuition money in advance. He factors in the cost of lab fees as well, since if he had gone, he argues, he would have been a chemistry major. When Cliff turns his wrath on his son, Theo retreats—partially: "Well, can I at least borrow three dollars for some pizza?" In another episode, Theo rhapsodizes about the merits of the University of California at Berkeley, daydreaming about cruising through campus in a convertible. Cliff, grouchy as ever, wonders aloud if the city has introduced a new fleet of convertible buses.

With a good deal of the series devoted to frustrations of the lesser and greater kind, *The Cosby Show* is less idealized than merely peaceable. Still, in many ways it is a throwback; it does not reflect much on its medium, nor does it seek to complicate the sitcom's essential simplicity. The sitcom, coming of age in the conformist 1950s, was devoted to presenting a whitewashed American family, stripped of conflict except of the most trifling variety. *The Cosby Show*, with its familiar living-room and kitchen sets, its nuclear family model, and its ever-present laugh track, is hardly ready to jettison all that came before it. And yet, by the very fact of its presence, it sought to widen the narrow funnel of the American ideal in order to include families like the Huxtables as well.

The Cosby Show made the unfamiliar familiar—and vice versa. A show about a wealthy African American couple and their ideal brood was hardly the stuff of *Good Times* or *The Jeffersons*. Would a mainstream American audience embrace the Huxtables? Cosby's sweaters, impossibly ugly and yet deeply familiar in a bad-Christmas-present sort of way, are the secret weapons. Cliff is black, bourgeois, a New Yorker, and a doctor, but he is also someone ordinary enough to have no fashion sense whatsoever. The sweaters domesticate him.

Cliff has his stubbornly undomesticated side as well. He is Groucho Marx as father, his whole family serving as his straight man and their escapades providing the ideal opportunity for Cosby to riff. Cliff is the responsible id. He dreams of hoagies, hides potato chips in the chimney, and regales Theo's friends with adolescent stories of skating across his kitchen floor. He is crafty, petulant, and often cutting in his sneak attacks on his wife and children. And yet Cliff is not an eternal man-child, like those who would follow in his wake; Brooklyn's answer to *The King of Queens* he could never be. The burdens of race, as well as the character's own medical persona, demand a fundamental devotion to family and profession that offsets such surface attributes.

The series itself walked the same line between playfulness and respectability. In a magnificently executed episode from its second season, "Theo's Holiday," that echoes many of the themes of the pilot, Theo informs his parents that he plans to make a living as a model. (Perhaps Theo and the George Costanza of the booming hand-modeling sideline in *Seinfeld*'s "The Puffy Shirt" could go into business together.) Intent on teaching him another lesson about economics, the family transforms their home into the Real World Apartments, with his parents and sisters playing the new people in his life: the landlord, the modeling agency secretary, the café owner, the bank loan officer. Theo's room, now unfurnished, goes for $600 a month. Does he want a bed? That'll be $200 extra. Denise, as the restaurant proprietor, charges him $24.50 for sneaking a snack out of the fridge. Diminutive Rudy, glasses perched on her nose, looks over his loan documents at the bank, and Cliff, a cigar stub clamped firmly between his teeth, is the ever-skeptical landlord. By show's end, Theo has learned his lesson: "I learned that when I go into the real world, I don't want to do business with *anyone* in my family."

The entirety of *The Cosby Show* is like the Real World Apartments, offering neatly packaged life lessons in the guise of witty games and practical jokes. When an elderly neighbor is in need of a health tutorial, Cliff fakes collapsing after consuming a gigantic hoagie. And when Vanessa is caught drinking with friends, the family plays a mock drinking game together to teach her a lesson. Cliff, his mouth crumpled sidelong into a parody of an afternoon drinker, shouts out encouragement: "Drink 'er down! Chug-a-lug!"

The series' carefully tuned balance—between the aspirational and the relatable, the responsible and the ridiculous—helped make the series into not only one of the most popular shows on television during its nine-year run on NBC, but one of the most beloved television programs of all time. In its first season, *The Cosby Show* was the highest-rated new sitcom since *Mork & Mindy*. It would go on to become the first show since *All in the Family* to top the Nielsen ratings for four straight seasons; it spent seven seasons in the top five and reached an average audience share greater than 50 (meaning that more than 50 percent of all viewers watching TV on Thursdays at 8 PM were watching *The Cosby Show*) in both 1985–86 and 1986–87. *Cosby* was the highest-rated show on television since *Bonanza* more than twenty years prior, in 1964–65. It was the highest-rated series of the 1980s, and no show since has achieved remotely comparable ratings. (For comparison's sake, the top-rated show of 2011–12, NBC's *Sunday Night Football*, achieved an audience share of 20 among viewers ages eighteen to forty-nine, less than half of *Cosby*'s at its peak.)

Premiering on television two months before Ronald Reagan (who had first announced his presidential candidacy in Philadelphia, Mississippi, where three civil rights activists had been murdered by the Ku Klux Klan in 1964) was reelected in a landslide, *The Cosby Show* was simultaneously about and above race. The series resides in its own handcrafted, effortlessly multicultural world, where veterinarians and naval officers are black, neighbors are white, and patients are Asian American, and yet discussion of the Huxtables' personal good fortune as successful African American professionals is drastically limited. Much is made of the Huxtables' wealth ("Let me get something straight, OK," Cliff tells Vanessa. "Your mother and I are rich. You have nothing."), but the show wears its blackness lightly, like a self-evident fact hardly worth explicit mention. Politics only sneaks in at the margins. Sondra and her husband name their twins Winnie and Nelson, but it is up to us to presume that their namesakes might be Winnie and Nelson

Mandela. "Racism is not funny to me," noted Cosby about his show's purposeful avoidance of racial issues.

The Cosby Show prefers to be a filter, not a megaphone. When it does address race, it does so in sidelong fashion, letting others say what it preferred not to. In one of the most quietly indelible moments of *Cosby*'s run, an otherwise typical episode, "Vanessa's Bad Grade" (Vanessa gets a D in school; Cliff falls asleep at a foreign film), transforms unexpectedly when the family shuffles into the living room, one by one, their mundane business interrupted by the sound of Dr. Martin Luther King spilling out from the television: "Let freedom ring from the snowcapped Rockies of Colorado! Let freedom ring from the curvaceous slopes of California!" For two minutes—a relative eternity in television time—we watch the family watching Dr. King. No one says a word, and when King's "I Have a Dream" speech ends ("Free at last! Free at last! Thank God Almighty, we are free at last!"), so does the show. That "Vanessa's Bad Grade" debuted on January 16, 1986, four days before Martin Luther King Day officially became a national holiday, was a subtext that viewers would have to provide themselves.

Eliding race as it does, *The Cosby Show* is more explicitly concerned with reeducating savage men in their responsibilities toward women. The series designates two official whipping boys, present mostly to be lectured to: Sondra's husband, Elvin (Geoffrey Owens), and Rudy's pipsqueak friend Kenny, a.k.a. "Buuud" (Deon Richmond). Elvin asks Claire whether she has checked with her husband before purchasing an expensive painting, and solemnly informs Sondra that she should not pump her own gas, since "women should not smell like gasoline. Women should smell like sandwiches." Kenny solemnly echoes the pronouncements of his unseen older brother on women's proper roles, only to be repeatedly put in his place by Claire, and even by Rudy. Race is too inflammatory to dwell on, but *The Cosby Show* solemnly lectures its audience on feminism through its designated straw men. One set of reactionary boors stands in for another.

More than just a war of attrition between parents and children or feminists and traditionalists, *The Cosby Show* is also a lovingly drawn portrait of a devoted marriage. Claire and Cliff may bicker (whenever Claire, in full attorney mode, begins a sentence with "Let the record show," Cliff instinctively flinches), but when Cliff leads Claire in a 2 AM dance in their living room or enlists the kids in putting together a mock high school prom for their parents, *The Cosby Show* offers a snapshot of a life devoid of that sitcom staple: petty bickering. Claire is tough on her husband at times, but she always laughs at his jokes. What more is there to a marriage?

There are hints of darker sentiments, problems too complex to be solved within twenty-two minutes. The specter of drug abuse is introduced, and summarily dispatched with a flick of the parental whip: "As long as you are living in this house, you are not to do any drugs. When you move into your own house, you are not to do any drugs. When I am dead, and you are seventy-five, you are not to do any drugs." Contrast *Cosby*'s approach to that of its contemporary *Roseanne* in its drug-themed episode "A Stash from the Past," in which Roseanne and Dan accuse their kids of doing drugs, only to then get high on what turns out to be their own supply (more about that episode in the following chapter).

Slower and more easygoing by a good measure than tightly paced successors like *Seinfeld*, *The Cosby Show* is more than willing to turn over three or four of its weekly twenty-two minutes to a musical number or comic bit, with Cosby serving as the impresario and master of ceremonies. The performances are often integrated into the show by the cast's presence, be it the family lip-synching to a James Brown number or attending a Lena Horne show for Cliff's birthday. Though hesitant to address the politics of race too explicitly or too often, *The Cosby Show* nonetheless gave Cosby a chance to school audiences in the glories of African American culture.

Lena Horne was far from the only legendary performer to make a personal appearance on the show. Every few episodes, sitcom devotion to plot hijinks gives way to a guest singer or performer: Tito Puente, Dizzy Gillespie, Stevie Wonder, Art Blakey, Placido Domingo, B. B. King. Comedians and clowns such as Bill Irwin and Danny Kaye are brought on to perform their own routines. (You have not truly lived until you've seen noted college basketball guru Dick Vitale as a gabby moving man in the episode "The Getaway.") *The Cosby Show* owes something to vaudeville in its embrace of variety and its leisurely sense of pacing. Kaye takes over the overwhelming bulk of "The Dentist," the episode he guest-stars in, as a mischievous tooth-puller with a pair of talking dentures. "Do I know you?" he asks them. "No, but you've taken out some of our friends." Cliff, the eternal child, asks on the way out, sotto voce, if he can see the teeth once more.

Cosby, meanwhile, was forever the educator, and he took his responsibilities seriously. He had, after all, played a teacher on *The Bill Cosby Show*, and, billed as "Dr. William H. Cosby, Ed.D." in his role as *The Cosby Show*'s cocreator, made no secret of his doctorate in education. The latter series served as a convenient mechanism for teaching his millions of regular viewers about jazz or the blues or the March on Washington. History became a personal affair; the march, in the episode of the same name, wasn't just about Dr. Martin Luther King but also about Cliff's singing that day on the bus, and his father Russell's recitation of King's "I Have a Dream" speech. When Russell sings "The Battle Hymn of the Republic," we understand: history is what happens to people just like the Huxtables—or us.

Later seasons found the show seeking to revitalize itself with new characters: Denise's navy-man husband (Joseph C. Phillips), her too-cute-by-half stepdaughter Olivia (Raven-Symoné), and Claire's inner-city cousin Pam (Erika Alexander), who pops up whenever the writers remember she exists. (Also look out for Seth Gilliam—*The Wire*'s Sgt. Carver—as one of Pam's friends.) It also leaned on increasingly implausible reasons—housing shortages on naval bases, Denise's and Theo's seeming inability to complete and return housing forms promptly—to keep all the children at home. (Why couldn't everyone just visit regularly?) Even Sondra's husband Elvin is overhauled, transformed from Neanderthal chauvinist to the kind of man who carries his baby strapped to his chest. None of the new performers are entirely successful; the original chemistry Cosby created with his on-screen children could not be replicated. Luckily, Malcolm-Jamal Warner kept the faith until the very end, with his Theo also subtly altered over the course of the show's run from teenage slacker into a youth mentor and high-achieving college student.

The Cosby Show's incredible success also led to a college-themed spin-off, *A Different World* (NBC, 1987–93), in which Lisa Bonet's Denise is sent off to her parents' alma mater, Hillman College. *A Different World* had its own surprisingly successful run, given Bonet's limited acting and the show's sharply politicized content, seemingly all women's studies courses and gender-integrated beauty contests. (The show had the good sense to rapidly jettison Bonet in favor of sharper performers like Kadeem Hardison's flip-up-sunglasses-rocking Dwayne Wayne and Jasmine Guy's southern belle Whitley.) But in a wider sense, *The Cosby Show* would have few if any successors.

The mid-1980s—that era of Michael Jackson and Bruce Springsteen—would spell the last hurrah of the crossover hit. *The Cosby Show* deliberately appealed to white and African American audiences alike, but with the advent of new networks such as Fox and UPN, future African American sitcoms would be relegated to niche broadcasting. How many white families would gather weekly around the television to watch *Martin* (Fox, 1992–97)? And how many black families would be sure never to miss an episode of *Seinfeld*? *The Cosby Show* existed in an effortlessly multicultural realm, but how much of an African American presence would there be on an NBC hit of the next decade, like *Friends*? There would be other worthy shows with majority African American casts—the underrated *Martin*, for one, along with *The Fresh Prince of Bel-Air* (NBC, 1990–96) and *The Bernie Mac Show* (Fox, 2001–06)—but the miracle of *Cosby* was never to be duplicated. Television, in the aftermath of *The Cosby Show*, would find it easier, and in some ways preferable, to cater to audiences that were homogeneous—not only racially but also culturally and demographically.

On April 30, 1992, *The Cosby Show* aired its two-part finale. While Theo was graduating from college, other young African American men were rioting in the streets of Los Angeles, irate at the seeming indignity of the Rodney King verdict, announced the previous day. Mayor Tom Bradley pleaded with Angelenos to go back home and watch *The Cosby Show* instead. (Cosby himself would appear on NBC's L.A. affiliate after the finale, begging rioters to demonstrate calm.) In the less violently fractured and racially polarized alternate world of the Huxtables, Cliff is amazed to find himself sitting in the stands as Theo graduates. Falling into reverie, he looks back at the very beginning of *The Cosby Show*'s story, doling out Monopoly money and explaining the facts of the real world once more to his immature son. Cliff, emerging from his daydream, looks at his wife, mouth agape: "What just happened?"

What had happened was the phenomenon of *The Cosby Show*, savior of NBC's flagging fortunes, recipient of an unprecedented $500 million syndication deal, and one of the top five shows on television for seven of its eight seasons. Cliff and Claire return home from graduation and dance one last time around their living room. Then, Huxtables no longer, Cosby and Rashad head off beyond the borders of the sitcom set and into the studio audience. Their fellow cast members stand and applaud them, and by extension themselves. *The Cosby Show* took a final victory lap, and for at least this once in sitcom history, the victory is not marred by the celebration. In fact, this acknowledgment of all of us, at home, watching the Huxtables live their lives is perfect in its own way. Cliff and Claire waltz out the door of the studio, never to return. All that remains are these 201 episodes, documents of a certain kind of situation-comedy perfection. The traditional sitcom— Mom, Dad, irrepressible kids—had been mastered, soon to be permanently retired in favor of sportier, jauntier models.

13

Roseanne

"Terms of Estrangement, Part 1"

September 15, 1992 ▪ ABC

It was the economy, stupid. Sitcoms had mostly existed in a hazy middle-class bubble, in which momentary eruptions of money panic—how will we pay for Sis's prom dress?—were mere blips in a larger panorama of placid, worry-free existence. The sitcom promised comfort and familiarity, the certainty of an eternal present free of all but the most fleeting concerns. And even as it matured, it found it mostly preferred the company of the well-off or the comfortably middle class, the problems of the working class being too deep-rooted, too intractable, to comfortably situate within its frame. Even series that were ostensibly about working-class heroes deracinated its characters; the hacks of *Taxi* all somehow lived in middle-class comfort or were too addled to know otherwise.

"If you knew how to run a business, he'd still have a job and he wouldn't be leaving. Now I don't have Mark, I don't have college, I don't have anything. You blew it, Dad! You blew it for everyone in this family!" Becky Conner (Lecy Goranson, for now) stands in the Conner kitchen in the *Roseanne* episode "Terms of Estrangement, Part 1," one foot out the door, and blows a hole in the calm facade of the sitcom. Her boyfriend, Mark (Glenn Quinn), has been working at the bike shop owned and operated by her parents, and a downturn in the economy has forced them to close the store and lay off Mark. Roseanne (Roseanne Barr) tells Becky to shut up, and Becky fires back, enraged, "Come on, Mother, you know it! Everyone knows it! I'm the only one with the guts to say it."

"Terms of Estrangement, Part 1," which kicked off the fifth season of *Roseanne*, aired some forty-nine days before the election that would sweep a theretofore obscure governor named Bill Clinton into the White House on the basis of widespread economic disaffection. The episode recasts the travails of the United States as a family-size recession story. It is pitched, as so much of *Roseanne* is, as a struggle between parents and children. Becky pleads with her father, Dan (John Goodman), to keep Mark on at the bike shop, and he bristles while pretending to placidly balance the scales of justice: "I don't have a job, and your mother doesn't have a job, but we'll make *Mark* our first priority." Becky storms out, and her wisecracking younger sister, Darlene (Sara Gilbert), steps gingerly into the fray. Roseanne turns on Darlene confrontationally: "Do you have anything that you want to say?" Darlene pauses thoughtfully, and wonders, "Can I have a pony?"

Youngest son DJ (Michael Fishman), meanwhile, graciously offers to help, pointing out that he still has some birthday money tucked away in his closet. "Aww, no you don't," Roseanne informs him, smiling gratefully. "But thanks anyway." Like *The Cosby Show*, with which it overlapped for a portion of its run, *Roseanne* thrives in the indeterminate space where sitcom treacle is undone by a bracing blast of reality. Cliff Huxtable runs roughshod over his son's plea to live his own aimless life, and Roseanne Conner blithely steals her son's life savings. The sitcom is no longer polite, and yet its new bluntness, domesticated in familiar-looking kitchens and living rooms, jars us hardly at all. Instead, it offers a new kind of intimacy, one predicated on our familiarity with the foibles and failings of its characters.

The recession trickles into every corner of the Conner household. Roseanne's ever-helpful sister Jackie (Laurie Metcalf) reads the obituaries to her, noting that eleven people with good jobs have died in the last week. Roseanne, only too aware of her own limitations, sighs regretfully that she is unqualified for any of those positions. "Didn't somebody get their head caught in an Orange Julius machine or something?" The language of the downward slope is the lingua franca of the Conner household. In another episode, Dan pumps his fist at one of DJ's school events, sure his son has clinched the spelling bee when he hears the final round's word: "foreclosure."

"Warped and depressing is what's cool now," a character notes when DJ gets in trouble for bringing one of Darlene's hand-drawn comic books to school. This could easily serve as *Roseanne*'s motto, as one of the first family sitcoms to push the heretofore closed boundaries of the form. The sitcom, it turned out, could be as much about affliction as comfort. "Terms of Estrangement," written by Sy Dukane and Denise Moss, offers no solutions, proffers no easy resolution to its conundrum. The American economy is not magically fixed by the Conners at the end of its twenty-two minutes. Roseanne promises Dan an evening of candles and massage to take his mind off their struggles, and he bristles: "Rose, this sucks. Nothing you could say is going to make it any better."

Instead, the show, as is its wont, offers a further complication. Mark has taken an offer for a better job in Minneapolis, and Becky has secretly run off to join him. She calls the family collect to let them know that she and Mark have gotten married. Roseanne grabs the phone away to scream at her daughter: "Fat cat!" The episode ends with the pay phone outside a gas station hanging off the hook, Roseanne shouting uselessly to the frigid air after her daughter and new son-in-law have driven away. No more helpless image of emotional disconnection and economic calamity would appear in the cautious world of the 1980s sitcom. Nor does the problem immediately disappear, a product of sitcom amnesia. In "The Dark Ages," two episodes later, the Conners lose their power because of unpaid bills, and Roseanne sighs wearily, "Well, middle class was fun."

Roseanne was the peak of a wave of working-class sitcoms that began to appear in the mid-1980s and continued through the mid-1990s. ("We know they're working class," John Leonard opined, "because they go *bowling*.") For a time, such series were the most popular shows on the air. *Roseanne* was a top-five show in the Nielsen ratings for much of its run, and the number one show in the country for the 1989–90 season. *Home Improvement* (ABC, 1991–99)—*Roseanne* with its protagonist relegated to the kitchen and Dan and his power tools moved front and center in the guise of Tim Allen—was also a ratings titan for ABC, and the top-rated show of 1993–94. Blue-collar was cool, and ABC specialized in these semi-gritty series. *Grace Under Fire* (ABC, 1993–98), with Brett Butler as a brash single mother, was essentially generic-brand *Roseanne*, weaker but with fewer side effects. Eventually an entire spate of CBS shows followed, such as *The King of Queens* (CBS, 1998–2007), about tubby men in blue-collar jobs and the lithe women who love them.

Married . . . with Children (Fox, 1987–97) was a harbinger of *Roseanne*'s gleeful crassness, without any of its delicacy or nuance. *Married* was so cheaply produced it made *Roseanne* look like *Lawrence of Arabia*. It was a show about male emasculation and the stunted efforts of Al Bundy (Ed O'Neill) to rebel against his obnoxious, sex-crazed wife Peg (Katey Sagal) and spoiled children Bud (David Faustino) and Kelly (Christina Applegate). Al was a love child of Ralph Kramden and Archie Bunker, his hand permanently down his pants, forever crafting a new, ironclad get-rich-quick scheme or bemoaning his creeping middle age. He and Peg are, needless to say, no role models. Bud struggles to remember which parent had told him it is always good to be good to others, and draws a blank from both of them:

"Must've been *Cosby*, then." For all its vaunted truth-telling, *The Cosby Show* practiced a politesse notably absent from this remarkably consistent one-note symphony of vulgarity.

None of these shows had the heft or resonance of *Roseanne*, but collectively they formed a flank of sitcoms devoted to repelling the urbane, urbanist, gang's-all-here tendency of the 1990s sitcom, epitomized by *Seinfeld* and *Friends*. These were shows about families, their boorishness worn proudly as a badge of relatability and ordinariness.

Much of *Roseanne* offers affliction as a fresh kind of comfort, retaining the format of the classic sitcom while emptying it of its easy solutions. Roseanne sidles up to her husband after Becky's kitchen table outburst in "Terms of Estrangement" and slyly insists that her daughter is entirely mistaken—she *would* have the guts to tell the truth about the family's disastrous financial choices. Roseanne offers a brand of consolation whose tone belied its content. As Roseanne mocks her husband in his moment of travail, perhaps it would be wisest for us to return to the very beginning of *Roseanne*, and bear witness to the method of attack that had allowed *Roseanne* to craft this moment of pain as humor, humor as pain.

Created by Matt Williams and originally called *Life and Stuff* (its title indicative of its weary, shrugging attitude), the show was transformed by producers Marcy Carsey and Tom Werner (who had also been responsible for *The Cosby Show*) into a vehicle for Barr, then a successful stand-up comedian with an HBO special. Roseanne had been a Denver housewife who belatedly discovered stand-up comedy, adopting the persona of a proudly outspoken "domestic goddess": "A lot of people say I'm not feminine. Well, they can suck my dick."

In her stand-up routines, Roseanne was disarmingly honest about sensitive issues like her weight and the everyday indignities of blue-collar American life. Barr was convinced that in transforming *Life and Stuff* into *Roseanne*, the show had gone from being Williams's to her own, unimaginable without her own pointed worldview. Williams would have argued that by tempering her excesses and creating a fully formed domestic sphere for her to inhabit, he had created the opportunity for Roseanne to shine.

From its debut in the fall of 1988, *Roseanne* established that its take on the family sitcom would differ notably from its ostensible rivals. This was family life as combat, a war of all against all. "Are you ever sorry we got married?" Dan asks Roseanne in the first scene of the show's first episode, a sitcom softball if there ever was one. But like *The Cosby Show*, *Roseanne* uses an easy sitcom teaching moment to underscore its own idiosyncratic take on the form. Cliff stifles Theo's heartfelt ode to ordinariness, and Roseanne smiles genially at her husband and tells him she regrets their marriage "every second of my life!"

As it was on-screen, so it was offscreen; Roseanne was furious that Williams received sole creator's credit on the show. She bickered with Williams, Carsey, and Werner from the outset, pushing Williams out (he would go on to oversee *Home Improvement*). Roseanne pledged to fire much of Williams's staff when her show hit number one in the ratings, and followed through on her threat. "This is no fucking character!" she yelled at a producer while threatening her with a pair of scissors. "This is my show, and I created it— not Matt, and not Carsey-Werner, and not ABC." Relentless squabbling also drove off *Roseanne*'s second head writer, Jeff Harris, who departed with a full-page ad in *Variety* that announced, "I have chosen not to return to the show next season. Instead, my wife and I have decided to share a vacation in the relative peace and quiet of Beirut." Roseanne was the ultimate winner of her battles with the show's writing staff, with ambiguous results for the long-term health of *Roseanne*.

In a later episode, a coworker asks Roseanne if she has ever been married. "Yeah," she responds, "and it kept dragging on and on." (The real-life Roseanne, meanwhile, married and divorced twice during the series' run, including to occasional supporting star Tom Arnold.) Roseanne and Dan struggle with their children, too. Becky is first a prim suck-up and then a white-trash princess married to slacker king Mark; Darlene is a tomboy-turned-misanthrope; DJ is just a weirdo. None of the kids are success stories, particularly. Nor do they fit the whiz-or-scamp dialectic of the sitcom family. The Conner children are too strange, too oddly delinquent to be comfortably slotted into a preordained TV category.

Roseanne and Dan are reluctant caretakers, their kids a burden as much as a blessing. And then there are the Conners' surrogate children: Roseanne's needy, pushy sister Jackie and the two Healy boys, the unimpressive Mark and his soft-spoken brother David (Johnny Galecki, later a star of *The Big Bang Theory*), who end up marrying Becky and Darlene, respectively. Even David, neglected by his mother, is only reluctantly welcomed into the family: "We don't let anybody grow up here unless we're forced to by law," Roseanne insists.

Roseanne's quintessential punch line is a nasty crack delivered by one family member at the expense of another. Dan, accused by his wife of being a good-for-nothing, offers to fix dinner for the family. Roseanne, knowing a juicy setup when she hears one, zings him: "Oh, but honey! You just fixed dinner three years ago!" On another occasion, Roseanne insists on leaving the kids at home and having a second honeymoon in Las Vegas. "You want to just take off and leave the kids?" asks Dan, incredulous. "Yes, Dan," Roseanne responds, belaboring the obvious, "that's all I've ever wanted!" Roseanne and Jackie scheme about a Halloween prank to put a good scare into Dan, and Jackie suggests telling him that Roseanne is pregnant. Taken aback, Roseanne responds, "I don't want to *kill* him."

Dan comes home, rattled by a close call at work, and is disappointed by his children's meager response to his brush with death. "You were sitting in a porta-crapper that got nailed by a wrecking ball. I didn't take one shot. Now *that* is love," the wisecracking Darlene argues. Once, Roseanne facetiously argues, all Becky had wanted in life was to see her parents dead. With her boyfriend in the picture, "Now that's not good enough for her. Now she's gotta have a car, too." Family harmony is a kind of prison sentence, with Roseanne, and by extension the Conners, the only ones honest enough to acknowledge its torments. In one memorable scene from the show's first season, they bicker playfully over splitting up the family. "I'd leave you the kids," warns Roseanne. "You wouldn't," says Dan. "I'd give 'em to Jackie," she suggests. "Hell, even I don't hate her that much," argues Dan.

Roseanne—show and character alike—coasts in the intermediate zone between viciousness and geniality. The show's opening credits conclude with Roseanne's trademark cackle, a staccato burst of amusement at her own plainspoken daring. Roseanne is tart-tongued but not mean, precisely, and it is this ever-familiar burst of laughter that is a marker of her simultaneous desire to tell it like it is and to soften the blow with kindness. In her family life, the same principle holds. Roseanne and Dan, struggling with letting Becky bring her "punk" boyfriend home to live with them, deliberate over what kind of parents they are, rejecting the hippie "live and let live" model as well as its obverse: "We ain't Robert Young and Jane Wyatt, either." This was most assuredly not *Father Knows Best*, and yet the endless bickering and squabbling and backbiting that are *Roseanne*'s very oxygen are also its proofs of that familiar sitcom emotion: love.

Like any family sitcom worth its salt, *Roseanne* imparts home-cooked wisdom, bite-size lessons to be chewed over and consumed by its audience. But *Roseanne* prefers to keep its lecturing to a minimum, tackling familiar sitcom topics from its own distinctly warped perspective. In "A Stash from the Past," the Conners face what is perhaps the quintessential sitcom-family dilemma of the era. Roseanne stumbles across a baggie of marijuana while cleaning the house and is convinced it belongs to one of her children. Her sister Jackie suggests getting Dan in a good mood before breaking the news to him, and Roseanne bristles. "Jackie, I hardly have the time to get Dan all liquored up, have sex with him, and make s'mores!" David is the first suspect called in, and his facade of never having touched drugs collapses under Roseanne's interrogation: "Me? No! Of course not! I would never! . . . Twice." Dan observes Roseanne's impromptu investigation with a beatific smile. "Only one thing wrong," he tells her. "This is your pot, Roseanne." He then collapses in a mock-junkie stupor. "I think I would remember hiding pot in the house," Roseanne huffily insists. "Not if you were stoned at the time!" Dan triumphantly concludes.

The three adults proceed to smoke the pot themselves, gathering in Roseanne and Dan's bathroom to get high. Everyone proceeds to get wildly paranoid. Jackie is all alone in the world, hiding out in the Conners' tub. She has no boyfriend, no family of her own: "It's just me and my ganja." Dan, meanwhile, is having no fun at all. "Were we ever really stupid enough to enjoy this?" he wonders. In the final scene, David insists that he is too smart to turn into a drug-addled "useless zombie," as the three responsible adults sit around the table in a woozy heap. David reaches into the fridge and pulls out one empty carton after another, the remnants, presumably, of a pot-fueled munchies binge. Drugs are bad, just like Cliff Huxtable told us, but *Roseanne* is ill-inclined to practice what it preaches. To be more precise, it prefers to demonstrate rather than lecture. *Roseanne*'s characters are not role models.

Let us begin with the physical evidence gathered before us. Roseanne and Dan Conner are—let us not mince words here—two of the fattest sitcom protagonists ever to grace the small screen. Ralph Kramden had been tubby, to be sure, and Homer Simpson has an inexhaustible fondness for doughnuts, but Roseanne and Dan inhabit an entirely new realm of portliness. Their very lack of Hollywood polish—Roseanne's modified mullet, Dan's hefty beer belly—is a guarantee of realism. "Food's the one luxury we can afford," Dan notes, and the proof is in their air of comfortable dishevelment. If this show would allow its two main characters to be anything but svelte, it indicated that perhaps the remainder of *Roseanne* would be similarly devoid of traditional television trimness. The unimpressive lighting and camera work serve a similar purpose. The show's production values are roughly on par with the Conners' decor, its artlessness hinting at *Roseanne*'s devotion to other, less surface attributes.

The promise of Barr and Goodman's lumpy bodies is underscored by the sets themselves, which are impromptu shrines to bad taste: ugly carpets, uglier sofas, an array of gruesome knickknacks that make the *Cheers* bar look downright elegant. There is even a poster of dogs playing poker on the wall, in case anyone missed the point. Inverting the traditional sitcom aesthetic, the Conners looked not as we wanted to be but as we were. Roseanne in particular is the guru of the hidden class distinctions of American life. In the episode "Home-Ec," she takes Darlene's class to the supermarket to give them a lesson in shopping and pauses at the deli counter to ask each girl to select a cut of meat. First, though, a question: "What does your dad do for a living?" Rib eye or hamburger was not a matter of taste; it was a question of economics. Vulgar Marxism was now suitable subject matter for prime-time network programming. It was also a reflection of the marked contrast between the proudly blue-collar Roseanne and her mostly Harvard-educated writing staff, whose head writer once famously required an explanation of a reference in a script to "lunch meat."

The Conners are too wise ever to be yokels but self-aware enough to know that others might confuse them for hicks. Dan in particular regularly lapses into an oafish face designed to embarrass his children, jutting out his chin, rolling back his lip, and rounding and elongating all his words, as if in unconscious anticipation of *The Simpsons'* Cletus the Slack-Jawed Yokel. *Roseanne* is smart about being stupid, its best jokes emerging out of its awareness of its characters' limitations. And Goodman is the show's secret weapon. As good as Roseanne is—at least before the show veers off a cliff—Goodman is her ideal partner, always game for a prank or a new two-handed riff, existing on the fine edge between working stiff and comic wizard.

The Conners also sound little like the other, perfect families on TV. Their wide, flat vowels and faulty grammar practically scream Middle America—fictitious Lanford, Illinois, to be specific—another constant reminder that this was decidedly not those familiar television strongholds of Los Angeles and New York. Moreover, the Conners are the rare television family actually engaged in that most popular, and least seen, of American family activities—watching TV. When Dan wonders if Roseanne will quit her job to keep an eye on teenage delinquent Darlene, she angrily responds, "No, Dan, I'm going to put her on top of the television so *you* can watch her all day!"

The Conners show their love by zinging each other, but approximately eighteen minutes into each episode, there will be an emotional turning point—a revelation, a confrontation, a conversation—and they pull together once more, united against the fates and the unrestrained harshness of a world that seems perversely devoted to punishing the Conners. Dan summons his courage and has the dreaded sex talk with Darlene. Roseanne confronts Jackie with her fears about her sister joining the police force. Jackie reveals that her boyfriend, Fisher (Matt Roth), beat her, and Dan silently marches out the door, intent on settling matters with his fists. Each turning

point advances the plot slightly, usually setting the table for the next episode's conflict, turning point, and resolution.

If this style sounds at all familiar, *Roseanne* is only too aware. For its
sixth-season opener, *Roseanne* invites soap opera stalwarts Luke and Laura
from *General Hospital* to stop by Roseanne's diner so that Dan can revisit
all of the preceding season's drama. "Seems like every week, something else
is happening to us," she observes. *Roseanne* is the sitcom as soap opera, its
occasional overindulgence in the surprise twists and open-ended resolutions
of the soap tempered by its essential devotion to its own brand of sardonic
humor. *Roseanne* would eventually be consumed by its own hubris, becoming, by its later seasons, the illogical-plot-twist-driven, visually depthless
soap it had once mocked. The show knew it, too. "My sister and my mother
are fighting over the same guy?" Roseanne exclaims after one particularly
absurd plot development. "The only thing left for this family is cannibalism."

The show is also an accidental documentary record of Roseanne's shifting hairstyles, weight fluctuations, and name changes—Roseanne Barr to
Roseanne Arnold to just plain Roseanne. Roseanne's trademark mullet
eventually gives way to a sleeker bob, and her weight balloons and plunges
at semiregular intervals. You can usually guess how far along into the show's
run any specific episode of *Roseanne* might be by how much effort seems to
have gone into her hairdo. Most other shows devoted to a single star strived
for a sense of timelessness. With or without Little Ricky, in New York or
L.A. or Connecticut, Lucy Ricardo is always the same. Roseanne, by comparison, is in a constant turmoil of change.

As *Roseanne* ages, it grows increasingly conscious of the medium to
which it owes its existence. In seventh season's "Couch Potatoes," the Conners are selected as a Nielsen family, their TV-watching habits determining
the audience ratings. In desacralized America, where television is the last
object of worship, this is an honor above all others. "Time to down a sixer
and help shape the culture of America," Dan says. (Would the Conners
watch *Roseanne*? One would presume so.) When DJ bristles at Roseanne's
insistence that the family watch only PBS and educational programs, complaining, "You're making me hate TV," Roseanne recoils in shock: "Hey,

don't you ever say that. Not even in jest." *Roseanne*'s bizarre eighth season—about which more momentarily—ends with a violent knockdown fight between Roseanne and Dan. Dan upends the coffee table, and Roseanne responds by destroying the television set—so intimate, so taboo an action that the show is initially reluctant to show us the damage.

Roseanne's anxiety about her place in television history grows as well. In later seasons, the series regularly summons the ghosts of sitcom past in order to place itself within the tradition and solidify its bid for television immortality. In the clip show "All About Rosey," Roseanne hosts the Sitcom Mom Welcome Wagon in her kitchen, offering the surreal sight of June Cleaver, Weezie Jefferson, and Norma Arnold of *The Wonder Years* gathered around the table, fondly reminiscing about their favorite *Roseanne* episodes. Roseanne is the anti-June, slyly invoking her own slightly dinged take on *Leave It to Beaver*: "I'm just as wholesome as any of you. I ain't the one who named my kid Beaver."

When June asks what "reefer" might be, referencing "A Stash from the Past," Roseanne suggests she ask Eddie Haskell. And when Roseanne whispers her annual salary into June's ear, June exclaims, "I'd make out with a chick for that kind of dough." This is all solidly in television's tradition of summoning has-been stars to poke fun at their congealed reputations, but there is something subtler happening here, too. Roseanne is placing herself at the tail end of a tradition of sitcom mothers that began with June Cleaver, drawing attention to all that had changed in forty years. Her character still raised children, still ministered to her husband, but she also had her own career. The show, Roseanne made sure to point out, was named after her. And she got all the best lines.

Later on, as *Roseanne* was rapidly, thoroughly heading off the rails, it devoted an entire episode to reimagining itself as a *Beaver*-esque 1950s sitcom called *That's Our Rosey*, and most of another to depositing Roseanne and Dan in famous sitcoms past, including *The Mary Tyler Moore Show* and *That Girl*. In *That's Our Rosey*, Dan is now a harried office worker, his fedora pushed perilously back on his head, worrying over that goshdarn Anderson account. Dangerous Mark is now a sweater-wearing letterman type. Rosey gets through the day, rescuing her children from their hijinks and salvaging that pesky Anderson account, with the assistance of Veritol, a magic potion that is essentially alcohol in a prescription bottle. Like Lucy with her Vitameatavegamin, Rosey gets sloshed in a socially prescribed fashion. The sitcom tradition is simultaneously upheld and trashed, its pieties trotted out so that *Roseanne* can tread all over them in its muddy boots.

The last two seasons of *Roseanne* are a master class in the ways in which a beloved show can betray its audience by staying true to its own wildly malfunctioning internal compass. *Roseanne* veers drastically away from the domestic sphere to become a series of fantasy set pieces: Roseanne wrestling with terrorists atop a train, Jackie falling in love with a Moldavian prince, the family appearing on *The Jerry Springer Show*. Dan has a heart attack at Darlene's wedding. The Conners win a $100 million lottery jackpot. No longer a frumpy housewife with a forked tongue, Roseanne is now a superstar in her own right. The show melds Roseanne Conner with Roseanne, media icon; it is as if some of her real-world fame has bled into the world of Lanford, without any suitable explanation for the sudden uptick in interest in the doings of a now-wealthy suburban housewife. Roseanne summarizes recent plot developments in the ninth and final season of the show: "It's almost like some insane woman made it all up." It was.

Late *Roseanne* aims for a casual brand of surrealism, in which its workaday characters are thrust into scenarios far beyond their ken. But in truth, there was simply no need for such elaborate and uncharacteristic shenanigans. For what could be more surreal, more casually unsettling, than the peculiar saga of Becky Conner, like Buñuel's *That Obscure Object of Desire* brought to Middle America? After her dramatic confrontation with her parents in "Terms of Estrangement" and her marriage to Mark, Becky, first played with snotty panache by Lecy Goranson, disappears for the remainder of the fifth season and the start of the sixth. When she returns, Becky is suddenly played by another actress, Sarah Chalke (soon to go on to stardom on *Scrubs*). "Our daughter Becky left home for a year and a half, and when she came back, we barely recognized her," Dan complains, to audible whoops of mirth from the studio audience. The family gathers around the

TV to watch a rerun of *Bewitched*, and Roseanne expresses disbelief at the show's artistic choices: "I cannot believe they replaced that Darrin."

Goranson eventually returns for *Roseanne*'s eighth season, and Chalke takes over for the ninth. Matters become so convoluted that *Roseanne* resorts to the kind of preshow announcement common to Broadway shows: in tonight's episode, the role of Becky will be played by Sarah Chalke. The alternation of Goranson and Chalke is more a product of circumstance than choice, but the end result is perhaps the single strangest character in sitcom history, as if Dick York and Dick Sargent alternated episodes as Darrin.

There was only partial redemption to be offered by *Roseanne*'s final episode, "Into That Good Night," which undid much of the bizarre plot developments of the final two seasons. *Roseanne* is recast as shadow autobiography, its excesses merely a reflection of the fantasies endemic to television. Though none of this undoes the colossal time suck that is late-period *Roseanne*, the plot twist returns the series to its plainspoken working-class roots just in time for a final farewell.

As the camera swirls around the dining room table, taking in the Conners and their friends eating dinner, Roseanne delivers a monologue in voiceover. This story, it turns out, is just that. Frustrated housewife Roseanne has taken the elements of her own life and spun out a story more to her liking. There was no lottery payday. Darlene is actually married to Mark and Becky to David, but Roseanne preferred them paired off with each other's husbands and switched them around.

Dan raises his eyebrows and smirks at the camera, and when the camera cuts back to him, we take in an empty chair. "I lost Dan last year when he had his heart attack," says Roseanne. Sentimental piano fills the soundtrack as the scene fades. Roseanne now appears alone, framed by a black backdrop. "He's still the first thing I think about when I wake up, and the last thing I think about before I go to sleep. I miss him." Roseanne is now a grieving wife, and *Roseanne*—or at least the baroque late-season *Roseanne* this finale plays off of—is the work of an artist intent on revising her own experience to suit her fantasies. The stories are her cushion after Dan's death. "I began writing about having all the money in the world," she notes in voiceover, "and I imagined myself going to spas and swanky New York parties just like the people on TV, where nobody has any real problems, and everything's solved within thirty minutes. I tried to imagine myself as Mary Richards, Jeannie, That Girl, but I was so angry I was more like a female Steven Seagal, wanting to fight the whole world."

Realism crept into the sitcom stealthily, infiltrating its tightly guarded panic rooms of filtered experience. *Roseanne* was the beginning of the charge—or perhaps just a peak in the perpetual challenge of reinventing the sitcom in slightly less stilted fashion. It burrowed into the familiar sphere of the female-driven situation comedy—that wonderland of Mary and Jeannie and That Girl—and emerged with something grubbier, dumpier, and less starry-eyed than its predecessors. Like its colleague and compatriot *The Cosby Show*, *Roseanne* widened the filter of the sitcom, expanding the scope of whose stories they could tell—and whom they could tell them to. It was more than just the economy; it was a way of seeing the world.

14

The Simpsons

"22 Short Films About Springfield"

April 14, 1996 ▪ Fox

Milhouse, do you ever think about the people in those cars?" Bart Simpson and his trusty sidekick stand atop an overpass, gazing down at moving traffic on the highway below. "There must be thousands of great stories out there," he adds. Milhouse, notably unmoved by Bart's philosophical digression, squeezes mustard out of a bottle and onto a passing convertible. Milhouse may not have noticed, but in introducing "22

Short Films About Springfield," a wildly inventive episode from its seventh season, *The Simpsons* reveals its most deeply held intentions. Having begun as a trifle about a dysfunctional family, an animated update of *The Flintstones*, *The Simpsons* kept expanding its frame, venturing farther and farther beyond the Simpson family home until there it stood, atop an urban overpass, taking in everyone and everything under its wing. *The Simpsons* is about Springfield—i.e., America.

When considering the show's longevity and dependability, it is perhaps best to revisit Bart's exchange with the Comic Book Guy after a disappointing episode of *Itchy & Scratchy*, *The Simpsons'* show-within-a-show doppelganger and all-purpose springboard for consideration of its own medium. "Worst. Episode. Ever," Comic Book Guy sneers in his inimitable clipped nerd-brogue. "Rest assured that I was on the Internet within minutes registering my disgust throughout the world." Bart bristles at his presumption. "What? They've given you thousands of hours of entertainment for free! What could they possibly owe *you*? I mean, if anything, *you* owe *them*!"

We do, all of us, owe *The Simpsons* for its remarkable reign as not only the longest-running sitcom in television history but also one of the most consistent, and for its first decade or so, perhaps, quite simply, the best. "We should thank our lucky stars that they're still putting on a program of this caliber after so many years," Bart's sister Lisa Simpson says of *Itchy & Scratchy*, and she and her brother gaze directly out at the screen, as if to challenge us to disagree. Were we really planning to voice any complaints about the sitcom that had likely brought more aggregate hours of pleasure to its audience than any other in the history of television? No, we were not.

The show began inauspiciously enough, as a recurring short on the sketch comedy series *The Tracey Ullman Show* (Fox, 1987–90). The Simpsons were squiggly, jittery caricatures—wiseacre children Bart and Lisa, baby Maggie, long-suffering wife Marge, sullen, sad-sack husband Homer. They were the creations of cartoonist Matt Groening, an alternative-newspaper fixture with his comic strip *Life in Hell*. Groening had initially been hired to provide short animal cartoons for *The Tracey Ullman Show*. When producers voiced concern about copyright issues related to using Groening's

Life in Hell characters, he came back the next day with a new set of figures sketched on a piece of paper: the goggle-eyed, overbite-sporting Simpsons. *Tracey Ullman* was not long for this world, but the Simpsons were so popular that they received a spinoff series of their own. It was that rarest of television commodities: a prime-time animated series.

From the start, *The Simpsons* (Fox, 1989–) was a contradiction in terms: an animated series devoted to realism, a family show that also took wild flights of fancy, a domestic sitcom able to range widely through history and pop culture. It was a children's cartoon whose foremost creators were veterans of the sitcom. James L. Brooks had helped create *The Mary Tyler Moore Show*, *Rhoda*, and *Taxi*; Sam Simon, the unsung genius of *The Simpsons'* early seasons, had been a writer and producer for *Taxi* and *Cheers*. Groening invented the Simpsons, but Brooks, and especially Simon, invented *The Simpsons*. Groening was the show's official front man, its foremost media presence, but *The Simpsons'* open secret was that its creator was not much involved in the day-to-day production of the show. "The thing about Matt is that he did supply the template for the show. And that's undeniable," said show writer Wallace Wolodarsky. "Sam was able to take that template and make it into an even bigger world and really flesh it out with characters. He brought a broader perspective to it. He made it bigger than just the family."

Early *Simpsons* episodes are rooted in the dysfunctional antics of its family. Homer regularly neglects Marge and throttles the irrepressible Bart. The family goes to a therapist and turns a trust-building exercise into an opportunity to give each other some nasty electric shocks. The Simpsons were not, as noted television theorist George H. W. Bush put it, the Waltons. Like the Conners, they were proudly flawed, their love and their rancor struggling for supremacy. But the show, innovative as it was in this earliest phase, was unsatisfied with life as a family sitcom.

By season seven, "22 Short Films" was hurtling headlong through *The Simpsons'* Springfield, named by Groening after the hometown of *Father Knows Best*. (The episode title, meanwhile, is borrowed from the film *32 Short Films About Glenn Gould*.) Written collectively by the *Simpsons* staff, including future *Office* showrunner Greg Daniels, it is composed of brilliantly interlinked, lightning-fast encounters among the series' wildly disparate cast of recurring characters. As it zigs and zags from character to character and from scene to scene, much of the episode is couched in the language of television, with individual segments given titles and theme songs like imaginary stand-alone sitcoms. Convenience store clerk Apu Nahasapeemapetilon stars in the latest installment of "The Jolly Bengali," convinced by a friend to let down his hair and leave the store. "For the next five minutes," he crows, "I'm going to party like it's on sale for $19.99!" He dashes to a party, where he eats a hot dog raw, drinks a beer, hits on a woman, and takes her into an empty cabana. He emerges smoking a cigarette, his clothing disheveled, knocks all the partygoers into the pool, and makes it back to the store with a minute to spare.

School principal Seymour Skinner and his boss Superintendent Chalmers star in the slapstick "Skinner and the Superintendent." Skinner seeks to pass off a sack of Krustyburgers—from the fast-food emporium of Bart's hero and merchandising inspiration Krusty the Clown—as home cooking, telling Superintendent Chalmers they are an old family recipe for "steamed hams." We peek in at the hillbilly-themed segment "Cletus the Slack-Jawed Yokel," whose dumb protagonist and sneakily catchy theme song appear to be beamed in from some alternate universe where *The Beverly Hillbillies* still dominates the Nielsen ratings.

Later, the Bumblebee Man—another Springfield TV star, already familiar from Homer's restless channel flipping—arrives home and tells his wife, in Spanish, about his horrible day on set: attacked by a woodpecker on a nude beach, electrocuted by strands of pasta, knocked flat by a giant baseball. After being pelted by a torrent of oranges, he leaps onto the chandelier and pulls down the kitchen ceiling. His wife serves him with divorce papers. *"Ay, donde esta mi tequila?"* he moans. We are touring not only Springfield but the television dial: bad sitcoms, rural yukfests straight out of the 1960s, Spanish-language variety shows.

We are whizzing between stories faster than we can keep up, the speed more essential than the plot itself. Do-gooder extraordinaire Lisa Simpson steps out of the house to recycle one of her father's beer cans, and Bart zooms past on his skateboard, nonchalantly tossing his gum into her hair. After a series of futile gum-removal tricks leaves her hair slathered with peanut butter and mayonnaise, a swarm of bees surrounds her, and now we take a bee's-eye perspective, swooping through Springfield until we spot nuclear-plant owner Montgomery Burns and his faithful factotum Waylon Smithers on their tandem bicycle.

Burns petulantly wonders why they have crawled to a halt, and Smithers explains that he has a bee in his eye: "I'm allergic to bee stings. They cause me to, uh, die." Burns, thrust into action, pledges to get Smithers to the ER the only way he knows how: by verbally browbeating his second-in-command until he puts his feet back on the pedals and bikes them to the hospital.

Bartender Moe reminds his most dependable customer, Barney Gumble, that he had sent away to NASA for a calculation of his bar tab. As Barney chuckles, Moe flips through the printout, coming up with a total: $70 billion. "No, wait, wait, wait," Moe corrects himself, "that's for the *Voyager* spacecraft. Your tab's $14 billion." As Barney takes in the news, perpetual recidivist Snake holds up the bar. Moe flees for a hidden safe room, and Snake helps himself to the contents of the till, to Moe's chagrin. "Goodbye, student loan payments!" Snake exults.

Later, we return to Krustyburger to the tune of a *Pulp Fiction*–style surf-rock ditty and the sound of a familiar conversation. "It's the little differences," says Lou, taking on the John Travolta role as he tells his colleagues Chief Wiggum and Eddie about a recent trip to a McDonald's in neighboring Shelbyville. "Well, in McDonald's you can buy a Krustyburger with cheese, right, but they don't call it a Krustyburger with cheese." *The Simpsons* is expert in its pastiche, capable of transforming a Tarantino film into source material the same way earlier episodes had *Goodfellas*, *King Kong*, *Cape Fear*, *Citizen Kane*—the list goes on and on.

The Simpsons was self-referential television with a vengeance. Everything was fodder for appropriation; everything could be integrated into the world of Springfield. *Fantasia* could be transformed into an *Itchy & Scratchy* cartoon. *All the President's Men* could be repurposed as a top-secret investigation into the Springfield mayoral campaign. Homer could imagine himself a Mafia don in a Little Italy straight out of *The Godfather Part II*, his vassals paying obeisance with offerings of his favorite foodstuffs. ("That's-a nice-a doughnut," Homer thanks one local.)

Hence yet another major echo of *Pulp Fiction* in "22 Short Films": Chief Wiggum, done with lunch, picks up some doughnuts for dessert and is run over by Snake. Creepy gun-store owner Herman points a shotgun at the two men, imprisoning them in his store/lair. Meanwhile, a doughnut tumbles through a grate and is whisked through the sewer to a spot under the Flanders home, where Reverend Lovejoy directs his dog to "do your dirty sinful business" on his least favorite parishioner Ned Flanders's lawn.

Milhouse and his father, wandering into the store to use the bathroom, free the ball-gagged Wiggum and Snake when Milhouse accidentally knocks out Herman with a mace. School bully Nelson finally laughs at the wrong person when an enormously tall man in a miniature car unfolds his limbs from the driver's seat, holds Nelson up by the head, and parades him down the street after pantsing him. "Hey, everybody, look at this! It's that boy who laughs at everyone. Let's laugh at him!"

Did you follow all of that? Any of it? *The Simpsons* rewards viewers for their diligence in remembering walk-on characters and tossed-off lines from earlier episodes or spotting passing references to movies and TV shows. After seven seasons and 149 episodes, the show also leans on our familiarity with its enormous array of secondary characters. (By some counts, the show has boasted about two hundred over the course of its run, a staggering number by traditional sitcom standards.) Thus, "22 Short Films" is the epitome of *The Simpsons'* universe not only because of its remarkable, interlocking bicycle-spoke narrative (shades of *Seinfeld*'s ability to intertwine seemingly unrelated anecdotes into an airtight whole) but also in its gargantuan supporting cast. What had begun as an intimate family show—Homer and Marge and the kids—expanded to take in a whole universe of eccentric television personalities, police officers, criminals, lawyers, doctors, clergymen, and disco studs.

Many of *The Simpsons'* most memorable episodes, like "22 Short Films," were turned over to supporting characters, at last given their chance to flourish in a star turn of their own. Kwik-E-Mart owner Apu is an illegal alien dreaming of American citizenship in the touching "Much Apu About Nothing." Homer is moved by Apu's plea for tolerance: "You must love this country more than I love a cold beer on a hot Christmas morning." (As Homer might say, this line works on so many levels. Homer's quiet awe allows us to feel some of Apu's pent-up emotion about his adopted country at the same time that it is a) about beer, and b) completely nonsensical.) Chief Wiggum arrives at the Springfield waterfront with orders for his officers: "All right, men, here's your order of deportations: first, we'll be rounding up your tired, then your poor, then your huddled masses yearning to breathe free."

Homer's friend and fellow barfly Barney Gumble reinvents himself as a cinematic auteur in the film-festival episode "A Star Is Burns," premiering his sensitive black-and-white study of alcoholism to rapturous applause. "Don't cry for me," he forlornly concludes, "I'm already dead." (Homer, once again, is momentarily transformed, pledging never to drink again, before being accosted by a beer vendor: "Beer here." Homer perks up: "I'll take ten.") Troy McClure, habitué of instructional films everywhere, steps out from his modest big-screen perch to woo Marge's sister in "A Fish Called Selma," marrying her before falling prey to his unspecified addictions to intimacy with salmon.

The Simpsons' subversion of the traditional sitcom order is so extensive and so widespread that it's easy to overlook its more pious tendencies. It is, contra *Seinfeld*'s unofficial motto, a show with both hugging *and* learning. Many, if not most, *Simpsons* episodes are carefully constructed morality plays, offering a tidy lesson, if one occasionally smeared by Bart's undimmed amorality and Homer's mountainous idiocy. Often its implied message is hidden by its stated one, with Homer in particular offering an array of warped life lessons to his children. "No matter how good you are at something," he tells Bart after being booted from the company softball team by his boss, Mr. Burns, who has imported a team of all-star ringers, "there's always about a million people who are better than you." "Gotcha," Bart nods. "Can't win, don't try." The Simpsons are perpetually tempted by the easy thing—a sultry country singer, a prized video game—but ultimately, often under the prodding of Marge, settle on doing the right thing.

In a way, however, the show's morality plays are themselves a rejection of the traditional sitcom order, the genre's lazy assurances that the easy thing is good enough. In one throwaway gag, Homer and the family watch a Garrison Keillor figure on TV, and Homer is enraged. He marches up to the TV and smacks it repeatedly, demanding improvement: "Be more funny!" *The Simpsons* said good enough wasn't, and the sitcom remade itself in its image, shamed into being better than it had been.

None of this would have seemed likely when *The Simpsons* debuted on Fox in 1989. Fox was then the fledgling fourth broadcast network, beginning to make a name for itself with programming like *Married . . . with Children* and the underrated *Get a Life* (Fox, 1990–92), which starred Chris Elliott as a thirtysomething paperboy living with his parents (with his mother played by Elinor Donahue, daughter Betty on *Father Knows Best*) and momentarily enamored of a series of ludicrous careers such as male modeling. The Simpsons were initially intended as an animated version of *Married*'s Bundy family. But animation had potential that the live-action sitcom lacked. Television, in its classical three-camera or modern single-camera incarnation, had crafted a style that was a non-style, invisible and unobtrusive. The camera never drew attention to itself, because to do so would be to damage television's intimate relation to its viewers. *The Simpsons* embraces a distinctly cinematic (if obviously artificial) language of crane shots and zooms and pans heretofore absent from most prior sitcoms. Only an animated series could be capable of such technical refinement. As a result, the show feels roomier and more elegant than its sitcom compatriots.

More than that, the ease of execution allowed the show's writers and producers to dream bigger than the sitcom had previously been able to. Unencumbered by the real world's limitations, *The Simpsons* could go anywhere it imagined, could transform its characters in any manner it desired. The credit, according to the show's writers, belonged chiefly to Sam Simon. "Sam opened our eyes to the possibilities of what an animated show could be, which is to say we could go anywhere in the world, we could do any-thing, and that was incredibly liberating, coming from live action, because you were obviously limited by so much," said Wolodarsky. Simon was also responsible for assembling *The Simpsons'* remarkable writing staff, that leg-endary graduate colloquium of former *Harvard Lampoon* writers who trans-formed his vision for the show into twenty-two-minute reality.

"Cartoons don't have to be 100 percent realistic," Lisa sagely observes in one episode, the show proving her case by having a second Homer pass by just outside the window as he sits on his couch. The normal limitations of reality—how could a bald actor grow hair convincingly overnight? how to depict outer space?—held no brief here. And cartoons, as Homer notes on another occasion, "don't have any deep meaning. They're just stupid draw-ings that give you a cheap laugh." They were that, to be sure; *The Simpsons* was unashamed to reach for a laugh by having Homer scratch his butt or fall flat on his face. But they were also a medium astonishingly rich in unex-plored possibility. "What is *The Simpsons* but a hallucination of the sitcom?" wondered Groening in a 1990 interview.

No live-action sitcom would have been capable of pulling off a feat of the imagination the likes of "22 Short Films About Springfield." Location shooting, extended cinematic parodies, musical numbers, action sequences, fleets of extras and supporting players, even 3-D (in the episode "Treehouse of Horror VI")—all fell under the *Simpsons* rubric. ("I feel like I'm wasting a fortune just standing here," a 3-D Homer wryly observes.) Writer Conan O'Brien's revelatory, wildly unrealistic "Marge vs. the Monorail," from the show's fourth season, also expanded *The Simpsons'* world, as did the switch in animation studios from Klasky Csupo to the more limber Film Roman.

The Simpsons is an artificial reconstruction of a familiar form—mother, father, 2.5 children, living room—that is simultaneously far more and far less real than its predecessors. "TV families were always hugging and tack-ling issues," Bart says on the faux *Behind the Music*–style documentary epi-sode "Behind the Laughter." Marge follows up on Bart's point, positing her husband as the mastermind of *The Simpsons'* legacy: "Homer kept saying he could do a more realistic family show." This is a depiction of family in which the cartoon squiggles belie the familiar contours. The Simpsons are gloriously, perversely dysfunctional. They are also us.

In a way, Homer *was* the show's creator, as much as Groening or Simon or *The Simpsons'* unparalleled writing staff. If a series that has lasted for almost a quarter of a century and more than five hundred episodes can be said to have a fulcrum, it is in the subtle shift of focus in the early seasons of *The Simpsons*. In short, Bart Simpson gives way to Homer Simpson.

Bart's kid-friendly antics were the centerpiece of the *Tracey Ullman* sketches and the early stand-alone episodes. "I'm Bart Simpson," he challenges us. "Who the hell are you?" Bart's cool disdain for authority made him the breakout star of the show. *The Simpsons* was well aware of its own explosive popularity among the preteen set, the figure of Bart a semaphore directed at every rebellious twelve-year-old boy between Seattle and Sarasota. It was aware, as well, that Bart's enormous appeal, built atop a rickety edifice of catchphrases ("Don't have a cow, man!") and ubiquitous merchandising, was in danger of imminent collapse from overexposure. In one early episode, Homer insists that no self-respecting parade could include a float devoted to flash-in-the-pan stars without turning into a farce—as an enormous Bart Simpson balloon drifts unnoticed across his television screen. In "Bart Gets Famous," the show references Bart's legend even more directly, with the boy becoming a star after coining an accidental catchphrase on Krusty the Clown's show. Bart later chides his hack-comic hero for cashing in on tacky goods distinctly resembling his own: "How could you, Krusty? I'd never lend my name to an inferior product."

Homer, on the other hand, was originally a relative afterthought, glum and woebegone. The essential transition of *The Simpsons*, which took it from potential flash in the pan to sitcom legend, was turning Homer into the face of the show and an icon of indefatigable doltish energy. Look up "stupid" in the dictionary, and you'll find a picture of Homer. No, really—see "Homer Defined," season three, episode five.

"Bart the Daredevil," from the show's second season, is the iconic moment for *The Simpsons'* switchover from being a Bart-centric to a Homer-centric series. Homer dashes to the Springfield gorge to keep Bart from performing a dangerous skateboarding stunt. Father and son hug, sharing a heartfelt moment after Homer rescues Bart from harm. All the while, Homer, crouched on Bart's skateboard, begins drifting out of the shot and down the incline. As he sails over the gorge, Homer experiences a fleeting moment of glee, confident that he will land safely on the other side: "I'm king of the world!" No sooner said than Homer sinks, Wile E. Coyote style, into the crevice. (In fact, the sequence was the cause of a significant dispute between the writing staff and Groening, who insisted that *The Simpsons'* realism demanded that such a fall would seriously injure Homer.)

Homer crashes headfirst into every rock and tree branch and outcropping on his thudding journey to the bottom. He clangs into them all again as he is airlifted out of the gorge by helicopter to a waiting ambulance. The ambulance then slams into a tree, sending his stretcher shooting back into the depths of the gorge. A tender moment is undercut by inspired silliness. *The Simpsons* refuses to jettison its essential sweetness even as it mocks its own proclivities for sentimental resolutions. (The penny drops further in "Behind the Laughter," nine seasons later, when a clip of the gorge sequence is followed by footage of Homer in rehab after the accident, gulping painkillers. Perhaps now Matt Groening was satisfied.)

Homer was paradoxically enriched by the narrowing of his intellectual horizons. Other shows had leaned on stupidity as an easy punch line, a life raft in the middle of the vast sea of the sitcom. *The Simpsons* chose to view Homer's increased stupidity as an uncharted territory, to be explored at leisure. Knowing nothing, Homer could go everywhere: Lollapalooza, Australia, New York, college, the future, outer space. "Homer always felt to me like a bigger, dumber version of Ralph Kramden," said writer Wolodarsky, but the reconceived Homer may in fact be one part Ralph, loser with dreams of glory; one part Ward Cleaver, sitcom dad; and three parts doltish sitcom sidekick granted center stage. Homer searches under the couch for a missing peanut and stumbles on a twenty-dollar bill. Disappointed not to have found the peanut, Homer's brain informs him that "Twenty dollars can buy many peanuts." "Explain how," Homer asks, greedy for information. "Money can be exchanged for goods and services," his brain tells him, offering an introductory lesson in microeconomics pegged to Homer's set of interests.

For Homer, life is a television program, its boring moments mere commercials to be bypassed. Having hounded the dutiful, hard-working Frank Grimes to his death in the shockingly scabrous "Homer's Enemy" (perhaps the darkest and undoubtedly the most unyielding of all *Simpsons* episodes), Homer falls asleep at his funeral, drooling on his suit and sleepily calling out, "Change the channel, Marge." In another episode, Homer gets excited about attending his high school reunion to see all the old gang: Ralph Malph, and Potsie, and did he mention the Fonz? Marge gently reminds him that those are characters from *Happy Days*, but Homer's enthusiasm does not wane.

By the 1980s, the sitcom had mostly turned away from its early hints of self-awareness toward traditionalist series like *Cheers* and *The Cosby Show*. *The Simpsons* made self-awareness an essential component of its comic palette. "Some of the most creative stuff we write comes from just having the Simpsons watch TV," said longtime showrunner Al Jean. Premiering at roughly the same time as *Seinfeld* and *The Larry Sanders Show*, *The Simpsons* was the third leg of a tripod of 1990s television self-awareness and self-referentiality. (Its contemporary *Roseanne*, as previously mentioned, also tackled similar material, although somewhat less successfully.) What TV wanted, more than anything, was to talk about itself.

Moreover, whereas 1950s shows like *I Love Lucy* and *The Honeymooners* had hilariously mocked television tropes in general, *The Simpsons*, along with *Seinfeld*, were targeting sitcoms in particular—and particular sitcoms. In "$pringfield (or How I Learned to Stop Worrying and Love Legalized Gambling)," Homer trips over an ottoman in homage to that other great paternal klutz of the sitcom, Rob Petrie, and an unseen studio audience laughs uproariously, as if to remind us how far the sitcom has come from its humble origins. "Flaming Moe's," from the show's third season, finds Moe's sleepy bar turning into the Springfield version of Cheers. The perpetually sodden Barney is recast as Norm, greeting the bartender's setup line upon his entrance with a burp, and Moe is the thickheaded Sam to a newly introduced Diane figure.

Best of all is the skewering given Bill Cosby, whose Cliff Huxtable is expertly parodied ("They don't know what the *jazz* is all about!") in an episode devoted to the death of Lisa's friend and teacher, saxophonist Bleeding Gums Murphy. (*The Simpsons* had been placed head-to-head with *The Cosby Show* on Thursdays starting in 1990, and the character of Dr. Hibbert was introduced as a longer-running Cliff Huxtable parody.) After *The Simpsons'* expert burlesques, one could never watch the originals in quite the same way again. Its borrowing was inspired, paving the way for a new era of sitcoms—including not just animated compatriots like *South Park* and *Family Guy* but also live-action series like *Arrested Development* and *Community*—that sought inspiration in pop-cultural ephemera.

The bee stings and tandem bicycles of "22 Short Films" are the perfect expression of *The Simpsons'* quiet rebellion against the conformity of the 1990s sitcom. "When you and I were kids," *Simpsons* writer George Meyer told a *New Yorker* writer for a 2000 profile, "the average TV comedy was about a witch, or a Martian, or a goofy frontier fort, or a comical Nazi prisoner-of-war camp. That was the mainstream. Now the average comedy is about a bunch of people who hang around in some generic urban setting having conversations and sniping at each other. I remember watching, in the sixties, an episode of *Get Smart* in which some angry Indians were aiming a sixty-foot arrow at Washington, and Max said something like 'That's the second-biggest arrow I've ever seen,' and I thought, Oh, great, shows are just going to keep getting nuttier and nuttier. I never dreamed that television comedy would turn in such a dreary direction, so that all you would see is people in living rooms putting each other down."

For all its family-show leanings, *The Simpsons* is driven by the desire to shoot its second-biggest arrows in every direction—to manifest the inspired hilarity Meyer found in fantasy-oriented 1960s sitcoms. *The Simpsons* expanded into a realm of gleeful, frictionless nuttiness far more sophisticated and less infantile than its forebears: Homer chomping potato chips in space, Springfield consumed by lust for a useless monorail system, Bart bringing home a pet elephant.

And yet *The Simpsons'* default stance regarding television is one of ironic skepticism toward its promises of frictionless entertainment. "Lis'," Bart lectures his younger sister, who is bubbling with excitement for the TGIF lineup of family-friendly TV, "when you get a little older, you'll learn that Friday's just another day between NBC's Must-See Thursday and CBS's Saturday-night crap-o-rama." Homer flips channels and comes across an NBC promo: "Tonight, on *Wings* . . ." "Ah, who cares," sighs Homer, summing up, in three pithy words, eight seasons of indifferent audience response to that emblem of sitcom mediocrity.

Still, the show's characters devote themselves to watching TV with religious devotion. Marge's sisters, Patty and Selma, are loyalists of 1980s duct-tape warrior *MacGyver*, and Grandpa Abe Simpson and his fellow nursing-home cronies are passionate followers of Andy Griffith's legal eagle *Matlock*. "TV sucks," Bart says on another occasion, and Homer dramatically leans in, suddenly fierce: "I know you're upset right now, so I'll pretend you didn't say that." Homer, like Roseanne Conner, is a zealous defender of the medium that gave him life.

It was *The Simpsons* itself that gave life to the modern prime-time animated program. Before it there had been *The Flintstones* (ABC, 1960–66), itself an homage to *The Honeymooners*, and *The Jetsons* (ABC, 1962–63), but by resurrecting and defining the category, *The Simpsons* cast a long shadow over its descendants. The anxiety of influence was omnipresent, and the prevailing mood was, as one episode of *South Park* was revealingly titled, "Simpsons Already Did It." *Beavis and Butt-head* (MTV, 1992–97), *South Park* (Comedy Central, 1997–), *Daria* (MTV, 1997–2002), *Family Guy* (Fox, 1999–2002, 2005–), *King of the Hill* (Fox, 1997–2010), and the Groening-produced *Futurama* (Fox, 1999–2003; Comedy Central, 2009–2013) struggled to mark out territory not already claimed by their progenitor, with varying degrees of success. Coasting easily in *The Simpsons'* capacious wake, they would mostly transform themselves into pop-culture slot machines, paying off with an endless dribble of quarters imprinted with pictures of old TV shows and movies.

Each inheritor of *The Simpsons'* mantle picked one aspect of the original it could expand, or pilfer, or undermine. *South Park* amplifies *The Simpsons'* shock value, as if Bart Simpson were not only the series' protagonist but also its showrunner. Creators Matt Stone and Trey Parker are unapologetic flamethrowers, spewing fire at an array of bloated targets, from Barbra Streisand to the Church of Scientology. Their South Park, Colorado, is another microcosm of America, like Springfield, but one more informed by the excesses of celebrity. Metallica drummer Lars Ulrich—a noted opponent of illegal downloading of music—sobs by his pool in "Christian Rock Hard," unable to afford that new shark tank because of rampant piracy. Tom Cruise dashes into Stan's bedroom on a Scientologist quest in "Trapped in the Closet," and then locks himself in the closet when Stan has the temerity to compare his acting work unfavorably to "that guy who played Napoleon Dynamite." The remainder of the episode mostly consists of Stan and everyone else complaining, "Tom Cruise won't come out of the closet."

South Park's protagonists are like four Bart Simpsons let loose on an unsuspecting world, adorable prepubescent boys with filthy mouths and insatiable appetites for chaos and disorder. The remarkable Eric Cartman—one of the most indelible characters in sitcom history—is like Bart's untrammeled id, untempered by Marge or his own tardy conscience, fed by a steady diet of Cheesy Poofs. In "The Death of Eric Cartman," he believes himself to have died when his friends ignore him and lists some of his sins in the hopes of ascending to heaven; they include having taken a crap in the principal's purse—twice—and attempting to exterminate all the Jews.

Cartman is not to be trifled with. "Scott Tenorman Must Die," which echoes "Homer's Enemy" in its unyielding ferocity, has Cartman repeatedly falling prey to an older boy's pranks. He buys a shaving of Scott's pubic hair for ten dollars and is humiliated when Scott shows a video of Cartman on his knees, begging for his money back. Cartman tells his friends he is planning his revenge in typically crude fashion, training a pony to "bite off his wiener." Having planted this childish scheme as a ruse, he springs a more fiendish trap, having Scott's parents killed and feeding their corpses to him as part of a chili cook-off.

In the heartfelt "Kenny Dies," Cartman stumbles upon a cache of aborted fetuses, and after failing to sell them to research laboratories (he tells one potential client, in full salesman mode, "I'm just like the fetuses, Chuck, I wasn't born yesterday either,"), he pledges to save his pal Kenny from a rare disease. But, as is Cartman's wont, he has merely misled his friends, preferring to use fetal stem cells to clone his own Shakey's Pizza franchise. Cartman interrupts Kenny's funeral to announce that all he needs is one hundred more aborted babies to finish his kitchen.

South Park's animation is deliberately crude, its characters seemingly pasted together from mismatched pieces of construction paper, its motion an awkward, flat-footed shuffle. Denying itself the easy pleasures of pictorial beauty, it also denies the easy emotional attachments of other shows. For a while, Kenny would die in every episode. After setting up the mystery of Cartman's parentage for much of the first season, Parker and Stone summarily cancel the big reveal. Instead, we are given thirty minutes of nattering, farting Canadian caricatures Terrance and Phillip, whose aimlessness makes *South Park* seem like a model of concision in comparison.

Where *South Park* took up *The Simpsons'* challenge to shock and satirize, *Family Guy* is most enamored of its flashbacks and dream sequences, turning one arrow in *The Simpsons'* quiver into its primary weapon. Talking dog Brian wonders if a harrowing flight to Europe can get any worse, and is immediately stuck sitting next to *60 Minutes'* Andy Rooney and in front of Jerry Seinfeld, each of whom offer their pithy observations on flying.

Family Guy's best jokes are its throwaway ones. Brown, where Brian goes to complete his college degree, plays football against the Board of Education. Peter, coming across the reincarnated Jesus posing as a record-store clerk (he catches him by threatening to piss on the store's Amy Grant CDs), brings him to the White House to reenact the Marshall McLuhan scene from *Annie Hall* ("You know *nothing* of my work") with President George W. Bush.

Paterfamilias Peter Griffin is the designated Homer Simpson stand-in, another bumbling, well-meaning father who has laid in an inexhaustible supply of stupid. In the Y2K episode "Da Boom," Peter eats a year's supply of dehydrated meals in one go, washing it down with a glass of water. "Everyone leave," he orders the assembled crowd as his body perilously inflates. "I have to poop. Now!" (There is no shortage of poop jokes on

Family Guy.) But the anxiety of influence is sometimes unconscious. The alternate-world hypothesis of the episode "Road to the Multiverse," in which Brian stumbles on a universe-altering remote control, was perhaps already familiar from Homer's adventures in "Treehouse of Horror VI." *The Simpsons* had, indeed, already done it.

The freewheeling, anything-goes style of *The Simpsons* seemed to be a sitcom style that could only work in animation. We would recoil, the theory went, from *Simpsons*-style adventures if acted out by flesh-and-blood actors. Fox, flush from *The Simpsons'* success, tested the theory with *Malcolm in the Middle* (Fox, 2000–06), a live-action family sitcom composed of wildly exaggerated caricatures. Hal (Bryan Cranston, not yet *Breaking Bad*'s Walter White) is a direct descendant of Homer, sweet and dim in roughly equal measures. Like Homer, Hal means well but is often fatally waylaid by his own aimless enthusiasms.

Hal is a father of four (eventually five) who functions as the oldest of his wife's children, sticking his head in the fridge and wondering, "Honey, which juice don't I like: apple or grape?" In the episode "Surgery," his son Malcolm (Frankie Muniz) is laid up in a hospital bed awaiting an emergency appendectomy, but Hal moans and clutches his own stomach in Homer fashion: "Between the stench of disease and all those waffles, I don't feel very well." Hal reassures a police officer that he plans to give his mischievous sons a stern talking-to in "Stock Car Races," before kicking the cop in the shins and encouraging the boys to make a run for it. Hal lives in his own world of fantasy, enthusiastically narrating his imagined competition in the new Olympic sport of competitive shaving before dashing downstairs in the hope of snagging the last piece of breakfast bacon. Homer would undoubtedly have approved.

"Yup," Milhouse agrees with Bart at the end of "22 Short Films," "everybody in town's got their story to tell." Notes Bart, "There's just not enough time to hear 'em all." As if on cue, mad scientist Professor Frink comes rushing into the frame, out of breath and flailing his arms. "Sorry I'm late. There was trouble at the lab, with the running and the exploding and crying and one of the monkeys stole the glasses off my head." The screen fades to black, even as Frink tempts us with a snatch of his show's prospective theme song: "Professor Frink, Professor Frink, he'll make you laugh, he'll make you think, he likes to run, and then the thing, with the person . . . Oh boy, that monkey is gonna pay." There is no end to *The Simpsons*, no conclusion to Springfield's adventures. There is only the twenty-two-minute frame, offering a brief glimpse of a world so vibrant that it seems to carry on existing even when the television fades to black.

The Simpsons had gone from a flash in the pan, a Bart-hijinks delivery system, to a television institution. Like *Saturday Night Live*, it transcended the ordinary television show concerns of cancellation and disappearance. *The Simpsons*, it was understood, would be on in perpetuity. And like that other TV-comedy icon, it would ebb and flow, falling out of sight for a season or two and then reappearing in the public eye after a fresh skit or a clever episode. The glory years—the run stretching from "Bart the Daredevil" to "Homer's Enemy"—would likely never be replicated, but that did not mean that *The Simpsons* could not still impress, and occasionally stun, with its inventiveness.

"They'll never stop the Simpsons. Have no fears, we've got stories for years," goes the chorus to the "We Didn't Start the Fire"–ripping ditty from the episode "Gump Roast." Whether it was a threat or a promise was unclear, but it was undoubtedly true; that episode, from *The Simpsons*' thirteenth season, now hovers somewhere around the middle of the show's run. *The Simpsons* is now both definitively part of the sitcom's past, its present, and likely its future. It is in the hall of fame while still on the field, its position as a legendary sitcom solidified even as new episodes unspool every Sunday evening. Up and at them!

15

Seinfeld

"The Pitch"

September 16, 1992 ▪ NBC

"See, this should be the show. This is the show." "What?" "This. Just talking." "Yeah. Right. . . . Just talking? What's the show about?" "It's about nothing." "No story?" "No, forget the story." "You've got to have a story." "Who says you gotta have a story? Remember when we were waiting for that table in that Chinese restaurant that time? That could be a TV show."

Balding, bespectacled, frazzled George Costanza (Jason Alexander), he of the grandiose ideas and minimal follow-through, has latched onto a new one: for his best friend Jerry Seinfeld's forthcoming sitcom pitch, he should present the gathered NBC executives with an idea for a show about nothing. Jerry, initially intensely skeptical, soon warms to the concept of nothing: "I think you may have something here."

At the pitch meeting, George steals the spotlight from Jerry, announcing to the dubious execs that "I think I can sum up the show for you with one word: nothing." Following through on his pithy initial summation, George notes that "nothing happens on the show. You see, it's just like life. You know, you eat, you go shopping, you read. You eat, you read, you go shopping." Over the increasingly frantic objections of his partner, George engages in a pointed back-and-forth with one of the skeptical executives: "No stories? So, what is it?" "What did you do today?" "I got up and came to work." "There's a show. That's a show." "How is that a show?"

As it happened, viewers could testify that it was indeed a show, for what George was describing matched, in nearly every pertinent detail, the show we were already watching: *Seinfeld* (NBC, 1989–98). George and Jerry's waiting for a table at a Chinese restaurant was not just an episode from their lives but also an episode of *Seinfeld*: "The Chinese Restaurant," a standout from the show's second season. And so, having introduced an entirely new mode of comedy—highly stylized, exuberantly mundane—*Seinfeld* sought to pitch itself, as it were, into the stratosphere with this self-referential thrust. Though self-awareness had been a component of the sitcom's comic arsenal since Lucy and her TV commercial, *Seinfeld*'s version took a deeper interest in the clichés and stereotypes that served as the sitcom's building blocks. None of this was precisely new; *Father Knows Best* had covered much of the same ground with the episode "Father Is a Dope." But self-awareness was newly highlighted, newly essential to the task of crafting a sitcom.

This was the sitcom as Mobius strip: not only does fiction imitate reality, but the fiction within the fiction mimics the fiction as well as the reality. The series would fold in on itself, its characters confronted with doppelgangers, funhouse-mirror versions of themselves. Years before he played

Ari Gold on *Entourage*—but around the same time as his stint as Larry Sanders's head writer on *The Larry Sanders Show*—Jeremy Piven auditions for the role of "George" on George and Jerry's sitcom-to-be in the episode "The Pilot." Kitted out in ill-fitting sweatpants and bulky glasses, Piven reduces everyone except George to helpless laughter. George balks, seeing no resemblance whatsoever between himself and this pseudo-George. In that same episode, Kramer (Michael Richards) demands the opportunity to audition for the part of Kramer—after all, who is better equipped to understand the role?

What was this strange thing we were watching? Who had invented it? The questions could be asked of *Seinfeld*, but *Seinfeld* preferred to ask it first, interrogating television, and the sitcom in particular, for answers. The show enjoyed undercutting its medium, ridiculing its traditions and its unspoken assumptions, even as it maintained its most basic injunction to entertain. "Don't you hate 'to be continued' on TV?" Jerry asks the audience, even as we sat on our own living-room couches, watching *Seinfeld* wrap up the first part of its own two-part tale. "If I wanted a long, boring story with no point to it, I have my life."

Seinfeld is, in essence, "a long, boring story with no point to it," at least as we generally understand "points." Its plots don't arc; its characters do not develop. The show's unofficial mantra was "no hugging, no learning," and it stuck to it assiduously for its nine seasons. (There were even jackets made up bearing the directive.) Jerry, George, Elaine, and Kramer never grow, never change, never adapt. They merely are, and their lives are less the stuff of art than accretions of the sort of niggling details art traditionally avoids—the petty annoyances, minor scuffles, and bits of personal housekeeping that form the barely audible background hum of everyday existence.

Seinfeld is a masterful exploration of minutiae, inspired by (and featuring, in bite-size bursts) star Jerry Seinfeld's pointillist stand-up routine. Alive with taglines, punch lines, and bursts of near-Dada nonsense poetry ("yada yada yada"), *Seinfeld* reinvents the sitcom as an experimental art form, its hyperrealism ultimately eschewing realism altogether in favor of a religious devotion to the oddball. Turning life inside out, *Seinfeld* empties

it of all emotional or intellectual content—all that hugging and learning—
and keeps only the dross, making it into a memorable potpourri of instantly
recognizable details. Shrinkage. The puffy shirt. "Not that there's anything
wrong with that." Spongeworthy. The Pez dispenser. Fusilli Jerry. Festi-
vus. The Bubble Boy. "Shiksappeal." Mulva. The mimbo. The Soup Nazi.
"Serenity now!" "They're real, and they're spectacular." And what of the
epic question posed by the series' most justly beloved masturbation-themed
episode "The Contest": "Are you still master of your domain?" Daily life
was *Seinfeld*'s domain, and it was unquestionably the master there. It may
have been about nothing, but that nothing grew until it seemed to include
practically everything.

Before we enumerate the many ways in which *Seinfeld* revolutionized
the sitcom, it might be wisest to mention the ways in which it did not. The
show still had three cameras and a laugh track, an anomaly in the era of
M*A*S*H and a dinosaur by the early 1990s. It insisted on welcoming the
series regulars—particularly its house eccentric, Kramer—with deafening
rounds of applause entirely not in keeping with the show's aesthetic. *The
Larry Sanders Show* debuted on HBO the month before "The Pitch" aired
on NBC, and its free-wheeling, single-camera, laugh-track-free style made
Seinfeld's seem positively ancient.

Perhaps, having decimated so many of the traditions of the network
sitcom, *Seinfeld* preferred to preserve some tenuous link to what had come
before it, as if to remind viewers who echoed that NBC executive's concern
that yes, this *is* a television show. It is also a nervous nod in the direction
of those same executives, providing confirmation that *Seinfeld* was just as
interested in crowd-pleasing entertainment as those earlier NBC smash hits
The Cosby Show and *Cheers*. "You don't think I could put asses in the seats?"
Elaine huffily asks of her friends in the episode "The Shoes," skeptical of her
erotic hold over a waffling NBC bigwig, and the same question could be
seen as *Seinfeld*'s silent query. Even as it rewrote the rules for what a television sitcom was—what it might be—*Seinfeld* still assiduously devoted itself
to putting asses in seats, in a manner that its more acid contemporary *The
Larry Sanders Show* never did. One approach was not necessarily preferable

to another; but the arc of sitcom history was clearly tilting away from the one and toward the other.

NBC executives had, indeed, approached Seinfeld, a thriving stand-up comic, in the late 1980s and asked him to pitch a show. Seinfeld, whose television experience ran to appearances on Johnny Carson's *Tonight Show* and a guest stint on the *Soap* spinoff *Benson* (ABC, 1979–86) alongside fellow future sitcom star Ted Danson, approached fellow comedian Larry David. Seinfeld and David realized that their joint taste for aimless conversation, like talking smack about the products on offer at a Korean grocer's, had never really been seen on television before. They initially planned for a one-time ninety-minute special following a comedian through his day, collecting shards of material. The show would culminate in the performer onstage, his material inevitably reflecting the course of his day. (The same kernel of an idea would inspire David's first post-*Seinfeld* television endeavor, the 1999 HBO special *Larry David: Curb Your Enthusiasm*.)

Later, Seinfeld and David came up with a similar sitcom idea, about two stand-up comedians much like themselves who used their mundane adventures as source material for their comedy. Both ideas were eventually scrapped—ninety minutes was too long for the special, and Seinfeld and David did not want to pepper a twenty-two-minute sitcom with two separate stand-up acts. But the kernel of both—the link between the boredom of the everyday and the keenly honed observation of stand-up—became the fulcrum on which *Seinfeld* turns. They pitched the series to NBC—reportedly, the phrase "a show about nothing" was never uttered—and the network tentatively agreed to take it. NBC president Brandon Tartikoff, himself Jewish and from New York, worried that "it's too New York and it's too Jewish" but had the patience to leave *Seinfeld* on the air as it found an audience.

The show began as a midseason replacement in 1989–90 called *The Seinfeld Chronicles*. In the pilot episode, instead of Elaine, there was a wisecracking waitress at Monk's. And George was more of a romantic guru, a successful real-estate mogul who belted out show tunes and dispensed relationship wisdom to Jerry. (It is hard to imagine the George of later seasons offering up any of his favorites from *Les Miserables*—or even having enough interest in the world beyond his testicles and his hairline to attend a performance of the show.) Soon enough, George was the Costanza America grew to love, observing in mock-professorial fashion that "I know less about women . . . than anyone in the world." And after auditioning the likes of Megan Mullally and Rosie O'Donnell, David and Seinfeld happily settled on Julia Louis-Dreyfus for the role of Elaine.

The first two seasons of the show are decidedly uneven, but "The Chinese Restaurant," from the end of the second season, is a hint of where *Seinfeld* planned to go. Jerry, George, and Elaine head to their favorite Chinese joint for dinner and proceed to . . . wait. George attempts to commandeer a pay phone to call his girlfriend, Elaine moans about her hunger pains, and Jerry fails in his attempts to bribe the maître d'. Jerry offers Elaine fifty dollars to grab an egg roll off some elderly patrons' table. As soon as they leave the restaurant, too hungry and frustrated to wait another minute, the maître d' calls their table. End of episode. There are no interruptions here, no breaks in the action, none of the compressions and elisions native to the sitcom. It is television comedy unadorned and unafraid. By the time of "The Pitch," written by Larry David, George is offering up this very incident—an anecdote from his life or an episode from our *Seinfeld* life—as the epitome of what his *Seinfeld*-esque series will feature.

There are, functionally speaking, two stand-up comics on *Seinfeld*. There's Seinfeld himself, less an actor than a comedian parachuted into the war zone of television, his voice ascending into its whinier upper registers when he is inevitably agitated, and there is Alexander's George Costanza, a lightly disguised version of the phobic, disheveled, hyperarticulate David. George is socially maladjusted, romantically inept, and professionally incompetent, a connoisseur of diminished expectations whose list of potential conversational gambits with women begins and seemingly ends with "How I'm good at going in reverse in my car." He and Jerry are joined by their two compatriots and partners in crime: wild, magnificent Kramer, his tangled shocks of hair an exact correlative for his personality, prone to such flights of fancy as rebranding himself as an underwear model or designing a coffee table book about coffee tables; and Elaine, a tightly bundled mass of neuroses, given to slugging her friends ("Get out!") and ditching her boyfriends for not being "spongeworthy."

Transforming Larry into George was not the only sleight-of-hand trick the series played; *Seinfeld* is, at its core, about the self-absorbed lives of four lightly disguised neurotic New York Jews, their sensibilities transmogrified into more generic Manhattan personae that likely fooled no one. The Gentile backstories and non-Semitic last names—Benes? Costanza?—are hardly convincing evidence, given the show's recurring interest in mohels, babkas, marble ryes, Chinese restaurants, and South Florida. And what Italian in the history of the world has ever asked his host at an impromptu screening of *Breakfast at Tiffany's*, as George Costanza does, "So, anything to, uh, nosh?"

One is reminded of the brilliant cold open to the fourth season of *30 Rock*, and NBC network exec Jack Donaghy's suggestions for making their show within a show more marketable to mainstream America: "We'll trick those race-car-loving wide loads into watching your lefty homoerotic propaganda yet!" For nine seasons (including five in the top three of the Nielsen ratings), *Seinfeld*'s brand of Jewish Manhattanite propaganda was one of the most popular shows on television.

To fully grapple with the miracle of *Seinfeld*, we must turn our attention to perhaps the most perfect of its 180 episodes, written by David and airing later that same fourth season. In "The Contest," as in every *Seinfeld* episode, the ineluctable, intermeshing gears of comic fate are set into motion by an improbable sequence of events. George is caught in an embarrassing position by his mother while flipping through a copy of *Glamour* magazine at his parents' house: "I didn't know whether to try and keep her from falling or zip up!" Humiliated, George pledges to never pleasure himself again—a pledge his friends believe him highly unlikely to fulfill. After all, as Jerry observes to Elaine about men in general, "We have to do it. It's part of our lifestyle." Elaine pleads to be included in the bet, arguing that it is best compared to shaving: just as men shave their faces, women shave their legs. ("Not every day," Kramer sagely observes.)

And so a four-way competition is established, with the last one to stay master of his—or her—domain declared the winner. The contestants are faced with an array of unprecedented erotic trials: a naked woman in the apartment across the street; the stunning nurse sponge-bathing an equally stunning patient in the bed ncxt to George's mother; the temptation of Jerry's girlfriend Marla, the prudish virgin (played by Jane Leeves, later *Frasier*'s Daphne); and for Elaine, the sight of John F. Kennedy Jr. on the mat in front of her at the gym. Contestants drop, one by one. Kramer spots the nude beauty, retreats to his apartment, and returns, slamming his hundred dollars on the counter and shouting "I'm out!"—hand saucily posed on hip.

That night, Elaine, George, and Jerry toss and turn in their beds as Kramer sleeps the sleep of the satiated. A few days later, Elaine strolls in, calmly removes the cash from her wallet, and announces defeat, murmuring a new name to herself like a mantra: "Elaine Benes Kennedy Jr." George and Jerry are reduced to shouting at each other about matters of deep import like socks and coffee, their sexual frustration transmuted into a crabby *Odd Couple* dynamic. The episode doesn't reveal which of the final two contestants wins the wager—though George will claim the following season that he was the victor. The true champion, however, is Kramer, who is spotted by his friends in the naked woman's window across the street, waving, at episode's end. Jerry, on the other hand, loses a girlfriend in the bargain; horrified to learn of Jerry's bet with his "perverted friends," Marla the virgin storms out—into the arms of John F. Kennedy Jr.

The miracle of "The Contest" is that, following network strictures, no one ever says the word "masturbate." Instead, *Seinfeld* provides its own brand of instantly understandable jargon. George is "king of the county"; Jerry is "lord of the manor." Everyone is (at least temporarily) "master of their domain." Divergent subplots—George getting caught in the act, Elaine's run-in with JFK Jr., Jerry's girlfriend's prudery—are brilliantly woven together, with each unexpectedly bouncing off the other in a game of high-stakes comic ping-pong.

If there is a platonic ideal of the *Seinfeld* episode, it is the foursome encountering a new patsy and promptly proceeding to destroy his or her life.

Babu the Pakistani immigrant, his restaurant dreams destroyed by Jerry; the Bubble Boy, his protective sac trampled; George's girlfriend Susan's father, whose beloved cabin is burned to the ground with one of his own cigars, and whose secret homosexual relationship with the novelist John Cheever is exposed; Poppie the restaurateur, whose pro-life abortion views doom his flourishing pizza business. Jerry, George, Elaine, and Kramer are like roving assassins of others' well-being, their modus operandi the uncovering of others' secret shames.

An inordinate amount of the series is set in those receptacles of the tragically mundane: trains, buses, dry cleaners, coffee shops, restaurants. Over the course of its nine seasons, *Seinfeld* develops an urban cosmology akin to *The Simpsons'*, with its four central protagonists surrounded by a roiling scrum of memorably quirky supporting characters like Jerry's Uncle Leo (Len Lesser), who makes a habit of fishing discarded wristwatches out of the trash and shoplifting books; George's hideously neurotic parents (played by Estelle Harris and the inimitable Jerry Stiller); New York Yankees boss George Steinbrenner (voiced by Larry David himself as an update on *The Dick Van Dyke Show's* petulant, mostly absent Alan Brady), with a taste for calzones and a tendency toward ranting; and above all, Wayne Knight's gleefully odious postman Newman, who serves as Jerry's neighbor and all-purpose nemesis. Knight is the inspiration for the most cutting greeting in the history of television: Jerry's gritted-teeth "Hello, Newman." The show's grubby realism is borne of these eternally recurring, unshakable presences. They are emblems of an entire world of nagging, harassment, and petty hostility, which are *Seinfeld's* preferred methods of interaction.

This penchant for unveiling and shaming extends to their own lives; *Seinfeld* is devoted to the ritual humiliation of its own featured characters. In "The Raincoats," Newman busts Jerry making out with his girlfriend during a screening of *Schindler's List*, to the eternal chagrin of his fretful Jewish parents. Jerry, unable to understand Kramer's "low-talking" fashion-designer girlfriend at dinner in "The Puffy Shirt," accidentally agrees to wear a career-damaging ruffled shirt for an appearance on the *Today* show. Jerry and George are wrongly exposed as gay lovers by an intrepid college reporter in "The

Outing," reducing them to increasingly unlikely disavowals of homosexuality and pleas for tolerance: "Not that there's anything wrong with that!" ("My father's gay!" George blurts out.) In "The Implant," Jerry schemes pathetically in order to determine whether his girlfriend (played by future *Desperate Housewives* star Teri Hatcher) has had a boob job. She discovers his ruse and memorably kisses him off: "They're real, and they're spectacular."

Much of *Seinfeld* is turned over to its star's observation of contemporary phenomena, passing judgment on the minute questions of propriety to which it—and only it—turns its attention, like the world's quirkiest advice column. Who controls a parking spot—the car backing in or the one pulling in? What is the appropriate amount of time to surreptitiously glance at a woman's cleavage? Is it permissible for a man to steal another man's signature move in bed? Is cinnamon the "lesser babka"? Seinfeld's stand-up turns on such points of etiquette, and the show itself functions as a dramatization of the issues enumerated in Jerry's routines.

Seinfeld is, like *The Mary Tyler Moore Show* and *Cheers* before it, a show about single people in a big city, but unlike those will-they-or-won't-they soap operas, it is abundantly clear that there will be no happy endings on *Seinfeld*. "The idea," Jerry tells Elaine early on, attempting to sell her on a no-strings-attached sexual relationship, "is to combine the this"—his hands rapidly dance between the two of them in a speed-walking maneuver, indicating the back-and-forth of good conversation—"and the that," jerking his thumb backward to point at the bedroom. Peter Mehlman, soon to be a writer on the show, watched this scene being filmed and decided that this moment, with its judicious depiction of a quintessential human conundrum, was "the greatest single scene in the history of sitcoms." Yet the entire crux of *Seinfeld* is that, like Jerry's beloved Superman and Kryptonite, there is no genuine combination of the this and the that that does not result in calamity. During a stand-up tour after the episode aired, Seinfeld polled audiences about whether they wanted Jerry and Elaine to wind up together. He returned to the show convinced that the characters would have to be kept apart, and the intimation of their friends-with-benefits bliss was unceremoniously dropped.

Seinfeld is a show about the eternality of small annoyances, and its fundamental tone—speedy, easily agitated, fundamentally shallow—could never be altered by marital bliss. The show about nothing feints at something before pulling back, taunting us for even considering the possibility of maturity and responsibility for its characters. "What in God's name are we doing?" George cries out at the start of the seventh season. "We're like children—we're not men!" Jerry and George pledge to become responsible adults but prefer bickering about who may or may not have reneged on their agreement to settle down than actually, you know, settling down. Jerry meets the perfect woman (played by Janeane Garofalo), his identical twin in every quirk of their shared personalities, and rashly proposes marriage before reconsidering: "I can't be with someone like me! I hate myself!"

Would we prefer emotional honesty? In another episode, Jerry cries over the latest in his interchangeable array of here-today, gone-tomorrow girlfriends, experiencing something new. "What is this salty discharge?" he wonders, rubbing at his wet eyes. "This is horrible. I care." The new, emotionally open Jerry is a much improved human being. What he is not, as he well knows, is himself. "Sure, I'm not funny anymore," he excuses himself, "but there's more to life than making shallow, fairly obvious observations." Not in the world of *Seinfeld* there wasn't. Emotion would only have clogged the pipes.

Even George's impromptu engagement to Susan (Heidi Swedberg) is merely a dodge, an extended jab at the very notion of maturity, audaciously unraveled by her unexpected death from licking defective envelopes for their wedding invitations. (Taking a page out of *MTM*'s "Chuckles the Clown," her death is played primarily for laughs.) Girlfriends and boyfriends are dismissed for reasons so patently ludicrous even the characters themselves must admit their inadequacy. One fails to place an exclamation mark after a phone message announcing a friend's new baby; another is dismissed for liking an annoying commercial for Dockers pants; a third bites the dust because Jerry failed to remember her name, which he knew rhymed with a female body part. (Was it Mulva?) "So essentially," Elaine wonders in "The

Soup Nazi," "you chose soup over a woman?" "It was a bisque," Jerry mutters in his own defense. It is, as Elaine diagnoses Jerry, a disorder rapidly heading toward outright dementia: "So now you're finding fault at a subatomic level?"

Seinfeld was so popular, and so thoroughly unlike what had preceded it on television, that a legion of imitators were introduced over the next few seasons, each hoping to capitalize on its enormous success. Its television shadow was long enough to encompass other near-legendary shows that emerged in its wake. One pictures legions of television executives—close kin to Bob Balaban's fictional NBC president Russell Dalrymple—throwing telephone handsets at their underlings, demanding they be brought the next *Seinfeld*. There would be no next *Seinfeld*, but there were numerous imitators and impersonators that sought to capture some fleeting measure of the original's quirky magic.

Ellen (ABC, 1994–98) began life as *These Friends of Mine*, a title so generic it could have been pressed into service as an alternate name for *Seinfeld*—or another show debuting that same season on NBC, *Friends*. Eventually, *These Friends of Mine* would be renamed after its star, but it would remain a show about aimless Gen Xers sipping coffee and getting into low-impact scrapes. Star Ellen DeGeneres was, like Seinfeld, another stand-up vet with a charmingly frictionless affect, as if she had just been awoken from an afternoon nap, and a fondness for observational humor.

Ellen honors *Seinfeld*'s commandment to elide all emotional content but never connects with audiences until the landmark "The Puppy Episode." Ellen comes out as a lesbian through an experience of the very kind *Seinfeld* is least interested in—a genuine encounter with another human being (played by Laura Dern). *Seinfeld* deflects uncomfortable sensation with humor and aimless chatter; *Ellen* mostly fails to entertain, but on this one occasion, it succeeds by rendering homosexuality less "not that there's anything wrong with that" than another matter for pointed observation. Ellen comes out to her friends, and Joe (David Anthony Higgins) offers his congratulations, then turns to the others: "OK, pay up." This landmark moment in television is also an opportunity to revisit *Cheers'* fondness for relationship-themed betting.

Then there is *Everybody Loves Raymond* (CBS, 1996–2005), with Ray Romano stepping in for Seinfeld as the designated straight man surrounded by eccentrics and paranoids. In this case, the oddballs are all members of Raymond's family, living next door to him and his wife (Patricia Heaton) and doing their best to spoil their version of middle-class Long Island bliss. This being a CBS show, the entire mood of *Raymond* is less subtle, less devoted to wordplay, and more aggressively normal than *Seinfeld* could ever have been. And yet, something of *Seinfeld* lingers in the Kramer-esque convolutions of Brad Garrett as Raymond's police officer brother (who had played Jerry's hectoring mechanic in the *Seinfeld* episode "The Bottle Deposit"), he of the gangly limbs and gravelly voice, and the persistent nagging of Doris Roberts and Peter Boyle as Raymond's irrepressible parents. It is as if Morty and Helen Seinfeld had left Florida to move in with Jerry and refused ever to go home.

The King of Queens (CBS, 1998–2007) made so bold as to hijack George's dad, Jerry Stiller, to play star Kevin James's rambunctious father-in-law. The gap between Frank Costanza and Arthur Spooner is so minimal as to be unnoticeable, with *King* functioning, as a result, as an off-license spinoff of *Seinfeld*.

NBC, meanwhile, attempted to re-create the magic time and again, usually with more heart but mostly to indifferent results. There was *The Single Guy* (1995–97), in which Jonathan Silverman's urban ne'er-do-well is surrounded by a passel of quirky friends, including Dan Cortese, who had memorably played Elaine's "mimbo" boyfriend. Paul Reiser and Helen Hunt's Paul and Jamie are like a kinder, gentler Jerry and Elaine on *Mad About You* (1992–99), its aura of Manhattan madness like *The Thin Man* without the mysteries and the martinis. Reiser and Seinfeld even appear to be related, with Jerry's Uncle Leo also Paul's Uncle Arnold, as documented in the *Citizen Kane*–flavored episode "Citizen Buchman." Paul and Jerry are each anxious Jewish men, their fragile equilibrium rattled by the

meddling of others. Like Jerry, Paul spends much of his time fending off the
well-meaning interventions of his relatives. Like Jerry, Paul's female companion—his wife, in his case—is an outsider to his neurotic Jewish world, a
blatant case of mainstream-skewing "shiksappeal."

The two shows share a fascination with the brusqueness of New York
living, where even a pregnant woman's trip to the hospital (as in *Mad About
You*'s "The Birth") could become a squabble over which expectant mother
was first in line for the delivery room. And yet, there the similarities mostly
end. Reiser is never the transformational figure Seinfeld was, and his show
exists in a lower, less daring register than its inspiration. The entire tone
of *Mad About You*, its fascination with the relationship dynamics between
spouses Paul and Jamie, is downright mushy in comparison with the acerbic
Seinfeld. It would be *Seinfeld*, in fact, that would have the definitive last word
on the show, when George, having proposed marriage to Susan in "The
Engagement," is doomed to a lifetime of snuggling in bed while watching
Mad About You. Hell is Paul Reiser.

Above all, there was *Friends*, which numerous critics immediately
labeled as a *Seinfeld* knockoff, but which parlayed its predecessor's only-in-
New-Yorkness and quirkiness in a less abrasive, more conventional package.
Friends, easily the most successful of the *Seinfeld* acolytes, and the only one
to match its popularity, borrows its New York setting and its gang-of-friends
dynamic (and *Mad About You*'s quirky waitress Ursula, played by series regular Lisa Kudrow), while ignoring its "no hugging, no learning" aesthetic and
its astringent brand of comedy. Could anyone imagine Elaine and Kramer
commencing a romance, or George fathering a baby with Susan? "No hugging" gave way to the roundelay of bruised hearts that was *Friends*' bread
and butter (about which more in chapter 17).

While most of *Seinfeld*'s imitators celebrated the ordinary, none could
capture the comic audacity of its relentless pursuit of the prosaic, or its
expert juggling and intertwining of initially divergent subplots. Given that
the only show that has ever approached *Seinfeld*'s sophistication is its quasi-
successor *Curb Your Enthusiasm*, one might presume that this particular
form of multistranded sitcom genius is reserved for Larry David alone.

By the latter third of its run, *Seinfeld* was somewhat exhausted by its own commitment to mundanity, even as it continued to occasionally turn out classic episodes and discover untapped nodes of absurdity in new secondary characters such as catalog mogul J. Peterman (John O'Hurley), Elaine's boyfriend Puddy (Patrick Warburton), and George Steinbrenner. Larry David left the show after the seventh season, and *Seinfeld* became, in the words of one David associate, "more postmodern." "I can't spend the rest of my life coming in to this stinking apartment every ten minutes to pore over the excruciating minutiae of every single daily event," Elaine moans. Jerry responds by immediately launching into a story about his trip to the bank. The self-referentiality of "The Pitch" is returned to time and again, if on less inspired terms, with Elaine turning Kramer's meandering stories into sellable material for the J. Peterman catalog, and Kramer peddling the Real Peterman Reality Bus Tour (a play off a similar endeavor by the supposed real-life inspiration for Kramer).

Instead of happy endings, or some *Mary Tyler Moore* huddle of friends, *Seinfeld* decided to go out the way it had come in: rubbing against the grain of the medium that had borne it. Larry David returned to pen "The Finale," *Seinfeld*'s last episode, which is generally considered to be a textbook example of a disappointing conclusion to a beloved television series. Jerry, George, Elaine, and Kramer are flying to Paris on NBC's private jet after a new executive expresses interest in Jerry and George's long-discarded sitcom pitch. "Do you think this is the plane that Ted Danson gets?" George wonders, still concerned about his place in the sitcom hierarchy. (In "The Ticket," the episode after "The Pitch," George insists, "I can't live knowing that Ted Danson makes that much more than me.") The plane hits some unexpected fierce turbulence, and George has a confession to make, thoroughly reorienting our understanding of what took place in "The Contest." This is *Seinfeld*'s deepest concern, the truth that emerges when its characters appear to be headed toward an imminent and fiery death: who did or did not secretly cheat during a masturbation contest some five years prior.

During an impromptu layover in Massachusetts, the quartet are arrested for standing by idly and cracking jokes while a man is being held up at gunpoint. "This time," proclaims the district attorney arguing their case, "they are going to be held accountable. This time, they are the ones who will pay."

Seinfeld is setting up a belated reckoning for its criminally negligent protagonists, allowing the real world to have its revenge on these clinicians of narcissism. Their victims—the Bubble Boy and Babu and the Soup Nazi and the puffy-shirt designer and Marla the virgin—return to testify to their callousness and cruelty. But even this audacious narrative gambit— a sitcom's characters on trial!—has no effect on the four defendants. We close on them locked into a lone jail cell, the camera receding down a long hallway as Jerry and George discuss the placement of shirt buttons. Astute viewers would remember this as the very first conversation from the very first episode of what was then called *The Seinfeld Chronicles. Seinfeld* was a closed loop; we ended exactly where we began.

Audiences were furious, and Larry David's next series, *Curb Your Enthusiasm*, would devote an entire season to, in effect, apologizing for having left fans in the lurch. But *Seinfeld* had always been about upsetting sitcom viewers used to bland comfort. Its final act was merely the last twist of the knife, reminding audiences that sitcoms no longer existed merely to please them. The joke was on them.

Like the stars of *M*A*S*H* or *Cheers*, the *Seinfeld* foursome were weighed down by the burden of their success. How do you top having starred in the defining sitcom of its era? Jerry Seinfeld wisely opted to mostly leave television behind, honing his stand-up act, writing an animated film, and producing a documentary about stand-up comedy. He also made a memorable appearance on the third season of *Louie* as Louis C.K.'s backstabbing rival for a late-night talk show host job. Julia Louis-Dreyfus put together the strongest resume of the *Seinfeld* stars. After the short-lived *Watching Ellie* (NBC, 2002–03), she rebounded with a strong guest run as Jason Bateman's love interest and foil on *Arrested Development*, and a popular if undistinguished CBS series, *The New Adventures of Old Christine* (2006–10). Louis-Dreyfus went on to win consecutive Emmys as the star of Armando

Iannucci's HBO series *Veep* (2012–), playing an underutilized vice president desperate for some political traction.

Jason Alexander, perhaps the most acclaimed performer of the *Seinfeld* quartet, struck out with each of his next two sitcom efforts, *Bob Patterson* (ABC, 2001), about "America's #3 Self-Help Guru," and *Listen Up* (CBS, 2004–05), costarring *The Cosby Show*'s Malcolm-Jamal Warner. *The Michael Richards Show* (NBC, 2000), reuniting Richards with a team of *Seinfeld* writers, was also a bust. *Seinfeld* was a gilded prison, shackling its stars even as it feted them. The only roles they could truly be suited for, as their triumphant guest run on Larry David's *Curb Your Enthusiasm* would prove, was as their *Seinfeld* personae.

16

The Larry Sanders Show

"The Mr. Sharon Stone Show"

August 10, 1994 ▪ HBO

"For four decades, I've heard people talk about how shitty TV is, and how great movies are. Fuck 'em! You do what you're best at. That's what makes you a success." Artie Lange (Rip Torn), producer extraordinaire, is pumping up talk show host Larry Sanders (Garry Shandling) with this impassioned pre-broadcast speech, but he might as well be speaking to the medium at large. Television had always been the younger sibling to the glitzier, more urbane film industry, its reach more limited, its audience less discriminating, its goals circumscribed by its second-tier status. But TV—and the sitcom in particular—dreamed of leaving its hokey roots behind, embracing sophistication by transforming the television series into a hall of mirrors, chuckling at the misshapen figures caught in its reflections. The sitcom would be great by doing what it was best at—not what the movies were best at.

"It's not like a regular ha-ha sitcom. There's no laugh track, there's no audience. It's very stylized. It's about a bunch of guys in a ska band in Seattle. It's very dark." *The Larry Sanders Show* (HBO, 1992–98) is not, like the sitcom pitch of fictional head writer Phil (Wallace Langham), about a bunch of guys in a ska band in Seattle. ("Like *Friends*?" a coworker asks Phil about his show, perhaps missing the point.) Still, the description is apt for *The Larry Sanders Show* itself, which jettisons the familiar grasps and handholds of the sitcom in favor of something knottier, less friendly (or *Friends*-ly), more deeply unlikable. The setup familiar since the glory days of *I Love Lucy*—setup, punch line, beat; setup, punch line, beat—was jettisoned, the easy ha-has of sitcoms past left behind for a humor sculpted out of its deeply flawed characters.

Larry Sanders arrived at a crucial moment in the sitcom's evolution, when the television comedy series shed some of the trappings of its callow youth and embraced the complexity of maturity. *Seinfeld* had begun earlier, but it was *The Larry Sanders Show* that redefined the sitcom as something more than light entertainment: it wanted us to work for our pleasure—a trend that has only grown in the decade and a half since the show went off the air.

The Larry Sanders Show was, once again, television about television, this time a series about the production of another series sharing the same name as the one premiering on HBO in August 1992. The show within a show was a struggling late-night talk show, scrabbling for ratings with real-life talk show hosts like Jay Leno and David Letterman. This was a sitcom about a talk show that was also, in some fashion, actually a talk show. (The format echoed Norman Lear's syndicated mock talk shows *Fernwood 2-Night* [1977] and *America 2-Night* [1978], which had host Martin Mull and sidekick Fred

Willard entertaining an array of oafish guests.) Garry Shandling (who created the show along with Dennis Klein) actually delivered a monologue as
Larry Sanders on many episodes, and guests came on to promote their new
projects, much as they would have with Leno or Arsenio Hall, if in more self-
aware fashion. Alternating between film and video footage, the show toggled
between views of the show within the show. We were inside and outside all at
once, television watchers and privileged backstage onlookers.

Like his putative rivals, star Garry Shandling was a former stand-up
comic now granted a wider platform for his work on television, but the job of
talk show host was as much performance-art provocation as genuine pursuit
for Shandling, an expression of self-loathing transformed into amusement.
(Shandling had even been offered David Letterman's late-night slot before
deciding to do the HBO series instead. A fake talk show was preferable to
a real one.) "No flipping!" Larry calls out before heading to a commercial
break, his playful banter a scrim stretched over an abyss of anxiety and self-
doubt. If we flipped channels, would Larry still exist?

Shandling had been a marketing student at the University of Arizona
when he drove from Tucson to Phoenix to see George Carlin perform one
night around 1970. He brought along a sheaf of comedy bits he had written,
and badgered Carlin after the show to take a look at them. Carlin suggested
coming back the next night, so Shandling did, and Carlin told him there
was enough good material there to justify a future career in comedy. Shandling went on to write for sitcoms like *Sanford and Son* and *Welcome Back,
Kotter*, and then to a flourishing career in stand-up. Shandling also garnered
significant experience as a talk show host, occasionally filling in for Johnny
Carson on *The Tonight Show* from 1983 to 1985.

"Stand-up comics who think they're actors make me fucking sick,"
Larry says of fellow comedian Richard Belzer, but the joke bounces back on
Garry Shandling himself, who had already turned from stand-up to a kind
of self-reflective, self-aware performance with the little-seen but critically
respected sitcom *It's Garry Shandling's Show!* (Showtime, 1986–90). Like
Larry Sanders, it is a burlesque of television mores, its explicit intention to
undo the easy, uncomplicated relationship we had with our favorite shows.

Garry Shandling was a sitcom with a vengeance, amplifying the absurdities of the form until we could not help but take umbrage at its embrace of escapist foolishness.

In each episode of *It's Garry Shandling's Show!*, Shandling emerges onto his living-room set to the roars of the studio audience, as if he is some combination of Mary Richards, Cliff Huxtable, and Mahatma Gandhi, and basks in the glow of his supposedly well-deserved adulation. The laugh track, too, is so raucous, beyond all possible measure of any real-life audience's actual mirth, that it is clearly intended less as a reminder to chuckle than a poke in the ribs: who had come up with this odd delivery system for television comedy? (*The Larry Sanders Show* would also tamper with the traditional laugh track, its yuks layered over the talk show scenes but absent elsewhere.)

Shandling's character is also named Garry Shandling, and his life is the subject of a sitcom. The traditional barriers between fantasy and reality, between television and life, are demolished, making for a series composed almost entirely of tweaks on the ever-familiar sitcom form. Scenes take place both within the frame of the show—Garry's living room, the basketball court where he and his best friend Pete (Michael Tucci) hang out—and without, with Shandling stepping beyond the cameras to speak to the studio audience or address the audience at home. (George Burns and Gracie Allen had done something similar three decades prior, on *The Burns and Allen Show* [CBS, 1950–58].)

Garry polls the audience about how to handle a knotty situation and passes them slices of cake from his mother's surprise birthday party. Characters clamor for the comforting glow of the camera. Pete's son Grant (Scott Nemes) comes by to whine about quitting the show: "I mean, Opie had more lines than I do!" Even Garry's metaphors are drawn directly from the world of television. Meeting an exciting but fickle woman he would like to see more of, he asks her, "Do you ever think about settling down and becoming a regular on a series?"

The sitcom's most basic unstated assumptions are undone. Characters are aware of the duration of episodes and remind each other to move the plot forward in the interests of time. In "Dial L for Laundry," Shandling emerges for his opening monologue in order to tell us that nothing much is planned for this week's episode. As it turns out, all the big excitement of the past week—Garry swallowing a harmonica, his best friends developing amnesia—had happened while the cameras were off. Following up on this line of thought, Garry slyly wonders just how it is that all those other sitcoms on television happen to catch the most exciting moments in their characters' lives in the half-hour each week that they film.

On one episode of *It's Garry Shandling's Show!*, Garry is a fill-in host on a local morning show, and in his real-life counterpart's head an idea began to sprout: what about an entire series about a talk show host? "The curtain is a good metaphor for how we want people to see us versus what we're really like," Shandling would later observe of the talk show's trademark separation between onstage and offstage. He left *Garry Shandling* behind for another funhouse-mirror version of himself, the flip side of that series' faux naïveté. Both shows are devoted to undoing the sitcom, but where *It's Garry Shandling's Show!* renders all of the sitcom's clichés null and void by treating them with an excess of respectfulness, *Larry Sanders* obliterates them by drawing on a rich array of grotesques, none of whom could ever be confused for Cliff Huxtable.

Shandling is now brittle, insecure late-night star Larry Sanders. Rip Torn is Artie Lange, who once produced Jackie Gleason on television and has now graduated (devolved?) to become Larry's capo and aide-de-camp. Jeffrey Tambor is the show's terminally dim second banana Hank Kingsley, all mirth and barely suppressed rage. A talented array of comedians including Janeane Garofalo, Jeremy Piven, Scott Thompson, and a never-ending array of guest stars round out the cast.

Perhaps the most significant of *Larry Sanders*'s achievements was the liberation of the sitcom from the strictures of family friendliness. Not every prior sitcom had been intended for children; *M*A*S*H* and *All in the Family* had been intended for a more mature audience than *Leave It to Beaver*. But network television maintained a certain propriety—still upheld today—that forbade the use of profanity on air and limited the amount of graphic violence or sexual conduct on-screen. For all its prurient interest in sex, *The*

Larry Sanders Show did not much embrace nudity, leaving that to contemporary and future HBO series like *Dream On, Sex and the City*, and *The Sopranos*. Instead, *The Larry Sanders Show* was the first comedy series to entirely remove its language filter, allowing its Hollywood-veteran characters to speak like Hollywood veterans. Torn in particular is charmingly profane, with nearly every sentence studded with some variety of the word "fuck." ("NBC can eat shit and die," Artie says of a rival network, apropos of nothing.)

The show's characters are joyfully, perversely inappropriate, and their lack of sensitivity is part and parcel of its appeal. When Hank is moved off the couch on the *Larry Sanders* set and away from Larry, he lashes out with the first historically inaccurate comparison that comes to mind: "This move to the band is like getting on the fucking bus to Auschwitz." Cable networks like HBO, Showtime, FX, and Comedy Central, and their interest in producing original programming distinct from the networks' offerings, permanently altered the landscape of the sitcom, creating opportunities for series whose profanity, sexual explicitness, or lack of traditional sitcom structure would have kept them from ever being broadcast on CBS, NBC, or ABC—or even Fox. *The Larry Sanders Show* was merely the first in a litany of cable-sitcom successes that would come to include *South Park, Sex and the City, Entourage, Louie, It's Always Sunny in Philadelphia*, and *Girls*.

The show looks different, too. In part, this is its expert evocation of the familiar routine of late-night television in the talk show segments: the montage of supposedly hilarious past moments (Larry gets hit in the nuts by a monkey!), the synthesizer-jazz theme, the zippy graphics. But it is also the deliberately shaky, interrogative camera work in the behind-the-scenes portion of the show that made *The Larry Sanders Show* feel more closely related to a contemporary drama series like *Homicide: Life on the Street* than the likes of *Mad About You*. Procuring a Steadicam for the moving-camera shots was too expensive for this low-budget HBO series. Cinematographer Peter Smokler, a veteran hockey player, instead shot many of the show's walking-and-talking scenes, especially those taking place backstage, while on Rollerblades, towed forward and pulled backward to follow the actors' movements. *Larry Sanders* was as serious as a drama about its comic ethos, and in its jettisoning of the familiar trappings of comedy, it would set the stage for many of the laugh-track-less, single-camera series of the future, like *30 Rock* and *Community*. It also cleared the way for the increasingly metafictional, self-absorbed Hollywood series of the future, such as *Entourage*, *The Comeback*, and *Episodes*.

The Dick Van Dyke Show had gone into the writers' room at a variety program much like *Your Show of Shows*, and *Seinfeld*, right around the time of *Larry Sanders*'s premiere, was having its characters Jerry and George pitch NBC executives their idea for "a show about nothing." *The Larry Sanders Show* ventured further down the rabbit hole, unable to find—or uninterested in locating—a real world beyond the reach of the camera and the cathode ray. Fame, and the notoriety that went with being a fixture on millions of Americans' television screens, was a narcotic so powerful it rendered regular, unfilmed life a matter of minimal interest. Everyone on *The Larry Sanders Show*, from Larry to head writer Phil to Hank's loyal assistant Darlene (Linda Doucett, for a time Shandling's offscreen girlfriend), is convinced that fame is both imminent and everlasting, if they could only grasp hold of it.

A steady stream of guest stars to both the show and the show within the show artificially augment the fictional fame of Larry and Hank. Much of *The Larry Sanders Show* is devoted to the last-minute scramble to book guests, or to unbook them, or to unravel the difficulties they have created. Joe Pesci cancels at the last minute, and David Spade, who had scuffled with Larry over appearing on a rival program, is reluctantly booked. Michael Richards of *Seinfeld* is bumped from the show because of a time crunch. After Larry complains about stale guests, Garofalo's show booker Paula books a daring gay performance artist—far too daring for Larry's staid tastes. He is booted from the show, only to be picked up by Leno as a cause célèbre, and replaced on Larry's talk show by the dependable but vanilla George Segal. Fame is the lens through which the entire world is viewed; even the O. J. Simpson trial, which is a *Larry Sanders* obsession, is thought of as a lost opportunity for a booking coup: "Who knew he was going to get this hot?"

Some guests, like Jon Stewart, who plays the popular fill-in host threat-ening Larry's tenure as his show's star, or David Duchovny, who is Larry's sexually ambiguous bosom buddy, become fixtures. Roseanne helps Larry through an addiction to prescription drugs and has an abortive romance with the newly clean star that echoes her own tumultuous relationship with real-life ex-husband Tom Arnold. Meanwhile, legions of others, from Ben Stiller to Helen Hunt to Jennifer Aniston, make one-off appearances as warped versions of themselves, their phobias and anxieties magnified mirror reflections of Shandling's own imaginary star. When Stewart guest-hosts and sees the guests booked for his stay—Zsa Zsa Gabor and *M*A*S*H*'s Jamie Farr—he has only one question: "Are you guys mad at me?" *The Larry Sanders Show* allows its visiting celebrities to display a self-deprecating sense of humor about themselves, while giving the show an opportunity to bull-doze the stale self-congratulation of Hollywood and of the sitcom.

The show's prevailing mood is insecurity—professional, sexual, bodily, interpersonal. Larry, that minor major star, senses himself perpetually in danger of losing his place in the world. No episode sums up *The Larry Sanders Show*'s toxic cocktail of frustration, dissatisfaction, and barbed humor as thoroughly as "The Mr. Sharon Stone Show," from the series' third season, written by Shandling and the show's head writer, Peter Tolan. Larry, who starts the series boldly flirting with actress Mimi Rogers on his show and then turning unsure about where entertaining banter ended and genuine attraction began, finds himself in the unusual position of dating Sharon Stone, still in the first flush of her post–*Basic Instinct* notoriety. Their relationship begins when Larry has Stone as a guest on his show and scurries to escort her back to her dressing room after her segment, to the unsuppressed mirth of his crew: "Good, there's a lot of gang activity in this part of the hallway," cracks Paula. After a relaxed chat with her by her dressing-room door, Larry dashes back to the set, late for his next bit—and too besotted to care.

Larry goes out with Stone after the show and has the good fortune to bed her, but the ecstasy is short-lived, soon replaced by another, far more intense emotion: wounded pride. Artie, well-known purveyor of gift-wrapped harsh truths, explains the problem to Larry: his new girlfriend is far more famous than he is. An impromptu news conference in the show's hallway gives the talk show host a sense of his new, diminished status. As Sharon pontificates on matters small and large, including her costar Sylvester Stallone's nude scene, Larry is left standing alone. Only a lone cameraman recognizes him: "Larry Sanders! You're standing on my cable."

Larry had been bragging to Artie that he was invited to a showbiz dinner being given for President Bill Clinton in Los Angeles. As he and Sharon lie in a tangle of limbs on his bed, Larry discovers that while he is seated at table 20, she is at table 1, next to Bill and Hillary. Most men would be thrilled to be in bed with the voluptuous blonde movie star with a penchant for regular displays of nudity. Larry clutches his forehead in pain, troubled by the mortal wound to his sense of importance. Fame's tribulations move Larry more than the prospect of sex with Sharon Stone. After pausing to gather himself, Larry returns to the wound: "Table 1?" Knowing of only one possible means of gathering himself, he suggests they turn on the television and watch some of his program before continuing on with their evening. Fame is the ultimate aphrodisiac.

Stone eventually breaks up with Larry, her assistant informing Larry's loyal assistant Beverly (Penny Johnson) that Sharon is looking to date someone outside showbiz. Larry is seemingly less stung by the breakup than by the fact that his ex-girlfriend's assistant has the temerity to place him on hold. At the end of the episode, Larry spots actress Julianne Phillips near the elevator. He has only one question before engaging in hot pursuit: "She's not more famous than I am, is she?"

Narcissism is the intoxicant of choice on *The Larry Sanders Show*, with every character imbibing of its dark brew, some more deeply than others. Unlike its predecessors, and in tandem with *Seinfeld*, *Larry Sanders* made little effort at constructing likable characters. They are all odious, selfish and petty and unkind. Larry and Hank in particular are shallow, self-absorbed, petulant, moody, and occasionally tyrannical. That's the joke. Series such as *Taxi* and *The Mary Tyler Moore Show* had underpinned, and occasionally undone, their sophistication with heart-warming television moments, and even Archie Bunker had his rough edges softened by his abiding concern for his family and the inhibitions of the sitcom. Though *The Larry Sanders Show* occasionally stretches for a moment of pathos, often granted to the otherwise irredeemable Hank, it ultimately offers no escape from its airless world of grasping ambition and haplessness. Hollywood is a snake pit, and it must be accepted on its own hissing merits.

In the words of Judd Apatow, who was a member of the show's writing staff before becoming the executive producer of *Freaks and Geeks* and then a cinematic wunderkind, Shandling "always talked about how it's incredibly rare for people to say what they mean"—expanding on Shandling's trademark curtain metaphor. "People are lying a great deal of the time." Shandling even resisted the urge to cast *himself* in an attractive light. In the show's final episode, Sean Penn comes on to plug his film *Hurlyburly* and badmouths his costar—a guy named Garry Shandling—for being "the most insecure man I ever met." And the gap between Larry and Garry was perhaps narrower than one might expect. After breaking up with Linda Doucett, Shandling also fired her from the show, necessitating a lawsuit and an out-of-court settlement. Larry might very well have approved of the maneuver.

Larry Sanders is a wizard of damaged self-regard, his stardom a cocoon preserving him from unnecessary interaction with the non-stars who frustratingly permeate his life when cameras are off. Wives and girlfriends, too, are less partners than annoyances, lumped in with network executives and needy underlings as problems to be passed off to producer Artie. "Artie's not here" is Larry's code for "I'm not home," his all-purpose get-out-of-jail-free card releasing him from wrestling with the knotty difficulties of other human beings. Instead, he can permanently reside in his sealed chamber of self-obsession. "Does my ass look fat?" Larry's perpetual question, mocked by the likes of Dana Carvey, becomes a mantra, an invocation of the nagging doubts that perpetually plague him in his long hours away from the camera.

Hank is like a less polished, less talented version of Larry, a buffoon comically obsessed with his own status and devoted to perverse grudges against the likes of Vince Vaughn. Tambor plays Hank as a man only vaguely aware of his own stupidity, a walking catchphrase ("Hey now!") in search of corporeal form. He is, as Larry dubs him in an unforgiving moment, "a talentless fat fuck," but he is *our* talentless fat fuck, a living, breathing mass of anxieties and delusions and confusions unredeemed by Larry's saving graces of charm and humor. He is an abused puppy, slavishly devoted to Larry no matter how many times he is kicked. When his relationship with his wife is on the rocks, Hank delivers a public, heartfelt tribute to the compassion and thoughtfulness of . . . Larry, thereby cementing the demise of his marriage. He is also convinced of his own eminence, even as his pride is damaged at every accounting: by a hilariously inept television wedding gone wrong, or a leaked sex video in which he tells two women that "the snake doesn't like Artie."

Hank is always a step behind. He requires the use of cue cards and a rehearsal to tape a birthday greeting for Larry. As the office buzzes over Larry's romance with an eighteen-year-old intern, Hank is oblivious to all but his own lustful interest. "Wouldn't I like to give her the old pork sausage," he cracks, mock-cranking a meat grinder. "Hello, Jimmy Dean!"

Hank's dimness takes on epic proportions. He asks film critic Gene Siskel to explain the excitement over the movie *The Crying Game*: "What's all the hoopla about?" When Siskel explains the crucial plot twist of the film, in which the character played by Jaye Davidson is revealed to be a man, Hank shakes his head regretfully, sorry for a fellow professional's mistaken impressions: "I don't think so." Hank is the sitcom sidekick—Ted Baxter, Latka Gravas, Ned Flanders—turned inside out and exploded, all petulance and burning anger.

As for Artie and the rest of the show's staff, their job is to protect Larry, and to a lesser extent Hank, from the slings and arrows of the outside world. A young boy dying of cancer comes to visit the show, and Artie does his level best to keep him away from Larry: "Don't you know how sensitive and fragile Larry is?" Larry offers a few words at a coworker's funeral and obsesses afterward over having run long, as if death were merely another Tuesday night at the Laugh Factory. In one episode, Hank furtively approaches Artie and tells him he wants to ask him a question he has never asked anyone before.

The bait has been set for a revelation, immediately undercut by Hank's self-serving question: "Do you think I skew to an older demographic?"

The characters' narcissism is reflected in the show's own narcissistic absorption in its making. *The Larry Sanders Show* expertly plays off the battle for late night then raging, in which Jay Leno was tapped to replace Johnny Carson on *The Tonight Show* and a jilted David Letterman left for CBS to compete against him. Larry is imagined as both a rival and an alter ego for Letterman and Leno, and the show references Bill Carter's book on the late-night wars, *The Late Shift*, extracting some of its juiciest nuggets of gossip. Larry, seeking to return to television after an abortive Montana exile, hides in a closet to spy on a network meeting, much as Leno was said to have done. References are made to Leno's purportedly puny contract, and late-night luminaries Chevy Chase and Letterman appear as themselves. Like the fictional *Larry Sanders Show* itself, "live on tape from Hollywood," reality and television are conflated, their strands conjoined until the one cannot be entirely distinguished from the other. Just where is Hollywood, anyway?

Larry is a television star who has been warped by the demands of television. "You should try to think of a performer as a small, helpless child," Artie tells Larry's wife Jeannie (Megan Gallagher) in the show's first season, seeking to assuage her dissatisfaction with the show's preeminence in her husband's life. "I have sex with him," she replies. "I'm so sorry," Artie says in return, and it is unclear whether he is apologizing for his remark or for the fact of their sex life. Larry later offers to make up to his wife for his absence by booking her as a guest on the show. The only way he knows to communicate with others—even his wife—is as a talk show host, dispensing punch lines and flattery and then scurrying off to the next guest. "No flipping!" he shouts at her as she threatens to leave him, echoing the naked plea that is Larry's pre-commercial trademark.

Later, Larry and Jeannie get divorced, and as in "The Mr. Sharon Stone Show," girlfriends are judged as potential guests and guests as potential girlfriends. "Hey," Larry says to one date as they sit on his living-room couch, "why don't you come back, tomorrow night, and we'll watch the show again?" Illeana Douglas, whom Larry briefly dates, is coached assiduously before her appearance on Larry's show, her future as a mate entirely dependent on her success as a guest.

Douglas went on to serve as a regular on another series devoted to exploding Hollywood's self-serving myths, as a hooker making the logical career shift to Hollywood film production. *Action* (Fox, 1999) was the networks' own version of the scabrous *Larry Sanders Show*. It was also a record of paths not taken, of approaches to the sitcom attempted and discarded. Cable series could slowly nurture an audience, but network shows had to produce on impact, or else. *Action* stars Jay Mohr as a gleefully morally bankrupt Hollywood agent surrounded by prostitutes, pimps, and other paragons of relative moral rectitude. Mohr's Peter Dragon is an antihero in the vein of Tony Soprano and Larry David, stranded on the network of Homer Simpson.

Action's visual language is lifted off the page, with screenwriting directions printed on the screen and notes reading DAY FOR NIGHT and TIME LAPSE indicating the tricks of the trade being employed. The restrained language of the classical sitcom has been replaced by the visual pyrotechnics of the cinema.

The tone is knowing, insidery, as if its audience were composed entirely of William Morris junior executives and *Hollywood Reporter* editors. "If writing's hard," Peter asks schlubby screenwriter Adam Rafkin (Jarrad Paul), "how come Matt Damon and Ben Affleck have Oscars?" Salma Hayek shows up to slap Peter for past sexual indiscretions, and Sandra Bullock knocks him out for his illegally promoted sex tape *While You Were Sleeping on My Face*. But what might work on HBO—sex with prostitutes, strung-out movie stars, a studio boss with a comically intimidating package—was a nonstarter for network television, even for a network as wonderfully crass as Fox. *Action* was proof that the sitcom would increasingly be heading in two directions: a more daring cable variety, and its tamer network sibling.

Better served by *Larry Sanders*'s model is its HBO compatriot *Dream On* (HBO, 1990–96), another sour take on dating and the working world—this one punctuated by gratuitous nudity, which is slathered atop the show like so many pats of melting butter. As the credits indicate, Martin (Brian Benben) was a television baby, raised by the comforting glow of the screen, and his frame of reference is formed by old TV shows and movies. *Dream On* is essentially one clever joke extended for six seasons, with Martin's mental frame of reference alluded to by a steady stream of clips from old movies and TV shows. When Martin is tempted by a joint uncovered in his teenage son's sock drawer, *Dream On* flashes to an old lady from some forgotten movie enthusing, "Let's have ourselves a high old time." Such footage often serves as an ironic commentary on the newly divorced Martin's overstuffed sex life, with Benben always smiling like a man struck by an unexpected streak of good fortune.

Good fortune was not a prevailing theme as *The Larry Sanders Show* wrapped up its own six-year run. *The Mary Tyler Moore Show* had ended with the entire staff of WJM, other than the odious Ted Baxter, being fired, but it had been more of a final, barbed joke than an actual plot point. *The Larry Sanders Show*, by contrast, follows through on its air of ever-increasing entropy by bearing witness to the slow collapse of its talk show. Larry and Artie come under increasing fire from clueless network executives, who demand that the tragically uncool Larry dash through the crowd before each show, Arsenio Hall–style, exchanging high-fives with the audience. They shackle him with a "hip" new set and flirt with the idea of bringing in a more youth-friendly host like Jon Stewart. Eventually, the network pulls the plug on Larry's show, and the staff members scramble to find their next jobs. Beverly is hired by Pat Sajak, Artie joins Roseanne, and Hank plans to follow in the footsteps of singer Andy Williams and entertain heartland patrons in Branson, Missouri.

The center cannot hold, and *The Larry Sanders Show* embraces the chaos of things falling apart. "You may now flip," Larry announces at the end of his final show, a catch in his throat. A product of the warped world that had nurtured him, it was hard to imagine Larry outside the cocoon of his fame. "Larry, we're off the air," Jim Carrey warns Shandling during the taping of the last show. "Real life now." No more terrifying words could possibly be uttered. The sitcom had always been about stasis—the establishing of a guiding premise, which could be threatened but never entirely altered. *The Larry Sanders Show* is a comedy with the heart of a drama, preferring to let some of the real world's bedlam creep in and tamper with its well-manicured garden. Even Larry's fond farewell with Artie—the true romantic center of the show—is sideswiped by Hank, who departs in a huff, cursing his two friends and antagonists on his way out: "All I gotta say is fuck you!"

If *The Larry Sanders Show* has taught us anything, though, it is that life is, more than anything else, messy. Hank comes back a beat later, sobbing his apologies and announcing that he has crashed his Bentley into a Dumpster. We leave the holy trinity of *The Larry Sanders Show* there, departing and yet forever stuck in the same cycle of abuse and dissatisfaction and desperate clinging. We laugh because we know them as well as we do ourselves, the tragedy of these denuded souls warped by show business undercut by the essential comedy of their circumstances. This is Hollywood, the show tells us. Time to flip?

17

Friends

"The One with the Embryos"

January 15, 1998 ▪ NBC

The sitcom, in its purest essence, is a proxy: a substitute family, or sub-stitute circle of confidantes. It is a group of people whom you spend time with weekly, shooting the shit and exchanging confidences. The crux of the challenge, for a good sitcom, is creating scenarios familiar enough and resonant enough to mask the otherwise obvious fact that this is strictly a one-way relationship. We know all about our substitute loved ones on television, and they know—and care—nothing about us.

And yet, a sitcom savvy in the ways of attracting—one might, in a crabbier mood, say manipulating—an audience knows that shrinking that gap is essential to creating the necessary tone of well-worn familiarity. We must be made to feel that we know these strangers on the screen intimately and that their foibles are our own private property, to be lovingly cataloged and chuckled over in the intimacy of our own homes.

In the history of the form, perhaps no series so thoroughly embodies the essence of the sitcom's promise, and its appeal, as *Friends* (NBC, 1994–2004). The wildly popular series, created by Marta Kauffman and David Crane, was the last sitcom to dominate the Nielsen ratings before a wave of police procedurals and reality programming permanently swept them from the upper reaches of the television ratings.

Now, when families gather around the television of an evening, they are far more likely to watch *Dancing with the Stars* than any sitcom. In the wake of *Friends*, the most popular network comedy shows, like CBS's *Two and a Half Men* and ABC's *Modern Family*, have lagged noticeably in the ratings behind dramatic procedurals like CBS's *CSI* and reality programming like Fox's *American Idol*. The sitcom is as good today as it has ever been, if not better, but the era of *The Cosby Show* and *Seinfeld*, of Americans gathering in unparalleled numbers to watch their favorite funny people, appears to be over.

Friends was like a well-worn pair of Rockports: it wasn't stylish, necessarily, but it got you to all the places you wanted to go, and you had accumulated a lot of history with it. "The One with the Embryos" was a reminder of just how much mileage had been accrued, without resorting to the tired sitcom clichés of the clip show or the montage. Not that *Friends* was above either of those crutches—far from it. It was just savvier about its allure for viewers starved for connection with a replacement family.

As its prosaic title might indicate, *Friends* is a paean to the glories of companionship. It devotes itself with single-minded dedication to the quirks and foibles of six single twentysomething Manhattanites: dim aspiring actor Joey Tribbiani (Matt LeBlanc); kooky masseuse Phoebe Buffay (Lisa Kudrow); wisecracking Chandler Bing (Matthew Perry); control-freak chef Monica Geller (Courteney Cox); her brother, geeky paleontologist Ross (David Schwimmer); and the newest addition to the gang, spoiled Long Island girl Rachel Green (Jennifer Aniston). It is not a show about work, nor is it, like *Seinfeld*, about the travails of New York life. These young men and women live a short subway ride from Jerry, George, Elaine, and Kramer, but the grubby, lived-in New York their NBC colleagues reside in is nowhere to be found here. Their apartment building and Central Perk, their coffee shop hangout of choice, could just as easily be in Seattle as New York, with little nuance lost in the transition.

Friends gestures at sophistication—the New York setting, the urbane twentysomethings—but rarely tests its audience the way *Seinfeld* did. (There are no babkas or references to John Cheever here.) Kauffman felt like NBC had a double standard, allowing *Seinfeld* to get away with plot-lines that *Friends* could never touch: "They're masturbating on *Seinfeld* and we can't show a condom wrapper." But *Friends* never wanted to leave a single viewer behind. It is pretty much the last sitcom to be so inclined; television was splitting up into an infinite array of microtastes, and *Friends* was one of the very last series to hold the splintering masses together—or to want to.

Kauffman and Crane had created the raunchy sex comedy *Dream On* for HBO, and the draining experience of filming an entire show revolving around a lone protagonist had convinced them that their next series would be an ensemble comedy. They gathered a cast of mostly unfamiliar faces that included Kudrow, the comic-relief waitress from *Mad About You*; Cox, who had played Alex Keaton's girlfriend on *Family Ties*; and Perry—an actor who, when *Friends* was being cast, was starring in a pilot about futuristic LAX baggage handlers. Kauffman and Crane also recruited James Burrows, who had directed the bulk of *Cheers* and *Taxi* episodes, to helm the pilot. *Friends* was establishing a line of succession, setting itself up to inherit the classical-sitcom kingdom from its most distinguished predecessors.

"The One with the Embryos," written by Jill Condon and Amy Toomin, from *Friends*' fourth season, is the ideal example of the show's calculated blend of broad humor, sentiment, and the comfort of the familiar. The episode begins by winking at the carefully nurtured connection between the series and its audience. In its first three and a half seasons, we had already borne witness to Rachel fleeing her impending marriage to a bland dentist named Barry, Ross mourning the end of his marriage to a woman who turned out to be a lesbian and the burgeoning crush he developed on Rachel, along with a plethora of less emotionally resonant developments: Monica accidentally buying a bed in the shape of a race car or Chandler suggesting "Joseph Stalin" as a potential stage name for Joey. What better way, then, for a series to illuminate the ways in which the explicit emotional bonds between characters are stand-ins for the implicit ones between viewers and their favorite shows, than a rapid-fire quiz show about its characters, in which the audience could chime in with their own answers? Having been present for so much, viewers could easily believe, as Chandler and Joey argue at the outset of this episode, that they already knew every possible detail of their friends' lives. Chandler correctly notes that Monica is wearing her old-lady underwear since it is wash day, and that there is a half-eaten box of cookies in Rachel's bag. ("You're good!" Ross enthuses.)

The boys bet ten dollars that they can name every item Rachel has purchased at the grocery store. They easily get the first handful—apples, tortilla chips, yogurt, diet soda—before stumbling over the last object. Chandler whispers one possibility into Joey's ear, but he instantly demurs: "No, no, not for like another two weeks." (Might there be a connection to be made between Joey and *Community*'s Abed, both freakishly aware of their female friends' menstrual cycles? At least Joey doesn't keep charts in his notebook.) Regrouping, Chandler digs deep to come up with the correct answer: Scotch tape.

Monica and Rachel demand a rematch, to the tune of a hundred dollars, and Ross is employed as game master for a *Jeopardy!*-style contest. The four contestants compete in categories including Fears and Pet Peeves, Ancient History, Literature, and It's All Relative. Joey names Monica's biggest pet peeve (animals dressed as humans), but Rachel and Monica whiff on the name printed on the address label of Chandler's *TV Guide*: Chanandler Bong. They do, however, nail the name of Chandler's father's all-male Las Vegas burlesque show: Viva Las Gay-gas.

With the four contestants jammed onto the couch, at the edge of their seats, Ross pulls an envelope from his pocket: "The lightning round!" (Ross, ever the overachiever, has even designed cards with a lightning-bolt theme.) The bet, too, has changed: Monica and Rachel demand the expulsion of Joey and Chandler's exasperating pets, a rooster and a duck, from their apartment across the hall. If they lose, they will trade apartments, exchanging their tidy, light-filled West Village two-bedroom (only on TV could a short-order cook and an aspiring fashionista afford this place, lame explanations about rent control notwithstanding) for the boys' slovenly dorm room.

The lightning-round questions shoot across the room with dazzling rapidity: What was Monica's nickname when she was a field-hockey goalie? What does Rachel claim is her favorite film? What actually is? Monica's towels are divided into how many categories? (The answers, for those of you curious to know, are Big Fat Goalie, *Dangerous Liaisons*, *Weekend at Bernie's*, and eleven, respectively.) It is the ladies' turn next, and after successfully naming Joey's favorite food (sandwiches) and Joey's imaginary childhood friend (Maurice the space cowboy), and missing Chandler's age when he first touched a woman's breast (it was nineteen, not fourteen), they stumble on a gimme: "What is Chandler Bing's job?"

Rachel and Monica are silent for a moment before Rachel takes a stab: "Oh, gosh. It has something to do with numbers." "And processing," Monica notes. "And he carries a briefcase," Rachel helpfully adds. "It has something to do with transponding," observes Monica, rapidly rotating her hands in agitation. Rachel jumps up and down, sure of herself now: "Oh, he's a transpond—transpondster!" Monica shouts in pain: "That's not even a word!" Chandler and Joey leap in the air, and Rachel lets out a slow-motion howl: "*Nooo!*"

Monica and Rachel want to go double or nothing, but Chandler, knowing the value of his prize, is suddenly calculating: "I would never bet this apartment. It's too nice." Joey wheels Chandler triumphantly into their new home as he sits astride their gloriously ugly ceramic dog sculpture, soon followed by their equally grotesque matching Barcaloungers. (Each ceramic dog and canoe is the totem of a past adventure, their mute presence in the background a subtle reminder of the show's bounty of anecdotes.) They scroll back their chairs in unison, grunting with pleasure at their unexpected real-estate bounty. (Chandler, deliriously pleased with his comfort on another occasion, imagines a high-noon showdown between himself and a fellow remote-control gunslinger, drawing his lounge chair and firing: "I don't think this town is big enough for the both of us to relax in.")

Perhaps the most intriguing, and representative, aspect of "Embryos" is the way in which *Friends* simultaneously gestures at the rich tradition of rapid-fire screwball comedy while remaining determinedly true to a cautious brand of sitcom humor. The jokes come hard and fast while still pausing for laughs after each and every punch line. *Friends* is the last of the hugely successful traditional sitcoms, laugh track and all. It is the kind of show that finds no shame in having one of its characters recap the previous season's developments, in character, at the start of a new season. After *Friends*, NBC would ditch the laugh track for far smarter, far less popular series like *30 Rock* and *Community*, and canned yuks would become the exclusive province of CBS and its older-skewing, less sophisticated audience.

Even *Friends'* occasionally risqué subject matter—homosexuality, threesomes, pornography—is counterbalanced by its deeply traditional emphasis on character and emotion. Pivotal moments in the show—Rachel kissing Ross in "The One with the Prom Video," Monica popping up in Chandler's bed in "The One with Ross's Wedding," the kiss at Chandler and Monica's wedding in, yes, "The One with Chandler and Monica's Wedding"—are greeted with explosive applause and cheers of delight from the audience. Is what we are hearing a reflection of the genuine pleasure of an actual studio audience, or a not-so-gentle prod to those of us at home? Suffice it to say that it is likely both, and that *Friends* is not above shoving its audiences toward a preconceived sentiment. It would be precisely this habit that would distinguish *Friends* from its more avant-garde, self-reflexive successors, and that would make the show feel more distant from the present day than might be expected from a series that went off the air barely a decade ago.

Like *Roseanne*, this is a comedy that is also a soap opera—or is it a soap opera with a laugh track? *Friends*' copious references to *Days of Our Lives*, the long-running NBC daytime series on which Joey is cast as Dr. Drake Ramore, are a not-so-hidden acknowledgment of its own noncomedic ancestors. The first few seasons of *Friends* are signed over to Schwimmer's sad puppy eyes and his assortment of hangdog looks as he moons over the flighty Rachel. (Rachel's mother is played by Marlo Thomas of *That Girl*, as if to suggest her sitcom lineage.) His crush is the primary focus of the show's first season, culminating in Chandler's accidental revelation of Ross's feelings and Rachel's scramble to the airport to confront him.

Friends soap-operatically extended its will-they-or-won't-they? melodrama to a mind-boggling ten seasons and 238 episodes. Rachel and Ross have so much history together that entire episodes of *Friends* are devoted to picking through the rubble of their relationship: Ross being ditched for a better offer at Rachel's high school prom, their encounter after Rachel's abortive wedding to Barry, their copious missed opportunities, their brief relationship, derailed by a squabble over the definition of a "break," their drunken Las Vegas marriage, their child.

The show's success, then, is the product of two competing urges: to melodrama and to comedy. Emotion is delicately balanced by laughs, but at peak moments, comedy is scuppered entirely in favor of sentiment. When Ross and Rachel break up in "The One Where Ross and Rachel Take a Break," a brutal relationship fight is punctuated by the other characters eavesdropping behind a door, openly sobbing. Ross and Rachel's saga is the through-line of *Friends*, their decade-long, winding path to happiness the emotional heart of the show.

The saga of Ross and Rachel is matched and offset by the quasi-romantic bond of the eternally childish Chandler and Joey, and in particular by Matthew Perry's comic chops. Chandler and Joey discuss purchasing a dining table like a couple tentatively grappling for the next rung on the relationship ladder, and when Joey temporarily moves into his own place, their friends treat the rupture like a breakup. The Laurel & Hardy poster prominently displayed in their apartment is the perfect symbol of both their inseparability and their chaste romance.

Chandler, in the show's early seasons, is like a nebbishy extra from *Seinfeld* given a weekly platform from which to pontificate about his fatally charmless life. Joey complains about his poor luck attracting women at Ross's ex-wife's wedding, and Chandler chimes in with his own strikingly apt complaint: "The world is my lesbian wedding." Joey suggests a competition between the roommates over who can bring the most beautiful woman home, and Chandler sardonically assents: "It's a good idea, Joe. We could call it life." Chandler gradually shifts from an antsy, antisocial runt to a fully fledged adult once he is paired off with Monica, ditching the show's earlier intimations that he is headed for a lonely, loveless adulthood. Chandler and Monica's late-blooming romance is the inverse of Ross and Rachel's, placid where theirs is stormy, easy where theirs is endlessly complicated.

And yet, for all its occasionally forced bonhomie, the funniest moments in *Friends* pit the six bosom buddies against one another in no-holds-barred fraternal combat. Everyone on *Friends* is constantly intruding on everyone else's private affairs, and any burst of pique can be enough to expose secrets to the cathode-ray light.

A Thanksgiving visit by Monica and Ross's parents in "The One Where Ross Got High" prompts them to an escalating bout of sibling warfare: exposing who stole Dad's *Playboy*s, who broke the porch swing, who secretly lost their job over a year ago, who married Rachel, who is secretly living with her boyfriend. Monica, pestered by her friends for dating her ex-boyfriend's son (yes, this really *is* a soap opera) in "The One with Chandler in a Box," lashes out at them, pointing at each guilty party in turn: "Judge all you want to, but married a lesbian, left a man at the altar, fell in love with a gay ice dancer, threw a girl's wooden leg in the fire, live in a box!" Everyone has a secret shame, and everyone has a secret weapon, kept behind glass, to be wielded in case of emergency. In "The One with Rachel's Assistant," Ross and Chandler spill their own secrets from their time as college roommates: Ross's incident on Space Mountain had temporarily rendered Disney World "the crappiest place on earth," and Chandler had, to his eternal shame, once won a Vanilla Ice lookalike contest.

Even Ross and Rachel, the sentimental heart of the show, are not immune from the irrepressible desire to squabble. After one particularly nasty breakup, Rachel extracts an especially razor-sharp arrow from her quiver with which to zing Ross one last time: "Just so you know—it's *not* that common, it *doesn't* happen to every guy, and it *is* a big deal." *Friends* often treads perilously close to treacle, from its musical references (Hootie and the Blowfish?) to its bizarre first-season insistence on heartwarming plotlines involving Ross's monkey, Marcel. ("Hey, remember when I had a monkey?" Ross asks the gang at the beginning of an episode late in the show's run. "Yeah, what was I thinking?") It is these moments of gratuitous nastiness, of spilling others' secrets, that undercut *Friends*' otherwise terminal politeness.

In the wake of its outsized success, seemingly every sitcom on television was a *Friends* knockoff. There was working-class *Friends* (*The Drew Carey Show*), gay *Friends* (*Will & Grace*), guy *Friends* (*Men Behaving Badly*), girl *Friends* (*Caroline in the City*), black *Friends* (*Living Single*), nerdy *Friends* (*The Big Bang Theory*), and rebooted *Friends* (*How I Met Your Mother*). Everywhere you turned on TV, there was a posse of pals sitting around a living room or a bar or a coffee shop or a science lab, trading quips and exchanging furtive glances. Some, like *Men Behaving Badly*, barely made a blip on the radar; others, like *Will & Grace* and *How I Met Your Mother*, became television stalwarts in their own right.

Living Single (Fox, 1993–98) is like *Friends* cross-pollinated with *Sex and the City*, embossed with a distinctly African American take on those two distinctly white shows. Hip-hop star Queen Latifah is the ringleader of a group of four upwardly mobile African American women balancing the drive to succeed with the ups and downs of relationships. Like *Friends*, *Living Single* professes warmth while preferring to play the dozens. "I didn't know they made bougie in such small sizes," one character says of another's fashion taste.

Like *Friends*, *Will & Grace* (NBC, 1998–2006) is, at its heart, a chaste love affair between pals. Straight, single Grace (Debra Messing) and gay, single Will (Eric McCormack) live together in platonic bliss, aided and amused by their far more exuberant, unhinged friends Jack (Sean Hayes) and Karen (Megan Mullally). *Will & Grace* was something of a relic even as it aired, its laugh track and its exaggerated, kitschy gayness—all picnic baskets at the soccer game and jokes about "baby's first 'fabulous!'"—increasingly out of date in the era of gay marriage (although Vice President Joe Biden credited the show with helping turn the tide in favor of gay rights). Gays were like this and straights were like that, and an impromptu sexuality test devised by Karen could have served as a stand-in for the entire comic attack of the show: "There's a penis and a vagina in a tent, and it's on fire. Which do you save?"

Gayness, on *Will & Grace*, is a matter of performance, like Jack slipping a handful of *kippahs* into his suit to bulk up his shoulders at Grace's wedding. (The *kippahs* are also indication of *Will & Grace*'s less-acknowledged, but equally obvious, debt to *Seinfeld* as another show with a New York Jewish sensibility.) But like its obvious inspiration, *Will & Grace* manages to be consistently amusing while never venturing more than a half-step beyond previous NBC sitcoms. Sexually daring chatter ("I hate when people have huge things behind my back . . . usually," Jack says, smirking, about a soiree to which they have not been invited) meets aesthetic conservatism—NBC's official formula for ratings success in the post–*Seinfeld*, pre–*30 Rock* era.

Friends offered so well-rounded a model for television success that it could be essentially rebooted, re-created with a new cast of five pals, an attachment to the follies of youth, and an emotionally charged plotline threaded through the series. The peg of *How I Met Your Mother* (CBS, 2005–14), as its title indicates, is that Ted (Josh Radnor), recollecting his aimless twenties, is filling in his two children on the backstory of how he met the love of his life. Procrastinating on providing any closure in much the same fashion as *Friends* held off on bringing Ross and Rachel together, *How I Met* prefers the bad-boy antics of Barney (Neil Patrick Harris), who embraces something called "the Naked Man" as a go-to seduction move. The show is naughty without ever really being surprising. "Do you want my Xbox?" Ted asks Barney, who is hyperventilating over having slept with

Ted's ex-girlfriend, Robin (Cobie Smulders). "Ted, she has a name!" he responds through gritted teeth. The show's sentimental voiceover is grating, but even marooned on the ferociously conservative CBS, the talent of gifted performers like Harris, Jason Segel, and Alyson Hannigan could not entirely be stifled.

The Big Bang Theory (CBS, 2007–), created by Chuck Lorre (also responsible for *Two and a Half Men*), is an unapologetically geeky take on the *Friends* aesthetic. A single episode is laced with references to Richard Feynman, Marie Curie, the Klingon language, and Carl Sagan alongside its jokes about *The Bachelor* and its general vibe of Central Perk slackerdom. *Roseanne*'s Johnny Galecki stars, the romantically hapless David now a romantically hapless experimental physicist. Jim Parsons's quirky, quasi–Asperger's candidate Sheldon is the show's breakout star, though, offering a steady stream of arch, multipart observations like "Hawaii is a leper colony on top of an active volcano where the disappointing finale to *Lost* was filmed." His voice cracking on the high notes of his witticisms, Sheldon is like Chandler Bing with a PhD and an inability to relate to others.

Though *Friends'* influence can still be felt, watching the original is like flipping through an old photo album, a simultaneous experience in nostalgia and humiliation. It is an illustrated guide to the more unfortunate dim corners of 1990s fashions: Joey's fringy mop-top haircut; Ross's flannel shirts and dinosaur ties; Chandler's sweater vests. It is, above all, a show about a hairdo: the Rachel, whose textured, layered look swept the nation, migrating from the television screen into hair salons across the country soon after *Friends* premiered in 1994. This was unprecedented and at the same time entirely to be expected. After all, Clark Gable had taken off his shirt to reveal a bare chest in the 1934 Frank Capra film *It Happened One Night*, and nationwide, undershirt sales plummeted. *Friends* collapsed the distance between television and real life, offering its passel of buddies as fill-in companions for a nation of stay-at-home television watchers. That we should be influenced by our new, more stylish compatriots—that we would want to remake ourselves in their image—was no surprise. Who wouldn't prefer a reserved seat at Central Perk to a spot on the couch, parked in front of the TV?

Having put its audience through its paces for a decade, *Friends* made no bones about ultimately giving them exactly what they wanted. "Having seen the *Seinfeld* finale and knowing when you depart from who you are it doesn't make the audience happy, let's deliver to the audience what they want and what they've earned," Crane said about wrapping up the series.

Friends ended in 2004, and its overwhelming popularity and familiarity would spell doom for many of its stars' future television endeavors: Perry in *Studio 60 on the Sunset Strip* (NBC, 2006–07), *Mr. Sunshine* (ABC, 2011), and *Go On* (NBC, 2012–13); Kudrow in *The Comeback* (HBO, 2005); and LeBlanc in *Joey* (NBC, 2004–06). (Cox would star in the more successful *Cougar Town* [ABC/TBS, 2009–], and Aniston would move on to big-screen comedies like *Horrible Bosses* and *We're the Millers*.) The likeliest measure of success for *Friends* alumni would be in playing some version of themselves, recreating their own peculiar personal conundrums as actors nagged by a success they could never shake. The inspiration was less *Friends* itself than *Curb Your Enthusiasm* and *The Larry Sanders Show*, and the actors' own fascination with the machinations of the show-business industry that had made them stars. As the last of the mega-sitcoms, *Friends* inspired its own cottage industry of metafictions. Schwimmer starred as himself opposite Larry David in *Curb*'s fourth season, cast as Leo Bloom in their production of *The Producers*, and both Kudrow and LeBlanc found critical approval as washed-up stars desperate for a new hit, inured to the callousness and cruelty of the world that had once feted their every step.

Kudrow was only granted one season as washed-up sitcom star Valerie Cherish on *The Comeback*, a faux reality series filmed in *The Office*'s mockumentary style. Valerie had been the widely proclaimed "It Girl," star of a semipopular series called *I'm It* (her moniker evoking the classic 1960s sitcom *That Girl* and echoing what Valerie had been and no longer was), brought back into the television limelight as a bit of reverse eye candy for a sitcom about nubile twentysomething roommates. *The Comeback*'s default mood is a kind of furious embarrassment, with Valerie hastily papering over an endless stream of setbacks (getting ditched by her costars for lunch, not being called onstage at the network's upfront presentation to advertisers) with a jittery stream-of-consciousness narration and an emptily dazzling smile.

"This is *my* comeback!" she crows at the start of the first episode, and is immediately interrupted by the unseen director, who requests a retake. What we are watching, we are told, is raw footage from the reality series following Valerie's return to prominence. It is actually a ritualized series of humiliations, with all of Valerie's best-laid plans for success coming to naught. Her own starring turn on the show is summarily canceled by the network executives, who cattily observe that her episode "was *Sex and the City* meets *Cocoon*." Valerie is not Phoebe, by any means, but her fundamental question—without television, do I still exist?—was one that TV shows were increasingly asking.

LeBlanc was cast against type as himself in *Episodes* (Showtime, 2011–), cocreated by *Friends*' David Crane, as a dingbat with surprising reserves of self-awareness. He plays "Matt LeBlanc" as a wealthy has-been still coasting off the fumes of Joey Tribbiani in this sitcom about the making of a sitcom, cast against all logic in the American remake of a critically beloved British show set at a tony private school. The fictional show's cocreator Sean Lincoln (Stephen Mangan) moans in frustration. "For the erudite, verbally dexterous headmaster of an elite boys' academy, he's suggesting . . . *Joey*?"

LeBlanc's headmaster role is soon retooled into a hockey coach, and the show within a show is craftily retitled *Pucks!* Matt is forever to be Joey. Broken down at the side of the road after a car accident, he is spotted by a tour guide, who cheerfully greets him with his own *Friends* catchphrase: "How *you* doin'?"

Episodes' version of LeBlanc—self-absorbed, sexually voracious, and enmeshed in an array of poorly planned investment schemes as he might be—is not to be confused with Joey. When Sean and his wife and cocreator Beverly (Tamsin Greig) vehemently deny the obvious source material for their show, Matt immediately plunges to the root of their artistic weakness: "So, it's *History Boys* meeting you saying it's not *History Boys*?" He is a savant of the sitcom, an adept of its mysteries. Matt successfully convinces Sean and Beverly to change his character's love interest from a frumpy lesbian to a frisky librarian, imparting a lesson learned from the very show we had once watched devotedly. "That's *one* season for us," he notes of their elegantly plotted narrative arc. "*Friends* did 236 episodes. [There seems to be some disagreement about the exact number of *Friends* episodes.] You gotta give yourself places for stories to go. How long do you think Ross and Rachel would've lasted if Rachel had been a lesbian? Or Sam and Diane on *Cheers*? Or Frasier and . . . I don't know, I never watched that show."

Each sitcom is a self-enclosed universe of referents and in-jokes, of familiar faces and well-worn places. Therefore, it is surprising, during *Friends'* decade-long run, to see George Costanza—or the actor who embodied him, Jason Alexander—appear as a suicidal office manager, or to spot Cheryl Hines—the future Cheryl David of *Curb Your Enthusiasm*—turning down the amorous advances of another inappropriate, sex-obsessed son of the outer boroughs, Joey Tribbiani. These incursions of one sitcom into another, infecting one specimen with the DNA of another, are disorienting. We rapidly grow accustomed to seeing familiar performers in their own place, their own surroundings. And the six *Friends* belong here—or so audiences have decided—and nowhere else. They are, now and forever, Ross, Rachel, Monica, Phoebe, Chandler, and Joey. "We could never leave that stage, metaphorically speaking," the real Matt LeBlanc says of his experience. "Still can't. Still on that stage. That will follow us around forever."

The sitcom is a blanket we wrap ourselves in to provide us with the TV-fueled illusion of stability; these sneak attacks are a reminder that the walled garden is a myth. Our friends are performers, and the shows we love are paychecks for actors. Central Perk is constructed out of papier-mâché and pasteboard. But to whom should we turn for consolation in our solitude, other than to television?

18

Sex and the City

"My Motherboard, My Self"

July 15, 2001 ▪ HBO

Four women sharing good times and swapping stories of their escapades with men. Four women gathering around a table and sharing desserts. Four women cracking one-liners about being single and frisky in the big city. Four women talking about lesbianism, casual sex, menopause, and handymen who overcharge. A group that includes one sex-starved eternal flirt, forever scanning the room for the next rich man to entrance, and one plainspoken

Everywoman with a tart tongue and a gift for pithy zingers. Four women dealing with incontinence, nursing homes, and browsing the obituary column for dates. Are we *sure* we're talking about the right show here?

OK, so it is unlikely that Darren Star, Michael Patrick King, and the other creators of *Sex and the City* marched into the HBO offices sometime in the late 1990s and pitched their new series as "*Golden Girls*, only with women three decades younger, and set in New York, and with more nudity," but the resonances between the two quartets, and the worlds they inhabit, are striking. And so, in order to appreciate the changes *Sex and the City* wrought on the world of television, it might be most useful to begin about a decade and a half earlier, and one thousand miles south of the Manolo Blahnik store in Manhattan. As Estelle Getty's Sophia might have said, a wistful note of longing in her voice, "Miami Beach, 1985 . . ."

The sitcom had always been a friendly sphere for women, offering female stars like Lucille Ball and Mary Tyler Moore perches far more comfortable, and longer-lasting, than film ever did. But in order to properly domesticate them, they would have to be surrounded by a network of men: husbands, neighbors, bosses, colleagues. Lucy had Desi and Fred; Mary Richards had Murray and Lou and Ted. Most shows preferred their women in subservient roles, as wives and mothers and babes to be ogled, and little more. Considering the networks' similar lusting after youthful viewers for their sitcoms and general indolence regarding older ones, the idea of a comedy series about four women of a certain age, dressed in housecoats, living in that eternal punch line of early-bird specials and salmon-colored pants, Miami Beach, with men as little more than glorified walk-ons, likely gave most television executives night sweats.

Like its eventual successor, *The Golden Girls* (NBC, 1985–92) is a collision of distinct types, mostly borrowed from prior series and prior roles. Bea Arthur's Dorothy is a ranter and a heckler, irrepressibly irritable like her earlier incarnation as the title character of *Maude*. Her mother, Sophia, is a font of earthy wisdom from 1912 Sicily. Betty White's Rose is a good-natured ditz, Sue Ann Nivens without the ambition or the lustiness.

Blanche Devereaux (her name echoing the magnolia-scented South of *A Streetcar Named Desire*'s Blanche DuBois) is perhaps the most notable television precursor to *Sex and the City*'s Samantha Jones. Man-hungry, flamboyantly sensual, intoxicated by the nearness of sex, Blanche, played by Rue McClanahan, is a postmenopausal Samantha, chasing the fathers, and in some cases the grandfathers, of Samantha's one-night swains. (The whipped cream is stored in Blanche's bedroom, not the kitchen.) In the flashback episode "The Way We Met," Blanche recommends smoked oysters as a remedy for "sluggish" men, thanks a fellow grocery store patron for praising her cantaloupes, and shushes her roommates when they squabble over the groceries: "Would you two please keep your voices down? I have shopped and dated extensively throughout this market." One could picture Samantha saying precisely the same thing, if demonstrably less decorously, to Carrie and Miranda.

Given its network home, *Golden Girls* is surprisingly raunchy. An entire generation of children grew up listening to, and probably not entirely understanding, Blanche's double entendres, Sophia's raunchy-old-lady asides, and Dorothy's quips. "He's still interested," Blanche says suggestively of one suitor. "In what?" Rose asks, befuddled. The show is still interested too, the bulk of its humor stemming from the potentially icky subject matter of late-middle-aged and elderly women and their sex lives (a topic Arthur explored on *Maude* as well). It is also open-minded in a way not entirely associated with 1980s television, let alone a series about senior citizens. "Isn't It Romantic," from the show's second season, has Dorothy's female friend Jean falling in love with Rose. While getting in more than its share of jokes about Jean conducting a "membership drive" for lesbians, it is also surprisingly sensitive about same-sex desire.

The women of *Golden Girls* exist in a predominantly female cocoon, their friendship insulating them from the blows of the world outside their front door. Theirs is a world of pathetic, shriveled, neurotic, whining, disobedient men (although Dick Van Dyke comes off decidedly better in a guest turn). Ex-husbands, boyfriends, plumbers, teachers, grandsons—they are all cut from the same cloth: whining for sex, sniveling after other women, comically unable to accept parity with the women around them.

And here we leap from the ladies of Miami Beach to those of Manhattan, from the neon 1980s to the chichi 1990s. The surroundings have changed, but the men have mostly not. For both sets of women, their bonds with each other supersede any links, temporary or otherwise, to the men in their lives. *Sex and the City* (HBO, 1998–2004), like *Golden Girls*, is a paean to female friendship as balm for the world's aches. But for all the striking similarities to their South Floridian predecessors, Carrie, Samantha, Charlotte, and Miranda are emblems of the post–*Larry Sanders* sitcom. They replaced the mercurial talk show host as the designated representatives of the newer, freer sitcom, as it was first blooming in the protected wilds of HBO.

When *Sex and the City* premiered, in the summer of 1998, it was not quite the show that its ardent fans would eventually come to embrace. Darren Star was the creator of prime-time soap operas *Beverly Hills 90210* and *Melrose Place*, and some of those shows' pulpy scandalousness crept into the new project. Star had been filming his latest series, *Central Park West*, in New York, and stumbled on Candace Bushnell's column in the *New York Observer*, also called Sex and the City. After Bushnell interviewed Star for a magazine article, he pictured adapting her column as a feature film—an R-rated comedy with female stars. Soon shifting gears, he began to seriously consider a television series based on her column, with the protagonist being Bushnell's alter ego, Carrie Bradshaw, and a supporting cast drawn from some of her regular characters. The idea of shopping *Sex* to the networks was a nonstarter. ABC was not even entirely sure it could allow the word "sex" to appear in one of its shows' titles. HBO leapt where the broadcast networks had frozen in panic.

The earliest episodes of *Sex and the City* have a sociological flair, with man-on-the-street interviews, characters directly addressing the camera, and a tight focus on the peculiarities of Manhattan dating. Three of the show's four main characters are easily summarized in a blunt, possibly offensive word: Samantha (Kim Cattrall) is a slut, Charlotte (Kristin Davis, a guest star on *Seinfeld* and *Friends*) a prude, and Miranda (Cynthia Nixon) a careerist. The fourth, Carrie (Sarah Jessica Parker, who had starred in the short-lived, underrated high school sitcom *Square Pegs*), is less exaggerated and easier to identify with, an Everywoman figure despite her wildly privileged lifestyle. As the show's narrator and as a sex columnist herself, Carrie is the chronicler of their collective adventures and unofficial court philosopher for single women of a certain age.

In the early going, the emphasis of *Sex and the City* is less on relationships than on dating. Almost every episode features Carrie and each of her friends dating a new man, with a new variation on the infinite masculine capability for oddity: the modelizer, the man who must shower immediately after sex, the guy into spanking, the baby-talk guy, the guy who screams out "You fucking whore!" at orgasm, the perfect man with the imperfect penis. This is realism of a distinctly fantastical kind, its brazen talk conjoined to a setting cocreator King dubbed "Eternal Spring." (No need for winter coats on *Sex and the City*, at least through the first four years of the show.) In the opening credits to the show, Carrie is splashed by a passing bus, but she is wearing a tutu and sashaying down the street at the time, and the bus bears a poster with her image on it. Star intended the opening credits to be similar to those of *The Mary Tyler Moore Show* and *That Girl*: a mini-movie that introduces and tells a brief story about the protagonist.

Sex and the City's crucial twist on earlier single-in-the-city series like *That Girl* and *Mary Tyler Moore* is its raunchiness. Star was pleased and delighted, on pitching the storylines for the show's first season to HBO, that the channel's president of original programming, Chris Albrecht, took no umbrage at hearing about the episode in which Charlotte debates whether or not to have anal sex with her latest beau, not wanting "to become Mrs. Up the Butt." Albrecht laughed, and *Sex and the City* flourished. (It was a little-known fact that HBO also retained final cut on the show, granting the channel the right to change storylines or reedit at will. Perhaps it was more accurate than television reviewers knew to describe a uniform artistic entity known as "the HBO series.") When the foursome discuss the most effective forms of dirty talk in bed (Carrie remarks that "a simple 'You're so hard' is often quite effective"), or Samantha complains of dating a guy with "the funkiest-tasting spunk," we marveled at the dazzling frankness of what we were hearing. Television had always been bound by its restrictions: what words its characters could and could not say, what activities it could and could not depict them doing. Now, suddenly, cable television had freed itself of all such shackles, and its characters were acting less like the articulate, wisecracking automatons familiar from sitcoms past and more like our own friends. That this, too, could eventually become a television cliché was not yet on the radar of *Sex and the City*.

In one notable episode of *The Golden Girls*, Rose meets a man and admits to her friends that she has not had sex since her husband's death fifteen years prior. Everyone treads cautiously around her, but Sophia wants the news as soon as she walks in the door: "So, did you and Arnie play Find the Cannoli?" *Sex and the City* is like a six-season-long version of that joke, uncensored and uninterrupted. Samantha, fortysomething and proudly unattached, is the resident "sexual anthropologist," as the show has it, defining her sexual affiliation as "trisexual—I'll try anything once." Samantha's existence is a male sexual fantasy come to life. (Some critics carped that Samantha was simply a gay man transposed onto a female body.) Her default facial expression is a radiant smirk, her eyes rolled back into her head, as if life were merely a lengthy prelude to orgasm. When Samantha announces to her friends, in the episode "What's Sex Got to Do With It?," that she has become a lesbian and is now involved with a woman, Carrie blanches: "Wait a second. *You're* in a relationship?"

Sex and the City's sexuality is flexible, polymorphous, unpredictable. It includes same-sex desires as well as straight ones, and frankly sexual gay characters alongside its female protagonists. Bald, bespectacled Stanford Blatch (Willie Garson) and bitchy Anthony Marantino (Mario Cantone) are the alpha and omega of gayness on *Sex and the City*, romantic hapless-ness and lip-smacking omnivorousness, respectively. In its recurring inter-est in gay life as a compatriot and precursor to the new zipless world of guilt-free female sexuality, *Sex and the City* was the boldest sitcom statement yet on the subject.

Stanford and Anthony come at the conclusion of a shadow history of gay sitcom characters. They are the unacknowledged offspring of *Soap*'s Jodie Dallas (Billy Crystal), the first openly gay sitcom character in television history. They are also the descendants of *Welcome Back, Kotter*'s Horshack and *The Odd Couple*'s Oscar Madison (Jack Klugman) and Felix Unger (Tony Randall), lead plaintiffs of an unofficial brief on gay marriage some four decades ahead of its time. Messy sportswriter Oscar and neat-freak photographer Felix squabble over doing the dishes and picking up dirty underwear, but *The Odd Couple* (ABC, 1970–75) is an exemplar of unremarked same-sex romance, devoted to a kind of lived-in, slobbish bliss.

Jodie was simultaneously groundbreaking and a relic, all at once. He was the straightest gay man ever on TV, marrying a woman, fathering a child, falling in love with another woman, and bemoaning his perpetual sexual confusion. *Soap* itself seems confused about just what being gay might actually consist of, and more than a little uncomfortable with depicting gay relationships. His obvious flaws notwithstanding, Jodie is a television landmark, paving the way for future gay sitcom characters like *Will & Grace*'s Will and Jack, *The Simpsons*' Waylon Smithers, *Roseanne*'s Leon (Martin Mull) and Nancy (Sandra Bernhard), and Ellen DeGeneres's much-hyped coming-out on her show *Ellen*.

But as far as television had come since the days of *Soap*, there is a certain defensiveness to *Sex and the City*'s erotic bravado. Samantha is forever defending her rights to sexual libertinism against a world intent on judging her and to friends occasionally shocked by what they perceive as her excesses. "I will wear whatever and blow whomever I want, as long as I can breathe and kneel," she announces defiantly, after Carrie catches her pleasuring a deliveryman in her office. Even Miranda, in the episode "Attack of the Five-Foot-Ten Woman," must stand up for herself against her overly judgmental housekeeper, who has kidnapped her vibrator and substituted a statue of the Virgin Mary in its place, and declare her first principles: she is a thirty-four-year-old woman who has premarital sex, prefers purchasing pies at a bakery to baking them herself, and occasionally enjoys the company of a battery-powered sex toy.

While the show had begun in distracting mock-anthropological mode, with a peculiar fondness for hazy slow-motion interludes and a tendency to break the fourth wall, by its second season it settled into a comfortable comic routine. *Sex and the City* expects us to be familiar with, or at least amenable to hearing about, the proper nouns of Manhattan life: Manolo Blahnik and Fendi and the Rabbit and Bungalow 8. It is a show not only about who its characters do, but what they do: the places they shop, eat, drink, party. It is about women in action, forever in the process of becoming who they are.

One of the series' favored visual motifs is to show Carrie with Miranda (or Samantha or Charlotte, or any other combination of the four women) high-stepping it along a Manhattan sidewalk, walking and talking in double time. The effect is surprisingly similar to that of a contemporary series drunk on conversation, *The West Wing.* Where Aaron Sorkin's show prefers the cramped corridors of the least trafficked corners of the White House, *Sex and the City* drops its characters into the midst of the overcrowded, exuberantly energetic city, letting them feed off Manhattan's energy. "The city to me was always the fifth character on the show," said Star. *Sex and the City* is a Manhattan fantasy, beginning with its designer wardrobes. What freelance writer can afford Jimmy Choos?

As the show matures, its emphasis also begins to subtly shift from dating to relationships. The "can-you-believe-he-wanted-to-do-*that*?" sociological reportage is still present but has mostly been shifted to Samantha's plotlines, and occasionally Miranda's. The characters, previously vague at the edges, begin to solidify. Charlotte is in search of the ideal WASP white knight on his Polo Ralph Lauren horse, and Miranda is the least glamorous and most grounded of the quartet, best able to spot the double standards that keep women in their place. Later *Sex and the City* episodes are about women in search of their "ridiculous, inconvenient, consuming, can't-live-without-each-other love," as Carrie would later put it, and the many indignities to be borne along the way.

But the show is steelier than its orgasms-and-Cosmos aura might suggest. Miranda, in a moment of pique, refers to their continued obsessing over men as "seventh grade with bank accounts," and *Sex and the City* simultaneously indulges in perpetual relationship navel-gazing while also clearly preferring the company of its women. The world of *Sex and the City* is composed of the bedroom and the brunch table, ping-ponging from one to the other in eternal procession, from the act to the discussion. It drops us headlong into intimate conversation among four old friends grown accustomed to one another's company and one another's foibles. That is ultimately *Sex and the City*'s strongest suit: its ability to allow viewers to pull up an invisible fifth chair at the brunch table and eavesdrop on fast, funny, emotionally revealing chatter about sex and relationships. Almost inevitably, the show cuts from the setup—relationship setback, sexual imbroglio—to the payoff: the four-way discussion and debate over the matters of the day. It is talk not action that is the sexiest and most compelling element of *Sex and the City*. Social theorist Michel Foucault argued that human sexuality encompasses both the moments of passion and the insatiable desire to talk about said moments. *Sex and the City* would just say it was about women.

Each episode of *Sex and the City* usually features three or four plotlines, with one a serious relationship drama and the others fizzy escapades. The ratio is essential to the show's appeal. Much of each episode is devoted to lighthearted sexual shenanigans, but it is the relationship drama that kept viewers hooked, like a soap opera with full-frontal nudity. Carrie and her recurring love interest Mr. Big (Chris Noth) are the new Sam and Diane, their will-they-or-won't-they seesaw the show's dramatic ballast. "Damn, it would have been so cool if I hadn't looked back," Carrie chides herself after one encounter, but the entirety of their relationship consists of Carrie peering over her shoulder, remembering what had been and was no longer, or assessing potential threats to their temporary union.

Big, supposedly based on Bushnell's on-again, off-again boyfriend, *Vogue* publisher Ron Galotti, is alluring and charming and utterly untrustworthy, and Carrie can never quite shake him, even when she is otherwise satisfied with her latest swain. "Tell me I'm the one," Carrie begs him. "You don't have to tell your mother, or the whole world. Just tell me." But this is precisely what Big cannot do, or simply will not do, for Carrie.

The series coasted in the well-oiled groove it established for itself, its broad humor conjoined to an underlying cynicism about relationships. But with "My Motherboard, My Self," from its fourth season, written by Julie Rottenberg and Elisa Zuritsky, the show touches a deeper nerve than it ever had before, exposing itself to the world beyond dating and sex in a manner that feels far riskier than what came before it. Journalist Carrie is upset, at the start of "My Motherboard," to discover that her Mac has crashed without her having backed up any of her documents. Her boyfriend Aidan (John Corbett), a furniture designer with bedroom eyes, floppy Eddie Vedder hair, and a taste for jam-band necklaces, gamely offers to assist with rebooting her laptop, and only succeeds in making matters worse. Carrie and Aidan trudge to the high priests of Mac-dom on Twenty-Third Street, Tekserve, where judgment is rendered from on high: "You're not compatible."

The techie is critiquing Aidan the PC guy's attempt to press Ctrl-Alt-Del on a Mac, but Carrie, stung, takes it as a final verdict on their increasingly unwieldy relationship. Carrie fell for Aidan while buying one of his beautiful leather club chairs but was driven by their old-brown-shoe relationship, and by Aidan's occasional bouts of schoolmarmish disapproval, back into the arms of old flame Mr. Big. On their first date, Aidan had pulled back from a kiss, complaining, "I can taste that cigarette." Big is another forbidden pleasure for Carrie to indulge in, like her postcoital smoke.

Though Carrie and Aidan broke up after she admitted her guilt, they've now gotten back together, their relationship rebuilt on decidedly rocky turf, likely to collapse at the tiniest breeze—even a dying computer. Carrie heads to the nearest pay phone (television series, repositories of the forgotten technologies of the past!) to bitch to Miranda, who lets her friend go on at some length about her computer crisis before breaking the news: she is in Philadelphia, where her mother has had a heart attack. Miranda calls again the next day, the camera tracking in on her tear-streaked, pale face, her lips moving inaudibly before any sound emerges from her mouth: "My mom died." Miranda instinctively rejects all offers of help from her friends, angry with herself that she had been away from her mother's side when she passed away.

Carrie, Samantha, and Charlotte convene at their brunch spot, where Carrie breaks the news to her friends and flagellates herself for having said all the wrong things to Miranda. Samantha, taken aback by the news, covers up awkwardly, her perpetually fabulous facade hiding some as-yet-unseen emotional shock. She expresses surprise at being told that her presence at the funeral is expected. Samantha chooses instead to concentrate on the acrobatic sexual workout she has been enjoying with a wrestling enthusiast. She discovers, to her disappointment, that her heart is not in her G-spot. "I lost my orgasm," she tells Carrie and Charlotte mournfully. "In the cab?" Carrie asks, incredulous.

Miranda, meanwhile, is shopping for a dignified outfit for the funeral, and is blindsided by a pushy older saleswoman who insists, all of Miranda's protestations to the contrary, that she is wearing the wrong-sized bra. Miranda, never one to take insults to her dignity lying down, is astonished when the saleswoman barges into the changing room to adjust her bra, and fights back fiercely, only to break down in tears when she realizes what this contretemps reminds her of. "Suddenly, Miranda realized," Carrie observes gently in voiceover, "she would never have a fight with her mother again."

Samantha, agitated by her sexual frustration, is "troubleshooting her own laptop," attempting to reboot her disappearing orgasm via application of vibrators and assorted other sexual implements. "Charlotte, I'm masturbating," she announces fiercely, vibrator at her side, when the phone rings. "I told you I'd be doing that all day today." Eventually, Samantha joins Carrie and Charlotte at the funeral, where she rapidly assesses the dismal array of disheveled losers on display: "Well, I'm not going to find my orgasm in this town." Miranda has been questioning herself and her commitment to her mother since her death, but the funeral itself returns the focus where the show's has always been: being single. Chatting with her friends, she bemoans the unspoken sentiments of her relatives: "Ignore the coffin! There's a single thirty-five-year-old woman walking behind it!"

Samantha shrinks from a sobbing woman sitting next to her, shifting into the farthest corner of the church pew. Miranda turns around and catches her eye after the priest repeatedly confuses her with her married sister. Samantha offers her condolences for the first time, mouthing, "I'm sorry"—then bursts into tears, sobbing, as Carrie puts it, "for things she didn't even know she felt." We have moved well beyond the show's easy stereotypes to something knottier and harder to pin down. Samantha is more than a walking libido; she is also a woman whose abiding love of *la petite mort* is a means of putting aside her fear of the larger, more permanent one. And the friendship of the four women is complicated by something darker and more troubling than the show's usual array of relationship troubles.

In its transposition of its fundamentally comic characters into a dramatic sphere previously beyond their ken, "My Motherboard, My Self" echoes a remarkable 1987 episode of *Designing Women* (CBS, 1986–93). In "Killing All the Right People," a dying AIDS patient (Tony Goldwyn) asks the women of Sugarbaker & Associates to decorate his funeral. Julia Sugarbaker (Dixie Carter) torches the episode's designated straw woman for her insensitivity to the horrors of the disease: "Imogene, get serious! Who do you think you're talking to? I've known you for twenty-seven years, and all I can say is, if God was giving out sexually transmitted diseases to people as a punishment for sinning, then *you* would be at the free clinic *all the time!*" The episode pulls no punches. Goldwyn dies, and while the bigots have been summarily told off, the toll of AIDS is not even temporarily, metaphorically halted.

Anticipating *Sex and the City*'s unstable brew of comedy and steely feminist vigor, both *Designing Women* and Diane English's newsroom sitcom *Murphy Brown* (CBS, 1988–97) are by, for, and about middle-aged women, exploring difficult or controversial material from a prickly, feminist perspective. Candice Bergen's acerbic television journalist Murphy is a feminist model without being much of a role model, an alcoholic, vindictive, late-middle-aged Miranda—or was she more of a Samantha? *Designing Women*, more enamored of its main characters—even Delta Burke's man-hungry Suzanne Sugarbaker, close kin to both Blanche and Samantha—has a similar faith in the intelligence of its audience, name-checking Freud and Virginia Woolf the way *Murphy Brown* drops references to Nixon and George Shultz.

In an unparalleled contretemps at the intersection of politics and pop culture, Murphy Brown would also become a single mother—over the public objections of Vice President Dan Quayle, who never seemed to entirely grasp that she was a fictional character. *Sex and the City* never became a culture-war flashpoint the way Murphy and her baby had, and yet the show has become emblematic of an era, much like *The Mary Tyler Moore Show* once was. It was more than a sitcom; it was a symbol of the rapidly shifting landscape of American culture, which had made room for these profane, sensual, assertive women.

"My Motherboard" ends with Carrie back at her desk, in front of her old laptop—now helpfully outfitted with a backup drive. Carrie sums things up by returning to the computer metaphor she had employed earlier: "After all, computers crash, people die, relationships fall apart. The best we can do is breathe and reboot."

Let us breathe and reboot, too, and return to *Sex and the City* before Carrie's computer crashes. "My Motherboard, My Self" marks a decisive turning point in the series. Before it, *SATC* was all Cosmopolitans and gallery openings and the fabulous lives of thirtysomething single women with disposable income to burn. After, it cracks open to let in more of the everyday heartaches that even fabulous Manhattan women must endure, and becomes a far better, and far less disposable, show than it had previously been. The switch from Darren Star, showrunner for the series' first three seasons, to Michael Patrick King undoubtedly played a substantial role in the gradual deepening of *Sex and the City*.

After "My Motherboard, My Self," *Sex and the City* deliberately lets some of the bloom come off the rose. Fantasy is eclipsed by reality. Charlotte fails to get pregnant, and her marriage to WASP beau ideal Trey (Kyle MacLachlan) collapses. Miranda does get pregnant, and after agonizing over whether to keep the baby—a painful debate for Charlotte to witness—decides to enter a new, wearying life as a single mother. "If he was thirty-five, this is when we would break up," she says about her newly arrived thirteen-pound bag of horrors. Carrie's relationship with Aidan flames out. Samantha's passion for wealthy hotelier Richard (James Remar) fizzles when she discovers his serial cheating. But friendship trumps all. Miranda gingerly breaks the news of her pregnancy to Charlotte, and after bursting into tears, Charlotte generously accepts Miranda's good news as her own: "We're having a baby?"

The newer, more difficult material is handled with the show's traditional savoir-faire. When Miranda's water breaks, it splashes directly onto Carrie's Christian Louboutin pumps. Steve gets testicular cancer, and Miranda, rattled, harangues him about doctors and treatment; later, when Carrie invites her to leave the city for the weekend, Miranda responds, "I can't go. Steve has cancer. Somebody has to stay in town and make him feel bad about it." Later, when Samantha begs Carrie to listen to her fears about being sick, it still emerges muffled as a joke: "I could die, Carrie, with really bad hair."

Countless *Sex and the City* imitators would follow in the wake of its success. The networks lusted after access to its upwardly mobile female audience, but without *Sex and the City*'s honesty and explicitness, broadcast imitators like *Lipstick Jungle* (NBC, 2008–09), also based on a Candace Bushnell novel, and *Cashmere Mafia* (ABC, 2008) were doomed to irrelevance. The best *SATC* imitator was another premium cable offering, one that pondered a very basic twist on the familiar setup: what if the four best friends were guys?

Entourage (HBO, 2004–11) is many things—Hollywood insiders' report, extended male fantasy—but fundamentally it is an all-male takeoff of *Sex and the City*, transplanting its New Yorkers to sunshine-and-palm-treed Los Angeles. Like the women of *Sex and the City*, the four guys of *Entourage*—movie star Vincent Chase (Adrian Grenier); best friend and manager E (Kevin Connolly); Vincent's brother, has-been actor Johnny Drama (Kevin Dillon, less-successful real-life brother of Matt); and all-purpose hanger-on Turtle (Jerry Ferrara)—are defined by their unbreakable bond. Women come and go, jobs are jettisoned with surprising nonchalance, but the four boys—they are hardly men—remain together forever.

Entourage's passion for aimless banter and sexual badinage is straight out of the Carrie Bradshaw playbook. *Entourage* is blatantly, shamelessly devoted to the fulfillment and exploitation of male fantasies (why, after all, are there beautiful women in bikinis and halter tops lingering in the background of practically every scene?), mostly without *Sex and the City*'s grounding in human frailty.

The walk-and-talk is the physical incarnation of *Entourage*'s default mood of impassioned wheedling. Hollywood is a cesspool of conflicting desires, and characters are forever striding one after the other, hoping to sway each other in their own direction. More than sex, even, Vince is turned on by the manifestations of his own power. "Say I have the juice," he tells Turtle after using his charm and his fame to secure a coveted pair of rare Nikes. "Say it." His agent Ari Gold, played by *Seinfeld* and *Larry Sanders* alum Jeremy Piven, puts Vince's self-absorption to shame, his charm not quite all-encompassing enough to offset his titanic ego. Piven is a gifted physical comedian, and he became *Entourage*'s breakout star on the basis of his tics: the "Did you just say *that?*" double take, the jittery "Who else is in the room?" scan of his surroundings, the limbs-flailing mad dash to secure a waffling client's latest demand.

The power games are ultimately a less joyous aspect of the show, playing second fiddle to its showbiz wish fulfillment. *Entourage* is a fairy tale whose happy endings are always guaranteed. It is a show where even Vincent's desire to mingle with the hoi polloi for a day, browsing the discount racks at Book Soup, still ends in a fantastic sex romp. Reality was for the birds.

By the end of *Sex and the City*, on the other hand, a new equilibrium had been achieved, an understanding that fairy-tale endings are appropriate only for fairy-tale princesses. The series delivers the expected happy endings—this is, after all, a Manhattan fable—while also extracting a measure of realistic heartache. Charlotte finds happiness and starts a family with sweaty, bald, uncouth Jewish divorce lawyer Harry Goldenblatt (Evan Handler); Samantha gets breast cancer and loses her hair but opens herself to a new kind of love with Absolut hunk Smith Jerrod (Jason Lewis); Miranda settles down in uber-domestic Brooklyn with husband Steve (David Eigenberg) and son Brady, but is also saddled with the care of Steve's mother, suffering from dementia. After Carrie leaves for Paris and a theoretically glamorous and substantively lonely new life with acclaimed artist Aleksandr

Petrovsky (Mikhail Baryshnikov), she's rescued by Mr. Big, stepping up at last and confessing that she's "the one." But even as the show provides a long-delayed catharsis for Carrie and Big, it insists on following it up with the most important reunion of all—between Carrie and her friends, in the city she loves.

As if in penance for its earlier frothiness, *Sex and the City* sends a symbolic stand-in to her death to acknowledge that the era of good times is over. Before Carrie leaves for Paris to join Aleksandr, she runs into an old party-girl friend (played by Kristen Johnston of *3rd Rock from the Sun* [NBC, 1996–2001]). Tipsy on too many glasses of champagne, she trips and tumbles out an open window to her death. In case we had not yet received the message, it is underlined for us: "It's the end of an era," Carrie offers. "Yep, the party is officially over," responds Samantha. There would be two feature films after the series' conclusion, but the party had definitely come to a crashing halt.

It would take nearly a decade for a show to emerge that would capture some of *Sex and the City*'s Zeitgeist-defining ambience. Another New York series, another four women, another epic conversation about relationships and careers and friendships. But this was Brooklyn, not Manhattan; internships, not jobs; boys, not men; twentysomethings, not thirtysomethings. The terms had changed, even as the fundamental structure remained the same.

The prominently placed *Sex and the City* poster, hung on the apartment wall of a college student named Shoshanna (Zosia Mamet), acknowledges the notable debt of *Girls* (HBO, 2012–) to its predecessor. But by displacing its influence onto the youngest and most gullible of its characters, and by allowing her to natter on inanely about the similarities between the adventures of her friends Hannah (Lena Dunham, also the show's creator), Marnie (Allison Williams), and Jessa (Jemima Kirke) and those of Carrie & Co., *Girls* was also inoculating itself against any critique of the resemblance.

In its details, *Girls* is notably distinct from *SATC*, its lack of gilding evident in more than just its one-word title. Its sex scenes are awkward and elongated where *Sex and the City*'s were smooth and frictionless. Its friendships are marred by dissension and its characters are sometimes-charming monsters of self-regard and self-absorption—so much so that one occasionally wonders whether there are jokes about narcissism that *Girls* itself is not entirely in on. But the fundamental outline of *Girls* is markedly similar to its predecessor, as is its desire to shock and unsettle its audience.

For *Sex and the City*, the formula was nudity and frank sexuality; for these younger women, a decade onward, that is no longer enough. It is not Hannah's nudity but her flabbiness that is shocking. *Girls* lingers on the sight of Hannah's untoned flesh and the intense awkwardness of her encounters with quasi-boyfriend Adam (Adam Driver), intent on unsettling a television audience too comfortable with HBO's traditional array of taut female flesh, featured on series like *The Sopranos*, *Boardwalk Empire*, and *Game of Thrones*.

Sex is the initial selling point, but *Girls* blossoms in its second season into a bittersweet portrait of know-nothing twentysomething dissension and anomie. It also serves as a rebuke to *Sex and the City*'s elegant facade, further indication that the anxiety of influence requires a rejection of one's forebears. Moreover, it marks the shifting attitudes of the sitcom, rejecting with one hand what it had so generously embraced with the other. One generation's realism is the next's out-of-touch fantasy.

19

Freaks and Geeks

"Dead Dogs and Gym Teachers"

October 10, 2000 ▪ NBC/Fox Family

A boy warms a grilled cheese sandwich on the stove, his TV tray positioned in front of the couch as he settles in for a lazy, lonely afternoon with his most dependable, trustworthy friend: the television. He laughs uproariously at the egghead-comedy noodlings of Garry Shandling, a dark clump of cheese smudged against his teeth. He laughs alone in front of the television, and we must admit, if we are honest with ourselves, that that boy is us.

Freaks and Geeks (NBC/Fox Family, 1999–2000), from the very outset, explicitly defines itself in opposition to the average run of sitcoms, summoning the ghost of countless TV shows and movies about adolescence that concern themselves with the emotional lives of cheerleaders and the first-string quarterbacks who love them only to summarily dismiss them. In the very first scene of the first episode of the show, the camera zooms in on a football player and a blonde, well-scrubbed cheerleader sitting in the stands as the football team practices. "I need you to talk to me," she pleads, and her boyfriend stammers, overcome with emotion, "It's just that I love you so much it scares me." The couple's embrace is unexpectedly interrupted by the opening chords of Van Halen's scuzzy anthem "Runnin' with the Devil," as the camera ventures below the stands to take in the stoners loitering underneath. We never see the two lovebirds again.

Freaks and Geeks is not about the cheerleaders and jocks, but about the likes of Bill Haverchuck, glimpsed at the outset of the episode "Dead Dogs and Gym Teachers" at his afternoon TV ritual. Bill (Martin Starr), with his friends and compatriots in high school Siberia, Sam (John Francis Daley) and Neal (Samm Levine), make up the "geeks" segment of the series' balanced equation, relegated to the bottom rungs of the social ladder. School is a series of indignities—flicked with towels in the locker room, ostracized by pretty girls in the lunchroom, humiliated in the classroom—but home is a beacon of TV-blessed solace.

At least until "Dead Dogs and Gym Teachers" (written by Judd Apatow and Bob Nickman), coming near the end of *Freaks'* lone season, when Bill learns that his mother's new boyfriend, coming over that evening for dinner, is his dreaded gym teacher, Mr. Fredricks (Thomas F. Wilson). Mr. Fredricks quizzes Bill about movies—his own favorite is *Rocky II*, impressed as he was by the glorious abdominals of Carl Weathers—and is horrified to learn that Bill is partial to the Bill Murray comedy *Stripes*: "Somebody ought to smack some respect into that guy."

Cajoled by Sam and Neal into going go-karting with Mr. Fredricks, Bill enjoys himself until an accidental bump sends him flying off the track, and he takes out his frustration on his mother's new suitor before stalking off: "You always have to win! All you care about is winning! You don't care at all about other people's feelings!" Mr. Fredricks finds Bill in his car, his eyes red and glassy from crying. The gym coach lumbers into the backseat, tentatively justifying himself to his student: "You know what I am? I'm a guy who loves your mother very much."

In the episode's final scene, Mr. Fredricks watches a basketball game on the Haverchuck family television, silently rooting his team on before Bill emerges from his room and commandeers the TV to watch *Dallas*. Bill tentatively begins to explain the baroque motivations of the nighttime soap opera's numerous characters, and Mr. Fredricks, deeply gratified to be included, peppers Bill with questions until he is gently shushed. "It's OK," Bill offers, "I'll tell you during the commercial." Mr. Fredricks, a fundamentally decent, if occasionally loutish, man, looks over at Bill and sighs heavily as the ghost of a smile flickers across his face, a hard-fought, well-earned victory in his grasp. TV is more than just the "boob tube"; it can also offer us a common language when all other words fail.

Meanwhile, Sam's sister, Lindsay (the superlative Linda Cardellini, the show's conscience and guiding spirit), is horrified to discover that she and her friend Kim (Busy Philipps) have accidentally run over her old friend Millie's dog, Goliath. Lindsay has been taking steps—at first tentative, then increasingly bold—to flee her past as a mathlete and star student, ditching her dowdy school garb for her father's army jacket and abandoning the hopelessly square Millie (Sarah Hagan) for a new set of burnout friends who congregate under the stairs at school. Kim is a jerk, Nick (Jason Segel) is a pothead, Daniel (James Franco) is manipulative, and Ken (Seth Rogen) is obnoxious, but Lindsay sees something in her friends that we do not, at least at first.

Lindsay and her fellow freaks are planning to see the Who in concert, and her ex-boyfriend Nick, inspired by lead guitarist Pete Townshend, has written a tribute to Lindsay cleverly titled "Lady L." "I couldn't use her real name," Nick explains. Ken has a ready-made rejoinder: "You shouldn't use *your* real name if you're writing that stuff." Later on, when Nick prepares to play "Lady L" for Lindsay, Ken intercedes, grabbing his acoustic guitar and smashing it, Townshend-style, against the pavement. *"This,"* he pointedly concludes, "is the biggest favor I ever did for you."

Millie, traumatized by the loss of her pet, defies her mother to join the freaks on their rock 'n' roll adventure, instantly transforming from goody-two-shoes into potential burnout. But Kim protects her from her worst impulses by blurting out the damaging truth: "I killed your dog!" Lindsay and Millie end up missing the concert, choosing to pore over old photos of Goliath, including one of two little girls in matching overalls and Indian feathers, their faces painted, standing next to an enormous dog that dwarfs them both.

Was this even a comedy? Not only was there no laugh track, there was hardly any path for viewers to follow at all; everything was marked with the same bittersweet brush. A hybrid of sitcom and drama, the hour-long, single-camera *Freaks and Geeks* also blends cruelty and kindness, its unexpected sweetness a respite from the everyday malice native to the struggle for teenage survival it depicts.

Freaks, premiering on NBC in the fall of 1999, was created by Paul Feig and executive produced by Judd Apatow. The latter, soon to achieve remarkable success as the writer and director of raunchy relationship comedies like *The 40-Year-Old Virgin* and *Knocked Up*, had gotten his start as a producer on the short-lived sketch comedy series *The Ben Stiller Show* (Fox, 1992–93). After that show's cancellation, Apatow served as a writer on *The Larry Sanders Show*, and some of that series' cringe-inducing style of comedy, simultaneously awkward and endearing, had made its way from the green room to the classroom.

Freaks mined Feig's and Apatow's pasts, as well as those of the show's writing staff, for hilarious and emotionally resonant material. Feig (who would later direct the enormously successful 2011 film *Bridesmaids*) had his writers fill out a questionnaire about their adolescent experiences, with questions like "Who were you in love with and why?" The answers were collected in binders, passed out to the staff, and used for artistic inspiration. Like the character of Sam, Feig really had worn a Parisian night suit to school; like Neal, writer Jeff Judah had indeed unexpectedly realized his father was cheating on his mother. "Weirder stuff happens to people in real life than it does on TV," said Feig.

Feig, himself a high school outcast, had been more comfortable writing the geeks than the freaks, leading Apatow to suggest finding talented performers and building the freak roles around them. Thus, *Freaks* served as a minor league for up-and-coming performers like James Franco, Seth Rogen, and Jason Segel, each of whom would also star in future Apatow cinematic productions.

As youthful scholars of television, Sam, Bill, and Neal would instantly recognize *Freaks and Geeks* as being built on the classical model of sitcom. Sam and Lindsay's mom and dad are prototypical sitcom parents: father Harold (Joe Flaherty) comically outraged, in Ward Cleaver fashion, by his children's minor scrapes, and mother Jean (Becky Ann Baker) loving but susceptible to emotional wounds at the hands of her kids. Lindsay and Sam, too, are familiar sitcom archetypes: the good girl experimenting with rebellion, and the modestly geeky younger son. Each episode of *Freaks and Geeks* is structured around a crisis or dilemma that might not have been out of place on, say, *Full House* (ABC, 1987–95): Daniel asks Lindsay to help him cheat on a math test; Lindsay crashes the family car; Sam is unsure whether to tell Neal he spotted his father with another woman.

And yet the expected payoffs, prompted by untold decades of unadventurous sitcom plots, never arrive. The setups are familiar but the resolutions are not, for *Freaks and Geeks* finds its comedy in the all-too-human disjunction between intention and action. Nothing ever quite works out the way anyone intends it to. Lindsay defends a mentally handicapped boy from bullies and accidentally insults him by referring to him as "retarded." She pushes Nick to be more hands-on with his music, only to see the ensuing tension break up the freaks' band. Sam dreams of untouchable cheerleader goddess Cindy Sanders (Natasha Melnick), only to find himself inexplicably bored with her once they do get together.

Much of *Freaks and Geeks'* resonance stems from the emotional morass of teenage love. Sam loves Cindy, who loves Todd. Cindy loves Sam, but Cindy turns out to be boring. Neal loves Lindsay, who thinks she might like

Daniel, but Daniel is dating Kim, so Lindsay loves Nick, but she doesn't really, so Nick takes up with Sarah. Sam and Neal and Bill all love new girl Maureen, who likes them all, but only as friends. Daniel falls for the punk-rock girl at the convenience store but goes back to Kim with his tail between his legs after a disastrous evening at a punk club. Sarcastic Ken falls for tuba player Amy, but she's intersex ("packing a gun and a holster"), which is confusing, to say the least.

The show's charm emerges from its deliberate confusion of tones—comedy giving way to pathos, pathos providing unintentional comedy. Nick comforts Lindsay after her house party spirals out of control, then (shades of Sam Malone) clumsily attempts to unclasp her bra. Popular cheerleader Vicki frostily keeps Bill at bay during their seven minutes together in a darkened room during a game of Spin the Bottle, then impulsively kisses him. After watching Kim's mother savagely wrestle with her for her car keys, her stepfather adds the ironic kicker: "You spoil her."

Freaks and Geeks is, in short, about the confusion inherent in being a teenager, alternating riotous good cheer and subdued anguish from moment to moment, scene to scene. It is a comedy whose emotional template replicates that of adolescence itself, keeping us off-kilter with its persistently off-balance rhythms. Farce gives way to gloom, only to unexpectedly veer back in the direction of comedy. If we didn't know how to respond, well—neither did any of the show's characters. As we're reminded in the show's opening credit sequence, in which the characters offer an array of forced, fake, or absent smiles to an unseen yearbook photographer's camera, being a teenager means wearing a mask. The only question is what kind of mask to wear.

The confusion is one not only of tone but also of our own assumptions. Jean Renoir famously noted in his classic film *The Rules of the Game* that "the tragedy of life is that everyone has their reasons"; *Freaks and Geeks'* take on Renoir is that those reasons provide much of the comedy of life, too. The series deliberately lays traps for its audience, prodding us into making snap judgments about its characters. We think we know them instantly, familiar with other sitcoms' telegraphing of attitudes, but everything we assume proves to be mistaken. The hard shells of many of *Freaks and Geeks'* characters cover the all-too-unprotected, quivering flesh.

This is true even of Alan (Chauncey Leopardi), the ninth-grade bully who torments the geeks for the better part of the season, his upper lip curled into a permanent sneer. In "Chokin' and Tokin'," Alan sneaks a fistful of peanuts into the allergic Bill's sandwich as revenge for an abortive scuffle. Reluctantly dragged to Bill's hospital bedside, he takes in the array of machines surrounding the unconscious Bill, and charges once more: "You're not faking, are you?" Anger gives way to remorse, and Alan begs Bill to recover, pleading that he will do anything if only Bill will not die. Even bullies have trampled hearts, for it turns out that Alan holds a grudge from the fourth grade, when Bill and his friends had excluded him from firing off rockets with them. (The story reminds us instantly of an earlier episode, when the beautiful Maureen is invited to join in that very same activity and notices Bill's silvery projectile: "God, Bill, your rocket is huge." Who says women don't care about size?)

Freaks and Geeks does not merely alternate the sour and the sweet, the charming and the brutal; it mingles them. There are times—too many to count—when we are unsure whether we are intended to laugh at *Freaks and Geeks* or to cry. When Bill, awaking in the hospital ICU, offers to feign further illness so that Neal and Sam will continue to benefit from the emotionally stoked largesse of their female classmates, is it funny? Is it sad? Is it both at once? No other show this consistently hilarious also made us cry so regularly.

Veering between and commingling such extremes, *Freaks* followed a path laid out, if rarely followed, by a shadow history of acclaimed series that probed the previously unexplored ground dividing television comedy and drama. (Let us delicately avoid the term "dramedy," which stinks of Burbank pitch meetings and Manhattan upfronts.) To violate the established order of television required some nimble footwork or explicit clarification of those violations. *M*A*S*H* was among the first shows to intertwine comedy and drama, the satiric looseness of its tone conjoined to an essential war-is-hell seriousness. *M*A*S*H* was a sitcom (thirty minutes long, with a laugh track) with aspirations to drama; 1980s shows inspired by its example were, often as not, dramas with occasional aspirations to comedy.

Hill Street Blues (NBC, 1981–87) and *St. Elsewhere* (NBC, 1982–88) revolutionized the network-television drama, their interconnected plotlines and multi-episode story arcs the inspiration for future dramas like *Homicide: Life on the Street* and *ER*. They also defined a new kind of hour-long drama distinct from their stodgy predecessors for their interest in comedy as an accent to the primary drama. Illustrating the sheer variety of life passing through the doors of a hospital or a police precinct means encompassing the frivolous as well as the weighty. Such secondary plotlines provide a necessary contrast to the often melodramatic swoop of the primary stories.

On the otherwise somber *St. Elsewhere*, Howie Mandel's Dr. Wayne Fiscus is the designated comic relief, his ever-present Red Sox cap a flashing neon sign of whimsicality. Encountering a difficult patient, he tells her roguishly, in full used car salesman mode, "This week we're running a special on abdominal distress. That includes parts, labor, a free checkup of all vital systems, a five-year, 50,000-mile warranty, whichever comes first."

Hill Street Blues prefers to parcel out its comedy more evenly among its cast. Sometimes the designated comic relief can itself unexpectedly shade into drama. Captain Freedom (Dennis Dugan), the outlandishly costumed mock-superhero devoted to cleaning up the streets on a multi-episode *Hill Street* arc, unexpectedly meets his death in a hail of slow-motion gunfire at the end of the episode "Freedom's Last Stand."

Perhaps no series so thoroughly articulated the new deliberate genre confusion of the 1980s as *Moonlighting* (ABC, 1985–89), simultaneously a stylish investigative procedural in the vein of its contemporary *Miami Vice* and a screwball comedy. The series, created by former *Taxi* writer Glenn Gordon Caron, preferred not to establish any clear hierarchy; comedy and drama grappled for the upper hand.

Moonlighting regularly introduces its cases with sequences that could have been taken directly from *Miami Vice*: booming drums, burbling synthesizers, stylish camerawork, and an array of gritty urban settings. A gun goes off, and we return to the cozy domestic sphere of the Blue Moon

Detective Agency, where the vibe is less Michael Mann than Preston Sturges. (The overlapping dialogue, straight out of *The Lady Eve*, is a broad hint of the show's sensibilities.) Maddy Hayes (Cybill Shepherd) and David Addison (Bruce Willis) are a screwball not-quite-couple, their pairing a union of opposites. Ex-model Maddy is a nervous newcomer to the private-eye business, and David is a wisecracking vet with a never-ending sense of amusement at his own antics.

Theirs is a self-aware Bogey-and-Bacall vibe, knowingly trading banter as a form of intellectual foreplay. When the partners pose as the waitstaff at an exclusive party to track down a spy in "The Murder's in the Mail," Maddy must put on a skimpy maid's outfit, and David stares directly into her cleavage, rapt with pleasure. "You're dressed like that for America, and I, for one, salute you," he says, snapping off a slow salute. Maddy is not amused: "Salute you, Addison."

Like episodes of *Cheers* from the Sam-and-Diane period, new installments of *Moonlighting* customarily end with a tender, ambiguous moment between its main characters. After Maddy falls for David's grifter brother in "Brother, Can You Spare a Blonde?" she and David engage in a playful exegesis of his having driven his brother to the airport. "You always this much fun this early in the morning?" David asks. "You're gonna die wondering," Maddy shoots back.

"Atomic Shakespeare" casts Shepherd and Willis, his performance one long wink, as Kate and Petruchio in an extremely loose adaptation of *The Taming of the Shrew*. Shakespeare's squabbling lovers are David and Maddy's distant forebears, their bickering bearing a distinct resemblance to the familiar brand being hawked weekly on ABC: "No, we will not," Kate tells Petruchio, struggling out of his grasp. "Not marry, not this Sunday, not next Sunday, not any Sunday from now until the end of time!"

Moonlighting's genre indiscretions—prime-time Shakespeare, drama and comedy intertwined—give way to a knowing mockery of television cliché. Maddy and David regularly break character, address the camera directly, and acknowledge their presence on a television show. "Maddy," David tells his foil, "I just had my hand on your behind. If I get any more serious, they're going to move us to basic cable." This is self-aware television, all too conscious that it is composed of TV stereotypes given herky-jerky life. "You can't just burst in here like that!" a cop shouts at David as he tumbles into an interrogation room, posing as Maddy's lawyer. "Tell that to the writers," he smirks back.

Style and comic verve interlock, each reinforcing the other. *Moonlighting* is interested in amusing and thrilling its audience in roughly equal measures. If the show seems more committed to the former than the latter, that is largely a testament to the comic strengths of its two leads.

Moonlighting ran out of steam as soon as Maddy and David got together, but its chief governing principle—of muddying the waters between comedy and drama—became a regular staple on television in the 1980s and beyond. As soon as TV shows could acknowledge the medium's arbitrary division of labor between comedy and drama, the rules began to fall away, their inherent illogic scrubbed away by the disinfectant of exposure.

Shortly after *Moonlighting*'s arrival, sitcoms like *The Days and Nights of Molly Dodd* (NBC/Lifetime, 1987–91), *Hooperman* (ABC, 1987–89), *Frank's Place* (CBS, 1987–88), *The "Slap" Maxwell Story* (ABC, 1987–88), and *Brooklyn Bridge* (CBS, 1991–93) followed in its footsteps, echoing its stylish allure and glints of dramatic heft. The shows made sure to hit sentimental and comic notes with equal regularity and ferocity; John Ritter's shambling detective Hooperman sobs in the kitchen of his murdered landlord only minutes after using a watermelon as an effective visual aid in talking down a suicidal jumper, and Blair Brown's bumbling Molly Dodd flirts with her date, bantering about the aphrodisiacal powers of oysters, before spotting her father, still married to her mother, on a date at the next table. These were comedies with an edge, thirty-minute series with a dramatic heft closer to *M*A*S*H* than to, say, *Cheers*. But *M*A*S*H*'s recipe for seriously funny fare was not so easily re-created, and few of these series found loyal audiences.

One of the few to succeed in that task was *The Wonder Years* (ABC, 1988–93). If *Freaks and Geeks* could be said to have had a single progenitor, it would be this winning period piece, another nostalgic show about adolescence recollected in tranquility. *The Wonder Years* is unabashedly sentimental where *Freaks* is bittersweet, even as Kevin Arnold (Fred Savage) is punched in the face by a vengeful ex or flops out of his chair while eavesdropping on a pretty girl's conversation. Kevin is a high school hero in the vein of Sam Weir, well-meaning but romantically inept. The gap between past and present on the show, between action and memory, is also the chasm separating comedy and drama. With no laugh track and Daniel Stern's ever-present, self-mocking narration, *The Wonder Years* is forever reaching for that lump in the throat, even as its first instinct is to amuse.

Many of the seriocomic sitcoms of the era chose to forgo the laugh track, which previously had been considered all but obligatory. The canned laughter of the traditional sitcom served as a click track for viewers, a prerecorded mix of chuckles and guffaws that cued them where to insert their own. The "laff box," designed by sound engineer Charley Douglass, had been used since the 1950s to fill in weak spots where the response of the studio audience was insufficient. Douglass's machine supplied a variety of artificial laughs, each targeted to a different kind of joke. The laugh track became a crutch for 1960s and 1970s sitcoms, even layered onto shows that had no studio audience and divorced from any sense of how actual viewers might respond. Later, savvier sitcoms avoided strictly canned laughter, preferring instead to rely on studio audiences alone, but unnaturally amplifying their responses to bulk up any weak laughs. By the 1990s, for sitcoms unwilling to draw a sharp distinction between comedy and drama, even that seemed forced and artificial.

Hour-long series—until now almost exclusively the province of dramas—also began to mingle the serious and the flippant. They discovered that they could be exaggerated and realistic all at once, tempering their traditional approach with surreal flourishes. Where *Hill Street Blues* and *St. Elsewhere* had carefully penned their comedic interludes in self-contained subplots, shows like *Northern Exposure* (CBS, 1990–95), *Picket Fences* (CBS, 1992–96), and *Ally McBeal* (Fox, 1997–2002) (the latter two series both productions of the prolific David E. Kelley) were genuine hybrids of drama and comedy, articulating both, favoring neither. On *Picket Fences*, a serial killer named Cupid shoots arrows at his designated targets, and a dentist dressed up as a giant tooth teaches schoolchildren about proper oral hygiene. The maudlin single-woman blues of *Ally McBeal* are also modulated by flashes of comic excess as Ally's overheated imagination spills over into reality: overbearing secretary Jane Krakowski's head swells to gargantuan size, or Ally shoots literal daggers at a chatty colleague to keep him from divulging a secret. Kelley's comic flourishes are robust but also serve to mask the creeping preachiness of his shows, all anguished wringing of hands over the latest newspaper headlines.

The pattern of intertwined drama and comedy reached a hyperverbal pinnacle on Aaron Sorkin's series *Sports Night* and *The West Wing*. The former is a comedy with pretensions to drama, and the latter a drama with comedic accents. Both are behind-the-scenes workplace series whose primary loyalty is to playful chatter. On *The West Wing* (NBC, 1999–2006), the general air of quick-witted, fast-talking, fast-walking bonhomie allows for characters who are deeply serious (they are working for the president of the United States, after all) and yet able to be justifiably witty about their high-stress professions. *Hill Street Blues* and *St. Elsewhere* had used comedy as a stress-release mechanism; *The West Wing* is a drama that is actually, regularly laugh-out-loud funny.

Gilmore Girls (CW, 2000–07), created by former *Roseanne* writer-producer Amy Sherman-Palladino, is another exemplar of the hyperspeed chatterfest style television was mastering. Like *Moonlighting*, its central premise—single mother cut off from her snobbish WASP family, and the brilliant daughter who brings them reluctantly back together—is less crucial than the air of antic screwball hyperverbalism, as if family life is merely the excuse for an endless array of pop-culture quips and freeform riffs.

Much of the new comic drama emerged from the desire to goose weary genres with a jolt of satirical energy. What could be done with the evening soap opera—that battleground of warring Carringtons and Ewings—that had not already been mapped out a dozen times before? Mingling parody, mystery, and broad comedy, *Desperate Housewives* (ABC, 2004–12) is simultaneously pulpy evening soap and burlesque of same. The hunky young gardener clips the hedges, making small talk with the husband of the woman he has just ravished as his still-bare behind enjoys the cool afternoon breeze. The supersaturated colors of the show's visual palette match the deliciously exaggerated sexual and personal hypocrisies of its emotional palette. No plot twist could be too absurd; the spillover of dramatic excess could be redirected to comedy.

By the turn of the millennium, even television's elite dramas had embraced the notion that they could be funny without violating their unwritten compact with audiences. In fact, the best dramas of the new television golden age, such as *The Sopranos* (HBO, 1999–2007), *The Wire* (HBO, 2002–08), and *Mad Men* (AMC, 2007–), were expected to provide comedic touches. (Otherwise, what were we to make of Christopher and Paulie Walnuts bickering while lost in the Pine Barrens, or that lawn mower running over an adman's foot?) Series no longer faced an either/or choice between comedy and drama but plotted a point along a spectrum: How funny could a drama be? How often would it reach for the lightest arrow in its arsenal? Characters could be both Hamlet and Falstaff, the tragic hero and the buffoon all at once. Tony Soprano could murder a snitch in one scene and play proud suburban father on his daughter's college tour in the next; *The Wire*'s Bunk and McNulty could investigate the scene of a brutal murder and communicate entirely in variations on the single word "fuck."

All dramas worth their salt became black comedies in disguise, and black comedies often bore the imprint of drama. After the fashion of *The Sopranos* or *Breaking Bad*, the half-hour suburban comedy *Weeds* (Showtime, 2005–2012) peels back the Band-Aid atop middle-class life to reveal the festering wound beneath. Like *Desperate Housewives*, it's about the secret lives of women, trapped in the amber of middle-class comfort and desperate to escape, but its lingering pleasures are mostly to be found in the aimless, drug-fueled conversation of its protagonists. Nancy's feckless brother-in-law Andy (Justin Kirk), sprawled on the living-room couch, asks the family housekeeper Lupita (Renee Victor) to settle an anatomical argument between him and his stoner pal Doug (Kevin Nealon): "What do you call the thing between the dick and the asshole?" Lupita responds, "The coffee table."

Nurse Jackie (Showtime, 2009–), starring *Sopranos* alum Edie Falco, is about another fatally damaged antihero in the vein of Carmela Soprano's husband, *Breaking Bad*'s Walter White, and *Boardwalk Empire*'s Nucky Thompson. But the mood of this thirty-minute hospital series is sprightlier than any of those shows, infected with a virus of galloping absurdity. A nurse spots medical staff sprinting down the hall and is immediately curious: "Is there cake?" Jackie, needing last rites for a patient, grabs a priest away from a dying man's bedside after first feeling for his pulse: "You've got ten minutes. Need him for five." This show about a harried nurse juggling husband and boyfriend and raging pill addiction has a wide sentimental streak just beneath its surface, even as it plumbs the depths of a darkness usually foreign to the sitcom. (The show's best laugh, of course, is a *Sopranos* in-joke; Carmela is, at long last, fucking Father Phil.)

The phenomenal success of so many of its seriocomic successors meant little for the fate of *Freaks and Geeks*. Bounced around from one time slot to another, including Saturday nights, when its natural audience would be unlikely to be home to watch it, *Freaks and Geeks* limped through part of one ratings-challenged season before being canceled by NBC. Network executives had been supportive of the show's breaks from sitcom orthodoxy but wanted more "victories" for the show's characters—something Feig and Apatow felt unwilling, or unable, to deliver.

Feig and Apatow wore 1970s tuxedos to the show's wrap party, and Feig had *Freaks* class rings made. *Freaks* was manhandled so thoroughly by the network that "Dead Dogs and Gym Teachers" never aired on NBC, premiering instead on Fox Family after the series' abrupt cancellation. Critically beloved and ignored by audiences, the show would have an unexpected afterlife, both on DVD, where it was belatedly discovered by all the fans who had missed it during its broadcast run, and in the *Freaks*-like series that would follow in its wake.

Stung by NBC's lack of loyalty to his show, Apatow regrouped with Fox and reemerged with *Undeclared* (Fox, 2001–02), which is essentially *Freaks* graduated from high school to college. While it never reaches the same giddy heights as its predecessor, *Undeclared* is another superb evocation of youthful turmoil, romantic bungling, and general buffoonery.

Jay Baruchel's Steven is *Freaks and Geeks'* Sam as a college freshman— well-meaning but clueless, a puppy-dog romantic let loose amidst an array of slavering pit bulls. Seth Rogen is back, too, this time as the sad sack Ron—a young man so self-consciously inept at romance that he coins the phrase "to Ron" as an all-purpose term of derision for others' awkward fumbling. Charlie Hunnam is in the James Franco role as the good-looking cad, and Carla Gallo is Lizzie, Steven's fickle, emotionally unstable crush, whom he sleeps with the first day of school and tries to win back ever after.

College is every bit as bewildering and disorienting as high school had been, and temporary infatuations—with religion, with the stock market, with fraternities, with that new boy or girl down the hall—only briefly distract the clueless from their fundamental confusion. Apatow feels the pain of loveless nerds like the hapless Marshall (Timm Sharp), preferring their company to that of the slick and romantically savvy. Even with its adjustments for increased mainstream appeal—half-hour episodes, more easily identifiable "sitcom" situations—the show was unable to find an audience. Just like *Freaks and Geeks*, *Undeclared* lasted only one season before being summarily canceled.

At first glance, the teenage musical series *Glee* (Fox, 2009–) bears little relationship to *Freaks and Geeks*, but its emphasis on romantic and emotional confusion (Does Finn love Rachel, or Quinn?), and its deliberate muddying of tones—often leaping from exaggerated farce to textured drama within the span of a single episode—marks it as a successor of sorts. Created by Ryan Murphy, *Glee* sought to capture something genuine about adolescence while inhabiting a deliberately artificial world, one in which teenagers' social lives are consumed by the performance schedule of their high school's glee club.

In its first season or two, *Glee* could be quite funny when it chose to be, with Jane Lynch's cheerleading coach and glee-club nemesis Sue Sylvester peddling a particularly deranged form of no-holds-barred comedic mayhem seemingly channeled from an entirely different, far more brilliantly malevolent series altogether. Much—if not most—of *Glee*'s humor, though, felt lifted from the *Freaks and Geeks* model: couldn't Sam, Neal, and Bill have easily been on the business end of a Slushying, if only their dull tormentors had had the creativity to have thought of it? *Glee*'s "gleeks" are both freaks and geeks, but next to Feig and Apatow's nuanced characters, the assortment created by Ryan Murphy are mere stereotypes: the sensitive jock, the Jewish princess, the African American diva, the snooty cheerleaders, and so forth.

Glee is undecided about whether it is an all-out burlesque of high school or a more earnest teen drama like *My So-Called Life*, so it splits the difference between the two, alternating clumsily between somber and absurd storylines. By comparison, the finely tuned balance of *Freaks and Geeks* seems even more masterful: it undoes the sitcom's order even as it lovingly preserves its exterior structure; it maintains the fundamental concerns of the form while trading its forced hilarity for smudged realism.

Freaks tips its cap to its comedic idols through the perspective of its geeks, who are deeply serious about comedy. To Sam, Bill, and Neal, with their posters of W. C. Fields and *Caddyshack*, their Groucho Marx Halloween costumes, and their extensive rehashing of Steve Martin movies, comedy is a religion, their taste functioning as their moral compass. Not only does Bill judge Mr. Fredricks for his dislike of *Stripes*, but also Sam breaks up with Cindy Sanders in large part because she doesn't think *The Jerk* is funny.

Many of Sam's lunch-table discussions with his friends are devoted to their preferred TV comedies: *Three's Company*, *M*A*S*H*, and *Saturday Night Live*. Sam is convinced, in "Dead Dogs," that *M*A*S*H*'s Radar O'Reilly always carries his clipboard because he actually has no fingers (there seems to be something about shrimpy sitcom characters and Radar; see *Community*'s Abed and his similar obsession). Neal believes that he can turn his skill as a ventriloquist into stardom, much like Jay Johnson of *Soap*. The Garry Shandling cameo in "Dead Dogs" should have been clue enough— Bill would love *The Larry Sanders Show*.

But *Freaks and Geeks'* self-reflexivity mirrors the entirety of the medium more than any one distinct genre. The series is less a sitcom about sitcoms than a series capturing the emotional roller coaster that is TV. Watching was like distractedly flipping the dial, catching a few minutes of *Square Pegs* (to reference another teen sitcom set in roughly the same time period) and a few minutes of *Dallas* and getting the storylines confused. The old boundaries—comedy to the left, drama to the right—gave way to a new TV model that preferred not to choose.

Television grew serious about its potential, and part and parcel of that newfound maturity was a desire to transcend the old categories of entertainment. Why did a comedy series have to be thirty minutes long, anyway? Sitcoms from earlier in the decade, like *Seinfeld*, *The Larry Sanders Show*, and *The Simpsons*, had revolutionized the traditional form. They were sitcoms about the form of the sitcom, about what it had been and what it could be. Now *Freaks and Geeks* came along to suggest that the comedy called life was too vast, too unpredictable, to be contained within half an hour.

20

Curb Your Enthusiasm

"Seinfeld"

November 22, 2009 ▪ HBO

Seinfeld had rechristened the traditional sitcom as something new: self-absorbed, pointillist, speaking a dialect of its own invention. At its peak, the show felt as if everything unnecessary about the form—its catering to the lowest common denominator of sentiment and predictability—had been stripped away, leaving only the irreducible core of its musings on the absurdity of the human endeavor. When *Seinfeld* ended in 1998, it left a hole where the highest-rated show on television had once been. The glorious beast created by Jerry Seinfeld and Larry David could not be matched, only baldly imitated. And then the bald man behind the scenes, the real-life George Costanza, decided to poke his hairless head out from behind the cameras, and a new show was born, even more unadorned and bare-bones than its predecessor.

F. Scott Fitzgerald famously said that there are no second acts in American life; in sitcoms, they are less nonexistent than tragically underwhelming. Who fondly remembers *Archie Bunker's Place* or *Joey*? To be sure, Mary Tyler Moore jumped from one triumphant series to another, and *Cheers* gave birth to *Frasier*. But mostly, great series are one-off endeavors, their magic destined never to be repeated. *Curb Your Enthusiasm* (HBO, 2000–), Larry David's triumphantly absurdist HBO series, is not quite a spinoff of *Seinfeld*, yet its comedic DNA, as well as its backstory, emerges from the marrow of its predecessor. In *Curb*, David portrays another version of himself: the hugely successful, wealthy creator of *Seinfeld*, now living a life of unimaginable leisure, and concomitant boredom, in the ritziest precincts of West Los Angeles. The question of just how skewed this version might be is an essential part of the show's comic allure.

The real Larry David was raised in West L.A.'s diametric opposite, the working-class Jewish neighborhood of Sheepshead Bay in Brooklyn. His father was a clothing salesman and his mother a secretary. David's father would bring home sport coats for him to try on after school. David attended the University of Maryland, where his "tales of woe" about his dating life made him realize other people considered him funny. After college, David worked at dead-end jobs like bra salesman while trying his hand at stand-up comedy. Other comedians loved David's cerebral, dyspeptic style, but audiences were not always as receptive. David legendarily came onstage for one performance, assessed the crowd, and muttered "forget it," dropping the microphone and stalking off.

David was so sure of his stand-up failure that he began scoping out Manhattan street corners for when he eventually became homeless. Forty-Fifth Street between Fifth and Sixth Avenues was particularly appealing.

But David was hired to write for *Saturday Night Live*, where he contributed all of one sketch throughout the entire 1984–85 season. Tired of being ignored, David marched in to executive producer Dick Ebersol's office one Friday and summarily quit: "This fucking show stinks!" Over the weekend, David realized how much money he would be giving up with his dramatic gesture and decided to slink into the office on Monday and act as if nothing had happened. This, as with so many other minor incidents in the life of Larry David, would eventually become a *Seinfeld* episode.

Seinfeld taught David the art of the multifaceted storyline, where characters' separate adventures would be woven together in an unexpected and comedically apt conclusion. The enormous success of the show made David a very wealthy man, but his interest in the frustrations of the mundane continued unabated. All that had changed, according to an interview with David at the height of his *Seinfeld* notoriety, was that "I don't have to shop for pants in stores anymore. I can just call up and they'll bring the pants right over to my house." David won an Emmy for *Seinfeld* and told millions of television viewers, "This is all well and good, but I'm still bald."

The ballad of the bald man was the theme song of David's post-*Seinfeld* stab at continued TV success, with his low-grade misery transported cross-country from the Upper West Side to West L.A. David was now not only writing and producing but also starring as a fun-house-mirror version of himself. *Curb*'s "Larry David" was, according to David, "my version of Superman. The character really is me, but I just couldn't possibly behave like that."

Life for the Larry David of *Curb* is "prettay, prettay, prettay, prettay good," as he would put it, and yet an endless emptiness—begging for diversion, for activity, for meaning—yawns before him. *Curb Your Enthusiasm* is about this wealthy, bespectacled, Jewish imp, card-carrying member of the "bald community," taking his revenge on the world. For all his advantages, though, the joke is ultimately on him. Larry is like Ralph Kramden moved to Malibu, all grandiose schemes that ultimately, helplessly backfire. He is the crown prince of a topsy-turvy moral world, forever bitten by his decent impulses and rewarded for his callousness.

Curb Your Enthusiasm began as an HBO special in 1999, a mockumentary in which Larry—or "Larry"—voluntarily appears before the cameras as he goes about his daily business, preparing for a stand-up concert film. The conceit of following a comedian through the minor scuffles and epiphanies of his day, watching the material being prepared before seeing it performed, was the same original idea David and Seinfeld had planned to use for *Seinfeld*. *Larry David: Curb Your Enthusiasm*, like an Albert Brooks film, ends with a chuckle-inducing whimper rather than a bang: Larry, convinced his material is not up to snuff, lies to HBO execs about his nonexistent stepfather being in a coma, bails on the show, and skates back to the safety of his *Seinfeld*-purchased bubble.

The outlines of what would become the series are already visible here: Larry the "social assassin," self-appointed judge of small social exchanges; his already-long-suffering wife Cheryl (Cheryl Hines), and his business manager and best friend, Jeff (Jeff Garlin). Cheryl and Jeff are the designated Greek chorus for Larry's unending parade of kerfuffles: Cheryl to cluck at his excesses, Jeff to uncritically support him in all his crusades. When *Curb* premiered as a standalone series in 2000, it ditched the mockumentary frame of the special and added two more recurring characters: Susie Essman as Jeff's shrewish Gorgon of a wife, and Richard Lewis (who had appeared briefly in the special) playing himself as another flinty middle-aged Jewish comic and a foil for Larry. (Other Hollywood figures, including Ted Danson, Mary Steenburgen, and Wanda Sykes, would take on similar roles.)

For each episode, David and his writing staff—including Alec Berg, David Mandel, and Jeff Schaffer—would hammer out a seven- or eight-page outline. They'd give the performers a broad sense of their motivation in each scene but allow them to improvise their own blocking and dialogue. David and the other actors had enormous leeway to find their way to the funniest version of a scene, and the series employed two handheld cameras to ensure that their unexpected moments were caught on the fly. The three-camera sitcom, shot on a soundstage, was a lumbering dinosaur by comparison.

Like *Seinfeld*, *Curb* is about the minutiae of mundane life: the cutoff time for evening phone calls, the propriety of offering wedding gifts more than one year after the event. Larry David's Los Angeles is merely a sun-dappled New York, crammed full of the same petty annoyances and low-level aggression that was *Seinfeld*'s métier and sole reason for existence. This show revolves around the same cramped set of familiar locales as its predecessor: restaurants, doctors' offices, studio lots, dry cleaners. Larry is always buying something, returning something, having something checked out, or consulting with a maître d'. He scrupulously follows a moral code only known fully to himself. He is opposed to chat-and-cutters in lines, to "schmohawks" on the road, to harsh toilet paper, to disrespecters of wood. He is forever attempting to get others—dry cleaners, fellow drivers, restaurant patrons—to understand the rules of daily life as he understands them, and forever failing.

But Larry's disapproval also extends to "*meshuggeneh* Muslims," to the creeping of his friends' wives into his masturbatory fantasies, to a relative who has committed suicide without leaving a note. As these examples might indicate, the tone of *Curb Your Enthusiasm* is keyed one level higher than *Seinfeld*. Simultaneously arch and scandalous, it maintains the same interlocking-puzzle-piece design of the earlier show while noticeably increasing its discomfort level. *Seinfeld* had been limited by the requirements of network censors, but *Curb* is free to explore all the deeply touchy subjects *Seinfeld* could not.

Curb Your Enthusiasm is devoted to the demolishing of others' fixed icons, to finding the most awkward, unpleasant topic imaginable and luxuriating in others' squirming—both within the show and for those of us following along at home. Impending terrorist attack: who should be tipped off in advance? Sex offender moves to the neighborhood? Invite him over for the Passover seder! Larry, over the course of eight seasons of rancorous badinage, poses as an incest survivor, is arrested for stealing forks from a restaurant, recommends a prostitute to the board members at a stuffy country club, informs the audience at a bat mitzvah about the tickle in his anus, and subtly suggests to his wife that, in the event of said terrorist attack, it's "a little . . . selfish" to not let him abscond alone.

The music, as James Parker notes in the *Atlantic*, is a clue to the show's preferred tone: "The puffings of buffonic tuba that announce *Curb Your*

Enthusiasm . . . tell us that we are entering the big top. Larry the clown will go down, get up, go down again, in a species of affective slapstick." Larry brings on every possible class of person—parents, in-laws, rabbis, hurricane victims, African Americans, religious Jews, lesbians, Parkinson's sufferers, evangelical Christians, Palestinians, the disabled—so he can affably insult them all. *Curb Your Enthusiasm* is equal-opportunity insult comedy; you haven't arrived in America until Larry David has demolished you.

Seinfeld's network-sitcom smoothness—of tone, of style—has given way to *Curb*'s patented HBO roughness, with its cameras jerking and bobbing restlessly around its characters. The show grows more assured-looking as it ages, graduating from the low-resolution camerawork of its earlier seasons to a more polished feel. But the improvised dialogue and playful performances—one cannot always tell whether it is the characters or the performers who are smiling at others' comic handiwork—gives *Curb Your Enthusiasm* a looseness that rubs against its stories' predestined disasters.

The relationship between *Curb Your Enthusiasm* and *Seinfeld* is perpetually hinted at, scattered like so many bread crumbs along the path of the series. Our memories of *Seinfeld* are being subtly tweaked, the tangled relationship between fiction and reality—or between fiction and metafiction—deliberately muddied. In the show's very first episode, Cheryl tells her husband to parlay his fame into a table at a crowded restaurant: "Try the *Seinfeld* thing." In the second season, Larry flirts with the idea of writing a new series for Jason Alexander, in which Alexander would play a successful actor haunted by the ghost of his most famous role—a lovable jerk from a hugely successful sitcom. As the inspiration for George Costanza, Larry visibly bristles every time another character inevitably refers to George as an "idiot": "So I'm a schmuck to be in a masturbation contest?"

Curb echoes *Seinfeld*, which echoed David's own life, which inspires *Curb*, a triangular procession of comedic repetition. A fan's promised encounter with Julia Louis-Dreyfus, in the episode "The Wire," takes on shades of Jerry's struggle with the odious Banya in the *Seinfeld* episode "The Soup," and their arguments over the nature of a promised meal. Larry goes shopping for a bra for his maid in "The Christ Nail," and the saleswoman at Victoria's

Secret is convinced he is shopping for himself. "Not that there's anything wrong with it," Larry reflexively notes, echoing George and Jerry in the legendary are-they-or-aren't-they *Seinfeld* episode "The Outing," before revising his opinion: "But there *is* something wrong with it."

Curb's fascination with its predecessor is nowhere more fully on display than in the show's brilliant seventh season, an extended meditation on the success of *Seinfeld* and a reminder that its triumph can never be repeated—even as it is, momentarily, resuscitated. Early in the season, Larry learns that NBC is eager for a *Seinfeld* reunion special. He rejects the idea out of hand, rightly insisting on the fundamental tackiness of all such reunion efforts (that means you, *Gilligan's Island*): "They never work. The actors are ten years older. It never looks right." He is swayed only when he realizes that by writing a plum role for Cheryl in a reunion show, he could win her back, as she has finally left him, fed up with his shenanigans. Jason Alexander, for one, is enthusiastic about the idea, believing it gives *Seinfeld* another crack at a more satisfying ending. The reunion would be an extended apology for "The Finale," or as he succinctly puts it: "We know. We know. We're sorry." Larry, once more, is vexed by any such criticism of *Seinfeld*.

Here are the real George and the fake George trading barbs. Seeing them bicker, for instance, over a pen the former has lent to the latter is to be thrust into a dazzling metafictional world in which fantasy and reality bleed into each other. (Perhaps Jerry could have lent them his astronaut pen.) Similarly, *Curb* achieves something remarkable by confining David and Jerry Seinfeld to a small room, letting them jabber about an assistant's exposed stomach flab and potential uses for Barbicide (Jerry posits that it is intended to assist depressed barbers in committing suicide). At long last, after a series of false stabs, these episodes of *Curb Your Enthusiasm* are the truest outgrowth of Seinfeld and David's initial idea for *Seinfeld*: watching the comedian at work crafting his material, preparing for a performance.

Against all odds, the final episode of season seven—named, conveniently enough, "Seinfeld" and written by David—grants us the unparalleled privilege of actually watching Jerry, George, Elaine, and Kramer back in the familiar confines of Jerry's apartment, a decade older but not a whit smarter.

There is, once more, a laugh track—a profoundly jarring confrontation of network style with *Curb*'s affectless technique. We are updated on what our friends have been up to since we saw them last: Jerry has donated the sperm for Elaine's daughter. George has invented the iToilet, an iPhone app that locates the nearest acceptable bathroom anywhere in the world, but has lost all his riches to the depredations of Bernie Madoff. (His ex-wife, played at first, of course, by Cheryl, pulled out her money from Madoff after spotting him on the street in a quilted jacket.) We are simultaneously present and at a remove. *Seinfeld* is miraculously back, even as we watch the proceedings from a distance, on another series entirely, aware that their reunion is only happening on a soundstage, populated by actors, written by a neurotic scribe.

Larry has recycled his "real life"—plotlines from earlier *Curb Your Enthusiasm* episodes—into plotlines for the reunion. Jerry is now the one who has given a little girl's doll a haircut; Kramer now hires the services of a prostitute to use the carpool lane. Off-camera, the *Seinfeld* crew are cast as the latest foils for Larry's socially awkward escapades. He is in hot water with Julia Louis-Dreyfus for supposedly having ruined a valuable wood coffee table by failing to use a coaster. Knowing himself, for once, to be innocent of the crime, Larry takes on a new role as "Larry David, Wood Detective." He also riles up Jason by critiquing his new book on acting, referring to it as an "acting pamphlet" and mirthfully suggesting that "I'll read it with dinner." (Jason's book party prompts Jerry's observation, equally applicable to the show, that "It's hiding the acting, and yet it's all acting.")

The familiar worlds of the two shows intertwine in unanticipated fashion. It is profoundly disarming to see Larry and Cheryl sitting together on the *Seinfeld* diner set, while Larry's pal Leon (J. B. Smoove) provides one of the biggest laughs of the entire season with his guileless response to the much-anticipated reunion of Jerry and Elaine in the familiar confines of Jerry's apartment: "Who are these two right here?" Even more disarming is to see Alexander flirting shamelessly with Cheryl, who appears, at least to Larry's jealousy-inflamed eyes, to be receptive to his attentions.

As the actor playing a version of Larry threatens to steal away his "real-life" wife, *Curb* provides audiences with one much-anticipated reunion even as it swipes another away. To keep his rival away from Cheryl, Larry immediately changes the blocking of a scene for the reunion show, shifting George from the living room to the bathroom. Larry insists he is fine, but Jerry, inveterate scholar of others' pettiest instincts, knows otherwise. Seinfeld and David have magical chemistry—one wishes there would be another show that consisted in its entirety of their aimless conversation—and Jerry gives Larry one of his iconic skeptical stares, silently studying his friend for clues to his dyspepsia.

Ultimately, Larry's jealousy drives him to drastically rewrite the script for the show so Jason and Cheryl's characters no longer end up together. "This is the show!" Larry insists, unconsciously echoing George's claim from "The Pitch." Alexander walks off the set, and Larry logically suggests that he take over the role of George. Jerry disapproves. "Do you understand what this is? It's iconic television here! The set's an icon. He's an icon. She's an icon. He was an icon. Icon," he shouts, pointing at each of the *Seinfeld* stars, before settling definitively on Larry: "No-con. There's no John, Paul, George, and Larry." "There were two Darrins on *Bewitched*," Larry pleads weakly, but the case is already lost.

When Larry steps through the door of Jerry's apartment as George, he is all wrong, herky-jerky and poorly timed, his voice at a near-hysterical pitch. Larry may *be* George, but he cannot play him on TV. The levels of irony swell, one atop the other, for who is Larry David playing on *Curb Your Enthusiasm* if not the real-life George? "You're not attracted to him," he pleads with Cheryl. "You're attracted to me! I'm George!" (Alexander, for what it's worth, can only do a passable Larry; his "prettay prettay good" sounds more like the cluck of a manic-depressive chicken.) Larry has made television history for the sole purpose of getting Cheryl back, caring less for *Seinfeld* than for his own bruised heart: "If I can't have her, what's the point?" This is both touching and infuriating. The man would even ruin *Seinfeld*! "We already screwed up one finale," Jerry argues, while Larry defends his revisions: "Who's gonna buy that? They get together? I mean, we don't do endings like that!" But here they are, providing the warm reunion they had never intended to deliver.

Seinfeld is back, for one brief, wonderful moment—and yet the other much-anticipated reunion, between Larry and Cheryl, is scuttled at the last second. When Cheryl is finally in his arms again at last, brought back to him by *Seinfeld*'s uncharacteristic happy ending, Larry immediately reverts to form, accusing her of being the one who stained Julia Louis-Dreyfus's antique table: "Do you respect wood?" Larry is as incorrigible as ever, and one warm television moment, generously granted to us by David, is undercut by another of quintessential Davidian foolishness.

There are no right answers on *Curb Your Enthusiasm*, only shadings of wrong. On *Seinfeld*, George and Jerry had been willfully amoral, discarding girlfriends like so many stale crackers, but Larry scrupulously adheres to his own carefully tended moral code. His theory is superb; his execution, subpar. There are times, watching *Curb Your Enthusiasm*, when the preordained slide into chaos is simply too much to handle. Approximately twelve minutes into every twenty-eight-or-so-minute episode, the outline of the story's arc begins to clarify and harden. Larry immerses himself in a touchy situation, attempts to improve matters, and momentarily succeeds before tumbling deeper into the morass of social chaos. That sinking feeling in the pit of viewers' stomachs is the premonition of what is to come. Things fall apart, the center cannot hold, and Larry David—both the show's creator and its protagonist—finds ways to sketch yet another in the infinite array of varieties of humiliation and social agony.

Perhaps the most entertaining recurring riffs are devoted to religion, which fascinates David without ever attracting him. Larry's tone-deafness, his cosmic inability to detect others taking offense, allows him to take his Gentile father-in-law's official *Passion of the Christ* commemorative nail to put up his mezuzah, or to let an assistant believe the spray of his urine is actually a tear shed by a portrait of Christ on her bathroom wall. *Seinfeld* was overwhelmingly Jewish in its concerns while camouflaging some of its characters as Gentile. *Curb Your Enthusiasm*, devoted as it is to Larry alone, is an extended meditation on the mixed blessings of Jewishness. Judaism is the cross, so to speak, that Larry must bear.

In the remarkable episode "Palestinian Chicken," from the show's eighth season, Larry is drawn into a battle over whether a new outlet of an openly anti-Semitic but delicious purveyor of chicken can open "next to the sacred ground" of Goldblatt's Delicatessen. The obvious reference is to the tempest in a teapot over New York City's proposed "Ground Zero mosque" (which was neither at Ground Zero nor a mosque, but that is a matter for another time), but is also about Larry's ambivalence toward his heritage. Larry is attracted to a beautiful Palestinian woman (Anne Bedian) he meets at the restaurant, and is blithely unconcerned when she renders his inimitable self into a generic representative of the hated other. "Fuck me, you fucking Jew!" she shouts, carried away by sexual bliss. Larry sees it as an issue of lost homes: "The penis doesn't care about race, creed, and color. The penis wants to get to his homeland." In both this episode and the thematically similar "The Baptism," in which Larry accidentally halts a Jew's conversion to Christianity, Larry stands, an uncommitted tribalist, torn between Jews and their putative oppressors, never entirely declaring his allegiances.

Larry is never more pleased or relieved than when he is told, in the show's fifth season, that he is not genetically Jewish. Having tracked down his birth parents in "The End," Larry lets out a gasp of relief: "Oh my God! I'm Gentile!" In perhaps the funniest shock cut in the entire series, Larry is immediately outfitted in the next shot in full-on *goyishe* garb: straw hat, turquoise T-shirt, shorts, athletic socks, fanny pack. The squabbles inherent to being Jewish—the squabbles that are *Curb*'s mother's milk—are no longer, replaced by genial WASP placidity. Gentile Larry is a new man: he does shots in a backward ball cap, fixes his new parents' roof, and has a noticeable milk mustache while eating his mother's Sunday roast. Larry is leaving Judaism—including its prohibition on consuming milk and meat together—behind, and he has never been happier. He is wheeled into the OR to donate a kidney to the ailing Richard Lewis with a smile on his face, just pleased as punch to be helping out. That is, until he is informed that, due to a terrible mishap, he is not related at all to the Cones of Bisby,

Arizona, and is, in fact, Jewish after all. "I'm not adopted," he roars with displeasure. "Get me the fuck out of here!"

Curb Your Enthusiasm served as the inspiration for a new wave of series— mostly on the guy-friendly cable channel FX—about similarly incorrigible men and their antics. Emily Nussbaum of the *New Yorker* referred to them as "dirtbag sitcoms," "crass, confident comedies that feature idiotic characters but are not themselves idiotic." The multiple heroes of *It's Always Sunny in Philadelphia* (FX, 2005–) or *The League* (FX, 2009–) are like a petri dish of Larry Davids, divided and regrown until reaching critical mass. *The League*, ostensibly about competitors in a fantasy football league, rapidly slides away from its who-are-you-starting-Sunday trash talk toward an all-purpose array of David-esque antics. And *It's Always Sunny* begins where *Curb* leaves off, with each episode a Swiftian mock proposal, acted out and dramatized by its socially inept, intellectually stunted characters.

The original dirtbag himself, Danny DeVito—Louie De Palma of *Taxi*— is back in *It's Always Sunny*, playing the buffoonish father of Dennis (Glenn Howerton) and Dee (Kaitlin Olson), two of the pushing-thirty proprietors of a gritty Philly bar. Like a traditional sitcom, each episode of *It's Always Sunny in Philadelphia* concludes with a return to the status quo ante, but the series' variations on the *Cheers* elbows-on-the-bar watering-hole routine are decidedly scuzzy: What if the bar became an underage hangout? What if Dennis and Dee went on welfare and became strung-out crack addicts? In the episode "Charlie Wants an Abortion," Dennis becomes an antiabortion zealot after meeting a comely protester. "Are you actually gonna throw away all your convictions for a chance to get laid?" his sister asks. Dennis chuckles into his beer, a dirtbag to the last: "I don't really have any convictions."

With its overlapping cascades of dialogue and its passionate absorption in heightened displays of awkwardness, *It's Always Sunny* is television under the sign of Larry David. Its ragged camerawork and deliberately awkward blocking only add to the show's subliminal suggestion that this is the work of gifted amateurs—that the polished professionalism of the sitcom has broken down by the side of the road, replaced by this jury-rigged jalopy of mismatched tones and styles.

The same was often true of *Curb*'s foremost descendant, and the inheritor of its mantle of socially maladjusted middle-aged male heroism. *Louie* (FX, 2010–) is written, directed, and edited by stand-up comedian Louis C.K., whom FX provided with a minuscule budget and complete creative freedom. Unlike most sitcoms, *Louie* actually looks good—a product of Paul Koestner's sterling cinematography—but the sense of amateurism, of television created by someone who does not actually belong on television, lingers.

Louie's template remains generally the same from week to week: an extended opening stand-up routine à la *Seinfeld*, followed by one or two longer sketches. Like Larry David, Louis C.K. is a teller of uncomfortable truths, his best jokes revolving around his mixed feelings about his children, his body's middle-aged failings, and encounters with strangers. The sketches that follow are all over the map, from an encounter with an elderly, racist aunt to a strained meeting with fellow comic Dane Cook, whom C.K. had accused—in real life—of stealing other comics' jokes. Louie, like Larry, is never allowed to skate on his misdemeanors. Approaching Cook for tickets for his daughter in "Oh, Louie/Tickets," he is made to squirm for his purported violations of the comedians' code. Out on a date with an attractive woman in the remarkable episode "Bully," he is humiliated at painfully extended length by an obnoxious teenager and secretly follows him back to his parents' home in the suburbs. *Louie* is a deliciously awkward show, touching on all the inexplicable weirdness and brutal bittersweetness of life.

Louie is also a primer course in comedy; this is stand-up with footnotes appended. Has there ever been another show on television that turned over five minutes to a gay comic explaining the etymology of the word "faggot"? ("So what you're saying is gay people are a good alternative-fuel source?" Louie asks, in wise-guy fashion.) Louie is forever explaining the nature of comedy to others: onstage hecklers, soldiers in Afghanistan, his kids.

Louie is not entirely above the lowest common denominator; it is perfectly content to end an episode about Louie's pregnant sister experiencing a medical emergency with her letting out a long, honking fart of relief. But C.K. is not satisfied with replicating the same comedian-gone-sitcom playbook. He reaches, with deliberate, impeccable awkwardness, for something deeper and more discomfiting than what television normally does, like a show whose goal is to re-create, week after week, that indescribable jumble of laughter and half-buried sentiment *Curb* occasionally strives for.

There are flashback episodes about Louie's tormented Catholic youth, and in the remarkable "Duckling," which barely skirts the edge of cheap sentiment, Louie's daughter smuggles a tiny duck into his suitcase for a USO trip to Afghanistan ("Holy shit on the tits of a dog," he exclaims when he discovers the duckling). Louie is awkward even in a war zone, making stilted small talk with a bored cheerleader. She is disgusted with his raunchy act and wants to know, "Why can't you say Christian things and be funny?"

The entertainers' helicopter makes a forced landing in uncertain territory, and the group comes face-to-face with a group of armed Afghans. The tense standoff is only broken when Louie's duckling hops out of his backpack, and Louie, chasing after it, tumbles into a ditch. Louie shames himself and makes us laugh. And in so doing, our presentiments of death are pushed off, delayed for another day.

Louie, unlike many of its contemporaries at the cutting edge of the twenty-first-century sitcom, is unafraid of approaching sentimentality in the name of transcendent emotion. Louie heads toward the helicopter taking him to safety, turns, and hands the duckling to an Afghan girl. Even "Bully" ends not with the comeuppance of the obnoxious adolescent but with Louie commiserating with his tormentor's father over the difficulty of raising children. *Curb*'s carnival music is replaced by a soundtrack of mournful jazz, ideal for the bittersweet dolefulness of a show about romantic failure and the onset of middle age.

In its best moments, *Louie* strives for a perverse kind of grace native to *Curb*, in which the show provides privileged moments of the sort *Seinfeld*—of the "no hugging, no learning" lack of sentimentality—would never have favored. *Curb* itself is not sentimental, precisely; it is more a designer of discrete instants of heightened comic wonder.

Curb's moments of perverse magnanimity are the culmination of entire seasons of subtle spadework. We had been set up without ever being aware of David's masterful manipulation. Mel Brooks and his wife, Anne Bancroft, are given the opportunity to live out a variant of Brooks's film *The Producers* in *Curb*'s fourth season, casting Larry as Max Bialystok in the Broadway musical version in the hopes of finally killing off the long-running golden goose. Unfortunately for them, their new star's ad-libbing skills—reminiscent of the star of *The Producers*' show within the show—doom them to eternal success. "No way out," Bancroft moans in frustration, echoing Max's famous line from the show. The show echoes the show within the show within the show, another hall of mirrors with Larry's shining pate pasted in over every face.

During the show's third season, Larry becomes an investor in a new restaurant. After a series of mishaps with chefs, Larry and his fellow investors hire a superb cook who, unbeknownst to them, also suffers from Tourette's syndrome. Larry, as always conscious of his baldness, was quietly touched earlier in the episode when he spotted some high school students who voluntarily shaved their heads in solidarity with a friend undergoing chemotherapy.

On the restaurant's opening night, the diners' enjoyment is unexpectedly interrupted by a foul-mouthed outburst from the chef, and Larry is reminded of his desire to emulate the teenagers' spontaneous generosity. Larry, inspired, seconds the gesture with a profane outburst of his own: "Scumsucking motherfucking whore!" Suddenly, everyone pitches in: Jeff contributes "Jism grandma cock," polite fellow investor Michael York gamely offers "Bugger and balls," and even Cheryl's conservative father shouts "Fellatio. Cunnilingus. French kissing. Rim job." The camera zooms in on Larry alone, arms crossed, at the center of the room, master of chaos.

Even more perversely touching is the belated television redemption of legendary World Series goat Bill Buckner, in the episode "Mister Softee." Larry runs into Buckner, famous for flubbing a Mookie Wilson ground ball and costing the Boston Red Sox a chance at their first World Series victory in sixty-eight years, after having a Buckner moment of his own: he is distracted during sex by the nagging jingle of the Mister Softee ice cream truck, whose persistent melody raises the specter of painful childhood memories.

Larry brings Buckner to a shivah gathering, where one of the mourners, an ardent Red Sox fan, insists he cannot be in the same room as the man who cost his team a championship. ("I hope there's no afterlife!" Larry shouts after him.) Buckner, remarkably good-natured about reliving the worst moment of his career, lets a Mookie Wilson autographed baseball slip through his fingers and out a window, prompting another round of angry-sports-fan recriminations. Buckner is like another version of Larry—a man famous for his errors, a schlemiel doomed to wander the earth doing penance for his crimes against humanity.

And yet Buckner is granted absolution for his crimes against Red Sox Nation, a symbolic stand-in for Larry and his wavering efforts to undo the damage he has wrought. At the end of the episode, Buckner and Larry, walking down the street, stumble on a terrifying scene outside a burning building. A desperate mother tosses her baby out the window, and Buckner dives and catches the baby, before being carried off triumphantly on the shoulders of the assembled firefighters. This is not quite comedy as *Seinfeld* might have understood it but something else entirely. It is the sitcom as a kind of secular grace. There is such a thing as redemption, even if it only exists within the frame of the television screen.

21

Arrested Development

"S.O.B.s"

January 2, 2006 ▪ Fox

"What has happened to us is a great injustice, that we were never really given a fair chance. But that's not the truth. We've been given plenty of chances. And maybe the Bluths just aren't worth saving. Maybe we're not that likable." Michael Bluth (Jason Bateman) is speaking of his father, George Bluth Sr. (Jeffrey Tambor, playing a hard-boiled businessman after his turn as *The Larry Sanders Show*'s sad sack Hank Kingsley) and his legal problems, but he is also writing the obituary, only slightly prematurely, for the show in which he is a character. *Arrested Development* (Fox, 2003–06; Netflix, 2013), the much-loved, mostly ignored series that originally ran for a mere two and a half seasons on network television, is holding a combined telethon and wake in "S.O.B.s," a pity party with laughs in the hope—ever so slight, but a hope nonetheless—that this exuberantly odd sitcom could be saved. "S.O.B.s" is a coda for this show, and all the other sitcoms deemed not worth saving, condemned to death before their time.

Television, unlike film or literature, requires the active cooperation of a mass audience in order to exist. A flop film, once it is made, still exists on DVD and in repertory, waiting to be discovered by the next generation. A book—even an out-of-print one—sits on shelves in libraries and secondhand bookstores, awaiting a new readership. With the passage of time, a new audience can always stumble over the forgotten gems of the past. But a television show is a serial endeavor, to which audiences must return, week after week, season after season, to follow the latest installment. If they choose not to, or if they never show up to begin with, that show will simply cease to exist. Television series' very existence is dependent on their popularity, and those shows that linger perilously close to cancellation depend on the goodwill of network executives and the hope of a rosier future. Neither of those last for very long. As a result, the story of the sitcom is also the story of those shows condemned before their time.

Often, this failure to locate an audience is a result of a certain confusion of tones. The sitcom was, traditionally, among the most rigid of formats; this is, after all, the television genre that required a laugh track to indicate to viewers what they might find worth chuckling about for more than forty years (sixty and counting, if you include CBS). Change arrived only haltingly and unpredictably, and often the series that did the most to advance the sitcom were the least likely to stick around. Consider *Arrested Development*, then, as a case study in the precariousness of challenging the sitcom's traditional values. *Two and a Half Men* (CBS, 2003–), the mind-numbingly predictable sitcom that premiered the same fall of 2003, is still running, some six seasons after *Arrested Development* was canceled.

Try not to scream silently in your chamber of solitude while considering this fact.

Arrested Development creator Mitchell Hurwitz was a comedic intellectual, but he received his training in the trenches of multicamera yukfests. He got his start as a self-described "gopher" for Witt/Thomas/Harris Productions, the production company responsible for *The Golden Girls*. Hurwitz eventually joined the *Golden Girls* writing staff, where he studied the hard craft of firing off an endless fusillade of jokes. He went on to write for the darker *John Larroquette Show* (NBC, 1993–96), about a recovering alcoholic who manages a bus station, and to serve as showrunner of the short-lived *Everything's Relative* (NBC, 1999) and *The Ellen Show* (CBS, 2001–02). After the cancellation of *Everything's Relative*, Hurwitz came up with an idea for a show about a family of quirky New York intellectuals. Then Wes Anderson put out his film *The Royal Tenenbaums* (2001), with the same basic premise, and Hurwitz regrouped, taking the germ of his original scheme—dysfunctional family thrust into the real world—and transferring it to Southern California.

Arrested Development was also an experiment in form. As a single-camera thinker trained in the traditional multicamera style, Hurwitz intended his new series to be a hybrid of the classical and avant-garde sitcom styles. He wondered, "What would happen if we applied the sensibility of multi-camera to single-camera?" He wanted the cleverness of the single-camera style, rigged to the consistent comedic attack of the multicamera style: *The Larry Sanders Show* meets *The Golden Girls*. Hurwitz's definition of the formula was "broad comedy done very dry." This also meant that the show's production would be far more complicated than that of its predecessors, bearing more resemblance to a cable drama than a straightforward sitcom. Where *Golden Girls* had eight scenes per episode, *Arrested Development* would have nearer to sixty.

Unfortunately, the era of *The Cosby Show* and *Seinfeld* had passed, and broadcast series with this level of artistic ambition were now often among the most ratings-challenged. "S.O.B.s," *Arrested Development*'s fifth-to-last episode before its untimely cancellation, is both a plea for viewers and a succinct reminder of why it would never find that audience. The episode, written by Jim Vallely and Richard Day, finds its laughs in the excesses of other shows scrambling to win an audience.

"The Bluths were desperate. The press had them all but finished," *Arrested Development*'s ever-present narrator (Ron Howard, back working in sitcoms after a quarter-century absence) observes. The Bluths—a once-prominent Orange County family brought low by scandal and malfeasance—need $100,000 to pay their attorney. They decide, in true Bluth fashion, to throw a lavish party to raise the money from friends and colleagues. If begging was the only means of survival, then begging it would be.

The pleading was happening both inside and outside the frame. "*Please,*" the narrator beseeches those of us who happened to be watching, "tell your friends about this show." A "promo" at the start of the episode promises "a shocking cavalcade of stars" and the guarantee that this week, one of these characters—rapidly shuffling through the images of the show's leading performers, and one unfamiliar elderly lady—will die. (The promised cavalcade of guest stars extends only so far as Andy Richter, of *Late Night with Conan O'Brien*, playing quintuplets, and seconds-long cameos by the likes of Ben Stiller and Zach Braff as guests at the Bluths' party.) PUT ON 3-D GLASSES NOW, flashes a message on-screen, before a tomato is launched in our general direction, splattering on the camera lens. A gauntlet had been laid down: the Bluths would survive at all costs. The world of the Bluths bled into our own—or, to be more precise, the struggles of *Arrested Development*, the critically beloved and commercially anemic sitcom, were ingeniously translated into a new crisis for the show's Bluths.

The rest of "S.O.B.s"—"Save Our Bluths," and an apt summary of the Bluths' character defects—is devoted to making *Arrested Development*'s case and subtly undermining it. The show was on life support and winking at its own status as a terminal case. It was also undermining its own halfhearted attempt at improving its odds by cleaning up its act. "Am I the only one that thinks that this family is finally starting to become sympathetic and relatable?" Michael asks his parents. "I mean, that's what people want to see, you know."

The Bluths' newfound relatability is no sooner mentioned than it is undercut, with Michael's brother, coddled mama's boy Buster (Tony Hale), bursting in the room with an announcement: "Sister's my new mother, Mother." Buster, his short-sleeved shirts buttoned to the neck, had been breaking away and crawling back to his mother, Lucille (Jessica Walter) in an eternal cycle of progression and regression. His job, in some manner, is to be the dutiful son; when caught in bed with his mother's maid, Buster is concerned he is the one his mother is firing, all references to cleaning the candlesticks to the contrary. After his latest announcement, their mother zings Buster right back: "Then why don't you marry her?"

Michael, weary as ever, watches it all slip away: "We're veering away from relatability again." Later, Lucille finds herself without a caterer only hours before the "Save Our Bluths" party is set to begin: "We have to make a good impression or we're finished!" The narrator, sensing an opportunity to chime in, adds his own pitch, as if quoting from an unseen network executive's note: "Now that's a clear-cut situation with a promise of comedy. Tell your friends."

For all their attempts to make a good impression, the Bluths of "S.O.B.s" are just as obliviously, gloriously strange as ever. Michael's spoiled twin sister, Lindsay (Portia de Rossi), embraces her new role as a housewife, unveiling her recipe for what she dubs "hot ham water." Michael's son, George Michael (future indie star Michael Cera), is misdiagnosed with obsessive-compulsive disorder when he hastens to shut off all the burners Lindsay has accidentally left on. Lindsay's husband, Tobias (David Cross), a former analyst/therapist now futilely pursuing a career as an actor, returns briefly to his old profession—he calls it, for short, "analrapist"—to diagnose George Michael. Older brother Gob (Will Arnett)—his name, pronounced with a soft *G*, and a long *o*, like the Biblical figure, hints at what he refuses to take on—poses as a waiter to play a prank on his mother and then finds himself attracted enough to the generous tips to stick around. George Michael's cousin Maeby (Alia Shawkat) has wheedled her way into an executive position at a film studio, despite being sixteen years old, and is embroiled in trouble on the set of *Snowboarding School 2*.

Try as they might, the Bluths cannot, will not, be normal, and it is this indifference to social convention that rendered them fantastically strange and comical—and ultimately rather unpopular as well. The inspiration, according to Hurwitz, was *The Sopranos*; he hoped the masses' response to the Bluths would emulate audiences' mysterious attraction to the oft-repulsive Tony Soprano. But what appealed to the devoted, self-selecting viewers of premium cable couldn't generate the broader audiences that network television demanded, and four episodes after "S.O.B.s," the series was canceled. It ended with Michael and George Michael adrift on a boat pointed south toward Mexico and studio exec Maeby pitching a show about her family to none other than Ron Howard, who politely passes while offering dedicated viewers hope for future endeavors: "Nah, I don't see it as a series. Maybe a movie."

Many other worthy shows might have been better off as a movie instead of a series, as well. If the shows dubbed by the cable channel Trio as "brilliant but canceled" could be said to have a unifying theme, it is that sometimes sitcoms appear before audiences are ready to accept them. Some superb comedy series failed because audiences were confused, *Freaks and Geeks*–style, about when to laugh. Others relied on a barrage of jokes to pummel audiences expecting a more orderly array of yuks. These shows are sitcom crime scenes, reminders that good series sometimes show up in the wrong place or at the wrong time. Sitcoms cannot innovate without making sure to bring audiences along.

The short-lived *United States* (NBC, 1980), created by *M*A*S*H*'s Larry Gelbart, exists on a razor's edge between physical comedy and brutal relationship drama. The series, about a couple hitting a rough patch in their relationship, is like a marriage counseling session scored with jokes—although one notably lacking a laugh track. The end result is like watching *The Honeymooners* played as much for drama as for comedy, where trading jibes is part of the fighting, and fighting is part of the show's ongoing two-man vaudeville routine. Before *Moonlighting* paved the way for a more genial, romantic blend of styles, Gelbart's series was simply too off-kilter for mainstream success. *United States* keeps viewers perpetually off-balance with its mixed platter of the bitter and the sweet; after a split, Libby (Helen Shaver) comes to her husband's hotel room to reclaim the remote control he pilfered from home, and the mood swings savagely from playful to embittered. "I'm convinced there's a conspiracy of married people never to tell single people what being married is really like," says Richard (Beau Bridges), in what could stand as *United States'* motto. "Couldn't they offer a class in high school? A training film!"

There was no confusion whatsoever about the comic bona fides of *Police Squad!* (ABC, 1982), created by the masterminds behind *Airplane!* (and eventually to be turned, after its inevitable failure, into the wildly successful *Naked Gun* films). But this parody of police procedurals, mocking the straitjacketed formal rigor and just-the-facts-ma'am vibe of the likes of *Dragnet*, failed to connect with audiences on first exposure.

Perhaps the avalanche of jokes and gags and puns ("ACT II: BRUTÈ," one typical on-screen chapter heading reads) and visual humor was too much for untrained audiences to keep up with. There was little else as visually rich on television in the early 1980s. Lt. Frank Drebin (Leslie Nielsen) regularly checks in with an informant who works as a shoe-shiner, and his visits are always followed by others looking for guidance while getting their wingtips polished: a Catholic priest scoping out the inside track on the afterlife, baseball manager Tommy Lasorda asking for assistance with handling his pitching staff. The moldy clichés of cop shows are roundly mocked. "Is this some kind of bust?" a voluptuous showgirl asks Drebin. "Yes, it's very impressive," he responds, poker-faced as ever, "but we'd just like to ask a few questions."

Like *Police Squad!*, *Bakersfield, P.D.* (Fox, 1993–94) is a cop show with laughs and a sitcom without a laugh track—but it's also a Fox show less gleefully raunchy than the likes of *Married . . . with Children*. The precedents are clear—*Barney Miller*, the funnier subplots of *Hill Street Blues*—but Fox audiences, lulled into complacency by other, weaker programs, could not figure out where to laugh. Similarly, *Action*, the broadcast-channel *Larry Sanders* starring Jay Mohr as an amoral, brutish Hollywood agent, lasted part of one season on Fox before being unceremoniously canned. Mohr's

Peter Dragon was, like the Bluths would later be, too conflicted and unlik-able to play the classical sitcom hero on network TV.

Sports Night (ABC, 1998–2000) attempts to split the difference between drama and sitcom with that contradiction in terms—a *subtle* laugh track. Show creator Aaron Sorkin was staunchly opposed to muddying his show's cascades of dialogue with pauses for canned laughter. More troublingly for its long-term future, the show was a lighthearted workplace comedy—*WKRP in Cincinnati* set at *SportsCenter*—with a persistent interest in affairs beyond its ken: the war on drugs, the Confederate-flag controversy, the afterlife. The same formula, relocated to the White House and slightly tweaked in favor of drama, resulted in the far more successful *The West Wing*. But as a thirty-minute series with a laugh track—even a subtle one—*Sports Night*, too, left audiences confused. In "The Apology," the finest episode of its two-season run, on-air personality Dan (Josh Charles) is raked over the coals for inopportune comments to a magazine writer about the legalization of marijuana, while his cohost, Casey (Peter Krause), obsesses over his fading coolness quotient and preference for 1970s one-hit wonders Starland Vocal Band's "Afternoon Delight."

"I don't know if you've noticed, but we're fighting a war on drugs in this country," a network executive chides Dan. Dan fires back: "How's it going so far?" Dan expresses confusion over just whom he is meant to apologize to for his remarks. He pauses dramatically on air, to the increasing consternation of the show's crew, before bringing up his brother Sam, killed in a car accident while high on drugs: "And there's no doubt that he'd be living a great life right now, except for that he's dead. . . . That was eleven years ago tonight, and I just wanted to say I'm sorry, Sam. You deserved better in my hands, and I apologize."

Comedy begets drama, and drama is undercut by comedy; Casey rolls his chair next to Dan's immediately after his apology, question in hand: "Can I just say one more thing about the Starland Vocal Band?"

When *Arrested Development* premiered on Fox in 2003, it was in many ways a show in the wrong place at the wrong time. It anticipated, in comedic fashion, some of the turmoil to come in American life; it was a comedy about the Great Recession five years ahead of schedule. The Bluths are a fabulously wealthy family fallen on hard times after the arrest of company patriarch George Bluth Sr. and the near-collapse of the family business. The show is about a group of spoiled hothouse flowers awkwardly acclimating themselves to the real world, 1 percenters finding themselves abruptly relocated to the land of the 99 percent. "Now the story of a wealthy family who lost everything, and the one son who had no choice but to keep them all together," Ron Howard's weekly introduction reads, pithily summarizing the show's fundamental conflict.

The Bluths' haplessness and delusions of grandeur are also deliberate echoes of the George W. Bush administration and its terrifying inefficiency and blindness. Gob, newly installed as head of the company, is dropped in by crane to the site of a newly built Bluth Co. home, outfitted as a construction worker. In case we missed the parallels with President Bush's flight-suited misadventures, a giant MISSION ACCOMPLISHED banner is draped behind him. George Sr., fleeing the authorities, is discovered hiding in the ground like Saddam Hussein; George Michael peers into his mouth with a flashlight, in a deliberate echo of the famous photograph of the captured Iraqi dictator. The "smoking gun" evidence of Iraqi weapons of mass destruction, sent around the world by American intelligence services, is actually, according to *Arrested Development*, a picture of Tobias's testicles, and WMDs found in one of the palaces George Sr. built for Saddam are dummy Bluth Co. armaments intended for home decor. As soon as Gob cuts the ribbon on the aforementioned Bluth home, the entire house collapses, an empty shell covering an abyss. (Metaphor alert.) But network TV watchers were not ready yet for such nuanced satire, or for the cantankerous cast of characters.

Arrested Development is a series whose structure and tone made it likelier premium-cable fare than Fox fodder—not just the unsympathetic characters but also the self-aware narration, copious self-referential touches, and reliance on exaggerated comic tropes like incest and homoeroticism. The show is composed almost entirely of these comic excesses. Tobias reveals himself as a "never-nude," always clad in a pair of jean shorts, even at the doctor's office, and nearly dies from a hair transplant gone terribly wrong.

The imprisoned George Sr. recruits Michael to arrange a conjugal visit, pleading "Daddy horny," and then balks when Michael sends George's wife and not his secretary (Judy Greer). In "Not Without My Daughter," everyone from police officers to security guards bring their daughters along for Take Your Daughter to Work Day, and George Michael, purse clutched firmly in hand, is dismayed to be left out of the fun. Buster loses a hand in an attack by a bowtie-wearing seal and spends the remainder of the series smashing delicate objects with his hook and thoroughly unnerving Gob. Even Michael, Jason Bateman's sympathetic Everyman, proves on closer inspection to be almost as deliriously weird as the rest of his family.

Arrested Development perpetually promises an emotional richness that it does its utmost to undercut. The show is forever gesturing at moments of catharsis, only for its characters to slip back once again to familiar habits of slothfulness. This is, of course, the pattern of the sitcom in general—the storm always giving way to the calm, the blank slate of a new episode—and yet *Arrested Development* is different. The pattern of "S.O.B.s" is repeated throughout the series: it knows what viewers want—sentiment, good cheer, tidy conclusions—and repeatedly feints in the right direction before undermining its own halfhearted attempts at angling for the lowest common denominator. George Michael, holding a tiny lump of fried corn, tells his father he is the most important person in his life. Michael responds, "That's a little cornball." Even as it provides neatly wrapped-up stories, it unwinds them. Gob, in the hospital after being stabbed in prison in the episode "Key Decisions," reunites with his girlfriend, Marta (Leonor Varela). They make up to the strains of a sentimental pop ditty, and the camera pulls in on Gob's peaceful expression. As we ponder a man redeemed by love, Gob mutters to himself, "I've made a huge mistake."

"I've made a huge mistake" makes its rounds as a catchphrase among all the Bluths. Each character is prone to making the same errors time and again. Gob's delusions of grandeur force him into roles he is too immature and too petulant to fill; Michael falls in love with inappropriate women and seeks to turn his son into a corporate drone; Lindsay looks to replace her disinterested husband with someone—anyone—else and perpetually strikes out; and so on down the line. Try as they might, none of the Bluths can stay unselfish for long. Their self-absorption always returns, undercutting the show's stabs at schmaltz. It is hard to feel overly sentimental about these monsters of excess.

The jokes could have worn thin, as with any other overly familiar sitcom, except that the familiarity was, in large part, the joke. The show is fond of repetition, doubling and redoubling familiar scenes, moments, and lines, and much of *Arrested Development*'s sophistication is in finding unique ways to make the same jokes and utilize the same punch lines. Part of the enjoyment of watching is in spotting these echoes; we know the Bluths well enough to grasp what they never realize: how much they are prisoners of their own familiar ways.

This is the sitcom as highly self-aware soap opera, piling wildly exaggerated mishap upon mishap while winking good-naturedly at its wised-up audience. None of this is meant to be taken seriously, even in the moment. The inappropriate women Michael falls in love with include Gob's girlfriend, his son's teacher, a shyster who is prosecuting his father while pretending to be blind (played by none other than *Seinfeld*'s Julia Louis-Dreyfus), a woman who turns out to be mentally retarded, and a prostitute whom he previously mistakenly believed to be his sister. She is, in actuality, Jason Bateman's sister, played as she is by *Family Ties* alum Justine Bateman. "Marry me!" he exclaims upon hearing she makes upward of $300,000 a year, echoing Maeby's all-purpose catchphrase, before catching himself. "That's weird, on so many levels." It was.

The ickiness of seeing real-life siblings shamelessly flirting is no accident, for *Arrested Development*, like *Seinfeld*, *Curb Your Enthusiasm*, and other notable sitcoms of the late 1990s and early 2000s, is devoted to our discomfort. *Arrested Development*'s preferred mode of heightening that discomfort is by emphasizing the Bluths' incestuous ties. George Michael, a shambling mess of hidden emotions and masked resentments, is in love with his cousin Maeby, forever attempting to wheedle his way into her affections while simultaneously standing back, horrified at his own desires. He searches high and low for a loophole that will allow him to pursue her openly. Could she possibly be adopted? Michael, oblivious as ever to his son's agony, arranges to have the cousins share a room, and gives George Michael a bit of accidentally pornographic advice about working with her at the family's banana stand: "You stay on top of her, buddy. Do not be afraid to ride her—hard."

Overgrown man-child Buster, meanwhile, is trapped in an unhappy romance with his mother, Lucille, simultaneously seeking to slip out from under her iron fist and to return to her familiarly icy embrace. Even when he finds another love (played with delicious zest by Liza Minnelli), she, too, is named Lucille, and is her mother's oldest friend—emphasis on *oldest*. "I'm leaving my mother for you," he tells Lucille Two, as she is known. "You're replacing my mother." Later, Buster dives through a plate-glass window rather than allow his mother to spot him with Lucille Two. In another episode, Michael asks Buster ("Hey, brother!") if he has a girl in his life, and he responds that he wouldn't exactly call his mother a girl.

The incestuous overtones are unceasing, becoming an in-joke in their own right. Maeby and Michael duet on 1970s AM-radio classic "Afternoon Delight" in the episode of the same name, only to realize, to their intense discomfort, just what kinds of delights the song proffers. (Did superlative sitcoms share an unconscious, or a CD collection? Note, also, Homer Simpson's Starland Vocal Band tattoo in the *Simpsons* episode "'Round Springfield.") Later, Michael and his son find themselves embarrassedly humming the song together.

Arrested Development's repertoire of sexual embarrassment encompasses more than just incest. In the same episode, Michael suggests to his hippie uncle Oscar (also played by Tambor), who has filled in for his father in his mother's affections, that he offer Lucille some "afternoon delight" of her own. Confusing the song's intended subject with a potent brand of marijuana he favors, Oscar provides his own suggestion, to Michael's immediate disgust: "Maybe I'll put it in her brownie."

Then there's Tobias, pound for pound perhaps the show's most laugh-out-loud-hilarious character, who is eternally unaware of the buried same-sex desires trapped inside his every unthinking statement. "I suppose we all do expose our inner desires, don't we?" Tobias remarks, and yet his inner desires spill out unnoticed every time he opens his mouth, in ever more ludicrous fashion. The aspiring actor, always performing for some imaginary audience, dreams of future success: "I can just taste those meaty leading-man parts in my mouth." Over time, Tobias's asides become less double entendres than single entendres with no meaning other than their own hidden sexual content, which only Tobias cannot hear. When he offers to serve as Michael's wingman for a night on the town, his proposal is impossibly convoluted: "Even if it means me taking a chubby, I will suck it up!" Michael suggests purchasing a tape recorder and recording himself so he can be aware of his phrasing. Tobias plays himself back, listening to him enthusing about chubbies, without noticeable concern. "Nothing wrong with that," he chirps, fast-forwarding the cassette.

How did Mitch Hurwitz convince a broadcast network to support a series so cheerfully perverse, in every sense of the word? In his estimation, it was partially due to the presence of Ron Howard as the narrator. In "kind of a manipulation," Hurwitz sold Howard to Fox executives as a drawing point for the show and argued that his voiceover responsibilities would ensure the respected filmmaker's input on the series in general. Howard serves a similar purpose within the show, the steady calm of his voice counteracting its hectic farce. His ever-present, self-mocking narration functions as the show's footnotes, supplementing our knowledge, explaining situations that have been set up in earlier episodes, and contradicting characters' ludicrous explanations. It also further encloses *Arrested Development*'s characters within a cocoon of lovingly designed Wes Anderson–style quirkiness. (In its visual style, as well, *Arrested Development* is reminiscent of Anderson's work, its bright primary colors and carefully orchestrated production design echoing the aesthetic of *The Royal Tenenbaums* and *Rushmore*.)

Howard's narration also keeps the story on course through a constant flow of visual information. Like *30 Rock* and the underrated 1990s HBO series *Dream On*, *Arrested Development* is visually ornate, with rapid inter-cutting, split-screens, flashbacks, still photographs, and ironic juxtapositions. The visuals pillage the cinematic language familiar from countless films and television shows, only to divest them of all expected meaning. The sentimentality of a glowing magic-hour shot of Michael and George Michael is undercut by Michael telling his son that George Sr. is "guilty . . . incredibly guilty." And in the show's first episode, bombastic tribal drums underscore the inherent drama of Michael's telling his family, "You're all going to have to start fending for yourselves." The next shot shows Buster banging those very same drums and sheepishly telling his brother that Lucille has said it is too windy to play on the balcony. We never know if we're being nudged toward a broad emotion or toward acknowledging the cudgels other television series use to garner cheap sentiment.

Well aware that it is a television show, *Arrested* makes regular references to its own existence, as if to remind viewers, much like *30 Rock* later would, not to let themselves settle too comfortably into its fictional world. Tobias hugs Buster in the episode "Forget-Me-Now," observing that "if this was a Lifetime *Moment of Truth* movie, this would be our act break." There is a long, awkward pause, then Howard chimes in: "It wasn't." Instead of cutting to commercial, the show awkwardly limps on. In "Making a Stand," a brief montage of Michael and Gob's dueling banana stands is accompanied by snippets from more than a half-dozen different songs, each rejected for failing to enliven the scene. The narrator then offers a commercial observation: "It was kinda funny to 'Yellow Submarine,' but who could afford it?"

The show is also in intimate dialogue with its fellow sitcoms, with *30 Rock*'s Jack McBrayer, *The Office*'s Brian Baumgartner, Funkhouser (Bob Einstein) and Jeff (Jeff Garlin) from *Curb Your Enthusiasm*, and Julia Louis-Dreyfus dropping by for cameos and guest runs. An accountant whom the Bluths plan to frame for murder is given the name Gilligan, primarily, it seems, to allow Gob to shout, "Gilligan killed the Skipper! I mean the stripper!"

More intriguingly, *Arrested Development* is like an extended reunion of *Happy Days*, with Richie Cunningham (Howard) serving as the narrator, Fonzie (Henry Winkler) playing hapless attorney Barry Zuckerkorn, and none other than Fonzie's late-season youth-audience substitute Chachi (Scott Baio) returning to television, after a lengthy absence, as Barry's replacement and Lindsay's love interest, Bob Loblaw (say it three times fast). The presence of Howard alone is like a guided tour to the sitcom's past, allowing the show's writers to make an extended *Andy Griffith Show* joke in the episode "For British Eyes Only," and for Howard, as narrator, to forswear all such levity: "No one was making fun of Andy Griffith. I can't emphasize that enough."

Andy Griffith's honor was indeed maintained, but *Arrested Development* was an extended riff on the self-absorption and absurdity of the sitcom as we knew it. It wanted viewers to both settle in to a comforting routine of absurdity and to stand back at a remove, enjoying the predictability of the sitcom's machinations. It was a guaranteed recipe for sitcom obsolescence.

And yet, some six years after its cancellation, *Arrested Development* was unexpectedly brought back from the dead, Hurwitz and its leading actors all returning for a new season of episodes released on Netflix in 2013. For a series that had already violated so many of the sitcom's rules, what was another? The "long tail" of popular culture, where low-rated but beloved television shows like *Arrested Development* could be rediscovered at leisure, also meant that even death sentences could be undone. The great injustice of the Bluths' fate could now become their surprising good fortune. And perhaps the underperforming sitcom could survive long enough to find an audience.

But, then, second acts are fraught with peril as well. What would the lengthy, inadvertent hiatus mean for the spell the show had cast on its most devoted fans? The fifteen episodes of *Arrested Development*'s long-awaited fourth season, released to viewers in a single undifferentiated clump, are like a television adaptation of an M. C. Escher drawing, with its familiar figures ascending and descending the same staircases in a crazy-quilt tapestry of interlocking activity. The result is something to be admired more than enjoyed—a remarkable magic trick of the kind Gob would have applauded but that left some audience members, expecting more traditionally comic amusement, occasionally scratching their heads. Perhaps *Arrested Development* was once more caught out in front of its ostensible audience. After a decade, the sitcom had finally been ready for more *Arrested Development*, but Hurwitz was already on to something else entirely.

The show fills us in on how its characters have kept themselves busy since their "future was abruptly canceled," as Howard's narration has it, before catching us up to the overly hectic present. Plot twist is piled atop plot twist, returning over and over again to familiar scenes (a campaign rally, a trial held at a seafood restaurant, a dinner double-date) from new perspectives, offering previously withheld scraps of information. The Escher effect is character-, not just plot-driven; the Bluths are forever in danger of turning into their parents, aping their parents, or transforming their children into warped versions of themselves. The effort required to sustain this vast canvas is heroic, rivaling the most mind-warping chronological conundrums of *Lost*. Some longtime fans were astounded by the new season's narrative intricacy, while others thought that *Arrested Development*, in its new incarnation, was so enamored of its complexity that it had forgotten its simple appeal.

Netflix had engineered a coup, but unexpectedly, the freedom from network constraints was seemingly a mixed blessing for *Arrested Development*. "I think movies are dead," Maeby, the former studio exec, tells her uncle Michael about the movie he plans to produce on the Bluths' trials. "Maybe it's a TV show." Maybe it was. (Or maybe it was an app; one of the show's cleverest hidden jokes was a Facebook ping dropped into the middle of an episode, sending a nation of viewers diving for their smartphones.) *Arrested Development* had come back in time for its belated audience to celebrate its return, but it had given them something decidedly different from what they expected.

22

The Office

"Casino Night"

May 11, 2006 ▪ NBC

"I was just—I'm in love with you." The camera zooms in, as if lurking behind the bushes, at the not-quite-couple as they linger outside their office's raucous casino night. "What?" "I'm really sorry if that's weird for you to hear, but I needed you to hear it." Jim (John Krasinski) is gawky, loping, endlessly mocking, a closet romantic in cynic's garb; Pam (Jenna Fischer) is polite, perky, with a streak of playfulness that matches Jim's. She is also engaged to the well-meaning doofus Roy (David Denman) and ill-inclined to listen to Jim's impromptu profession of love. "What are you doing?" she asks him, all traces of mischievousness erased from her face. "What do you expect me to say to that?"

Jim lifts his eyebrows and scrunches his mouth sideways, as if in partial apology. It is a facial tic that steady viewers of *The Office* (NBC, 2005–13) had already come to know intimately by the time of "Casino Night," written by Steve Carell, the finale of the series' second season. "I just needed you to know. Once." Pam nervously bounces from foot to foot, in search of an appropriate answer to Jim's declaration of love. "You have no idea—" "Don't do that," Jim interrupts. "—what your friendship means to me." "I want to be more than that," he insists. "I can't," Pam deflects, her face partially hidden by Jim's shoulder and back. "I'm really sorry if you misinterpreted things." Jim nods blankly, his eyes glassy, and as he turns to walk away he brushes a lone tear that has cascaded down his cheek.

When NBC announced an American remake of the brief but much-loved British comedy series *The Office* (BBC, 2001–03), it is likely that no one anticipated Pam and Jim's charged encounter. The UK series, starring the show's cocreator Ricky Gervais as David Brent, a well-meaning but dim-witted boss at a haggard paper company, specialized in the comedy of discomfort, drawing from the same well of irreversible entropy and unavoidable humiliation as its American contemporary *Curb Your Enthusiasm*. Although the American *Office* retains some of the original's skin-crawling awkwardness, it refuses to be bound by it. Nor does it adhere to the central precept of its NBC predecessor *Seinfeld*, "No hugging, no learning." It is an amalgam of the old and the new, a traditional sitcom cloaked in the garb of the new, acidulous comedy.

The Office is a satire of workplace mores in which practically every character is the oddball neighbor, and the straight men (chiefly represented by cute couple Fischer and Krasinski) are hopelessly outnumbered and outgunned. And yet the show expertly balances its mismatched parts, with workplace antics and romance and the narrative slipperiness of *Seinfeld* and *Arrested Development* each taking their turn onstage. In lesser hands, *The*

Office would have been an unbearable hodgepodge of worn sitcom tropes; instead, it was the most influential network sitcom of its era, crafting a style that rapidly became the default look for modestly adventurous shows with a quasi-realist bent.

Like its British predecessor, *The Office* is a mockumentary, in the style of *This Is Spinal Tap* and the films of Christopher Guest. It purports to be footage captured by an unseen camera crew as they follow the employees of a small paper company about their daily business. Ken Kwapis, who directed many of *The Office*'s early episodes, insisted on hiring camera operators who had actually worked in reality TV for an additional dose of verisimilitude. They were instructed to imitate the feeling of live television, occasionally shooting out of focus or arriving late on an actor's line. Kwapis also brought in Rollerblades-wearing cinematographer Peter Smokler, with whom he had worked on *The Larry Sanders Show*.

At the outset, the series offers no explanation for why a documentary crew would be interested in the Dunder Mifflin paper company of Scranton, Pennsylvania, and any semblance of narrative consistency regarding the premise is rapidly discarded. This is less a mockumentary than a mock-mockumentary, lifting the style, but not the substance, of the original series' documentary conceit. The British *Office* had stayed true to the camera-crew premise; its American counterpart is true to the notion of its action being caught on the fly while caring little about the details of the supposed documentary being filmed.

The camerawork on *The Office* is forever adjusting itself, fixating on something new or honing in on an intriguing detail. In Jim and Pam's fateful tête-à-tête at the end of "Casino Night," the camera casually cuts from an over-the-shoulder shot of Pam, framed by Jim's back, to a similarly composed shot of Jim. No camera crew in the world, no matter how intrepid, could have framed two such identical shots in such close order. This may sound like pointless critical carping, and perhaps it is. But the point is less to complain about *The Office*'s inconsistencies than to note the ways in which the show adopts the mockumentary style as a visual technique more than a narrative framework.

"Casino Night" lets the disappointment of Pam and Jim's fizzled romance sink in for only a moment before once more adjusting its frame. The camera slinks into the darkened Dunder Mifflin office, zooming back from behind opened blinds (a visual trademark of the show, emphasizing the show's recurring interest in secrecy and eavesdropping) as Pam calls her mother. She is interrupted by Jim walking in, with the camera zooming in as she hangs up the phone and seeks to pick up the conversation where they left it. "Listen, Jim . . ." Jim swoops in, grabs her around the waist, and kisses her. The two silently look at each other, their mouths hanging open with surprise, and the screen fades to black.

The Office would revisit the Pam and Jim romance after its summer hiatus, of course, but it is worthwhile to rewind to the show's introduction to see how cleverly it threads their relationship throughout as an emotional hook, baiting viewers to care about each new episode with promises of further installations of their saga while simultaneously devoting the bulk of its attention to the absurdist hijinks of boss Michael Scott (Steve Carell) and the rest of the Dunder Mifflin staff.

From the very first episodes of its abbreviated first season in 2005, when *The Office* was introduced as a midseason replacement, the cameras spy on up-and-coming salesman Jim as he lingers by the front desk, flirting with secretary Pam as a means of passing the time. The mock-mockumentary style gives us the sensation of spotting something overlooked by others, of observing without being observed ourselves. It allows viewers to feel clever while still being guided in their attention, subtly directed to silently monitor developments alongside the cameras.

Pam and Jim's budding feelings become less a matter of hackneyed television emotion-wringing and more something viewers are given the opportunity to slowly pick up on themselves. She and the lunkheaded, inattentive Roy have been engaged for so long that at the company's annual awards banquet, the Dundees, she is given the prize for Longest Engagement. (saleswoman Phyllis wins the award for Busiest Beaver, but an unfortunate misspelling on the statuette renders her the recipient, instead, of Bushiest

Beaver.) Pam gets drunk at the awards ceremony and kisses Jim before tumbling off her chair.

In "Booze Cruise," from the middle of the second season, Jim and Pam have a tender moment together during an alcohol-soaked company event aboard a boat. "Sometimes I just don't get Roy," she tells Jim, the smiles slowly fading from their faces as the unstated meaning of her words sink in, before she heads back inside. Jim is forever being lifted up and cast back down; by the end of the episode, Roy is setting a date for the wedding on the boat's PA system, and Jim has broken up with his girlfriend, sitting alone as he watches another happy couple share a moment of bliss.

Audiences were skeptical at first. Those familiar with Ricky Gervais's show were convinced the American *Office* could only be a pale imitation, and those unfamiliar with it saw little reason to tune in at first. "This episode is so good," Krasinski remembered NBC executives telling him week after week. "Unfortunately, it's the last one we're going to do." When the show was first introduced, its writing staff—show creator Greg Daniels, Michael Schur, and writer-performers B. J. Novak, Paul Lieberstein, and Mindy Kaling—were each tasked with bringing in one script for the six-episode season. Daniels had sought out performers who could also write in the hopes of forming a band of comedy warriors. "It feels like a small gang of people making their own vision," Novak said of Daniels's setup.

The Office struggled in the ratings, but it was rescued when viewers discovered the Pam-and-Jim dynamic and awareness of the show spread by word of mouth. It was also helped along by the iTunes Store; in late 2005, Apple began selling individual episodes, and by mid-2006, seventeen of the top one hundred most-purchased TV episodes were of *The Office*. The enormous success of Judd Apatow's *The 40-Year-Old Virgin*, starring Steve Carell, and NBC's realization that the hottest movie star of 2006 was under contract to the network, also boosted *The Office*'s flagging reputation.

As fans discovered the series and ratings built slowly, Daniels realized that this *Office* would not be limited to following the plot outline of its predecessor. "We've gotten positive feedback when we've gotten less like the

English show," said Daniels in a 2006 interview. "So I think that has given us the feeling that we don't have to mentally check in with that again so much." The show, boosted by the creative input of its cast, many of whom were veterans of the improv-comedy scene, grew looser, more unpredictable. And as it translated the British *Office*'s simmering relationship between Tim (Martin Freeman) and Dawn (Lucy Davis) into the extended up-and-down saga of Pam and Jim, it also grew more emotional.

After the "Casino Night" cliffhanger, *The Office* began its third season by revisiting that same charged moment between Pam and Jim. "You have no idea how long I wanted to do that," Jim tells Pam, and she agrees: "Me, too." But little actually changes between them, as Jim asks whether she plans to marry Roy, and she says she does. He slips his fingers out of her hands, and the next we see him, he is working in the Stamford office of Dunder Mifflin and casually flirting with new coworker Karen (Rashida Jones). If there is something surprisingly discomfiting about seeing Jim pursuing another woman, as if we're watching an ex use all the same familiar seductive moves on a new conquest, it's indicative of the easy intimacy of *The Office*—and of successful sitcoms in general. Good sitcoms manufacture a communion between themselves and their viewers, an instant shorthand that can convey profound emotions simply and straightforwardly.

Eventually, Jim and Pam do get together, but *The Office* manages to keep them entertaining. Jim keeps threatening to propose to Pam in inappropriate places, kneeling as they walk down the street, and asking her, in his huskiest voice, "Hey Pam? Will you . . . wait for me one second while I tie my shoe?" When Jim does settle on the ideal moment to propose, Andy (the brilliantly befuddled Ed Helms, introduced in the show's third season) steals the limelight by proposing to his girlfriend first: "Angela, will you do me the honor of giving me your tiny hand in marriage?" When Jim does finally have the opportunity to actually propose, at a rest stop halfway between Scranton and New York, we watch from a distance through a telephoto lens, silently, as they kiss, as if allowing them their moment of privacy.

The Office offsets Jim and Pam's healthy, mature, if long-in-coming union with a series of highly dysfunctional partnerships. Michael makes

out with his boss Jan (Melora Hardin), who ducks his advances before settling into a cozy relationship composed of passive aggression and assaults
on Michael's manhood. Andy and Angela (Angela Kinsey) are like a comic
inverse of Pam and Jim, laughably ill-matched and perpetually cranky.
Angela is having a furtive office affair with Dwight (Rainn Wilson), sneaking off for lunchtime quickies even as she plans—or better yet, puts off—
her honeymoon with Andy. Everyone in the office learns of Angela and
Dwight's affair by the time of "The Duel"—everyone, that is, except Andy,
who marches in and announces he wants to discuss the elephant in the
room. As Dwight tenses for a fight, Andy announces that no one from the
office has RSVP'd yet for the wedding. Andy, the Cornell graduate whose
cell phone ringtone is himself singing in four-part harmony, seems to want
to get married primarily to fly in his college singing-group buddies: Broccoli
Rob, Sandwich, Pubie Lewis and the News, and the rest of the gang.

The Office is only too aware of its antecedents, and it wittily pokes fun at
its own relative lack of inspiration. "We're like Friends," observes Michael,
with a surprising degree of honesty. "I am Chandler and Joey, and Pam is
Rachel, and Dwight is Kramer." Before we fully unpack that statement, let
us note that the emotional through-line of The Office bears a great deal of
resemblance to the one on Friends. Pam and Jim are not forced through as
many unlikely romantic mishaps as Friends' Ross and Rachel, but The Office
is similarly anchored in their relationship. Without them, Michael and
Dwight and the rest of their officemate sidekicks would float dangerously
untethered from reality. It is Pam and Jim who ground The Office in a familiar emotional reality—along with a surprising, late-blooming undercurrent
of economic collapse, which we will return to at the end of the chapter.

As for fumbling boss Michael, he is indeed both Chandler and Joey,
jokemeister and butt of the joke all at once. Before getting on the boat in
"Booze Cruise," Jim confidently predicts that Michael will re-create the
"King of the world" scene from Titanic within an hour, or he will give up his
next paycheck. Jim gets to hang on to his money. As his team boards the ship,
Michael sings the Gilligan's Island theme song, pegging Dwight as Gilligan
and African American grump Stanley as one of the Harlem Globetrotters

(evidently *he* was one of the people intrigued enough to watch that prime example of sitcom hackery). The allure of an open microphone, whether at Pam and Jim's wedding or a shareholders' meeting, can never be resisted.

Like Gervais's David Brent, Michael is a deep-rooted psychological nightmare for his employees, cleverly masked in the guise of a fun boss. He is immature, inappropriate, needy, petulant, and perpetually sidetracked from his work. Michael regularly pauses the work day to call his employees into the conference room and introduce a new distraction: a turn as hardened con Prison Mike to scare his workers straight on the dangers of the penitentiary in the episode "The Convict" ("You, my friend, would be da belle of da ball," he drawls at one employee. "Don't drop da soap! Don't drop da soap!"), or an impromptu lecture on tolerance. "I don't care if you are gay or straight or a lesbian or overweight," he announces, taking pains to point at a particular individual for each designation.

Carell's character expertly threads the line between laughing at him and laughing with him. Sometimes we suspect Michael is funny without being entirely sure why. After a roast goes terribly awry, Michael returns to the office with a vengeance, having planned an impromptu reverse roast of the roasters. "Jim, you're six eleven and you weigh ninety pounds. Gumby has a better body than you. Boom, roasted." He only degrades from there. "Stanley, you crush your wife during sex, and your heart sucks. Oscar, you're gay. Andy, Cornell called. They think you suck. And you're gayer than Oscar."

Michael's assistant Dwight, meanwhile, is indeed something like the show's Kramer, even if Michael's memory of the distinction between *Friends* and *Seinfeld* is hazy at best. Dwight is a dysfunctional attack dog, trained to be loyal only to Michael, who barely tolerates him; he enjoys the boss's kicks as much as the pats on the back. He is a totalitarian beet farmer who sees himself as an Übermensch, set to take over the Scranton branch of Dunder Mifflin and, from there, the world. Dwight is a creepy, emotionally neutered quasi-Amish mutant, expertly parodied by Jim in the episode "Goodbye Toby" when he reroutes all of Dwight's calls to his Bluetooth device as a prank: "Hello, *Mutter*," he greets Dwight's mother. "Good news. I've married. Tell *Vater*." Dwight is perpetually looking to sink his workplace enemies but is sidelined by Jim's pranks and taunts: Jim moves Dwight's desk into the bathroom, puts all his personal belongings into the snack machine, and turns him into the office equivalent of Pavlov's dog by linking the pinging of his computer to an offer of an Altoids mint.

In short, Dwight is a sidekick extraordinaire—yet the overlapping circles of *The Office*'s writing staff served to further deemphasize the traditional star-and-sidekick distinction of the sitcom. Each character is given his or her moment, like hard-drinking Meredith (Kate Flannery), romantically needy Kelly (Kaling, soon to star in her own series, *The Mindy Project*), sad sack HR rep Toby (Lieberstein), and temp turned megalomaniac exec Ryan (Novak). The show expertly plays its characters off one another, allowing individual episodes to revolve around the collision of well-established personae—prim, dogmatic Angela, say, with uptight, gay Oscar (Oscar Nuñez).

Best of all the supporting characters is Ed Helms's Andy Bernard— repressed, haplessly romantic, a dispenser of nicknames (Jim is dubbed Big Tuna for having once consumed a tuna sandwich in his presence). He is a man of the world whose world bears a distinct resemblance to a fraternity mixer: "Beer me *dos* Long Island iced teas, *s'il vous plaît*," he suavely requests of a bartender while on a Canadian business trip.

Andy is prone to turning his darkest feelings—of exclusion, romantic disappointment, professional calamity—into badly timed jokes, as if the whole world were a Dave Matthews Band concert and he had arrived just after the last encore of "What Would You Say." Dwight, taunting his erstwhile romantic rival in "Employee Transfer," arrives at the office in a Cornell sweatshirt, telling Andy he plans to apply to the school. Andy attempts to take this assault on his last bastion of pride with dignity, but it is simply too much for him. "Those colors are sacred," he upbraids Dwight, a goofy smile pasted on his face even as his voice hardens. These clashes of sensibility, of quirk meeting quirk, are the steady heartbeat of *The Office*. It is, as Andy would say, on like a prawn that yawns at dawn.

Through it all, the mockumentary camera is there, allowing the characters to subtly indicate their awareness of the lunacy surrounding them. The form even allows them to testify directly to the camera, a technique popularized by reality shows like MTV's *The Real World*, and a sham indicator of intimacy that *The Office* plays up to the hilt. This is not, like *The Mary Tyler Moore Show* or *Cheers* had been, a series about eccentrics glimpsed in the comfort of their habitat. Instead, it is a show in which the characters themselves are occasionally in on the joke, tipping their hand to us by playing to the camera. It is all a product of the same urge to self-awareness, whether it's Jim's array of winks and nods ("He's always looking at the camera like this," Rashida Jones's Karen tells the camera, perfectly imitating Jim's trademark shrug), or the silent importuning of Ryan when he is overwhelmed by the eccentricities of an unfamiliar office.

The mockumentary style was a surprisingly durable one for television comedy, even as it veered further and further from its original form. *Parks and Recreation* (NBC, 2009–) maintains the *Office* model for sitcom success, while paying even less heed to the fictional logic of its all-seeing documentary cameras. Created by *The Office*'s Michael Schur and Greg Daniels, *Parks* is another zany-workplace comedy, with Amy Poehler of *Saturday Night Live* in the Michael Scott role. Poehler plays Leslie Knope, a political functionary in the town of Pawnee, Indiana, with Hillary Clinton dreams and Roger Clinton talents. Leslie is a gentler figure than Michael, in keeping with *Parks* as a whole, which is a politer, less gut-twistingly awkward version of *The Office*. But like Michael, Leslie is forever admitting her failures only reluctantly, at the end of an internal struggle of which we have only glimpsed the very tip, and then instantly pressing on. "The only thing I'm guilty of," she says after a fracas with a rival town's parks official in the episode "Eagleton," "is loving Pawnee. And punching Lindsay in the face. And shoving a coffee filter down her pants." Leslie, even as she grows into a more assured and capable politician in her professional life, learns no personal lessons, acquires no wisdom. Reuniting her boss Ron (Nick Offerman, mustachioed and martini dry) with his toxic ex-wife in "Ron and Tammy," Leslie testifies to the cameras: "When you meddle in someone's personal life, it's just so . . . *rewarding.*"

Parks is blessed with an ensemble nearly the equal of *The Office*'s, with standouts like stand-up comedian Aziz Ansari, *Party Down*'s Adam Scott, wizard of snark Aubrey Plaza, and *West Wing* veteran Rob Lowe. As it grew from a shabby imitation of *The Office* into its own brightly pleasant, if not quite groundbreaking, creation, *Parks and Recreation* found its own voice in its cacophony of oddballs, each gloriously deaf to the world around them. "I can't make it to the telethon tonight," Tom (Ansari) tells Leslie, "because I have no interest in being there."

Modern Family (ABC, 2009–) is one step further removed from the mockumentary style, capitalizing on *The Office*'s aesthetic without even suggesting that there's a camera crew involved in capturing the private moments and zany adventures of three wildly disparate but interlocked families. The lingering, jittery camerawork familiar from *The Office* and *Parks and Recreation* is balanced out by the still compositions of individual characters' direct testimony to the camera. *Modern Family* is a deeply conservative reimagining of the classical sitcom decorated with contemporary touches: *Family Ties* with gay people. Paterfamilias Jay Pritchett (Ed O'Neill, enjoying a well-deserved resurgence after *Married . . . with Children*) is raising a second family with new wife Gloria (Sofia Vergara); his daughter, Claire (Julie Bowen), is married to the wannabe-hip Phil (Ty Burrell); and his son, Mitchell (Jesse Tyler Ferguson), has adopted a daughter with his partner, Cam (Eric Stonestreet).

Of the three couples chronicled on the show, the most amusing is the partnership of uptight, repressed lawyer Mitchell and Cam, whose idea of helpful behavior is to pass himself off as Native American at a private-school interview for their daughter to improve their gay-men-raising-an-adopted-Asian-baby pitch. "Leave it to the gays," Mitchell wistfully notes, "to raise the only underachieving Asian in America."

Modern Family is a coagulated mass of knowing stereotypes: the emotive Hispanic trophy wife, the zany, hapless dad, the overdramatic gay man. The stereotypes are redeemed only by the winking fashion in which they are deployed. Claire critiques Cam's choice of exercise wear, and when Cam returns, she asks if he has run off to the bathroom to cry. "Yes," he responds witheringly, "because that is what all gay men do," before weakening and admitting the truth: "Yes." Mitchell, accused by Cam of being fatally predictable, surprises him by participating in a flash-mob dance. Instead of being touched, Cam is furious: "You cheated on me with choreography, and that is the worst kind." *Modern Family* became a surprise runaway hit for ABC, charming audiences with its warmth and its tweaks to a predictable formula. It is like *The Office* if every character were simultaneously Dwight and Pam.

As with *Parks and Recreation* and *Modern Family*, *The Office*'s mockumentary style is a helpful veneer of aesthetic daring over a base coat of old-school sitcom conservatism. Pam and Jim are a will-they-or-won't-they couple in the long tradition of Sam and Diane, and Ross and Rachel. And there is nothing wrong with that. But it is Dwight who is the epitome of the series' discordant gooeyness, the deliberate shock tactics of *Curb Your Enthusiasm* conjoined to a *Friends*-inspired desire to please. Dwight is allowed to scheme and to fulminate, but he is practically never given the opportunity to triumph. How could *The Office* be sure of audiences' allegiance if it were to veer too far into David Brent / Larry David territory? This is not that kind of show, no matter what indications it occasionally makes to the contrary.

The Office may violate the *Seinfeld* precept against hugging, but it enjoys upholding its rule against learning. Michael is an immature little boy, snickering at his own gay jokes, sending around photos of his boss and occasional girlfriend Jan in a bikini to impress his pals, and delivering his one-size-fits-all punch line to any vaguely risqué double entendre: "That's what she said!" When his superiors inform him in the episode "Sexual Harassment" that such comments are inappropriate, he gloomily agrees to forgo them. Jim, preying on Michael's weakness, torments him with ideal setups like "You really think you can go all day long?" and "You always left me satisfied and smiling," and he quickly returns to his old habits.

In the episode "Gay Witch Hunt," Jim capitalizes on the boorish, dopey masculinity of both Michael and Dwight, selling them on a "gaydar" detector he tells them is on sale at the Sharper Image. (Michael panics when the detector beeps furiously as he passes it over his crotch.) As if in penance for his illiberal sins, Michael calls an emergency meeting and announces that he will be kissing Oscar as an expression of his newfound tolerance. The resulting embrace, with both Oscar and Michael cringing from the impact, and Pam gaping in open-mouthed shock, is one of the most memorably dysfunctional in television history, a clever riposte to the supposedly groundbreaking same-sex displays on shows like *Roseanne* and *Ellen*. But even after this awakening, Michael is still prone to flare-ups of homophobic inappropriateness, calling Oscar into his office to ask him what to expect, "in terms of sensation, or emotions," from an upcoming colonoscopy. "Should I have a safe word?"

Eventually Carell left the series and *The Office* started to falter, with neither James Spader as the creepy Robert California nor a fleet of celebrity drop-ins (Idris Elba, Kathy Bates, Will Ferrell) doing enough to make up for his absence. *The Office* was the epitome of the successful network ensemble show, and yet without its original star, the entire enterprise felt off-kilter, no longer capable of balancing its dual interests in improvisatory antics and emotional nuance.

Before that, however, the show kicked into a previously hidden gear, breaking Michael out of his reliable Chandler/Joey mold by thrusting him into the terrifying maw of the post-2008 American economy. Where *The Office*'s early seasons hummed with the background chatter of downsizing and cutbacks, the show's fifth season, in 2008–09, takes place against the backdrop of the United States teetering on the brink of a financial cliff. Michael unexpectedly announces he is quitting Dunder Mifflin (Jim hears the roar of terrifying beasts emerging from his office and quickly determines the cause of the trouble: "It's Monster.com—singular"), and ultimately decides to start the competing Michael Scott Paper Company, whose main task appears to be the daily preparation of a comically outsized stack of pancakes for himself and his staff. Pam, in a burst of misplaced enthusiasm, immediately regretted, agrees to join Michael.

The new company is an unmitigated disaster, but Michael puts enough of a scare into Dunder Mifflin to be bought out and given his old job back—in time to endure a revolt against the company in the following season's indelible "Shareholder Meeting." Michael grabs the microphone, as he is wont to do, and rescues the floundering board of directors by promising a forty-five-point, forty-five-day, carbon-neutral plan to rescue the company. The shareholders burst into raucous applause. That he has no points, no days, no carbon to offset, is no concern of Michael's. He has uttered the magic words of American business circa 2009, even if they have become, in this post-GM, post-AIG time, utterly without meaning. Michael Scott is no longer everyone's nutty boss; once the little man crushed by forces beyond his control, he is now the empty chair at the CEO's desk, the meaningless promises passed out like so many shares of worthless stock. *The Office* is our office, Michael Scott is America, and God help us all.

23

30 Rock

"Rosemary's Baby"

October 25, 2007 ▪ NBC

B egin with one large fistful of slightly dinged, Mary Richards–brand feminist spunk. Add in two clumps of zany, Larry Sanders star-power narcissism, and a generous sprinkling of Dunder Mifflin–style quirkiness, and season with *Arrested Development*'s brand of visual humor. Serve fresh from the oven, and you've got the triumphant showbiz farce *30 Rock* (NBC, 2006–2013), one of the most consistently funny sitcoms of the past decade.

Its humor and its mediocre ratings stemmed from the same root cause: it was a sitcom about the exhaustion of sitcoms, a summing-up and a parodying of all television's tired appeals. The sitcom was triumphing by acknowledging its failings. And who would want to watch that?

Emerging at the tail end of the sitcom's steady modernist accretion of self-reflexivity, *30 Rock* takes the conceit of the workplace sitcom—the land of *Cheers* and *Taxi* and *The Mary Tyler Moore Show*—and transforms its conjoined savagery and bonhomie into a condition of existence for Liz Lemon (show creator Tina Fey), the perpetually overstretched head writer of a television sketch comedy show that seems like a less successful version of Fey's own alma mater, *Saturday Night Live*. Liz is part no-nonsense comedy wizard and part pathetic single girl, stuck with the oddballs and narcissists who work on her TV show, *TGS*, because her devotion to her maddening job leaves little time for anyone else.

The series begins, in the very first scene of its first episode, by paying tribute to its predecessors while simultaneously enumerating the many ways in which Liz Lemon could never be Mary Richards. Liz stands in line outside 30 Rockefeller Center, where *TGS* is filmed, waiting to purchase a hot dog. Outraged by a middle-aged businessman's attempt to cut the line, Liz impulsively purchases the entire tray, passing out frankfurters to strangers and passersby as an impossibly perky, *Mary Tyler Moore*–ish theme song plays: "Who's that? I know that you're wondering. That's her! Who's got the kind of charisma that the boys prefer? Who's hot and you know that she knows it? That's her!" The tune, it turns out, is not Liz's theme song at all, but wafts over from a *TGS* soundstage, where rehearsals are under way for a sketch featuring Pam, the Overly-Confident Morbidly Obese Woman. Welcome to *30 Rock*.

Liz definitively lacks the "charisma that the boys prefer." She is diagnosed by her boss, foil, and soon-to-be mentor Jack Donaghy (Alec Baldwin) at their first meeting as "New York, third-wave feminist, college educated, single and pretending to be happy about it, overscheduled, undersexed, you buy any magazine that says 'healthy body image' on the cover, and every two years you take up knitting for," pausing and popping his lips for triumphant emphasis, "a week?" The series is given to denting whatever shreds of optimism and confidence remain for a single, thirtysomething Manhattan overachiever with too many overgrown infants to nurse and too little time for a life of her own. The main character of *The Mary Tyler Moore Show* would likely not have enjoyed romancing gentleman callers while wearing ice cream cone pajamas and futzing with her humidifier.

Mary Richards lived out the peppy-theme-song dream. Murphy Brown had been the bold feminist icon of a prior generation, proudly holding her own in a male-dominated workplace. The ladies of *Sex and the City* embodied the notion that women could have it all—fulfilling work, torrid sex, meaningful relationships, and good friends. Liz Lemon, in all her knock-kneed, poorly dressed, socially inept, sexually inexperienced, fun-hating glory, is the deliberate undoing of those fantasies.

Does that make her a satirical caricature, or a feminist icon in her own right? On the one hand, Liz is a strangely realistic depiction of modern, overachieving American women: dazzlingly competent, overworked, underloved, and exhausted. She is as efficient at work as she is hapless in her private life. She brings a live weekly television show to the air with a minimum of fuss but a maximum of hassle, the sole bulwark standing between *TGS* and utter chaos. On the other hand, Liz is the sort of person who sings hymns of her praise to her midnight snack of choice ("Workin' on my night cheese . . .") and creates a neologism, "lizzing," to define the phenomenon of simultaneously laughing and whizzing. The show itself cannot quite decide how seriously to take her. Skipping jauntily between wildly divergent modes of attack, *30 Rock* thrives by refusing to settle on a single style.

Both explicitly and implicitly, *30 Rock* is a clash of opposites. Its premiere episode is plunged into action by the unexpected arrival of washed-out movie star Tracy Jordan (Tracy Morgan, combining the worst of Eddie Murphy and Martin Lawrence into a surprisingly lovable whole) to join the cast of what had previously been known as *The Girlie Show*. And with that, sophisticated feminist humor meets the star of *This Honky Grandma Be Trippin'*.

The other core characters, too, are a deliberate hodgepodge of clashing styles, existing in their own echo chambers of self-regard, starring in their

own individual shows, only dimly aware of the existence of anyone lingering at the fringes of their spotlight. *TGS* star Jenna (Jane Krakowski) is,
like Tracy, a permanent inmate of the prison house of stardom, tirelessly
devoted to the maintenance of her fame. NBC boss Jack is a self-declared
master of the universe, breathing the rarefied air of the corporate elite and
permanently peeved at having to settle the minor squabbles of a third-rate
show. And network page Kenneth (Jack McBrayer) is the resident television
cheerleader and critic, the only one on the show who actually seems to enjoy
watching the finished product.

The clashing styles of *30 Rock* are vividly reflected in the second-season
episode "Rosemary's Baby," written by Jack Burditt. In its main storyline,
the episode explores Liz's feminism and her queasy relationship to power
in the form of the preternaturally self-assured Jack. Liz and *TGS* producer
Pete Hornberger (Scott Adsit) stand in line at a bookstore, waiting to have
a copy of the new memoir by Rosemary Howard (Carrie Fisher) signed.
Rosemary is not, as Pete suspects, "one of the ladies who tried to shoot
Gerald Ford," but a pioneering, legendarily outspoken comedy writer for
shows like *Laugh-In*.

Liz brings in Rosemary, her childhood role model, as a guest writer for
TGS, where she regales the writing staff with salacious stories of comedy's
glory days. "I'll never watch *Happy Days* the same way again," Liz exclaims
after one anecdote, awed to be in the presence of her idol. In Rosemary's
retelling, comedy writers had once been edgy, snorting cocaine at their desks
and writing sketches in which talking mailboxes were symbols of embattled
Nixon chief of staff H. R. Haldeman (echoing the drug-fueled golden age
of *Saturday Night Live*). Rosemary gets the *TGS* writers a bit *too* fired up
to do their jobs, which revolve more around the telling of fart jokes than
expert political satire—although the fact that *30 Rock* itself does traffic in
quite a bit of the latter adds to the richness of the joke. But *30 Rock*, arriving
long after comedy's glory days had come and gone, was not going to force
any presidents, or even White House chiefs of staff, from office. That would
have required a degree of trust in its mission—and an audience share—that
the show could not quite muster.

Liz admires Rosemary but is dismayed by the effect she has on the *TGS* staff, to whom her hero proposes such risqué sketch ideas as having Josh (Lonny Ross) appear in blackface. When Jack demands that Liz fire Rosemary, she refuses in feminist solidarity, and both women are fired instead. But what Liz finds outside the comforting confines of 30 Rockefeller Center is unsettling. She retreats with Rosemary to her idol's neighborhood of "Little Chechnya," where purse snatchers and drug dealers operate in broad daylight, as if *30 Rock* had accidentally stumbled onto *The Wire*'s turf. Liz rapidly pinwheels from spunky vigor ("We could start our own network, called Bitch TV—or the second idea that we think of") to a desire to flee from Rosemary and her roach-infested apartment as quickly as possible. "You can't abandon me, Liz," Rosemary shouts. "You *are* me!" Rosemary curses Liz like a mother damning an uncaring child: "You're never going to get married, Liz—you're married to your job. . . . You wouldn't have a job if it wasn't for me. I broke barriers for you."

Liz flees back to the comfortable corporate embrace of Jack Donaghy and NBC, determined never to turn into Rosemary. She pledges to send her idol $400 a month for the rest of her life and "to do that thing that rich people do, where they turn money into more money." She also instantly caves to Jack's demands that she rewrite a sketch about dog penises, preferring life as an employed conformist to that of an unemployed rebel. Not a groundbreaker, not passionately devoted to fighting the suits of the world, Liz is a woman standing up for herself in a tough business by craftily picking her battles—a refreshingly honest statement of purpose for a business in which, as the episode notes, women become obsolete as soon as no one wants to see them naked anymore.

Liz's predicament is also *30 Rock*'s. What taboos remain to be shattered after masturbation jokes on *Seinfeld* and blowjobs on *Sex and the City*? The heroic era of comedy, in *30 Rock*'s estimation, had come and gone, and trailblazers like Rosemary have been succeeded by the workmanlike Liz. Sitcom stars are no longer icons of American culture, nor are they symbolic representatives of larger shifts in society like Bill Cosby or Roseanne once were. There are no shocks left to be administered, no territory untouched by previous comic explorers of the sitcom, just some dog-penis jokes and a desire to survive.

But *30 Rock* was too modest by half, and its achievements were far greater than the expert recounting of dog-penis jokes or the making of money into money. (NBC would likely beg to differ with the latter characterization of the perennially low-rated sitcom.) Instead, *30 Rock* was brilliantly flexible, effortlessly riffing on the stray flotsam and jetsam of pop culture. Sitcoms had found their new voice, just in time for their audiences to shrivel. Was TV still funny if no one was watching?

Even "Rosemary's Baby" itself, as it articulates Liz's, and by extension Fey's, statement of purpose as a comedian and a woman after the heroic age of comedy has passed, is limber enough to be only half-devoted to its message. In a secondary storyline, Tracy develops a burning interest in dog-fighting after Jack casually mentions that it's the only vice a celebrity cannot be forgiven for partaking in. Fearing disastrous publicity for the network, and suspecting that Tracy's contrarian impulse is the result of unresolved parental issues, Jack employs a nifty bit of reverse psychology to coax his star into a private therapy session. When the therapist suggests a role-playing exercise, Jack takes the elements of Tracy's childhood—the North Phila-delphia–born father with the Campbell's Soup factory job and the droopy lip—as improvisational prompts, playing Tracy's father and a cast of other characters in an impromptu one-man show that draws liberally on rancid 1970s television stereotypes.

Tracy's father, emerging from Jack's mouth, sounds eerily like Redd Foxx from *Sanford and Son*, and his monologue (which Jack interrupts with the calls of their downstairs neighbor, "Mrs. Rodriguez") eventually devolves into a scene from some mediocre blaxploitation movie: "Da honkies shot me!" Tracy rushes to embrace his dying father, promising to give up dogfighting. Jack, invigorated, congratulates the patient on his unorthodox breakthrough, telling him, "It's too bad you didn't know Howard Cosell when you were growing up, because I had that one in my pocket the whole time."

The man of a thousand inflections, many of them buffed to a dull glow during his numerous turns as *SNL* host, Alec Baldwin treats his voice as, in some elemental fashion, the essence of Jack Donaghy. Critic Jessica Winter described Baldwin's voice as "a come-on, maybe, or a veiled threat, or a joke that you're not quite in on." Fey's original sitcom idea had been for her to play a harried cable news producer working with Baldwin's unruly right-wing pundit. When that pitch failed to achieve traction, Fey preserved Baldwin's character in all his essentials, transforming him into an NBC executive.

Baldwin's brilliant performance, Scotch smooth, knowing, and ever so slightly menacing, lifts Jack far beyond the incompetent corporate talking head he was initially intended to be to something substantially subtler and more compelling. Baldwin both embodies and mocks the figure of the square-jawed, blow-dried, pinstripe-suited corporate titan. He is the voice of AIG and Goldman Sachs and Bain Capital and, yes, NBC, convinced of his infallibility even as the ship he steers crashes headfirst into an iceberg. With his raspy voice and air of casually held authority, Jack specializes in weighty edicts and long pauses that lend even the most absurd pronouncements a veneer of wisdom. Even when we know he's wrong, we suspect, on the basis of that voice, if nothing more, that he may be right.

By season four, Jack had broken through what remained of the fourth wall separating him from the real-life NBC execs who eyed *30 Rock* itself with disappointment. Jack requests that the struggling *TGS* undo some of its elitist, East Coast, alternative, intellectual, left-wing ("Jack, just say Jewish, this is taking forever!") tendencies with some homegrown American talent in order to appeal to the average television viewer. Like its show within the show, *30 Rock* never found the devoted audience that a previous generation of NBC Thursday-night sitcoms such as *Seinfeld* and *Friends* had—a fact that the show was only too aware of. For all its Emmy success and critical plaudits, *30 Rock* was pulling in one-fifth the audience that *Friends* had in its prime.

"Though we are grateful for the affection *30 Rock* has received from critics and hipsters, we were actually trying to make a hit show," Fey sardonically notes in her book *Bossypants*. "We weren't trying to make a low-rated critical darling that snarled in the face of conventionality. We were trying to make *Home Improvement* and we did it wrong."

But one thing *30 Rock* assuredly did right was to maintain that clash of styles, playing its interest in matters political against its deliriously quirky sense of humor. This spared the series from the fate of its short-lived contemporary *Studio 60 on the Sunset Strip* (NBC, 2006–07). When *30 Rock* premiered in the fall of 2006, it stood in the long shadow cast by Aaron Sorkin's much-hyped *Studio 60*, which similarly concerned itself with the backstage goings-on at a fictionalized version of *Saturday Night Live*. But Sorkin's show proved itself in short order to be fatally self-serious and self-congratulatory, treating television comedy writers like the political operatives on Sorkin's previous show *The West Wing*. (In fact, *30 Rock* poked fun at the Sorkin style in its first season, with numerous characters engaging in his trademark brisk-walking-and-talking maneuver. And in its fifth season, Sorkin himself showed up to walk-and-talk with Liz.) By contrast, *30 Rock* is a sitcom about a sketch comedy show that feels like it was written by sketch comedy veterans.

This was apropos, for in addition to being a superb "Weekend Update" anchor, Fey had also been *Saturday Night Live*'s first female head writer—a notable accomplishment in that bastion of aggressive masculinity. Drawing on her *SNL* experience, Fey made her sitcom a comedy that was notable for its interest in the show's writers: nebbishy Lutz (John Lutz, another former *SNL* writer), outlandish-hat-rocking, cleaning-lady-knocking Frank (Judah Friedlander), and Toofer (Keith Powell), so named for being both black *and* a Harvard graduate, thus providing two sorely needed perspectives for the show. The stars are the writers, and occasionally the writers are the stars: Donald Glover, who got his start on the *30 Rock* writing staff while still working as an RA at NYU, went on to a leading role in *Community*. (He can be spotted in a handful of cameos in *30 Rock*'s first few seasons.) Rob Petrie, meet your successors.

There are times—Jack's brief stint in the Bush White House; the imaginary NBC reality program *MILF Island*; Liz's boyfriend the beeper king; and the tongue-in-cheek product shilling for the McFlurry, Snapple, and other corporate products—when *30 Rock* feels like a particularly inspired string of *Saturday Night Live* sketches. In numerous other instances, Fey shrinks down an array of *SNL*-style sketches into rapid-fire inserts, none lasting more than a few seconds, that allow *30 Rock* to reference everything from Jenna's starring role in *Con-Air: The Musical* to Tracy's disastrous appearance as a "stabbing robot" on *Late Night with Conan O'Brien*. These jolts of comic punctuation are *30 Rock*'s most recognizable stylistic feature, and they give the series, mostly enclosed within cramped writers' rooms and offices, the feel of a much more varied show.

The flash cutting is also an indication of *30 Rock*'s debt to shows it otherwise only loosely resembles. *Arrested Development* slots in occasional bursts of disconnected imagery as flashbacks or non sequiturs, often only loosely connected to the ostensible plot. *Dream On* repurposes scenes from old movies as commentary on the erotic escapades of Brian Benben's Martin Tupper. *Scrubs* (NBC/ABC, 2001–10), featuring *Roseanne*'s Becky Conner #2, Sarah Chalke, employs flash cuts as exuberant exclamation points to its wry take on hospital life. Heralding everything from musical numbers (in the wonderful episode "My Musical") to *Star Wars* lightsaber fights to blackface routines, *Scrubs*' familiar whirling-tomahawk sound marks the separation between the quirky-but-near-realistic tone of the show as a whole, and its regular interludes of anarchic weirdness.

Scrubs uses its knowing familiarity with sitcom clichés to fend off the danger of devolving into an *ER*-style medical drama. The fear is acted out most literally in "My Life in Four Cameras," in which Zach Braff's J.D. reimagines the single-camera *Scrubs* as a traditional sitcom. The lighting gets markedly brighter. Chalke's Elliot is now seeing patients in stilettos and a cleavage-baring top, and even J.D.'s idol, the middle-aged former *Cheers* writer now dying of cancer, is cracking wise: "Well, the good news is, I won't have to eat my wife's cooking anymore, right?" Sitcoms were where we went to escape, not engage, but even that refuge was now closed off. *Scrubs*, like *30 Rock*, underscores the extent to which the easy assurances of the sitcom had withered away. Every sitcom—even the most absurdist—was now devoted to some form of realism.

Of all *30 Rock*'s varied comedic modes, its most comfortable is the inside-showbiz humor already familiar from earlier efforts like *The Dick Van*

Dyke Show, The Larry Sanders Show, and particularly *NewsRadio* (NBC, 1995–99), whose DNA—beloved sketch comedy veterans like Phil Hartman and Dave Foley inhabiting slightly loopy behind-the-scenes showbiz characters—is notably similar to *30 Rock*'s. The two shows share a deep love for quirk (if not *NewsRadio*'s laugh track or steady drumbeat of punch lines), and both relentlessly mock their celebrity characters for their narcissistic self-absorption, their infantile antics, and their neediness. Hartman's Bill McNeal is in fact merely a quasi-celebrity, a local radio personality who, despite his minor-league status, is always enamored of his own opinions. In the episode "Arcade," he weighs in on the attractive qualities of some ancient sandwiches in the office vending machine: "They're an acquired taste. Like a good wine or cheese, a sandwich needs to be properly aged."

On *30 Rock*, Tracy in particular regularly reaps the unexpected benefits of his ludicrous and inappropriate celebrity behavior. He creates a pornographic video game that sells sixty-one million copies; he purchases Lehman Brothers to escape the grasp of some hard-partying ex-investment banker interns; he is hoodwinked into believing he is preparing for space travel on a *TGS* soundstage while engaging in his own version of banter: "When do I get some Tang? Also, I'm thirsty. Wordplay!" Morgan's affability conceals not-so-secret depths of profound strangeness regularly milked by *30 Rock*. Tracy is immature, helpless, and prone to finding himself at his local strip club when he had intended to head to the kitchen to bring his wife a sandwich. He is also, in his particular gift for non sequitur punch lines bellowed at top volume ("I think I voted for Nader. *Nader!*"), the secret source of much of *30 Rock*'s belly laughs.

Tracy is a master of surprise, thriving on others' perceptions of his inadequacies. In one episode, Jack summons him to play golf with NBC honcho Don Geiss (played by none other than Rip Torn of *The Larry Sanders Show*). Tracy calls out Geiss for the lack of black representation at NBC and then proceeds to embarrass Jack with his imitation of every Hollywood saintly-ignorant-black-man stereotype: "I studied fried chicken at the school of hard knocks, ain't that right, Mr. Jack?" Later, seeking to make it up to Jack for his golf-course impropriety, he delivers a deeply touching, and surprisingly coherent, speech at a charity benefit about his daughter's struggles with diabetes, impressing Geiss with his seriousness. On his way out, he leans in to share a word with Jack: "I don't have a daughter."

Repeatedly, hilariously, *30 Rock* bites the hand that aired it on Thursday evenings, raking NBC over the coals for its failing business model and mediocre reality programming. But *30 Rock* knows that this inside-showbiz material, too, has been done before. Where could it go that *Larry Sanders*, with its jaundiced view of the television industry, had not already been? And so *30 Rock* is less a backstage story than a burlesque of the same, elongated and exaggerated to the point of absurdity.

Enamored as it is with the ritual of television, *30 Rock* dives deeply into the arcana of the sitcom in a manner that would inspire its eventual Thursday-night colleague *Community*. In order to get all the jokes, it helps to be an initiate in the ways of the sitcom. (Without knowing about the inexplicably lengthy run of *Wings* [NBC, 1990–97], Jack's joke comparing Liz's plans for twenty more years of *TGS* to the mediocre airport sitcom would make little sense.) The show's characters live in a TV-drenched universe. In order to prepare for a *TGS* appearance, Jack watches the first season of *Friends*, enchanted by Ross and Rachel's on-camera chemistry. On another occasion, Tracy and Kenneth, jonesing for a satisfying conclusion to one of their favorite NBC sitcoms, write and shoot a new final episode of *Night Court* (NBC, 1984–92), complete with the (purportedly) long-awaited nuptials of Harry Anderson's Judge Harry T. Stone and Markie Post's defense attorney Christine Sullivan.

This series is haunted by the ghosts of television past—the sitcom heroes who had once knit together a nation of TV watchers. This is comedy for the era of terminal decline, pining for *The Cosby Show* and *Seinfeld* less for their comic chops than their Nielsen overnights. In an effort to boost the flagging ratings of his network in the episode "SeinfeldVision," Jack arranges for a series of computer-generated guest appearances by NBC's last sitcom megastar, Jerry Seinfeld, on everything from *Let's Make a Deal* to *Heroes*. Even the ghost of Seinfeld, it seems, is more popular than NBC's current stable of stars.

The era of the sitcom as cultural colossus had ended, and *30 Rock* was gleefully looting its desiccated corpse. The very building blocks of the form had begun to wear with age, and *30 Rock* was devoted to rubbing our faces in the rot. "I wish this were an episode of *Night Court*," says Tracy as he stands on the reconstructed set of the once-popular sitcom, "because then there'd be some big joke right now." Instead, he and Kenneth stand uneasily, waiting for a commercial to interrupt the awkward silence. In another episode, a bouncy interlude detailing Jenna and Tracy's lunchtime shopping extravaganza is brought to a sudden halt by Liz's whistle: "I get it. You went shopping. I don't need the montage."

When Tracy's contract comes up for renewal, Jack and Liz reminisce about all the wacky good times they've had with their show's star. Ignoring the immediately familiar sitcom cues to cut to a heart-warming montage, the show lingers on Jack and Liz staring into space, lost in their own memories. The series uses the history of the sitcom jujitsu-style against its audience, knowing our expectations but resolutely denying us the easy comfort of the familiar.

At the close of the sixth season, North Korean dictator Kim Jong-il, who has kidnapped Jack's wife, Avery (Elizabeth Banks), suggests a new plot twist—that Jack and Liz get together—while offering proofs from sitcoms past: "On *Friends*, was so satisfying! They do on *Cheers*, they do on *Moonlighting* . . ." They don't here. The series is not devoted to delivering that kind of pleasure. By the end of its final season, Liz does end up happily married—but not to Jack—while *30 Rock*'s only lasting love affair is with television itself. Like the staff of WJM on *Mary Tyler Moore*, the cast and crew of *TGS* find their show summarily canceled, and they go out with one last broadcast. Jack appoints Kenneth as his replacement as NBC president, and Liz adopts nonidentical twins who bear a startling resemblance to Tracy and Jenna.

The series craftily mocks what it loves, paying enduring homage to the glories of its medium through its designated TV authority, Kenneth. "More than jazz, or musical theater, or morbid obesity, television is the true American art form," he argues in the episode "The Head and the Hair."

"Think of all the shared experiences television has provided for us, from the moon landing to the *Golden Girls* finale, from Walter Cronkite denouncing Vietnam to Oprah pulling that trash bag of fat out on a wagon. From the glory and the pageantry of the Summer Olympics to the less fun Winter Olympics. So please, don't tell me I don't have a dream, sir—I am living my dream!" In love with the dream of TV, *30 Rock* was the embodiment of "the true American art form," even as that dream was dissipating in a premium-cable, Hulu-and-Netflix haze.

24

Community

"Modern Warfare"

May 6, 2010 ▪ NBC

A nd so we come to the end of our season, with one final episode to wrap up the loose ends, crack a few jokes, leave a lump of good feeling in your throat, and hopefully get you to tune back in next season. The sitcom spent its first sixty years slowly discovering its own contours: its traditions, its clichés, its ideals. In series like *Seinfeld*, *The Larry Sanders Show*, and *30 Rock*, the sitcom embraced its own version of modernism, ambition stealing into its inner chambers like a cat burglar in pursuit of a legendary diamond. With *Community* (NBC, 2009–), the sitcom fully comprehends its debts to television past. And yet the dazzling metafiction of the show, created by Dan Harmon, had an obvious Achilles' heel: hardly anyone was watching. What happens when you sum up the history of television and no one bothers to tune in?

To answer the question more fully, let us synchronize our DVD players and press play on "Modern Warfare," an episode from *Community*'s first season. The series had bubbled under the surface since debuting in September 2009, attracting a modest but passionate following from the outset, but "Modern Warfare" was perhaps the first *Community* episode to become essential Friday-morning water cooler conversation. In part, this was because it was the first episode to fully embrace what *Community* had been in the process of becoming: a show about other shows, an endlessly twisting rabbit hole down which we were unexpectedly dropped.

Community embraces its own self-awareness, refracting the predictable genre exercises of mediocre movies and television through its warped lens. Seven students of varying ages and backgrounds form a study group at Greendale Community College, last home for losers and misanthropes of all kinds: ex-lawyer Jeff Winger (Joel McHale), busted for practicing without a college diploma; middle-aged Christian housewife Shirley (Yvette Nicole Brown); feminist firebrand Britta (Gillian Jacobs); ex-jock Troy Barnes (Donald Glover); moist-towelette magnate Pierce Hawthorne (Chevy Chase); pill-popping high school overachiever Annie (Alison Brie); and quasi-autistic film student Abed (Danny Pudi). In another memorable episode, "Basic Rocket Science," the study group members pilot a space shuttle that is actually a creaky, circa-1980s flight simulator, sponsored by Kentucky Fried Chicken and housed in a dilapidated motor home. The show itself is much like that KFC space shuttle: quirky, jury-rigged, peculiarly self-referential.

"Modern Warfare," written by Emily Cutler, is less about TV than about the movies—specifically, apocalyptic fantasies of destruction like Danny Boyle's *28 Days Later*, and every grade-Z Cinemax shoot-'em-up of the late 1980s. Nevertheless, the referentiality is itself a weapon aimed at the screen, demanding our recognition that all this is, at long last, a series of familiar tropes, redeployed once more in the hopes of warding off anything that might smack of originality.

Jeff awakes in his car, surrounded by a blighted landscape instantly recognizable from a thousand B movies. The only difference is that here, everything is splattered not with blood and viscera but with brightly colored blobs of paint. As Jeff is the last to learn, Greendale has been decimated after a school-sponsored paintball competition went terribly awry, the grand prize of priority registration for next semester's courses proving all too tempting for its combatants. Succumbing to the temptation himself ("You could schedule all your classes on a Monday and then take a six-day weekend!"), Jeff enters into an alliance with the rest of the study group, with the knowledge that they'll eventually have to turn on one another to claim the coveted prize.

"Modern Warfare" playfully romps in the cliché-strewn forest of action movies. The episode's camera work is all clipped frames and jagged editing, matching the staccato style of *Black Hawk Down* or *Saving Private Ryan*. "Let's not resort to cheap ploys," Jeff pleads with his teammates, and perhaps with the show itself, undermining his case by stripping off his shirt to reveal his sculpted shoulders. He cocks his paintball gun in sidelong fashion, like macho action heroes, and his love interest / maiden aunt / nemesis Britta, in requisite action-chick leather vest, slides through Jeff's legs in slow motion to pick off a team of Afro-rocking disco roller-skaters. Shirley, like so many previous Bible-toting hit men from *Pulp Fiction*'s Jules Winnfield onward, recites the Twenty-Third Psalm to herself before letting loose with a fusillade of paintballs. The group gathers around a campfire in the school cafeteria, discussing what they would do with that priority registration were it to fall into their hands, like John Wayne and his troops in Monument Valley the night before a Comanche attack. The episode is masterful in its ability to incorporate the familiar tropes of the genre into *Community*'s insular sitcom world.

And yet "Modern Warfare" takes place in a sphere in which no good cliché goes unpunished. "That is so uninspired!" Annie shouts at the glee club's paintball team as they perform their rendition of Pat Benatar's "Hit

Me with Your Best Shot," before she herself is picked off. Shirley, shot by the disco assassins, lies motionless on the ground as the camera swirls upward. "I'm going home, Britta," she dreamily murmurs. "No, seriously, I'm going home. Can you help me up?"

Jeff and Britta trade their traditional snarky banter, prompting everyone else to interrupt a tense scene to point their guns at them in frustration. ("Will they or won't they? Sexual tension," Abed helpfully narrates in a different episode, summing up their Ross-and-Rachel vibe.) When Jeff is wounded in an attack, Britta nurses his injuries, and they both roll their eyes at the forced intimacy of this all-too-common dramatic scenario. "Can you feel that tension?" Jeff jokes. "It's a miracle we still have clothes on." Soon enough, though, they don't; the two have sex on the same desk at which their classmates study (soon to be a point of germophobic contention with them). Still locked in a postcoital embrace, Britta pulls a gun on Jeff, and he bristles. "Please tell me you didn't have sex with me to win at paintball." "No," she responds haughtily. "I had sex with you and *now* I'm gonna win at paintball. Don't be gross."

But Jeff and Britta's *Once Upon a Time in the West* guns-drawn showdown is broken off by the invasion of an entirely different set of action movie tropes. A Chinese pop ditty starts up on the soundtrack, and Greendale's Spanish teacher, Señor Chang (Ken Jeong), enters in slow motion. Chang, toting a tiger-striped, jumbo-sized paintball machine gun, is clad in a cream-colored suit and black sunglasses. The character is both himself and a hysterical mash-up of every John Woo action hero ever.

With moments like this, what *Community* demands from us more than anything is to acknowledge the artificiality of what we are doing. Why do we sit in front of our televisions, watching wisecracking young men and women hanging out together, week after week? More specifically, why is television the way it is? *Community* is an interrogation, episode by episode, of the unspoken clichés of the medium, decimating the world of TV even as it builds its own castle of acerbic, dazzlingly self-aware sitcom magic.

The figure behind *Community* is simultaneously a sitcom traditionalist and a raving formalist genius. Dan Harmon grew up in the Milwaukee suburbs, a latchkey kid like *Freaks and Geeks'* Bill Haverchuck, tuning in religiously to reruns of *Taxi* and *The Bob Newhart Show*. Harmon watched TV with such devotion, in fact, that he began to see patterns: the way *Moonlighting* bounced playfully from genre to genre, or how *The Bob Newhart Show* would sometimes freeze its final shot before the credits rolled, and sometimes unfreeze them.

Harmon grew up and became a writer, penning a legendary pilot for Fox called *Heat Vision and Jack*, starring Jack Black as a brilliant NASA scientist and Owen Wilson as his talking-motorcycle sidekick. The show wasn't picked up, but it led to Harmon eventually being hired for *The Sarah Silverman Program* (Comedy Central, 2007–10). *Sarah Silverman* was far more of a star vehicle than the ensemble-driven *Community* would be, but it was driven by a similar desire to chip away at its own gleaming facade.

Silverman was a pretty young thing who was also a potty-mouthed comedian, and her show is a perky, peppy, highly traditional sitcom (complete with next-door neighbors and friendly police officers) that is also a wholesale demolition of the sitcom's order. Harmon's tenure with *Sarah Silverman* was brief, but the structure of the show would carry over to *Community*.

After being fired from *The Sarah Silverman Program*, Harmon took a community college Spanish course and was inspired to pitch a show about a mismatched group of community college students. It was a thoroughly typical sitcom premise, but the mocking, stylized execution was entirely fresh.

The innovative arc of *Community* is found in its stealthy overthrowing of its entitled hero. Jeff Winger is everything a sitcom hero is supposed to be: white, male, good-looking, witty, effortlessly charming. He is, from the very first episode of the show, the unquestioned leader of the study group. Jeff is, as Abed describes him, a perfect amalgam of familiar sitcom heroes, with a little something extra: "10 percent Dick Van Dyke, 20 percent Sam Malone, 40 percent Zach Braff in *Scrubs*, and 30 percent Hilary Swank in *Boys Don't Cry*." Here, too, *Community* thrives on turning the expected wisdom inside out, as his easy white man's authority over the rest of the group turns to self-mockery. His patented motivational speeches become a more and more obvious crutch *Community* relies upon to wrap up its storylines, until in the fake flashback episode "Paradigms of Human Memory," the series stitches together a whole string of such declamations from imaginary episodes past (Remember that one in the ghost town? And the one with the Mexican drug runners?) into one single meta-speech that exposes the hollowness of Jeff's leading-man responsibilities.

Community also plays up and mocks the sexual chemistry between its characters. It hints at romantic fireworks between Jeff and Britta; in fact, Jeff forms the study group that brings all our characters together for the specific purpose of cozying up to the willowy, unapproachable blonde. Having established a central emotional thread—guy pursues unapproachable girl—familiar from countless other television shows, *Community* then proceeds to steadily unravel it. Jeff and Britta relentlessly bicker instead of flirt, their initial chemistry curdling into antipathy and snarkitude.

After their inevitable hookup in "Modern Warfare," the first season ends with a prototypical sitcom cliffhanger: Britta interrupts a school dance to profess her love for Jeff, leaving him to choose between her and the slinky, worldly Professor Slater (Lauren Stamile)—before the episode upends the choice altogether by having Jeff and *Annie* make out. Then, at the start of the second season, *Community* punishes its audience by giving them precisely what they want, haphazardly slapping Jeff and Britta together, much to Annie's chagrin. Another sitcom cliché—true love conquering all—is imploded, dynamited from within. The new couple, forced by pride and circumstance into a relationship neither wants, make out in class, each revolted by the tactility of their slithering tongues. Never content to follow when she might lead, Britta proceeds to one-up Jeff by proposing to him.

Audience assumptions—of who is star and who is sidekick, of which characters belong together—are discarded, replaced by an awareness that the rules of the sitcom, and of television in general, are essentially arbitrary. In one silent exchange of freighted glances, Abed lifts his eyebrows rakishly at Britta, then at Jeff. Pierce hungrily checks out each of the women. Shirley looks at Troy, who shrugs noncommittally. Britta and Annie exchange glances, then break off with a start. Jeff and Annie gaze into each other's eyes. Harmon and his writers could "let" Jeff and Britta get together, or opt for Jeff and Annie as a couple. *Community* could make us swallow Troy and Shirley together, if it was so inclined. Ross and Rachel could easily slip into Joey and Rachel if no one was minding the store.

Not only that, but *Community*'s characters could see what we were seeing, and comment on its inherent hokiness. After a sensitive musical montage (set to Sara Bareilles's "Gravity") tenderly celebrates Jeff and Annie's chemistry in "Paradigms of Human Memory," Jeff calls foul: "Give me a break! You could do the same thing with Pierce and Abed." Another montage immediately follows, set to the same song, celebrating perhaps the least likely emotional alliance of all among the show's seven characters. During the mockumentary episode "Intermediate Documentary Filmmaking," Jeff chides director Abed like a reality-TV contestant or a dyspeptic critic: "And don't you dare intercut this with footage of me freaking out!" The show, inevitably, intercuts this plea with footage of Jeff tossing his BlackBerry like a discus.

The characters are just as cognizant of what they can and cannot say to one another. Troy and Jeff stand on the Greendale gridiron in "Football, Feminism and You," the camera cutting back and forth as Jeff tries to convince his younger friend to join the school's football team. The rapid-fire back-and-forth is a hyperspeed refresher course in twenty-first-century political correctness, as if conducted by two NBC censors. "It's in your blood," Jeff says of football. "That's racist." "Your soul." "*That's* racist," Troy chuckles. "Your eyes?" "That's gay?" "That's homophobic." "That's black." "That's racist!" "Damn."

Community's characters are so highly self-aware that they begin "Modern Warfare" with a stinging critique of their own show's limitations. Abed explains to Jeff why *Community* will never scale the heights of popularity: "To be blunt, Jeff and Britta is no Ross and Rachel . . . ironically, and hear this on every level, you're keeping us from being *Friends*." (Shirley compares them, instead, to *Cheers*: "I *hated* Sam and Diane.") The point is not that Britta and Jeff are a poor imitation of Rachel and Ross but that modern audiences were all too aware of Rachel and Ross and the sitcom device they represent—and of the other clichés, lazy storylines, and ruts that are endemic to the form. Shows like *Community* still knew the spell to cast, but were also aware that its power had diminished through familiarity.

The principal embodiment of this growing familiarity is Abed. He is, as the show strongly hints, a likely Asperger's candidate, and his monomania latches exclusively onto pop culture. Each episode—each scene—is an opportunity for him, and by extension the show, to reference another movie, another TV show, another cultural milestone of the past. He is, in particular, a scholar of television, going mano a mano with a television studies professor to prove once and for all, with equations drawn on the chalkboard, that Judith Light's Angela, and not Tony Danza's Tony, was the unquestioned boss of the sitcom *Who's the Boss?* (ABC, 1984–92).

Possessed of an encyclopedic knowledge of the medium, Abed views life itself—or at least life at Greendale—through the lens of TV. He hums the *M*A*S*H* theme and demands to be called Radar, a quirky but lovable sidekick paying tribute to one of his forefathers. When Annie suggests he participate in a research experiment for her psychology class, Abed is taken aback: "I figured we were more like Chandler and Phoebe. They never really had stories together." In "Pascal's Triangle Revisited," the last episode of *Community*'s first season, he flicks the lights on and off, practicing potential farewells. When someone asks what he is up to, he tells them, "Just giving things a finale vibe." And when the series returns for its second season, Abed is first seen rising from his bed, announcing "And we're back . . ."

The most metafictional of *Community*'s already metafictional characters, Abed is perhaps the one that bears the closest resemblance to series creator Dan Harmon. Harmon gave himself online tests and has self-diagnosed as a high-functioning Asperger's candidate. He is given to drawing eight-pointed figures he calls "embryos," laying out the arc ("1. A character is in a zone of comfort. 2. But they want something. . . .") of every good television story.

Abed is the sitcom character as showrunner, suggesting and adopting new approaches for *Community* even as he is contained within its frame. He quizzes Jeff about whether he has any hillbilly cousins, rich uncles, or drinking buddies who may have had sex changes. "Abed," Jeff asks, "why are you mining my life for classic sitcom scenarios?"

Abed is forever trying to improve the show, as if in fear—all too real, if one stops to think about it—that if *Community* ceases to exist, so will he. He tries to convince Jeff to make over his abrasive personality into something more approachable, more closely resembling Alan Alda's Hawkeye: "He kept his upbeat humor and charm, even in the eleventh year of the Korean War." Abed is the show's guardian angel, its self-conscious acknowledgment that it has all been done already. There is nothing new under the sitcom sun. Abed's terrifyingly complete knowledge of TV only serves as confirmation.

I can tell life from TV, Jeff," he tells Jeff in one episode. "TV makes sense. It has structure, logic, rules. And likable leading men. In life, we have this. We have you." He and Troy—his sweet-tempered, slightly dim partner in crime, and roommate in what Jeff dubs "Indiana Jones and the Apartment of Perpetual Virginity"—are overgrown children tentatively playing at adulthood and finding they prefer the old, familiar routines of juvenility. Their high-concept playfulness is the jaunty analog to *Community*'s metafictions, with Troy and Abed crafting their own secret language composed of equal parts pop-cultural detritus and childhood fantasy. They construct a blanket fort in their dorm, host an impossibly perky "morning show" with their mostly confused fellow students as their guests, turn the spare bedroom of their new apartment into a "Dreamatorium," and regularly exchange a secret handshake—two hand slaps, two smacks of the chest—that Pierce, in full *Indecent Proposal* mode, sullies by purchasing from them.

For Abed, life is distinct from television, and yet, even at the height of its purportedly emotional moments, *Community* often reaches for a TV punch line for comfort. Jeff, distraught about a breakup, sobs on Pierce's shoulder: "We always used to watch the shows she wanted to watch. I hate *Glee*! I don't understand the appeal at all!" Pierce abandons the group in "The Art of Discourse," sick of serving as a collective punching bag, and Abed mourns his disappearance by way of a hooded critique of *Entourage*: "We've lost our Cliff Clavin, our George Costanza, our Turtle—or

Johnny Drama—or E. Man, that show is sloppy." Shirley takes umbrage with the depiction of middle-aged African American women on television as sassy, excessively spiritual walking clichés, only to immediately lapse into same: "Good Lord hadn't been watching, I'd have slapped him upside the head."

And when Shirley is at last reunited with her philandering husband, Andre, who is it—clad in an instantly recognizable hideous pullover sweater—but Theo Huxtable? Malcolm-Jamal Warner, forever a good sport, plays Andre as a spiritual descendant of, and homage to, a classic sitcom character. ("Nice sweater," Jeff tells him. "Thanks," Andre responds. "My dad gave it to me.") *Community* is yanked into a space-sitcom vortex, whereby *The Cosby Show* becomes not only a point of reference but a presence on the show. (A cameo by *Reading Rainbow* host LeVar Burton serves as similar nostalgic eye candy, rendering Troy speechless with shock.) As if prematurely aware of its own potential future as a "brilliant but canceled" special, the show even casts Tony Hale—Buster of *Arrested Development*—as a happy-go-lucky pottery teacher with rigid anti-*Ghost*-parody rules in his classroom. One classic but underwatched sitcom gestures to its predecessor, acknowledging that what made for superb television did not always make, at least on first viewing, for must-see TV.

As *Community* began its second season, it doubled down on its pop-culture mockery. In the season premiere, Abed announces that he wants the study group to get away from "soapy, relationship-y stuff" toward "bigger, fast-paced, self-contained escapades"—which, of course, is exactly what *Community* itself did. Haltingly, with some subtle shifts in tone along the way, the show increasingly turned to pastiche and parody as its preferred mode of attack, making "Modern Warfare" into a model for the rest of the series.

"Abed's Uncontrollable Christmas" absorbs and Greendale-ifies the DNA of overly sugary animated Christmas specials; "Regional Holiday Music" skewers *Glee*, a favorite target of *Community*'s ire; "Critical Film Studies" manages the remarkable feat of simultaneously lampooning *Pulp Fiction* (also the parodic subject of *The Simpsons'* "22 Short Films About

Springfield") and Louis Malle's legendary talkfest *My Dinner with Andre*; and "Messianic Myths and Ancient Peoples" features Abed as a meta-film-maker in the mold of Charlie Kaufman, who casts himself as the Jesus figure in his loose remake of Martin Scorsese's *The Last Temptation of Christ.* The series came to embody the spirit of a moment when all genres felt equally tapped out and equally worthy of mockery.

Community was not the only show of its era to truly embrace genre-savviness as a creative trope. *The Mindy Project* (Fox, 2012–), starring *The Office*'s Mindy Kaling, features a single protagonist whose warped ideas of romance were formed by romantic comedies like *Pretty Woman* and *When Harry Met Sally* . . . . Similarly, the HBO series *Bored to Death* and *East-bound & Down* are both devoted to subtly undercutting the genres to which they have pledged mock fealty.

Bored to Death (HBO, 2009–11) is a noir-flecked mystery series whose small-fry cases and chief detective, stifled novelist Jonathan Ames (Jason Schwartzman), bespeak the show's jaundiced view of the hard-boiled mode. Ted Danson is here, too, a long way from *Cheers* as a pot-smoking magazine publisher who prefers tagging along on Jonathan's cases to doing his job. *Bored* both is and is not a private-eye show, mocking its function even as it upholds its form.

And *Eastbound & Down* (HBO, 2009–13), detailing the halfhearted attempts of washed-up fireballer Kenny Powers (Danny McBride) to return to the major leagues, often reaches for a mock-heroic tone ("Welcome to the resistance," Kenny greets his friend and designated lackey on his arrival in Mexico) not at all in keeping with its perpetual air of self-inflicted foolish-ness. The soundtrack is straight out of Sergio Leone, but the action evokes Will Ferrell (a regular guest star), not Clint Eastwood.

The short-lived, sorely missed *Flight of the Conchords* (HBO, 2007–09) is comedy for music nerds, sweeping an entire universe of visual and aural associations under its wing and poking prodigious fun at the clichés of pop-ular music in the process. *Flight of the Conchords* mines comic gold from the gap between the lives of transplanted New Zealander folkie duo Bret (Bret McKenzie) and Jemaine (Jemaine Clement), adrift in low-rent New

York City, and their music, with the hampering circumstances of the former starkly contrasting with the lush pseudo-grandiosity of the latter.

In the debut episode of the series, the heartfelt breakup ballad "I'm Not Cryin'" features McKenzie (an elfin type whose scraggly beard is a comic visual effect in its own right) standing beside a rain-slicked window, singing, "These aren't tears of sadness because you're leaving me, I've just been cutting onions. I'm making a lasagna . . ."—his voice drops to a whisper—". . . for one."

For the Conchords' hip-hop battle song "Hiphopopotamus vs. Rhymenoceros," they take turns bum-rushing the camera like amped-up MCs anxious for their moment in the sun. Clement in particular gets a bit carried away, yanking the proverbial mic away from his partner with the audacious boast "I'm the hiphopopotamus, my lyrics are bottomless—" before immediately bottoming out, dazedly staring into the camera for the next few beats, unable to get another word out. Jemaine and Bret's already tenuous claims for hip-hop credibility are only further undermined by their decidedly un-street getup: Clement is wearing a tan blazer and jeans, like a college professor on summer holiday, and McKenzie is inexplicably clad in a bright yellow reflector vest more traditionally seen on suburban crossing guards.

Even for shows that did not seem to be mocking anything in particular, a certain knowingness persisted. Henry (Adam Scott) and Casey (Lizzy Caplan) of *Party Down* (Starz, 2009–10) are another Jeff and Britta, drawn together by their matching bone-dry senses of humor and sardonic wits, and pulled apart by the same.

Henry is an aspiring actor and Casey an aspiring comedian, and their dreams land them amid the fellow aspirants working at an L.A. catering company. Fame is a beacon calling them, and then stranding them in ruffled white shirts and bow ties, serving hors d'ouevres to the well-heeled in a no-collar echo of *The Office*'s workplace ludicrousness. Featuring such superlative performers as Ken Marino, Jane Lynch, and Martin Starr, *Party Down* is a showcase of up-and-coming comic talent couched in the now-familiar language of awkwardness and discomfort. "You're just pissed," Henry tells a romantic competitor, "because *I* shat where *I* ate, and now you want to eat at that same restaurant where I was shitting."

Caplan, whose dead-eyed stare is a punch line in its own right, did a multi-episode arc on *New Girl* (Fox, 2011–), another show that attempts to redeem and undermine the clichés of the sitcom. The ensemble comedy of bantering, well-dressed twentysomethings, that most tired and most appealing of setups, is redeemed by *New Girl*'s exaggerated quirkiness and its desire to undermine our expectations. *New Girl* is the *Three's Company* mismatched-roommates setup revivified. The highly appealing Zooey Deschanel is the putative star, but it is Max Greenfield's exuberantly odd Jewish frat boy Schmidt—supplying his own sushi platters, rocking his cardigan and his kimono, his penis in a cast, peeling off his Abraham Lincoln Halloween costume to reveal a *Magic Mike* stripper getup—who takes over the show, to *New Girl*'s undoubted benefit.

Then there's *Happy Endings* (ABC, 2011–2013), which, like *Community*, has its own line of patter and its own in-jokes among its incestuous band of best buds. Slobbish, amoral, gay Max (Adam Pally) prolongs the recovery of his laid-up friend Penny (Casey Wilson) to seduce her physical therapist ("He has been *Misery*-ing me!" Penny exclaims). Brad (Damon Wayans Jr., who starred in the *New Girl* pilot) poses as unemployed to please his wife, who prefers him to put aside the white collar and pursue hobbies like ventriloquism. And Max and Brad partner up as a bar mitzvah hype-man team called Boyz II Menorah.

Meanwhile in an alternative television universe coexisting with the forward-thinking present of *Community*, *Conchords*, *Eastbound*, and the like, the past is still alive and well and thriving on CBS. CBS's slate of throwback sitcoms regularly trounce NBC's far more creatively groundbreaking shows in the ratings. Series like *Two and a Half Men*, *How I Met Your Mother*, *The Big Bang Theory*, and *2 Broke Girls* (CBS, 2011–) have delivered a steady dose of familiar yuks via their slate of helpless man-child womanizers, clueless yuppies, nerdy science geeks, and snappy twentysomethings, respectively.

Turning on a CBS sitcom is like entering a sitcom time machine and returning to the predictable mediocrity of the pre–*Larry Sanders*, pre-*Seinfeld*

past. Most astonishingly of all, CBS series still have laugh tracks, booming splashes of guffaws informing viewers precisely when it is safe to laugh.
Even at the time of *Seinfeld* and *Friends*, it felt anachronistic to use the laugh
track; by 2012, it was itself the embodiment of these shows' bone-deep aesthetic conservatism. For all their vagina jokes, these CBS shows succeed
by providing a painfully predictable set of sitcom tropes and nothing more.
The future of the sitcom has arrived, but the past has only migrated along
the dial.

   Community, after some uncertainty, survived to limp toward a fourth
season, minus creator and showrunner Dan Harmon. David Guarascio and
Moses Port of *Happy Endings* took over for Harmon, who had famously
alienated his NBC bosses and squabbled with Chase. Surprisingly, NBC
then gave the go-ahead for a fifth season, with Chase departing the show
and Harmon, who had left in a haze of acrimony, returning. But regardless of where future episodes might take it, the show's air of good-natured
pop-cultural mockery, and its recurrent interest in the detritus of television
history—*Who's the Boss?* and *The Cosby Show* and the like—were indicative
of a medium that had turned its gaze definitively inward.

   The sitcom was still a mirror, but where once it had reflected ourselves
back at us, offering an image of well-scrubbed American families just like
its viewers were or wanted to be, it had now turned around. The sitcom now
reflected only itself, interested less in the real world—or what the sitcom
had once agreed to designate the real world—than the world of television
itself. We sought comfort in the sitcom's simulacrum of itself, and it was
more joyous, and more rewarding, than the sitcom's onetime simulacrum
of real life. Even as we were noting the absurdities of the form, we could
be moved by them as well; *Community* was not just a farce but a heartfelt
one. And its awareness of its predecessors gave it a more realistic feel than
its contemporaries that chuckled and guffawed as if nothing whatever had
changed since the days of *All in the Family*. A circuit had been completed.
A medium that had always been curious about its roots—just what was this
thing, TV?—since the earliest days of *The Honeymooners* and *I Love Lucy*
could now be a mechanism for exploring its own traditions.

Where could the sitcom go after *Community*? It might seem as if self-reflexivity was a dead end, a trap that the sitcom had stumbled into and could never profitably escape. And yet, *Community* itself offered a hint of how television might proceed forward after its surreptitious ascent from "vast wasteland" to cultural behemoth. In his self-directed stealth homage to *My Dinner with Andre* in "Critical Film Studies," Abed takes on the Andre Gregory role from the film and offers a searching monologue devoted to his time as, of all things, an extra on the sitcom *Cougar Town*, starring *Friends* alum Courteney Cox.

"If I'm a person that watches *Cougar Town*," he wonders, "how I can be in *Cougar Town*?" Pondering this existential dilemma, Abed comes to a realization about his life in television. "I realize I have to stop being someone who's ever seen the show and become a character on the show. Become a *man* from Cougar Town." The sitcom, like Abed, can be enclosed in itself and watching itself, all at once. The sitcom can be both genuine and self-mocking, interior and exterior, emotional and snarky. It can be a man from Cougar Town and a person who watches *Cougar Town*. The sitcom can now operate simultaneously on two levels, its humor both self-contained and endlessly reflecting the nooks and crannies of pop culture. It can now be free.

Acknowledgments

Writing a book is both a solitary and a collective process. While much of it happens alone, in a quiet room, no book would come to fruition without the assistance, in ways large and small, personal and professional, of many people.

My agent, William Clark, saw this project through from start to finish with his usual dedication and insight. Yuval Taylor, Devon Freeny, Mary Kravenas, Kathryn Tumen, and the entire staff of Chicago Review Press are models of diligence and devotion.

Sarah Rose, Ben Haimowitz, Larry Fisher, Eli Segal, and Helane Naiman generously shared their DVD collections and wisdom for research purposes. Ali Austerlitz and Ari Vanderwalde read segments of the book, and improved it with their sagacious comments. I would also like to thank the following people for simply being who they are: Josh Olken, Dan Smokler, Mark Fenig, Reuben Silberman, Jeremy Blank, Olia Toporovsky, Marina Hirsch, Annie Austerlitz, Abby Silber, Jason Seiden, Carla and Dan Silber, Ari Holtzblatt, Zev Wexler, Daniel Mizrahi, and Adi Weinberg.

Without my wife, Becky, this book would simply not exist. She is the presence behind every word.

Last, but assuredly not least, I am grateful to my son Nathaniel for arriving in this world during the writing of this book, and for having unwittingly sat through all ninety-eight episodes of *Gilligan's Island*. Life will only get better from here, I promise.

Bibliography

Abramson, Albert. *The History of Television, 1942 to 2000*. Jefferson, NC: McFarland, 2008.

Alley, Robert S., and Irby B. Brown. *Love Is All Around: The Making of* The Mary Tyler Moore Show. New York: Delta, 1989.

Armstrong, Jennifer Keishin. *Mary and Lou and Rhoda and Ted: And All the Brilliant Minds Who Made* The Mary Tyler Moore Show *a Classic*. New York: Simon & Schuster, 2013.

Baker, Nicholson. *The Anthologist*. New York: Simon & Schuster, 2009.

Barnouw, Erik. *Tube of Plenty: The Evolution of American Television*. New York: Oxford University Press, 1990.

Bloom, Ken and Frank Vlastnik. *Sitcoms: The 101 Greatest TV Comedies of All Time*. New York: Black Dog & Leventhal, 2007.

Edgerton, Gary. *The Columbia History of American Television*. New York: Columbia University Press, 2007.

Henry, William A. *The Great One: The Life and Legend of Jackie Gleason*. New York: Doubleday, 1992.

Jhally, Sut. *Enlightened Racism:* The Cosby Show, *Audiences, and the Myth of the American Dream*. Boulder, CO: Westview Press, 1992.

Kanfer, Stefan. *Ball of Fire: The Tumultuous Life and Comic Art of Lucille Ball*. New York: Alfred A. Knopf, 2003.

Kisseloff, Jeff. *The Box: An Oral History of Television, 1920–1961*. New York: Viking, 1995.

Kohen, Yael. *We Killed: The Rise of Women in American Comedy*. New York: Sarah Crichton Books, 2012.

Lackmann, Ron. *The Encyclopedia of 20th Century American Television*. New York: Checkmark Books, 2003.

Leonard, John. *Reading for My Life: Writings, 1958–2008*. New York: Viking, 2012.

————. *Smoke and Mirrors: Violence, Television, and Other American Cultures*. New York: New Press, 1997.

McNeil, Alex. *Total Television: The Comprehensive Guide to Programming From 1948 to the Present*. New York: Penguin, 1996.

Neuwirth, Allan. *They'll Never Put That on the Air: An Oral History of Taboo-Breaking TV Comedy*. New York: Allworth Press, 2006.

Ortved, John. *The Simpsons: An Uncensored, Unauthorized History*. New York: Faber & Faber, 2009.

Richmond, Ray and Antonia Coffman, eds. *The Simpsons: A Complete Guide to Our Favorite Family*. New York: HarperPerennial, 1997.

Roman, James W. *From Daytime to Primetime: The History of American Television Programs*. Westport, CT: Greenwood Press, 2005.

Ruuth, Marianne. *Bill Cosby: Entertainer*. Los Angeles: Melrose Square, 1992.

Samuel, Lawrence R. *Brought to You By: Postwar Television Advertising and the American Dream*. Austin: University of Texas Press, 2001.

Shales, Tom and James Andrew Miller. *Live from New York: An Uncensored History of* Saturday Night Live, *As Told By Its Stars, Writers, and Guests*. New York: Little, Brown, 2002.

Silvers, Phil, with Robert Saffron. *This Laugh Is On Me: The Phil Silvers Story*. Englewood Cliffs, NJ; Prentice-Hall, 1973.

Sohn, Amy. *Sex and the City: Kiss and Tell*. New York: Melcher Media, 2002.

Sorensen, Jeff. *The Taxi Book: The Complete Guide to Television's Most Lovable Cabbies*. New York: St. Martin's Press, 1987.

Sterritt, David. *The Honeymooners*. Detroit: Wayne State University Press, 2009.

Van Dyke, Dick. *My Lucky Life In and Out of Show Business: A Memoir.* New York: Crown Archetype, 2011.

Waldron, Vince. *Classic Sitcoms: A Celebration of the Best in Prime-Time Comedy.* Los Angeles: Silman-James Press, 1997.

———. *The Official* Dick Van Dyke Show *Book: The Definitive History and Ultimate Viewer's Guide to Television's Most Enduring Comedy.* New York: Applause, 2001.

Zoglin, Richard. *Comedy at the Edge: How Stand-Up in the 1970s Changed America.* New York: Bloomsbury, 2008.

Index

"One with Ross's Wedding, The" (*Friends* episode), 264
"One with the Embryos, The" (*Friends* episode), 260, 262–264
"One with the Prom Video, The" (*Friends* episode), 264
O'Neill, Ed, 194, 351
Oppenheimer, Jess, 9, 16, 17
Osmond, Ken, 54, 57
Our Miss Brooks, 15
"Outing, The" (*Seinfeld* episode), 233–234, 315
Owens, Geoffrey, 185

P
Paar, Jack, 11
"Palestinian Chicken" (*Curb Your Enthusiasm* episode), 319
Paley, William, 92
Palillo, Ron, 153
Pally, Adam, 381
"Paradigms of Human Memory" (*Community* episode), 374, 375
Parker, James, 313
Parker, Sarah Jessica, 277
Parker, Trey, 221, 222
Parks and Recreation, 350
Parsons, Jim, 269
Party Down, 380–381
"Pascal's Triangle Revisited" (*Community* episode), 376
Paul, Jarrad, 255
Perfect Strangers, 154
Perlman, Heide, 164
Perlman, Rhea, 148, 162
Perry, Matthew, 261, 265, 270
Persky, Bill, 100
"Personal Business" (*Cheers* episode), 166
Pesci, Joe, 249
Pete Hornberger (*30 Rock* character), 358
Petersen, Paul, 60
Petticoat Junction, 50
Peyser, Arnold, 82
Peyser, Lois, 82
Phil Silvers Show, The, 40, 46, 49, 51
Philipps, Busy, 293
Phillips, Joseph C., 187
Phillips, Julianne, 251
Phoebe Buffay (*Friends* character), 261
physical comedy, 10, 21, 69–70, 74, 85, 101, 181, 287, 330
Pickens, Slim, 93
Picket Fences, 301–302
Pierce, David Hyde, 172
Pierce Hawthorne (*Community* character), 370

"Pilot" (*Cosby Show* episode), 175–176, 189
"Pilot, The" (*Seinfeld* episode), 227
Pinchot, Bronson, 154
"Pitch, The" (*Seinfeld* episode), 4, 225, 317
Piven, Jeremy, 227, 247, 287
Plaza, Aubrey, 350
Pleshette, Suzanne, 107
Poehler, Amy, 350
"Point of View" (*M*A*S*H* episode), 137
Police Squad! 331
Port, Moses, 382
Poston, Tom, 154
Powell, Keith, 362
Price, Marc, 154
Prinze, Freddie, 124
Private Secretary, 15
Procter & Gamble, 70
"Producer, The" (*Gilligan's Island* episode), 89–90
Professor, the (*Gilligan's Island* character), 83, 91–92
"Proposal, The" (*Cheers* episode), 164
Pudi, Danny, 370
Puente, Tito, 186
"Puffy Shirt, The" (*Seinfeld* episode), 233
Pugh, Madelyn, 9, 16
Pulliam, Keshia Knight, 178
Pulp Fiction (1994), 211, 212, 378

Q
Queen Latifah, 267
Quinn, Glenn, 192

R
Rachel Green (*Friends* character), 261, 265
Radar O'Reilly (*M*A*S*H* character), 134, 138, 306
radio characters, 120–121
Radio City, 8
Radnor, Josh, 268
"Raincoats, The" (*Seinfeld* episode), 233
Ralph Kramden (*Honeymooners* character), 26–28, 30–32, 34–37, 150
"Ralph Kramden, Inc." (*Honeymooners* episode), 30
"Ralph's Diet" (*Jackie Gleason* sketch), 29
Randall, Tony, 279
Randolph, Joyce, 28, 33
Rashad, Phylicia, 178, 189
Ratzenberger, John, 167
Raven-Symoné, 187
Ray Milland Show, The, 15
"Ray Murdock's X-Ray" (*Dick Van Dyke* episode), 77
Real McCoys, The, 15, 50
Real World, The, 350